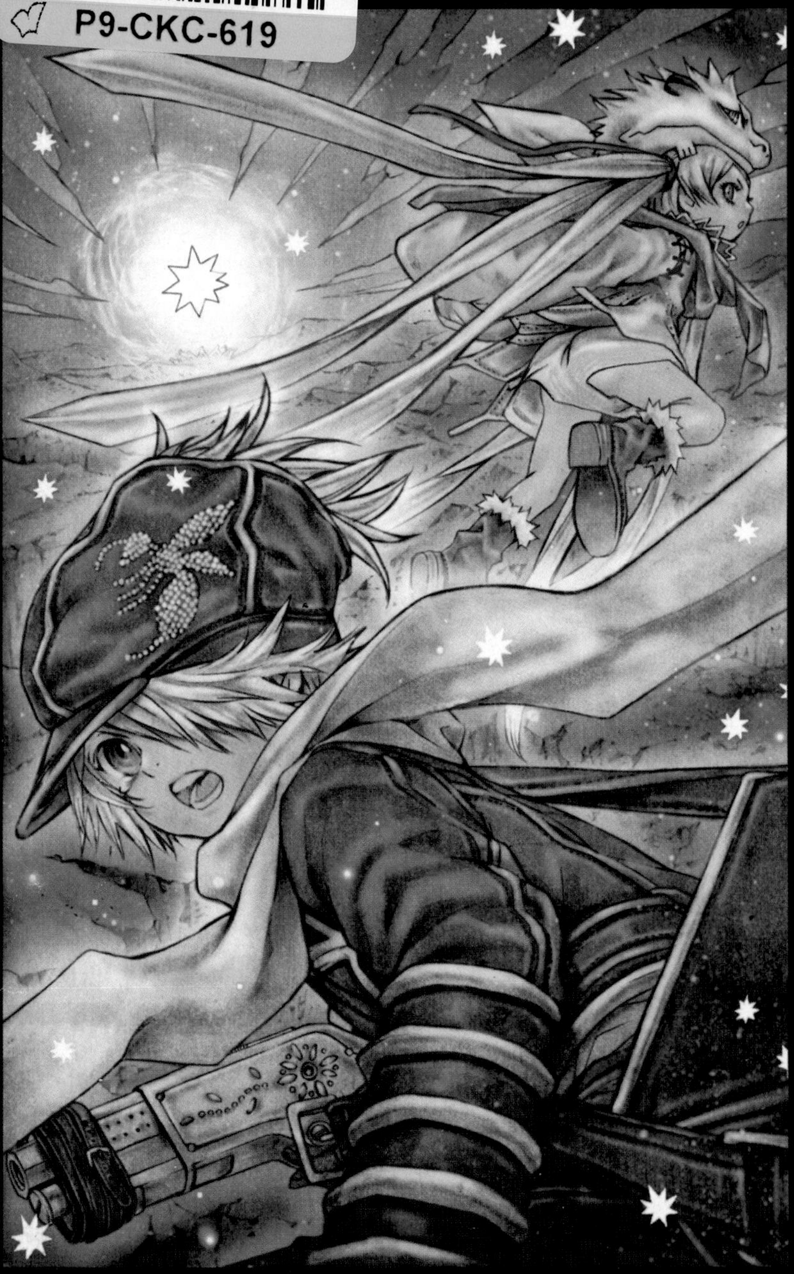

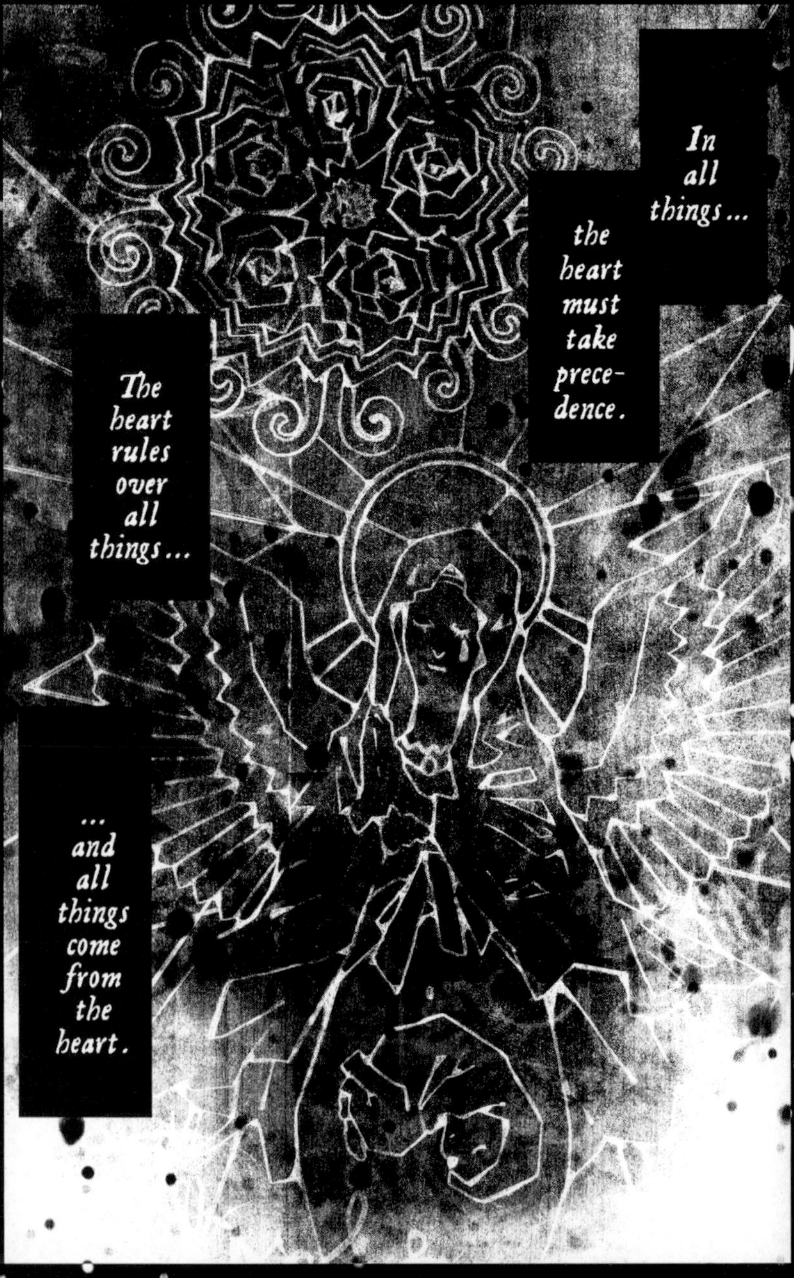
In all things...
the heart must take precedence.
The heart rules over all things...
... and all things come from the heart.

–THE SCRIPTURES OF AMBERGROUND, 1st verse

Tegami Bachi
LETTER · BEE

VOLUME 3
MEETING SYLVETTE SUEDE

STORY AND ART BY
HIROYUKI ASADA

This is a country known as Amberground, where night never ends.

Its capital, Akatsuki, is illuminated by a man-made sun. The farther one strays from the capital, the weaker the light. The Yuusari region is cast in twilight; the Yodaka region survives only on pale moonlight.

Letter Bee Gauche Suede and young Lag Seeing meet in Yodaka—a postal worker and the "letter" he must deliver.

Gauche is the sole support for his young, wheelchair-bound sister, and Lag has been marked for delivery to an unfamiliar place after his mother is abducted by strange men. Each begins the journey burdened with his own sadness, but as they endure the rain and fog and fight off the gigantic metal insects known as Gaichuu, they forge a strong bond of friendship. At their journey's end, they go their separate ways: Gauche is promoted to Akatsuki, where he can earn the money to cure his sister. Lag determines to become a Letter Bee like Gauche.

Five years later, Lag sets out for Yuusari to take the Letter Bee exam. On the way, he finds a strange young girl in a niche at the train station, marked for delivery with inadequate postage. Lag names her Niche and offers to deliver her. However, the recipient turns out to be the owner of a freakshow that plans on exhibiting Niche as the "Child of Maka." Lag rushes to save her, but Niche has already escaped to the forest, where she encounters a Gaichuu. In the nick of time, Lag arrives and destroys the Gaichuu, winning Niche's trust. And so Lag continues his journey with Niche as his trusty dingo.

At Kyrie, the town where the Bifrost Bridge connects Yodaka and Yuusari, their crossing pass is stolen by Nelli, a girl grieving over the death of her little brother. Lag confronts Nelli and ends up helping her deal with her grief. Lag and Niche continue to Yuusari after recovering their crossing pass. However, when Lag finally completes the Letter Bee aptitude test, Zazie the exam observer delivers some shocking news.

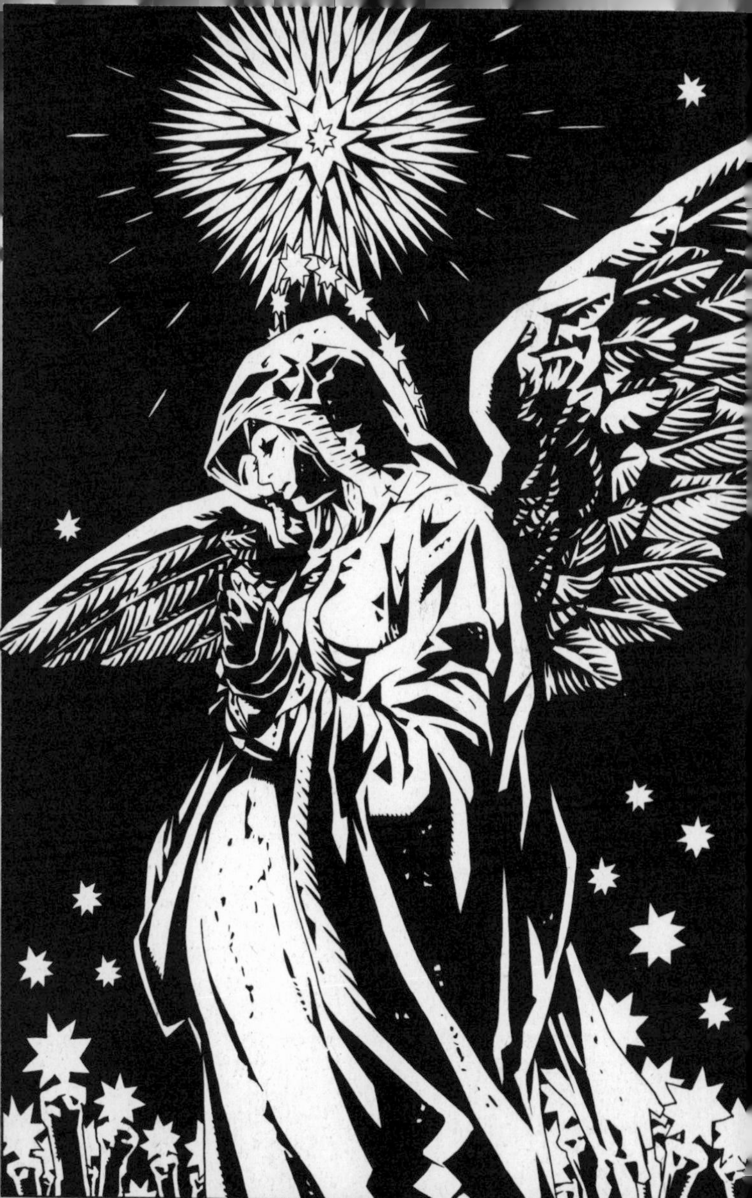

Tegami Bachi

LETTER · BEE

VOLUME 3

Meeting Sylvette Suede

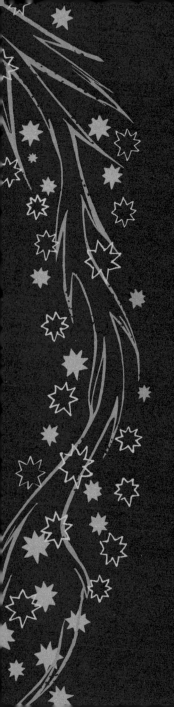

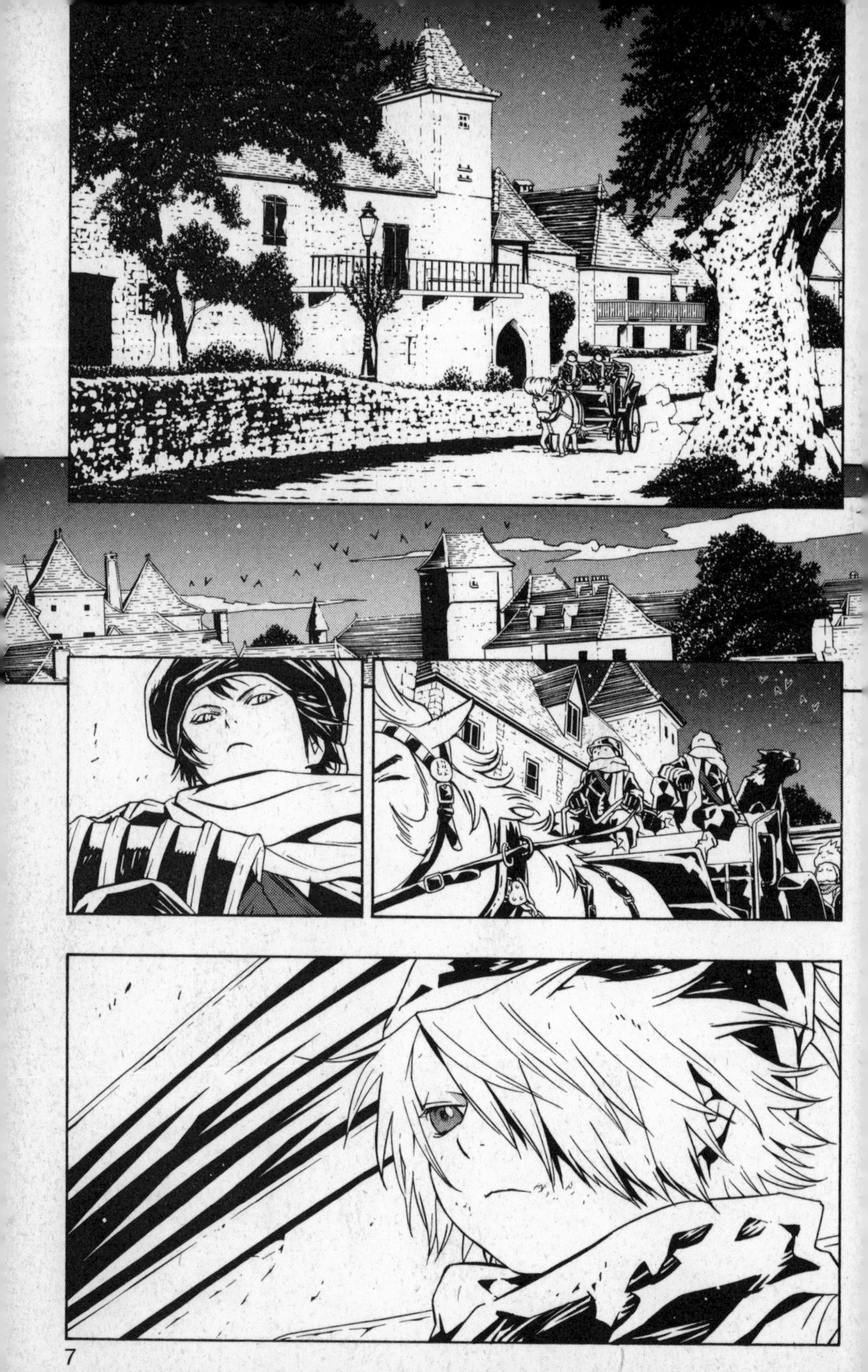

Chap[redacted]eting Sylvette Suede

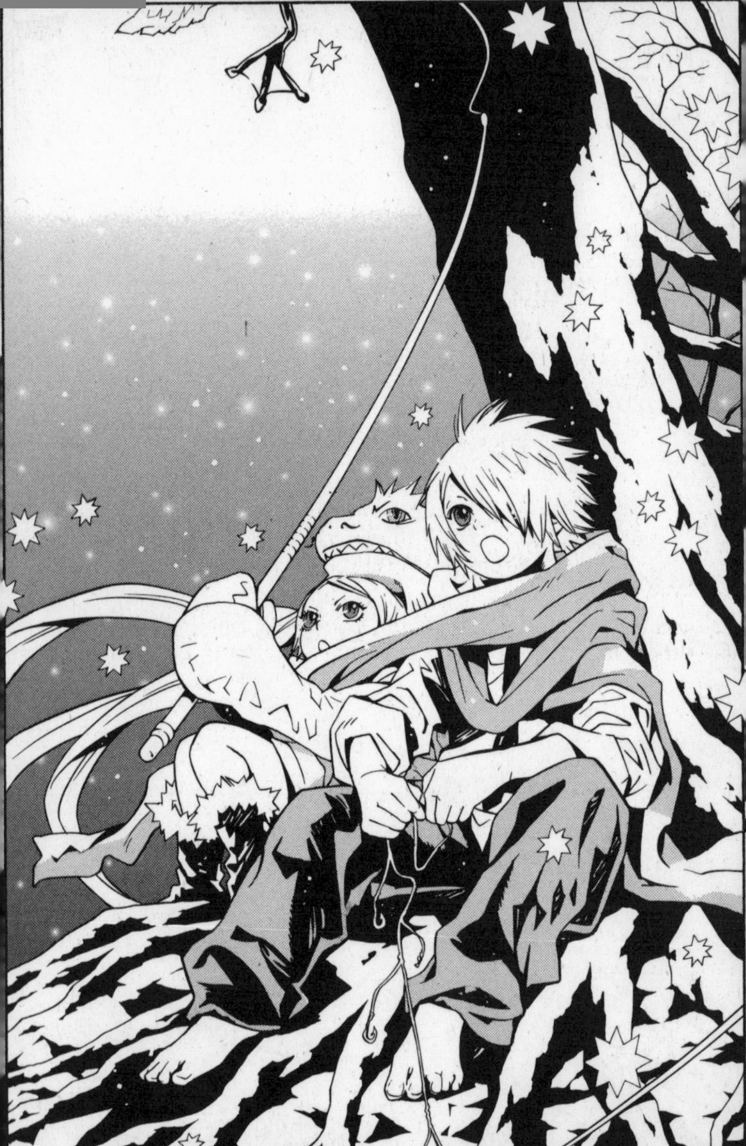

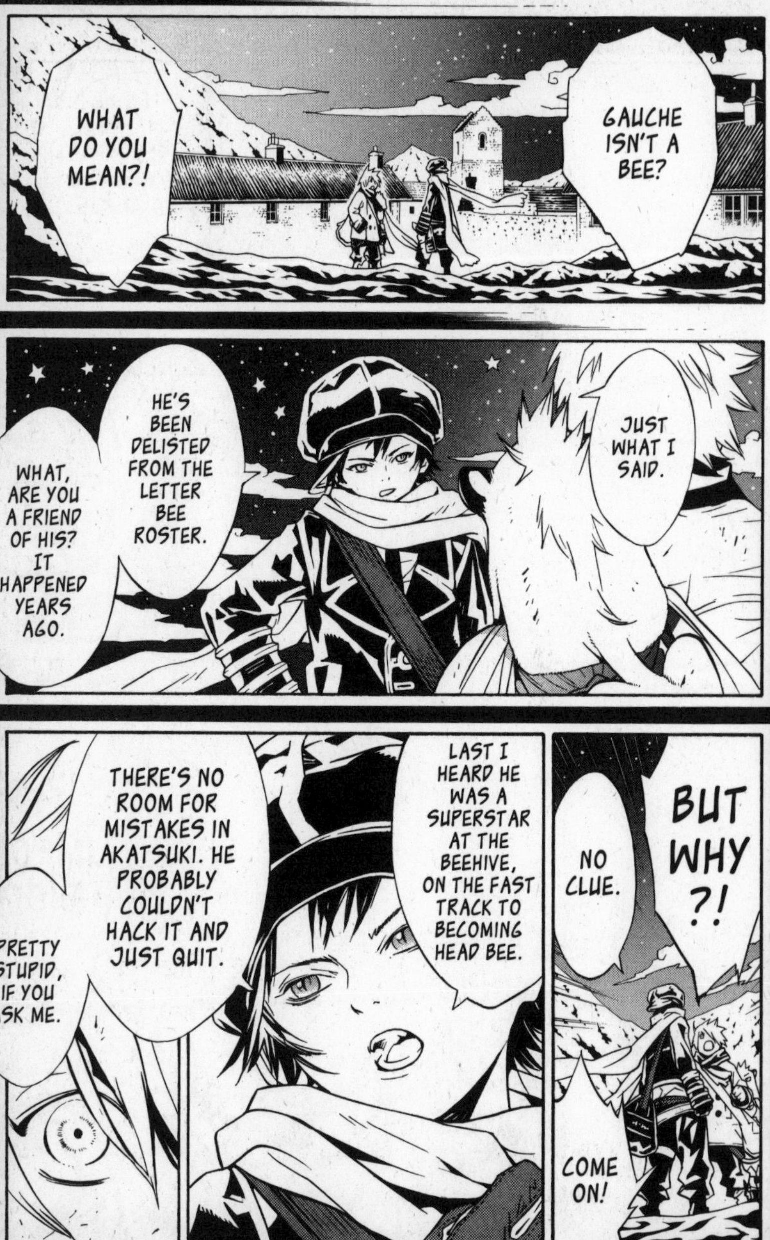
GAUCHE ISN'T A BEE?
WHAT DO YOU MEAN?!
JUST WHAT I SAID.
HE'S BEEN DELISTED FROM THE LETTER BEE ROSTER.
WHAT, ARE YOU A FRIEND OF HIS? IT HAPPENED YEARS AGO.
BUT WHY?!
NO CLUE.
COME ON!
LAST I HEARD HE WAS A SUPERSTAR AT THE BEEHIVE, ON THE FAST TRACK TO BECOMING HEAD BEE.
THERE'S NO ROOM FOR MISTAKES IN AKATSUKI. HE PROBABLY COULDN'T HACK IT AND JUST QUIT.
PRETTY STUPID, IF YOU ASK ME.

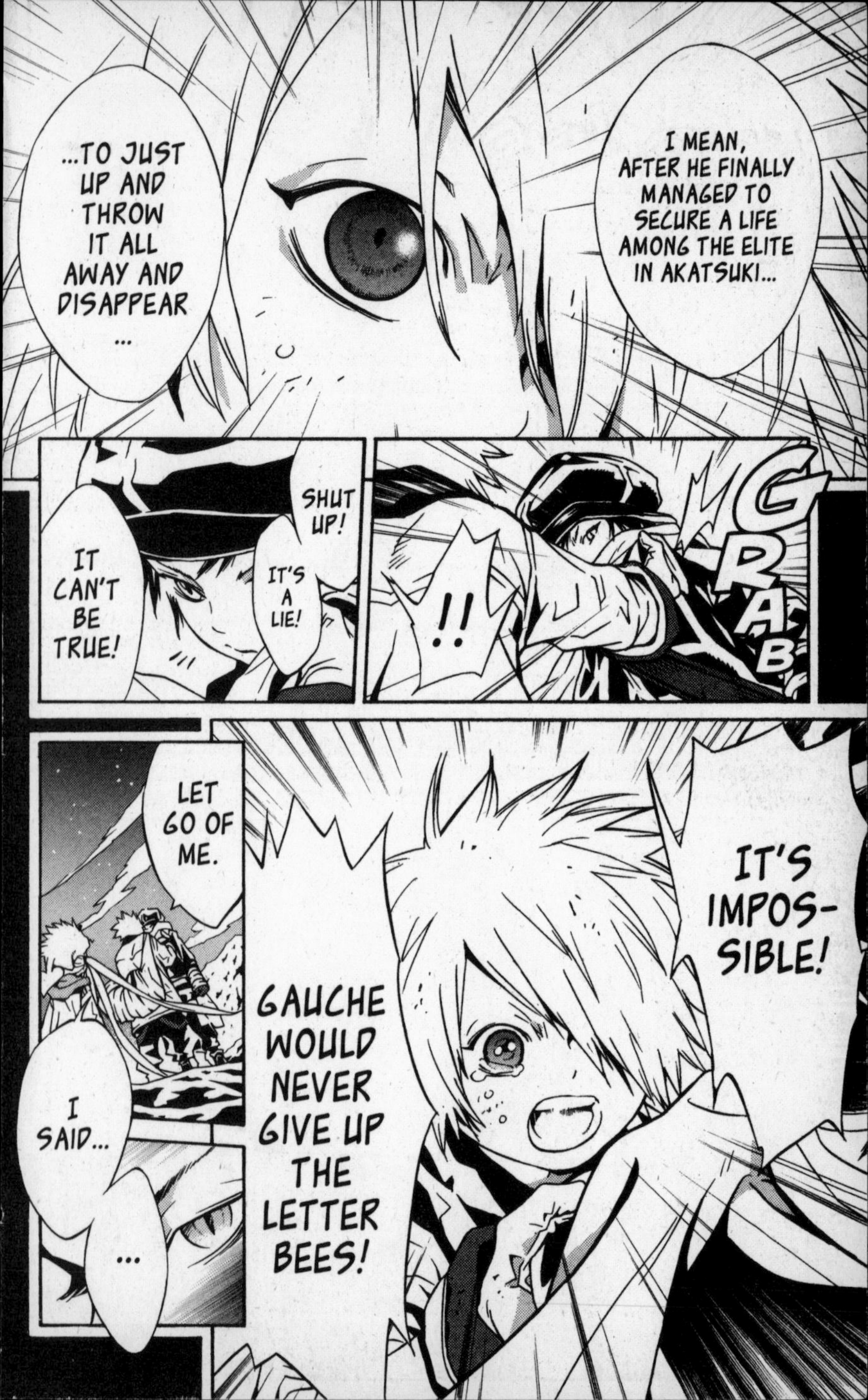
I MEAN, AFTER HE FINALLY MANAGED TO SECURE A LIFE AMONG THE ELITE IN AKATSUKI...
...TO JUST UP AND THROW IT ALL AWAY AND DISAPPEAR ...
GRAB
!!
SHUT UP!
IT'S A LIE!
IT CAN'T BE TRUE!
IT'S IMPOS-SIBLE!
GAUCHE WOULD NEVER GIVE UP THE LETTER BEES!
LET GO OF ME.
I SAID...
...

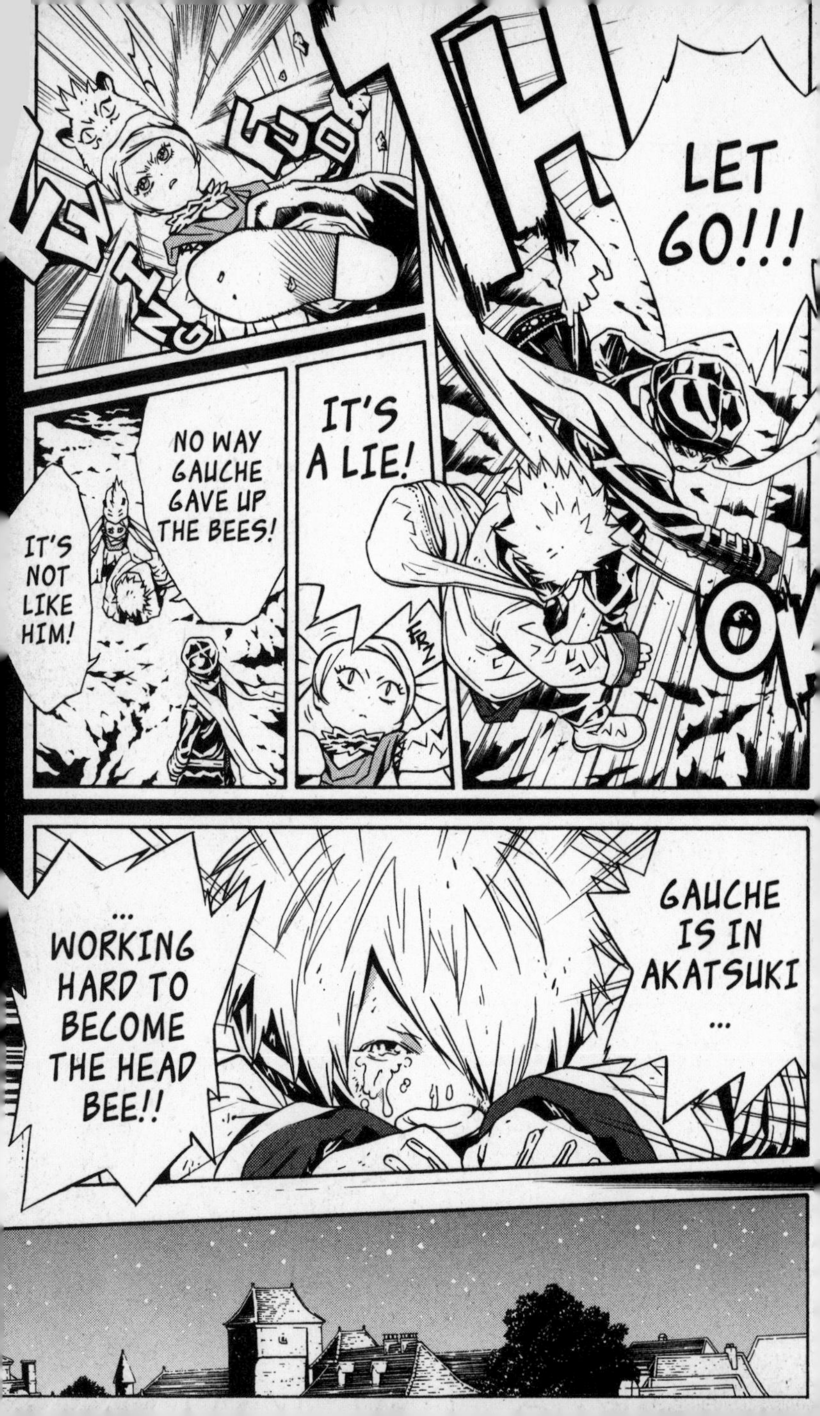
LET GO!!!
IT'S A LIE!
NO WAY GAUCHE GAVE UP THE BEES!
IT'S NOT LIKE HIM!
GAUCHE IS IN AKATSUKI ...
... WORKING HARD TO BECOME THE HEAD BEE!!

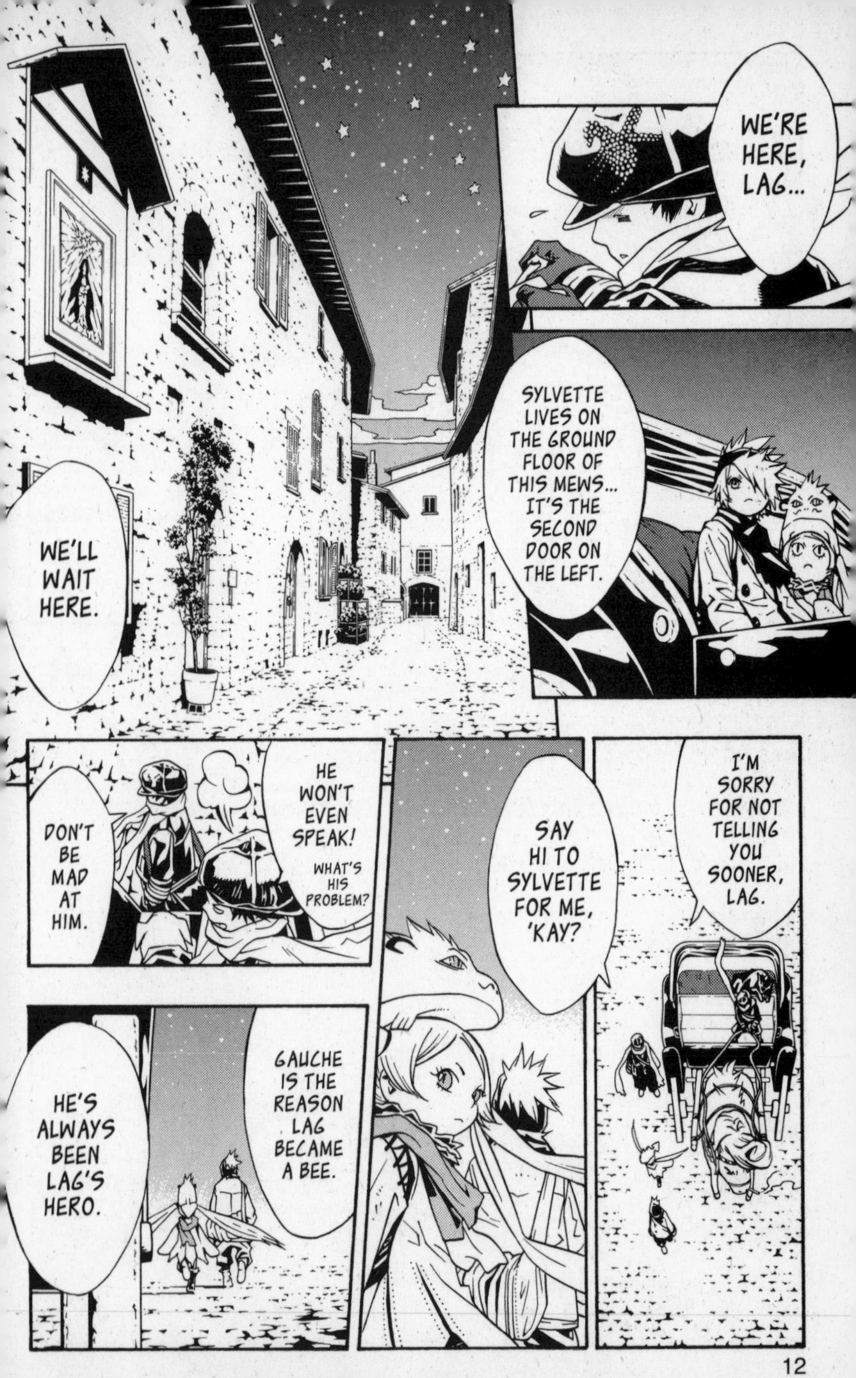
WE'RE HERE, LAG...
SYLVETTE LIVES ON THE GROUND FLOOR OF THIS MEWS... IT'S THE SECOND DOOR ON THE LEFT.
WE'LL WAIT HERE.
I'M SORRY FOR NOT TELLING YOU SOONER, LAG.
SAY HI TO SYLVETTE FOR ME, 'KAY?
HE WON'T EVEN SPEAK!
WHAT'S HIS PROBLEM?
DON'T BE MAD AT HIM.
GAUCHE IS THE REASON LAG BECAME A BEE.
HE'S ALWAYS BEEN LAG'S HERO.

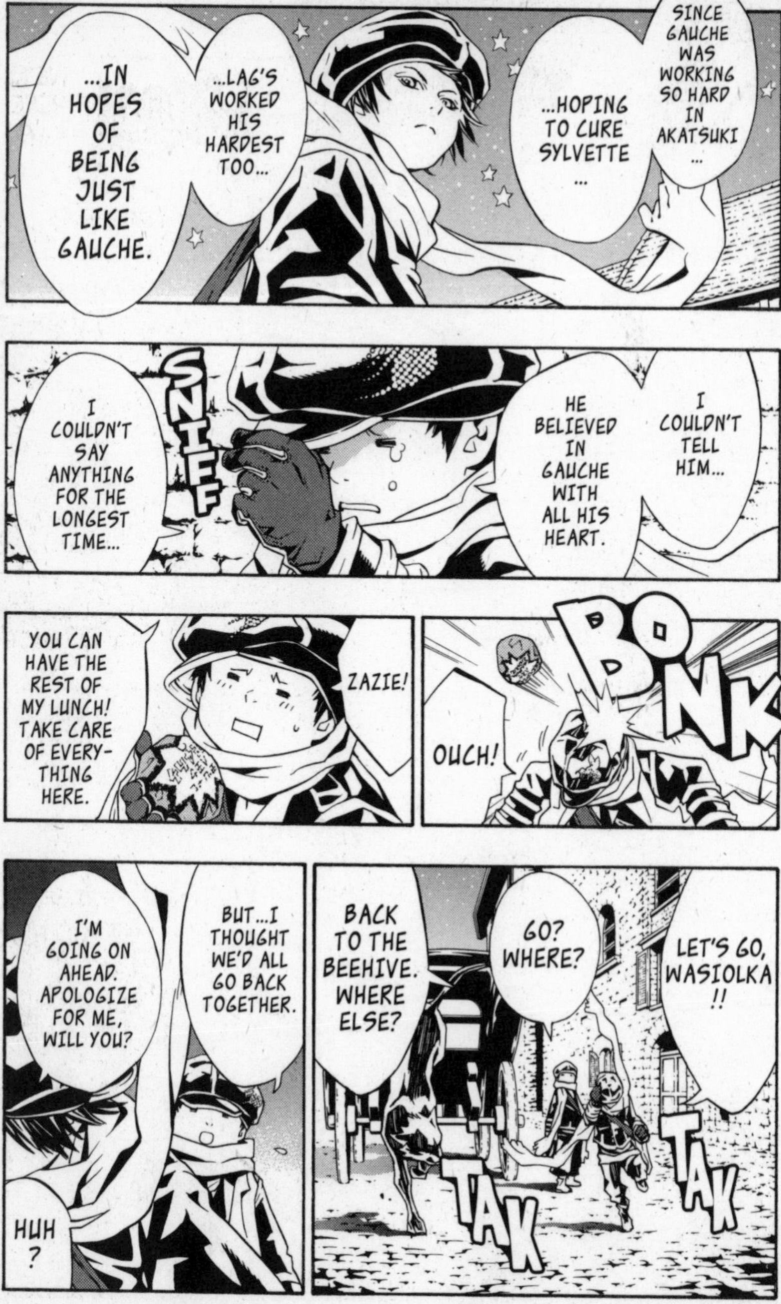
SINCE GAUCHE WAS WORKING SO HARD IN AKATSUKI...
...HOPING TO CURE SYLVETTE...
...LAG'S WORKED HIS HARDEST TOO...
...IN HOPES OF BEING JUST LIKE GAUCHE.
I COULDN'T TELL HIM...
HE BELIEVED IN GAUCHE WITH ALL HIS HEART.
SNIFF
I COULDN'T SAY ANYTHING FOR THE LONGEST TIME...
BONK
OUCH!
ZAZIE!
YOU CAN HAVE THE REST OF MY LUNCH! TAKE CARE OF EVERY-THING HERE.
LET'S GO, WASIOLKA!!
GO? WHERE?
BACK TO THE BEEHIVE. WHERE ELSE?
TAK
TAK
BUT...I THOUGHT WE'D ALL GO BACK TOGETHER.
I'M GOING ON AHEAD. APOLOGIZE FOR ME, WILL YOU?
HUH?

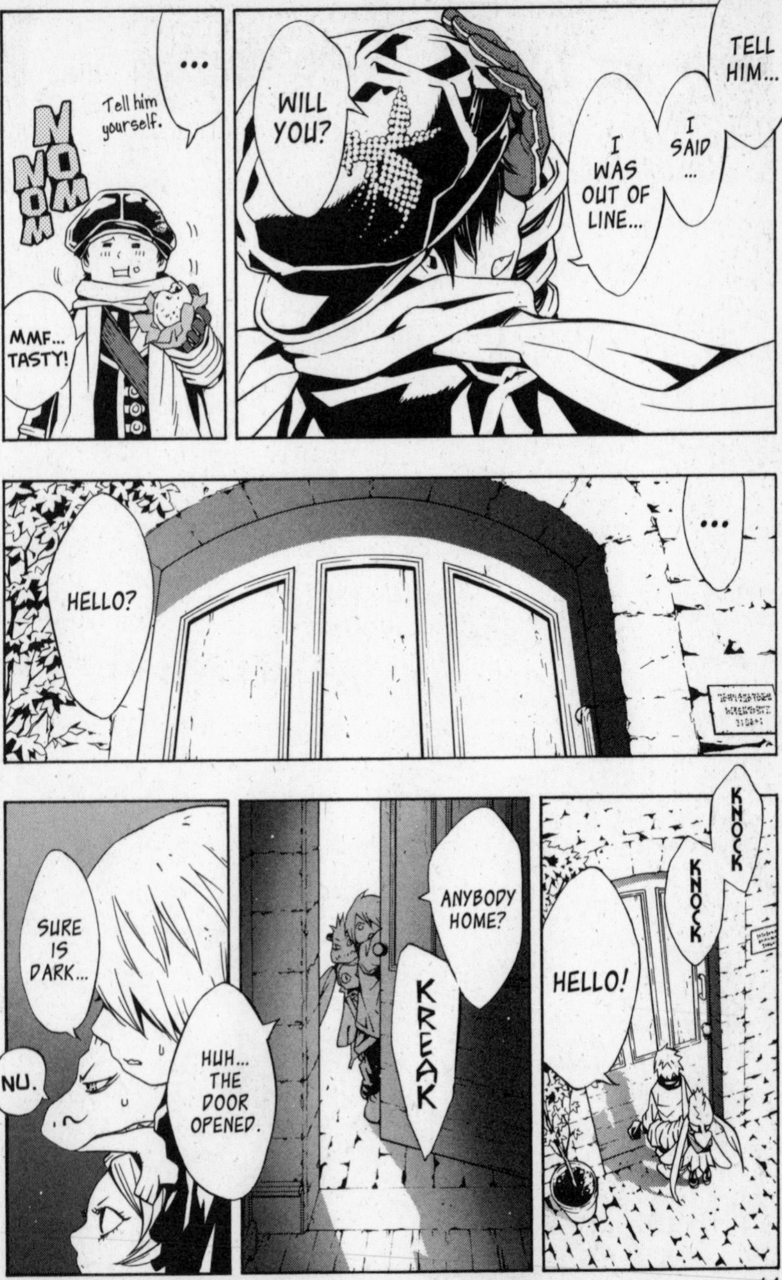
TELL HIM...
I SAID...
I WAS OUT OF LINE...
WILL YOU?
...
Tell him yourself.
NOM NOM
MMF... TASTY!
...
HELLO?
KNOCK KNOCK
HELLO!
ANYBODY HOME?
KREAK
SURE IS DARK...
HUH... THE DOOR OPENED.
NU.

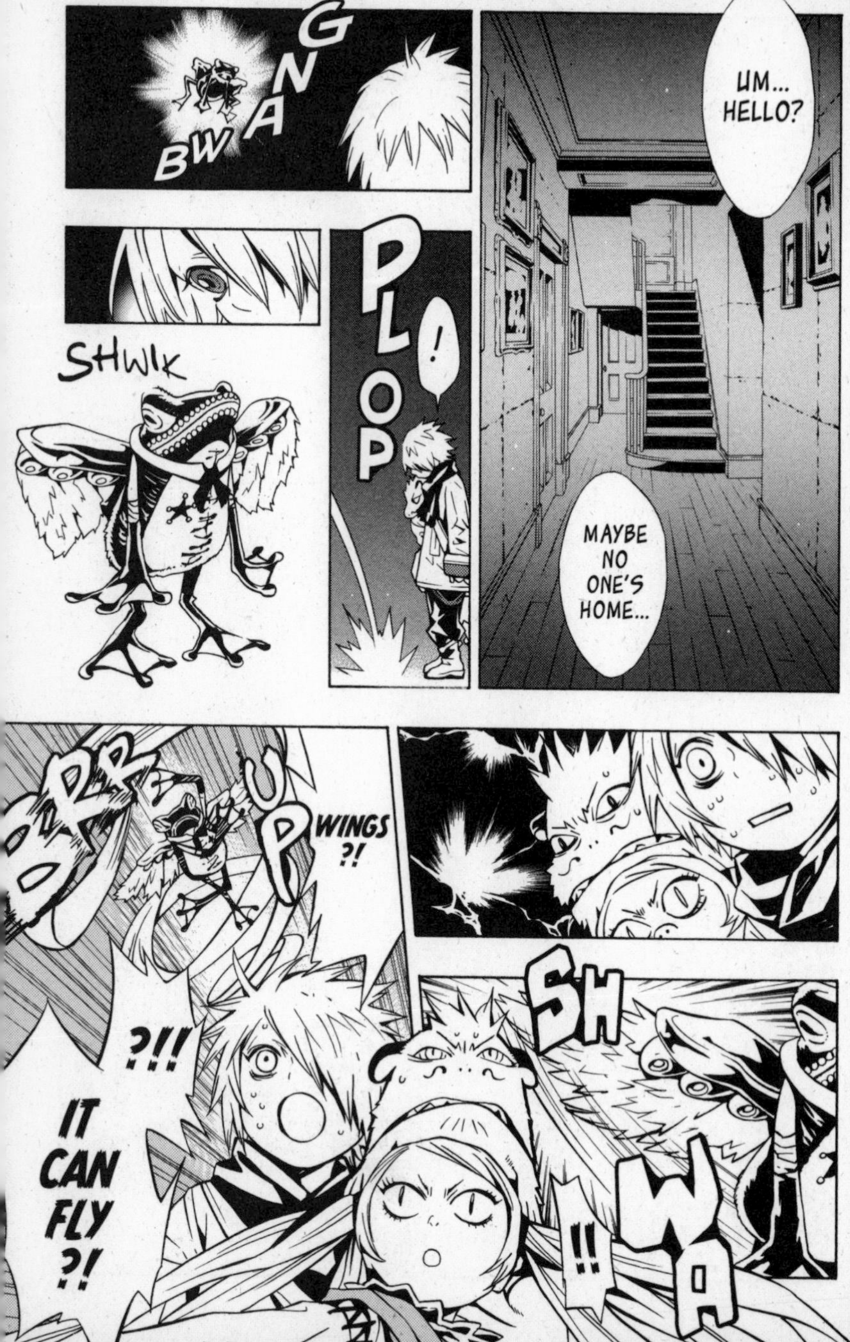
UM... HELLO?
MAYBE NO ONE'S HOME...
BWANG
!
PLOP
SHWIK
DRRUP
WINGS ?!
SHWA
?!!
!!
IT CAN FLY ?!

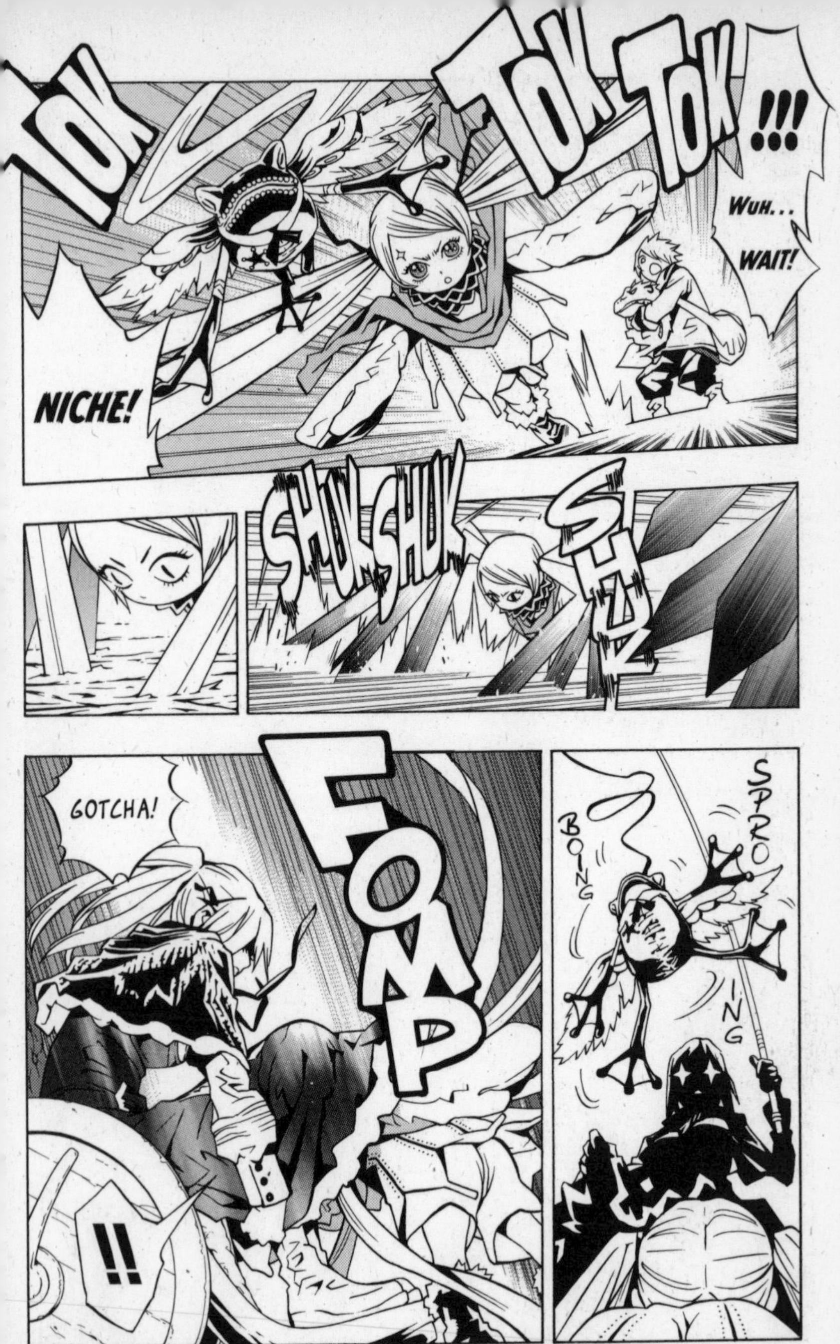
TOK TOK TOK!!!
WUH... WAIT!
NICHE!
SHUK SHUK
SHUK
SPRO
ING
BOING
GOTCHA!
FOMP
!!

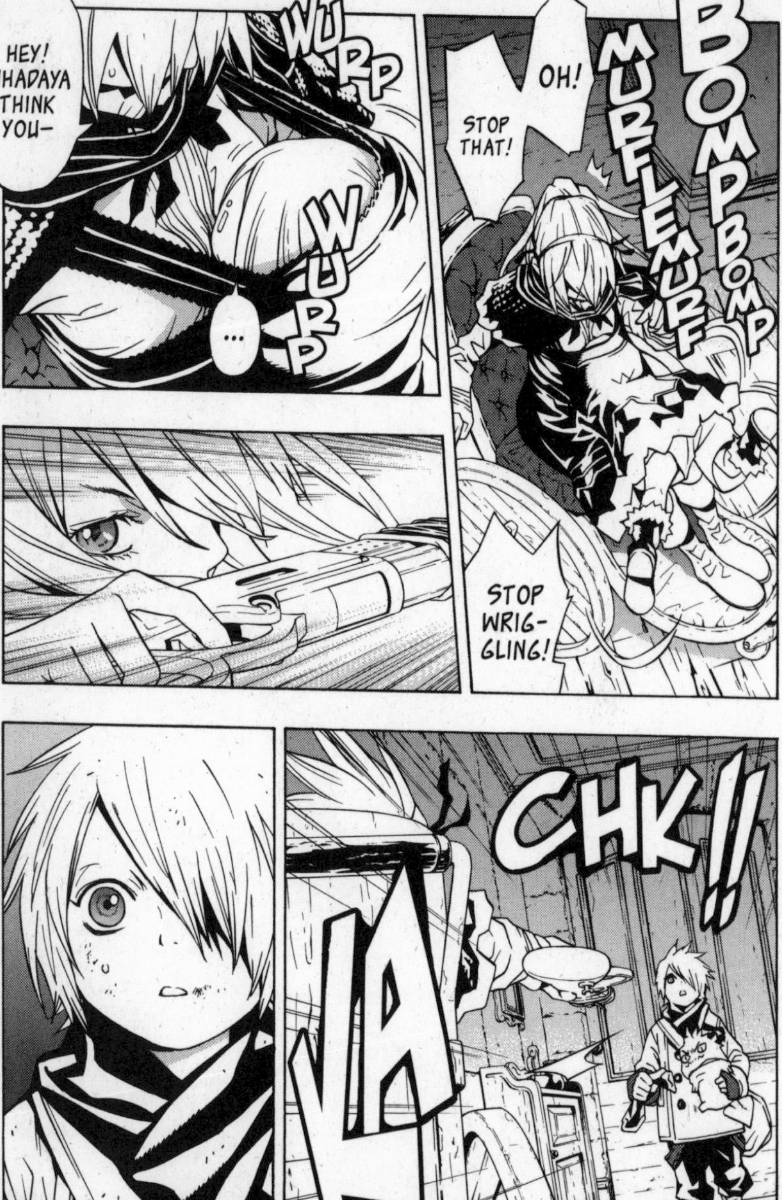
BOMPBOMP
MURFLEMURF
OH!
STOP THAT!
STOP WRIG-GLING!
HEY! WHADAYA THINK YOU—
WURP
WURP
...
CHK!!
KA

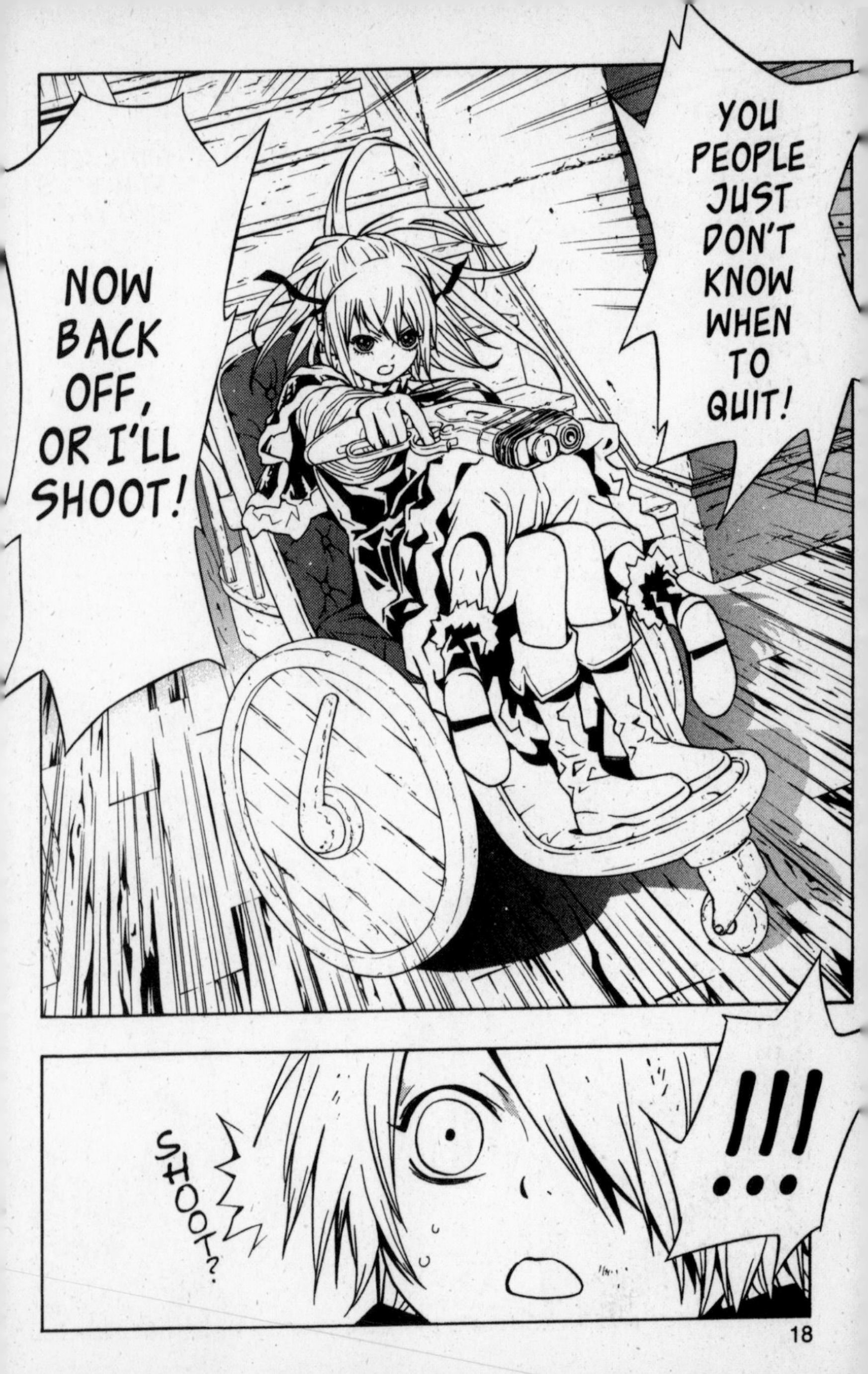
YOU PEOPLE JUST DON'T KNOW WHEN TO QUIT!
NOW BACK OFF, OR I'LL SHOOT!
!!!...
SHOOT?

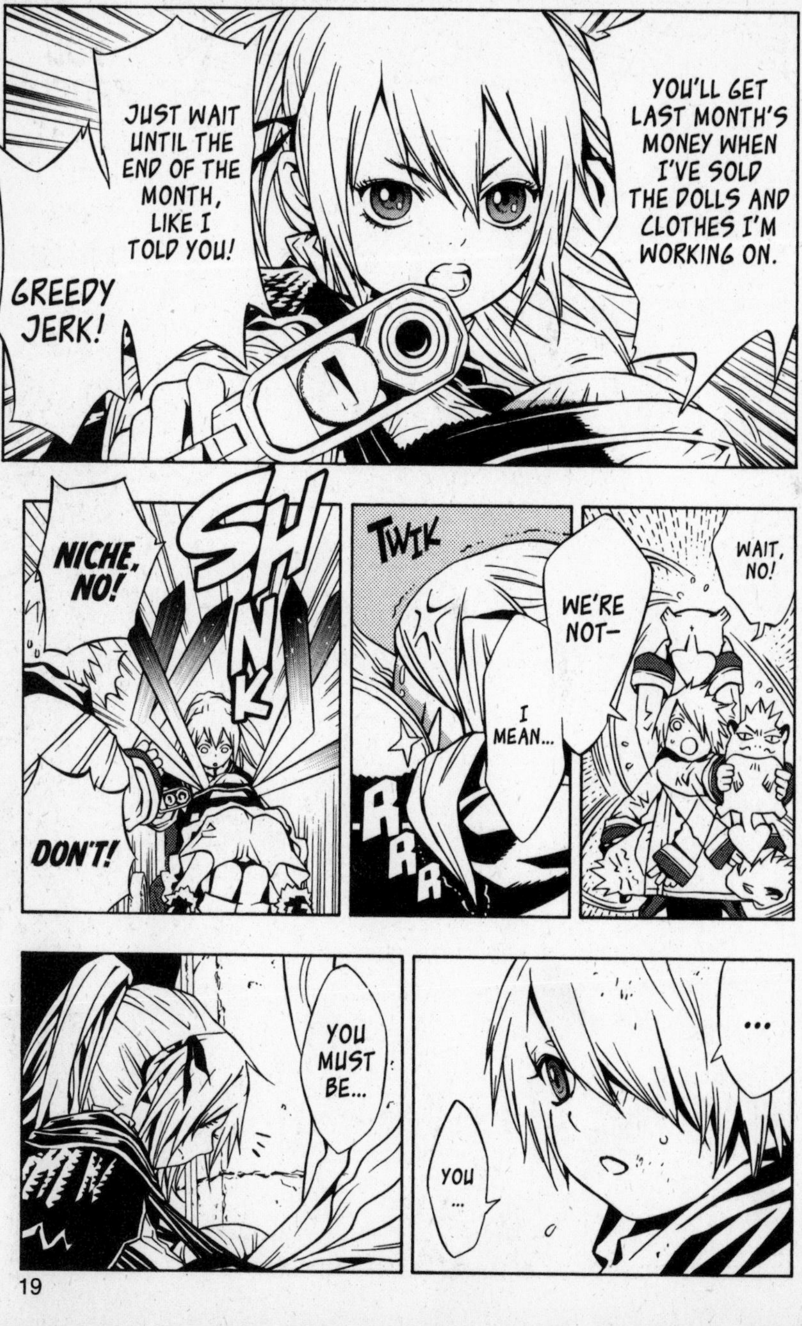
YOU'LL GET LAST MONTH'S MONEY WHEN I'VE SOLD THE DOLLS AND CLOTHES I'M WORKING ON.
JUST WAIT UNTIL THE END OF THE MONTH, LIKE I TOLD YOU!
GREEDY JERK!
WAIT, NO!
TWIK
WE'RE NOT—
I MEAN...
R-RRR
SHNK
NICHE, NO!
DON'T!
...
YOU ...
YOU MUST BE...

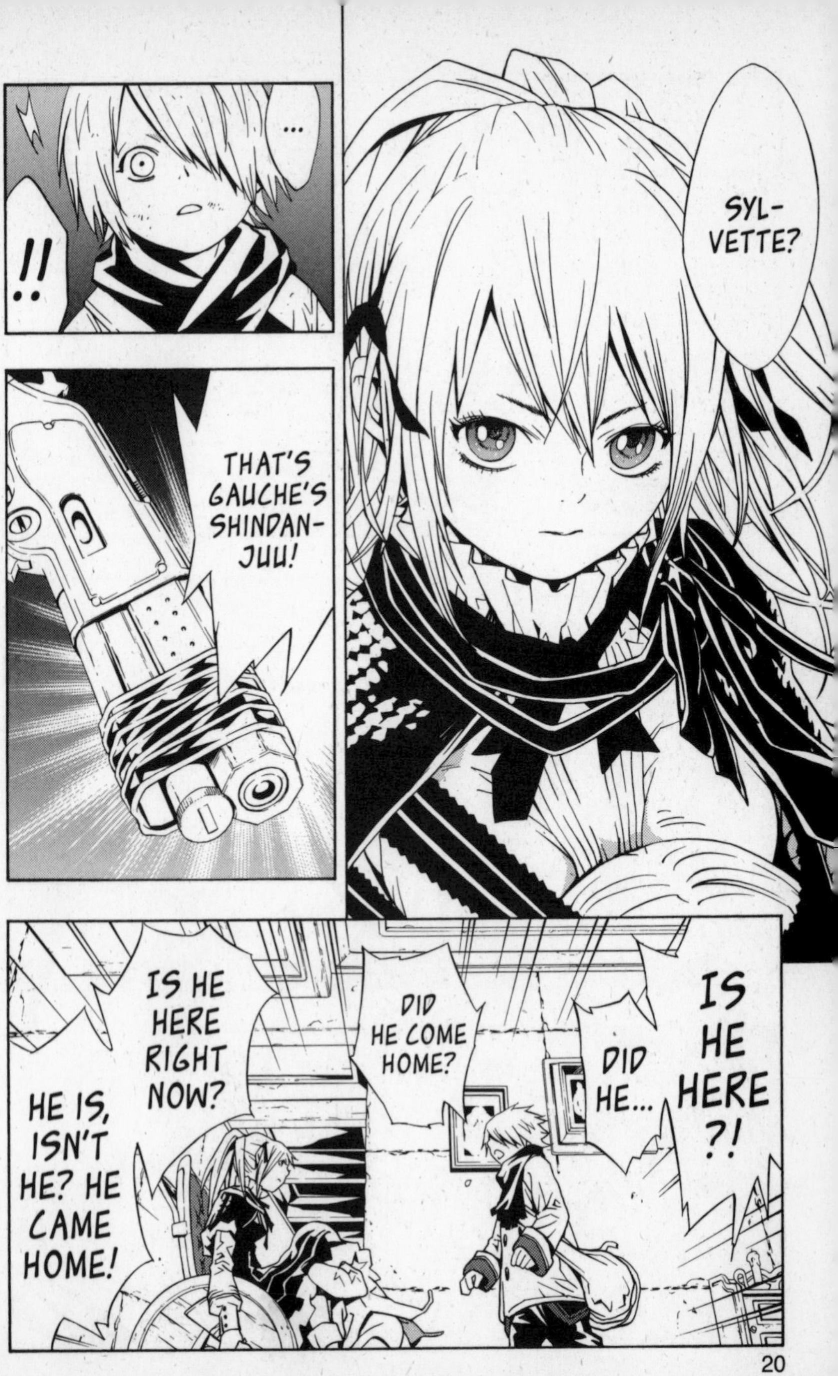
SYL-
VETTE?
...
!!
THAT'S GAUCHE'S SHINDAN-JUU!
IS HE HERE?!
DID HE...
DID HE COME HOME?
IS HE HERE RIGHT NOW?
HE IS, ISN'T HE? HE CAME HOME!

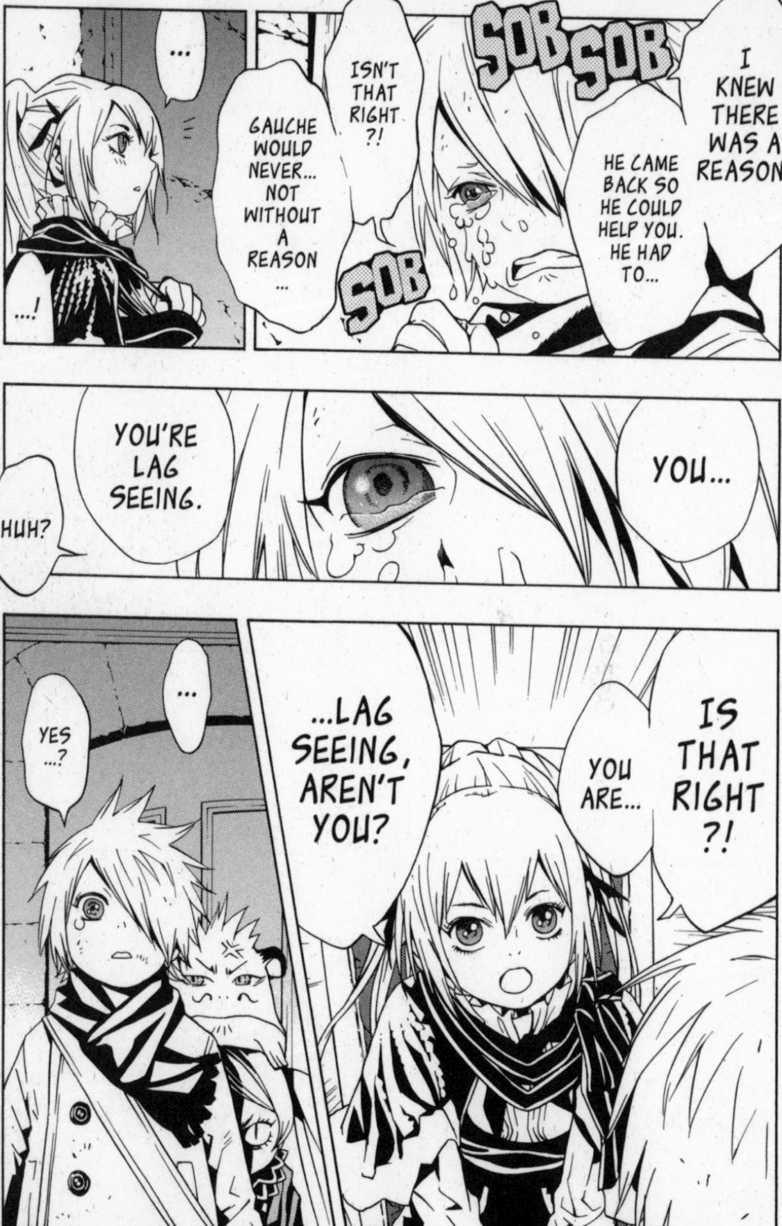
I KNEW THERE WAS A REASON!
HE CAME BACK SO HE COULD HELP YOU. HE HAD TO...
SOB SOB
ISN'T THAT RIGHT?!
SOB
GAUCHE WOULD NEVER... NOT WITHOUT A REASON ...
...
...!
YOU...
YOU'RE LAG SEEING.
HUH?
IS THAT RIGHT?!
YOU ARE...
...LAG SEEING, AREN'T YOU?
...
YES ...?

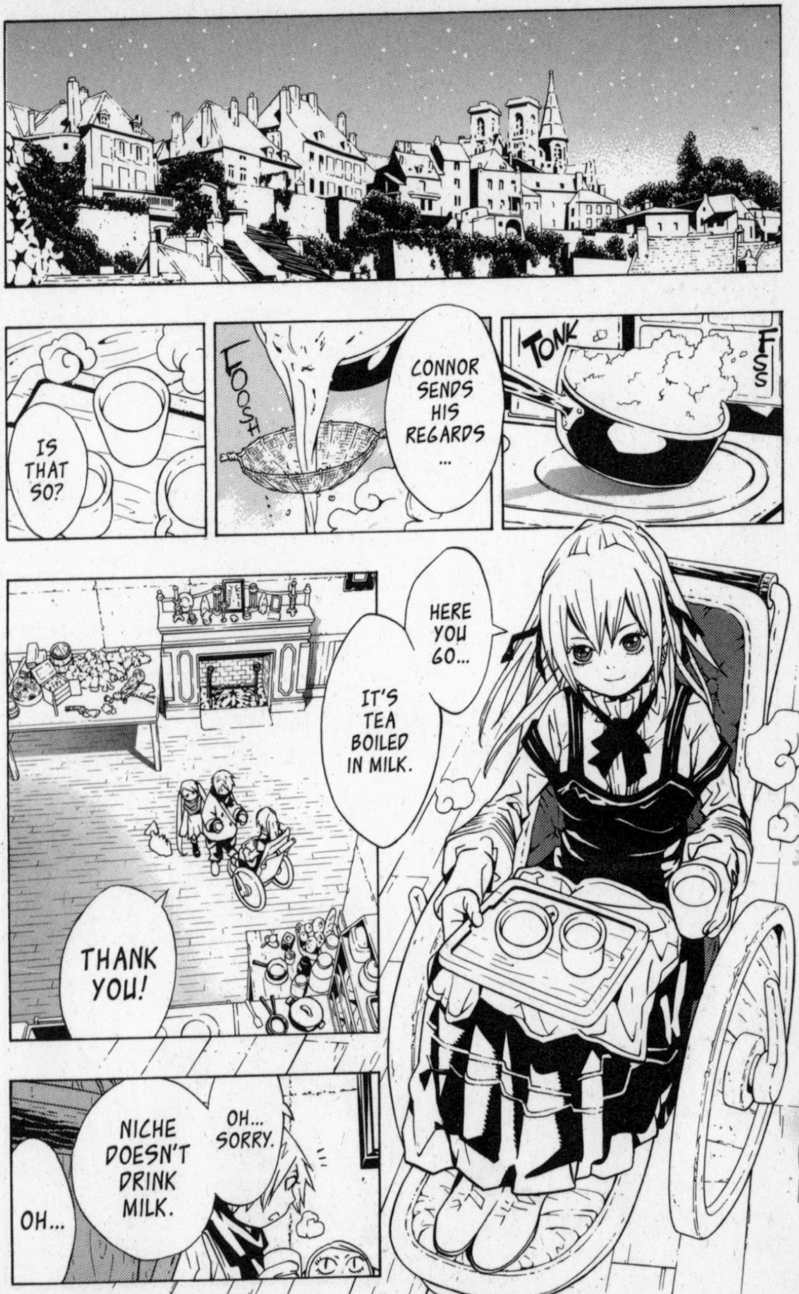
TONK
FSS
FOOSH
CONNOR SENDS HIS REGARDS ...
IS THAT SO?
HERE YOU GO...
IT'S TEA BOILED IN MILK.
THANK YOU!
OH... SORRY.
NICHE DOESN'T DRINK MILK.
OH...

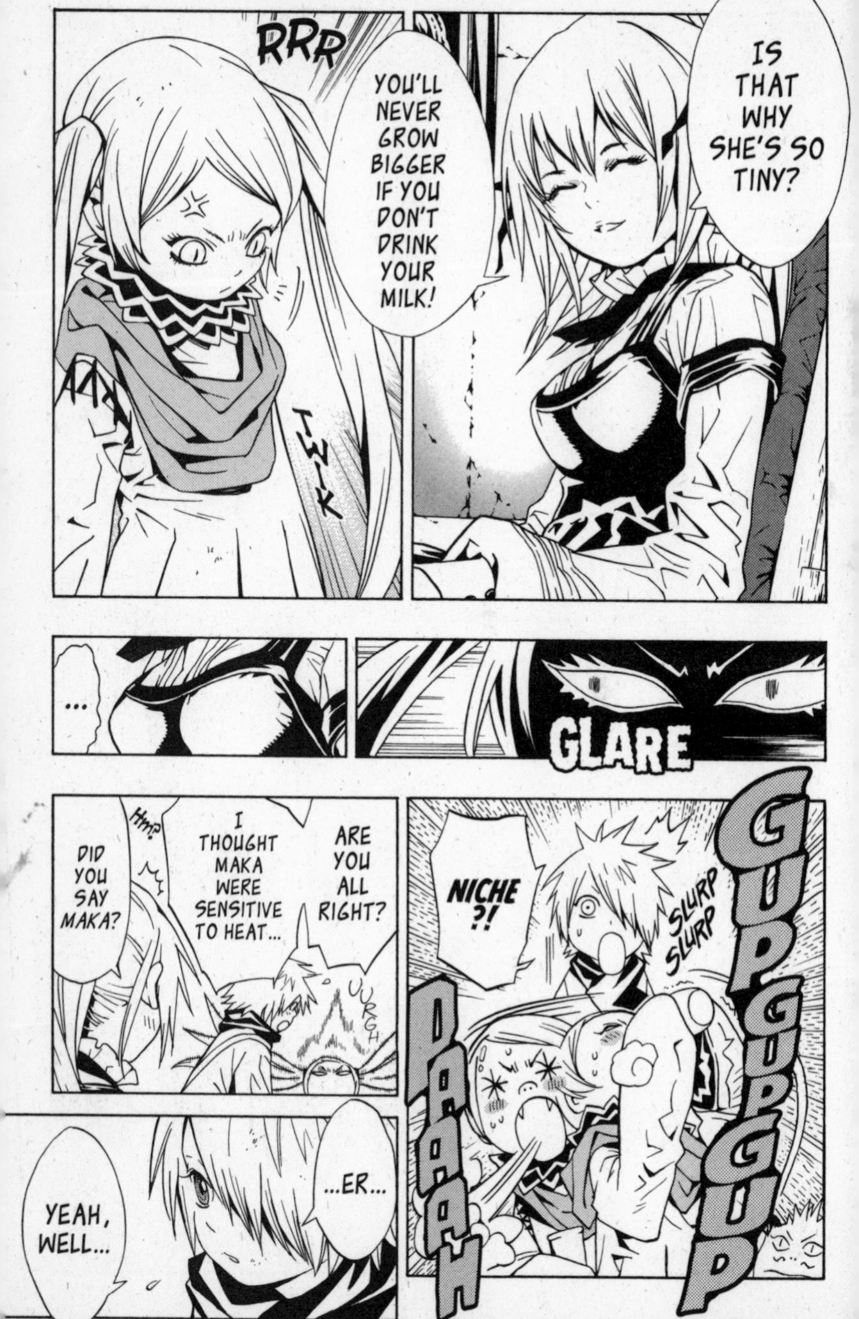
IS THAT WHY SHE'S SO TINY?
YOU'LL NEVER GROW BIGGER IF YOU DON'T DRINK YOUR MILK!
RRR
TWIK
GLARE
...
NICHE ?!
SLURP SLURP
GUPGUPGUPGUP
DAAAH
ARE YOU ALL RIGHT?
I THOUGHT MAKA WERE SENSITIVE TO HEAT...
Hm?
DID YOU SAY MAKA?
UURGH
...ER...
YEAH, WELL...

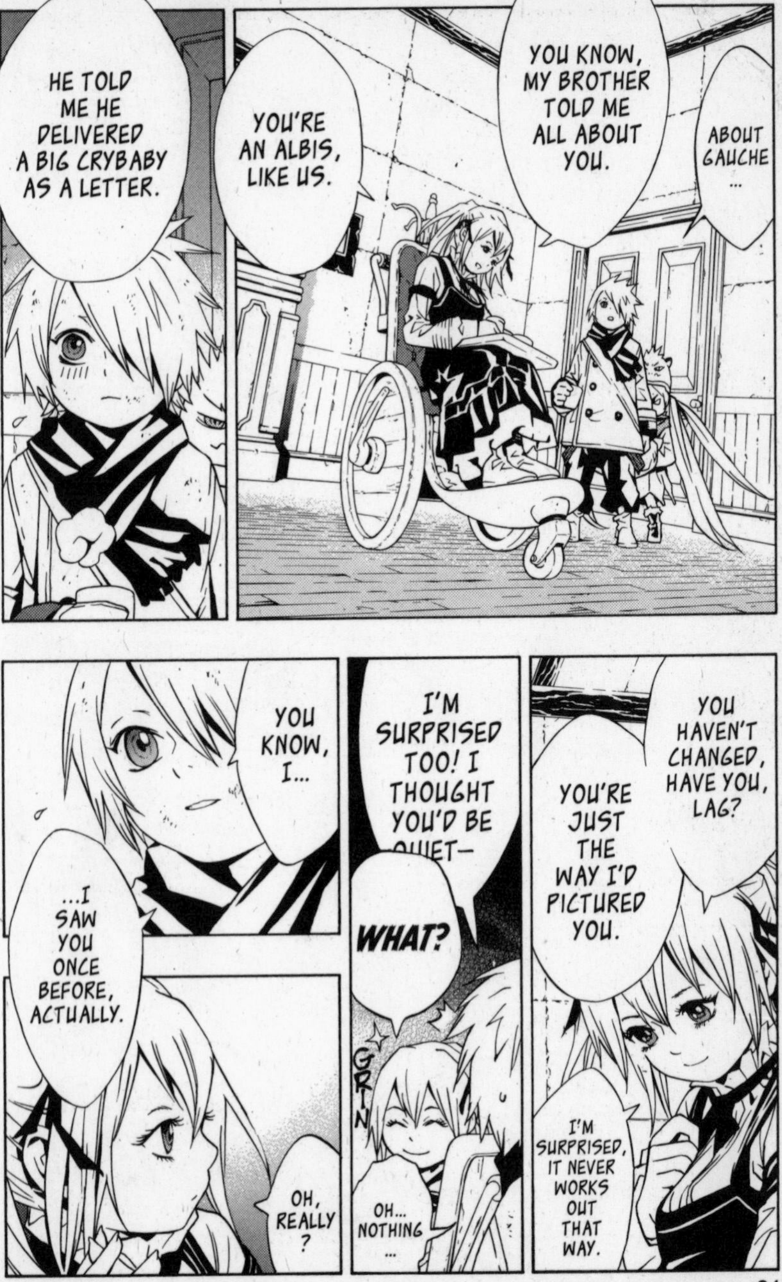
ABOUT GAUCHE ...
YOU KNOW, MY BROTHER TOLD ME ALL ABOUT YOU.
YOU'RE AN ALBIS, LIKE US.
HE TOLD ME HE DELIVERED A BIG CRYBABY AS A LETTER.
YOU HAVEN'T CHANGED, HAVE YOU, LAG?
YOU'RE JUST THE WAY I'D PICTURED YOU.
I'M SURPRISED, IT NEVER WORKS OUT THAT WAY.
I'M SURPRISED TOO! I THOUGHT YOU'D BE QUIET—
WHAT?
GRIN
OH... NOTHING ...
YOU KNOW, I...
...I SAW YOU ONCE BEFORE, ACTUALLY.
OH, REALLY ?

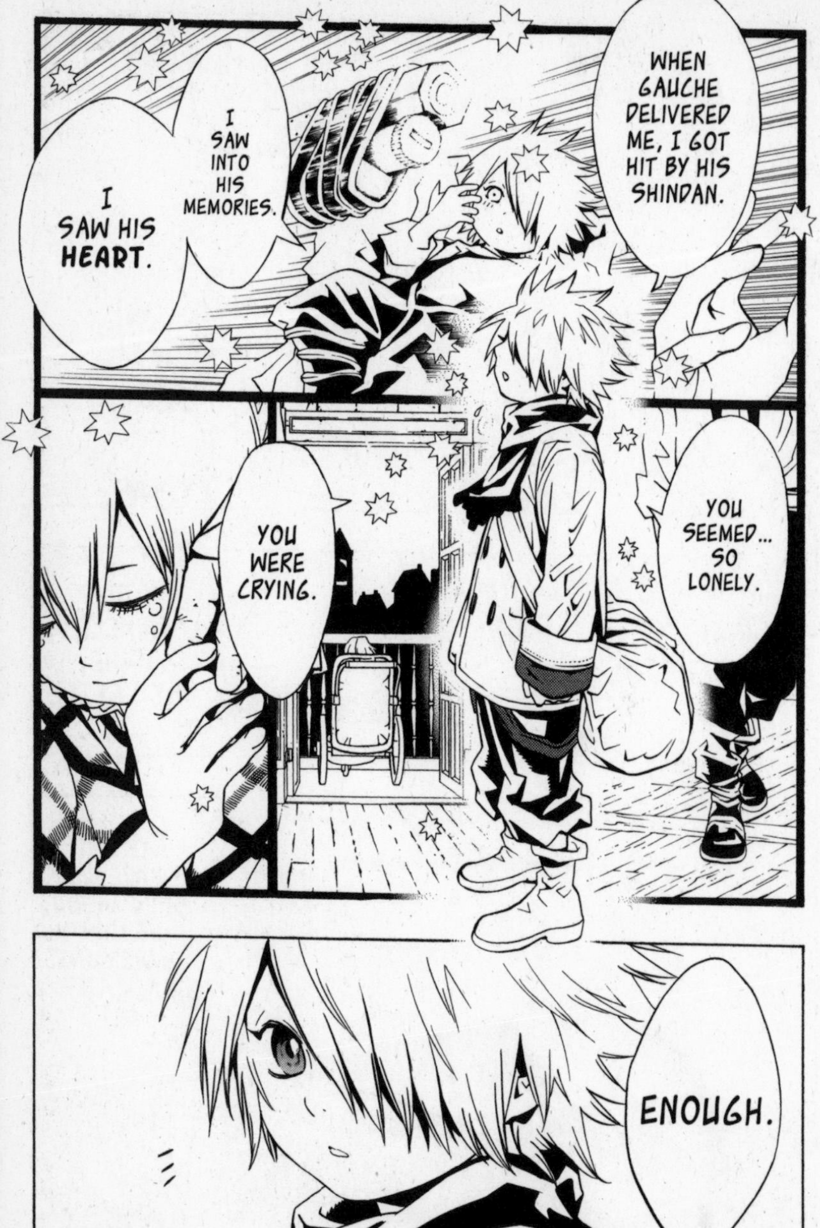
WHEN GAUCHE DELIVERED ME, I GOT HIT BY HIS SHINDAN.
I SAW INTO HIS MEMORIES.
I SAW HIS HEART.
YOU SEEMED... SO LONELY.
YOU WERE CRYING.
ENOUGH.

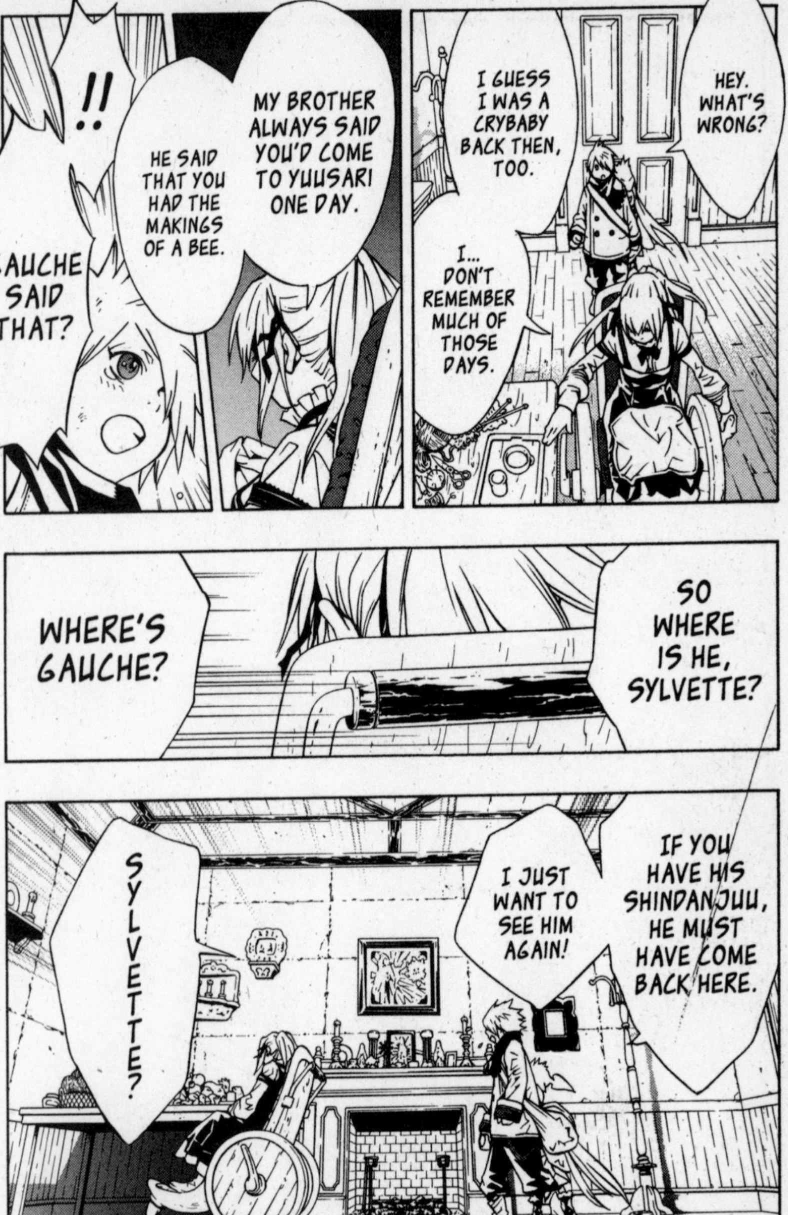
HEY. WHAT'S WRONG?
I GUESS I WAS A CRYBABY BACK THEN, TOO.
I... DON'T REMEMBER MUCH OF THOSE DAYS.
MY BROTHER ALWAYS SAID YOU'D COME TO YUUSARI ONE DAY.
HE SAID THAT YOU HAD THE MAKINGS OF A BEE.
!!
GAUCHE SAID THAT?
SO WHERE IS HE, SYLVETTE?
WHERE'S GAUCHE?
IF YOU HAVE HIS SHINDANJUU, HE MUST HAVE COME BACK HERE.
I JUST WANT TO SEE HIM AGAIN!
SYLVETTE?

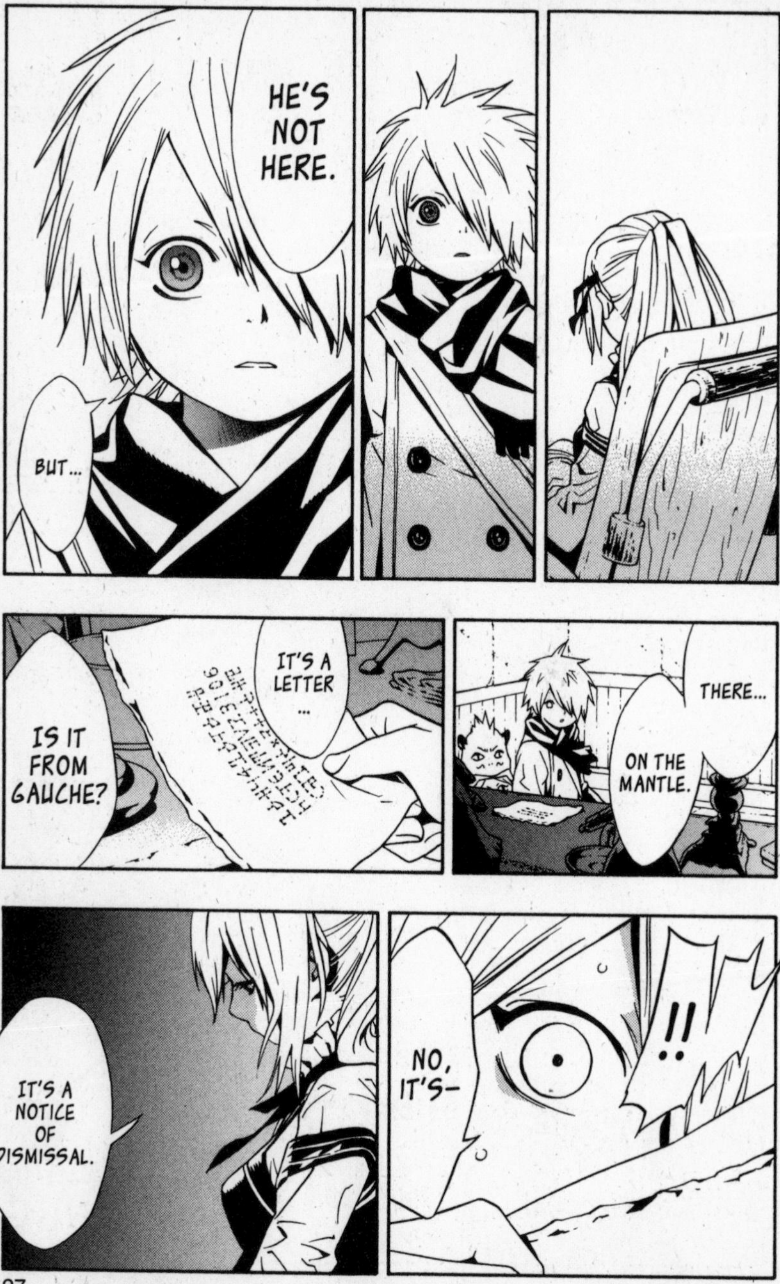
HE'S NOT HERE.
BUT...
THERE...
ON THE MANTLE.
IT'S A LETTER...
IS IT FROM GAUCHE?
!!
NO, IT'S—
IT'S A NOTICE OF DISMISSAL.

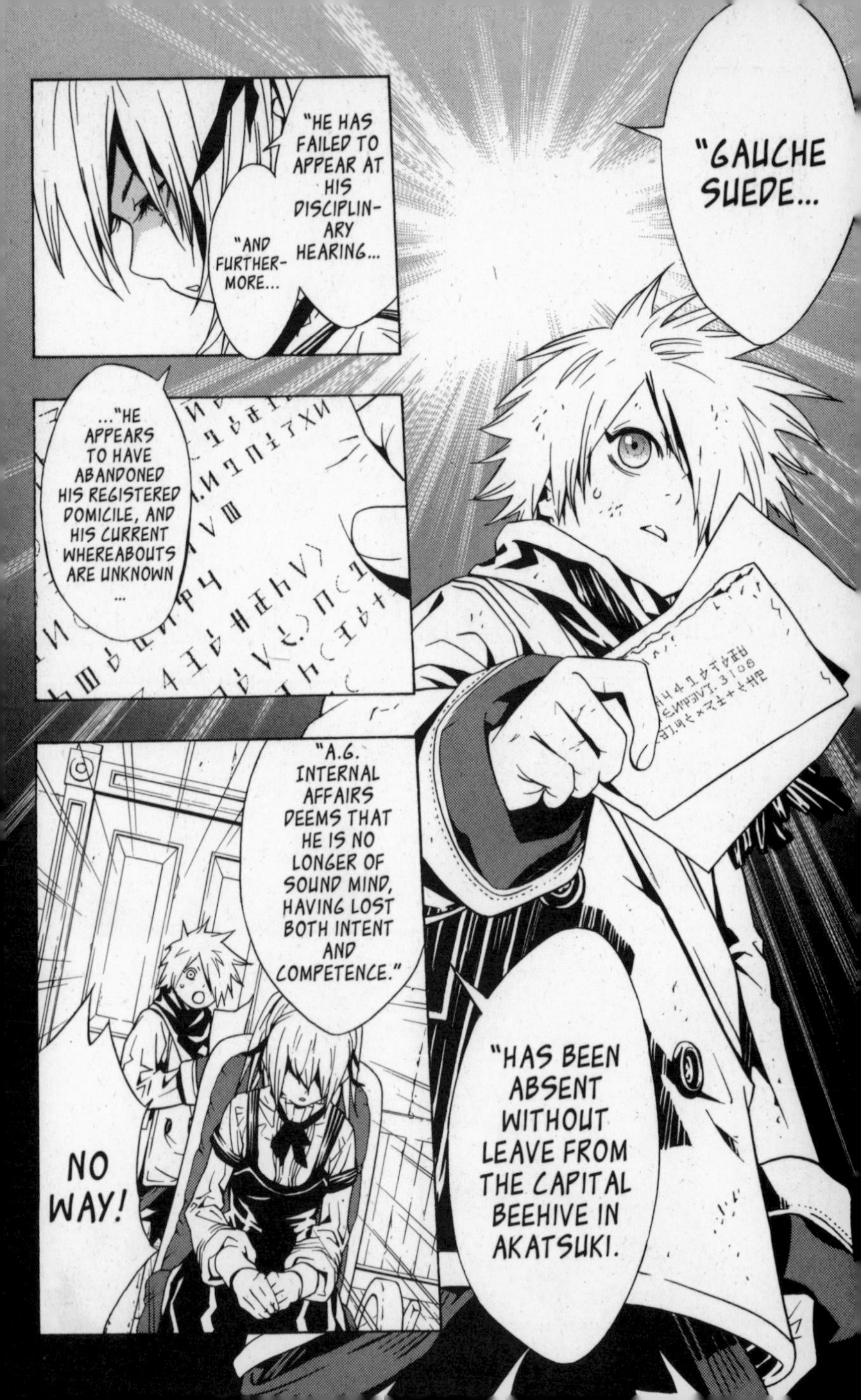
"GAUCHE SUEDE...
"HAS BEEN ABSENT WITHOUT LEAVE FROM THE CAPITAL BEEHIVE IN AKATSUKI.
"HE HAS FAILED TO APPEAR AT HIS DISCIPLINARY HEARING...
"AND FURTHERMORE...
..."HE APPEARS TO HAVE ABANDONED HIS REGISTERED DOMICILE, AND HIS CURRENT WHEREABOUTS ARE UNKNOWN ...
"A.G. INTERNAL AFFAIRS DEEMS THAT HE IS NO LONGER OF SOUND MIND, HAVING LOST BOTH INTENT AND COMPETENCE."
NO WAY!

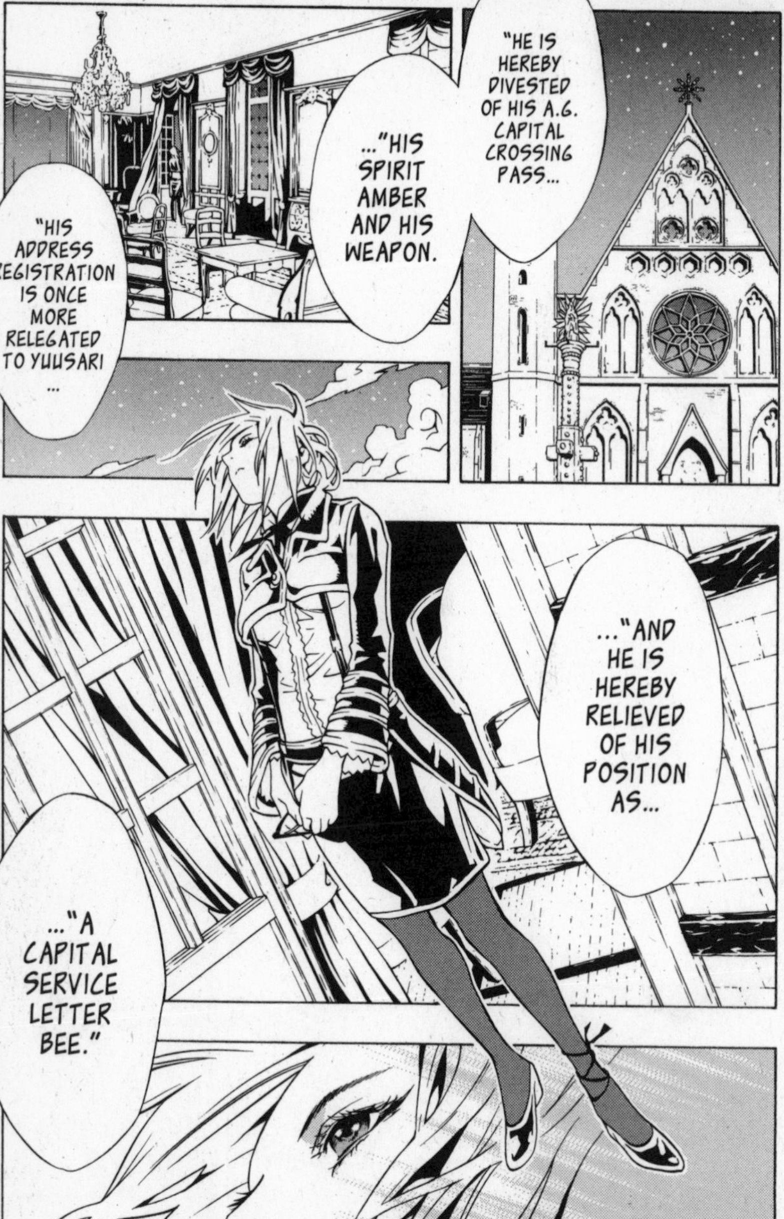
"HE IS HEREBY DIVESTED OF HIS A.G. CAPITAL CROSSING PASS...
..."HIS SPIRIT AMBER AND HIS WEAPON.
"HIS ADDRESS REGISTRATION IS ONCE MORE RELEGATED TO YUUSARI ...
..."AND HE IS HEREBY RELIEVED OF HIS POSITION AS...
..."A CAPITAL SERVICE LETTER BEE."

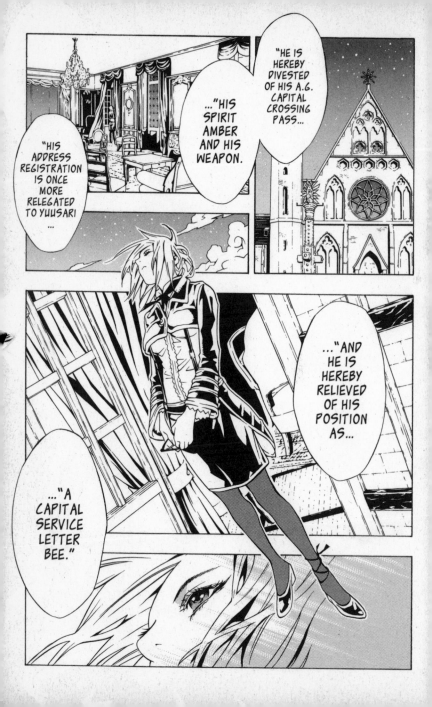

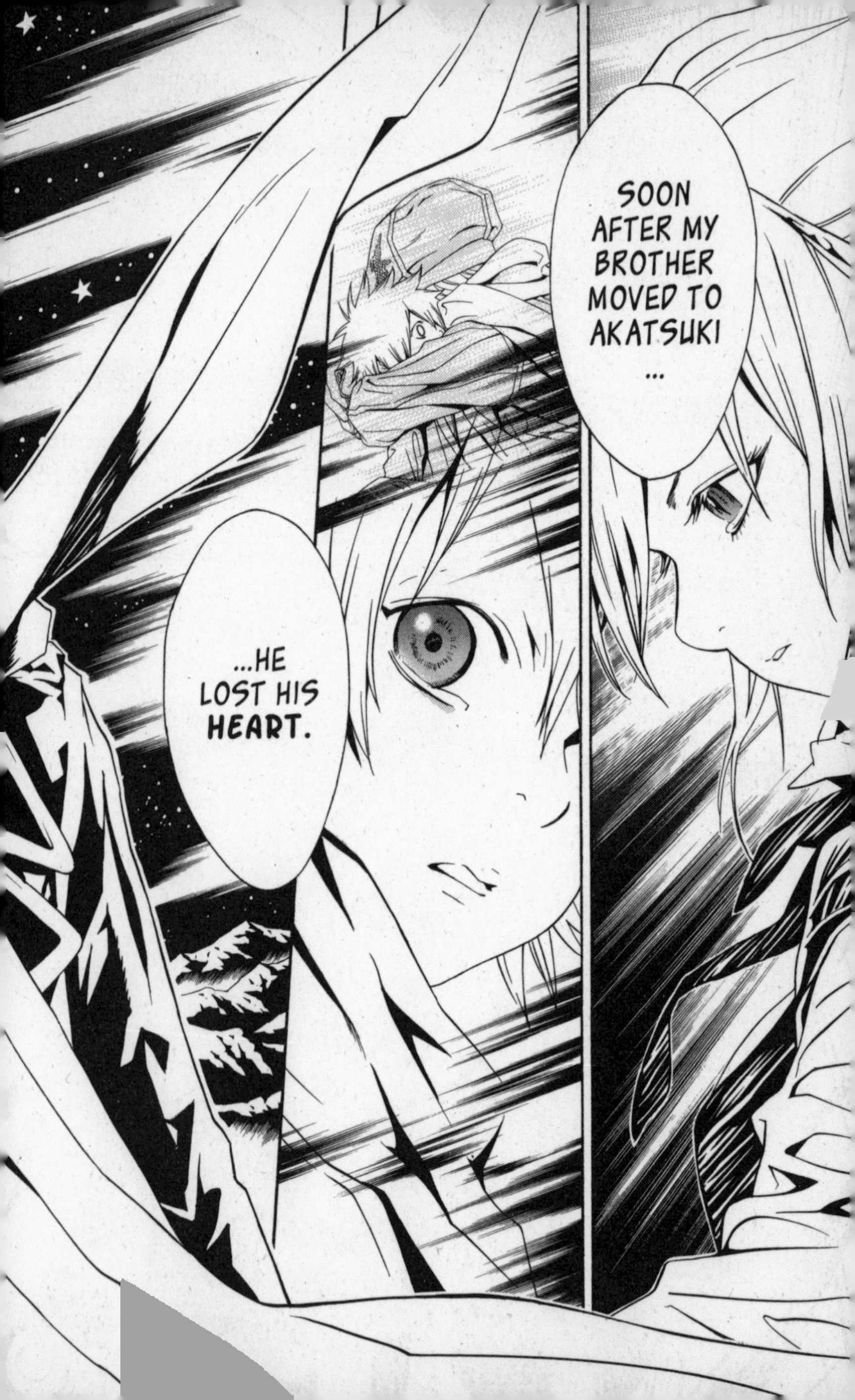
SOON AFTER MY BROTHER MOVED TO AKATSUKI ...
...HE LOST HIS HEART.

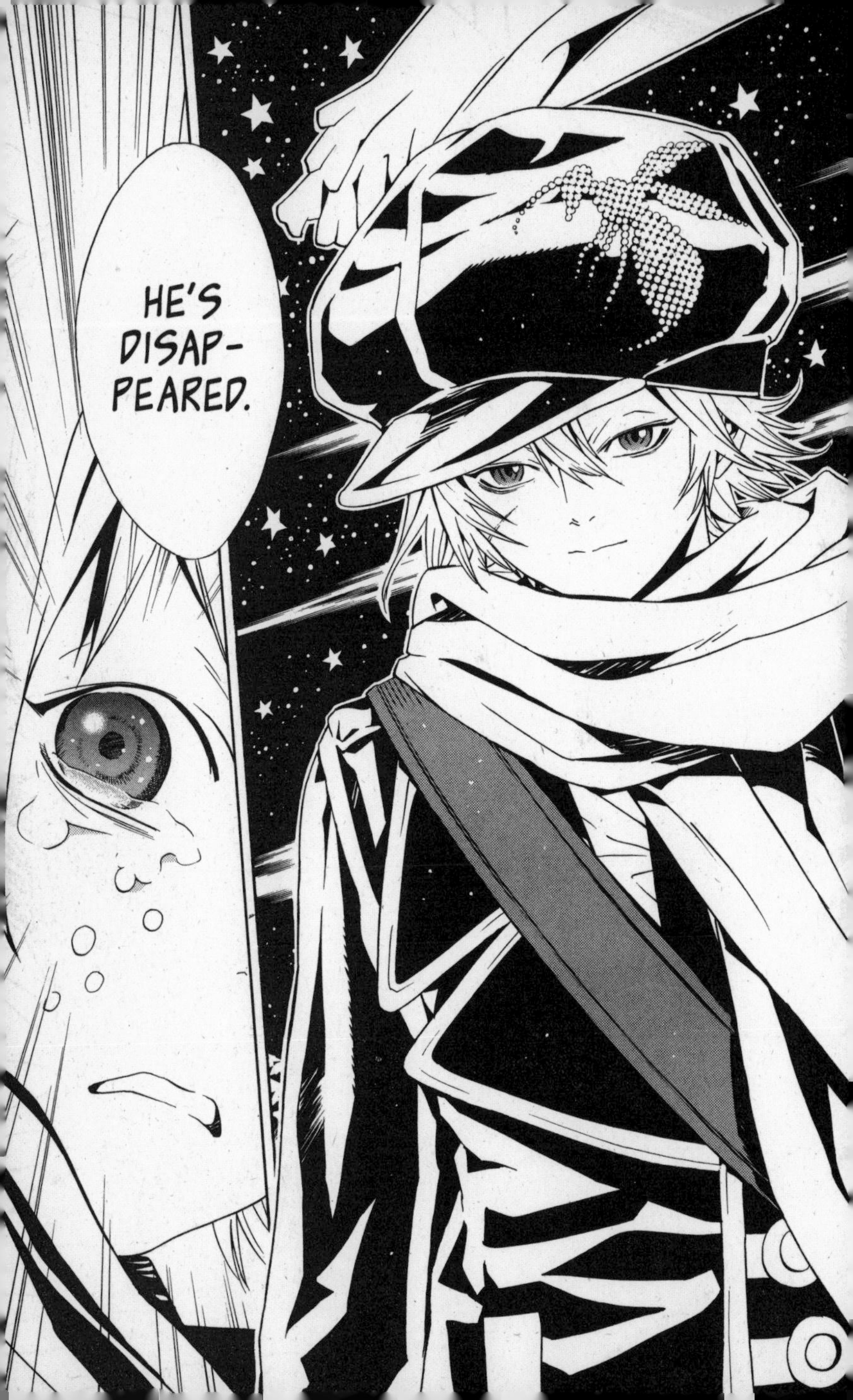
HE'S DISAP-PEARED.

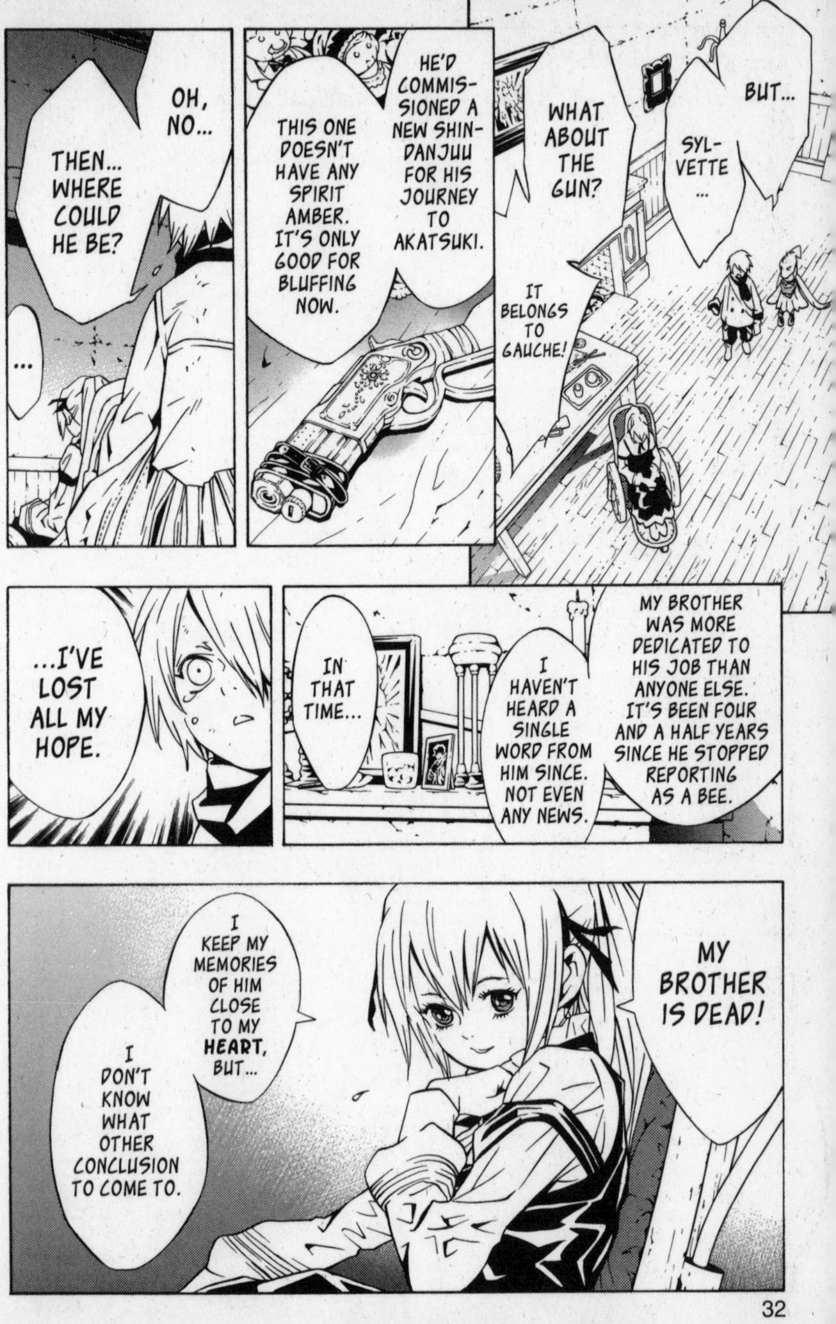
BUT...
SYLVETTE...
WHAT ABOUT THE GUN?
IT BELONGS TO GAUCHE!
HE'D COMMISSIONED A NEW SHINDANJUU FOR HIS JOURNEY TO AKATSUKI.
THIS ONE DOESN'T HAVE ANY SPIRIT AMBER. IT'S ONLY GOOD FOR BLUFFING NOW.
OH, NO...
THEN... WHERE COULD HE BE?
...
MY BROTHER WAS MORE DEDICATED TO HIS JOB THAN ANYONE ELSE. IT'S BEEN FOUR AND A HALF YEARS SINCE HE STOPPED REPORTING AS A BEE.
I HAVEN'T HEARD A SINGLE WORD FROM HIM SINCE. NOT EVEN ANY NEWS.
IN THAT TIME...
...I'VE LOST ALL MY HOPE.
MY BROTHER IS DEAD!
I KEEP MY MEMORIES OF HIM CLOSE TO MY HEART, BUT...
I DON'T KNOW WHAT OTHER CONCLUSION TO COME TO.

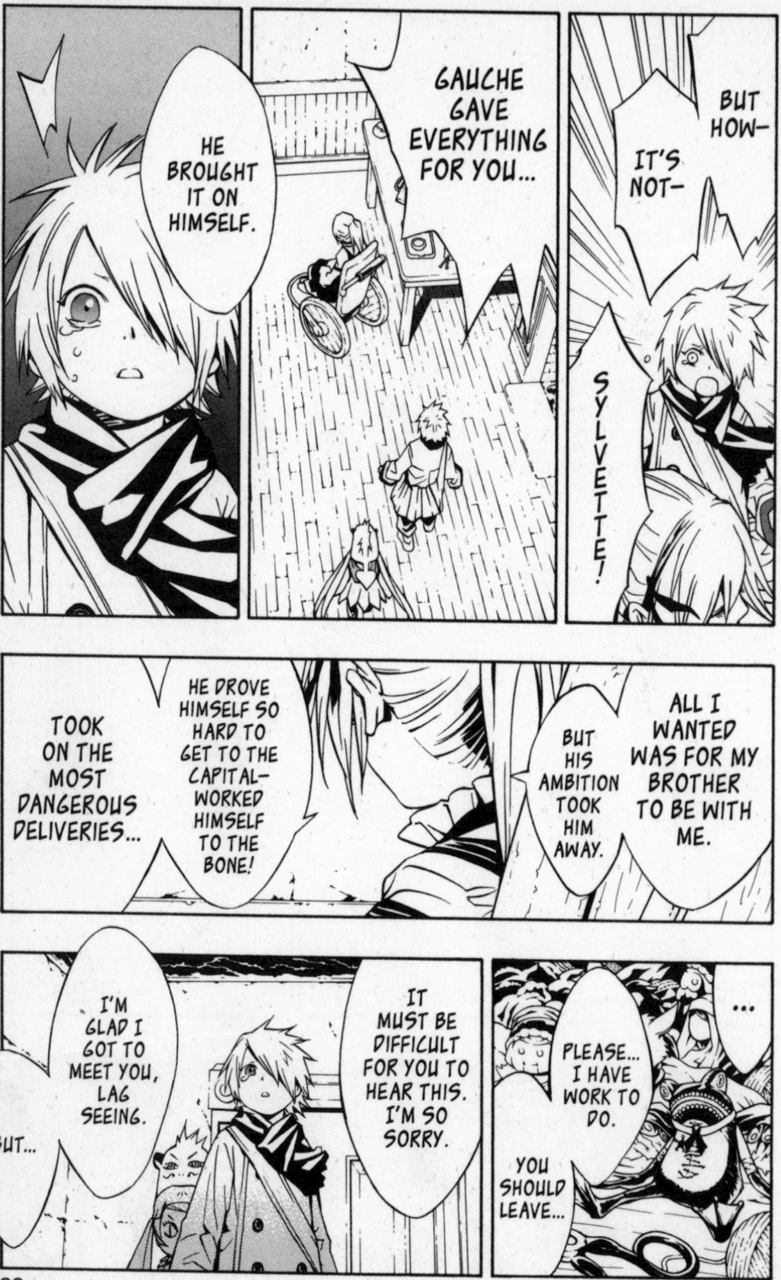
BUT HOW—
IT'S NOT—
SYLVETTE!
GAUCHE GAVE EVERYTHING FOR YOU...
HE BROUGHT IT ON HIMSELF.
ALL I WANTED WAS FOR MY BROTHER TO BE WITH ME.
BUT HIS AMBITION TOOK HIM AWAY.
HE DROVE HIMSELF SO HARD TO GET TO THE CAPITAL—WORKED HIMSELF TO THE BONE!
TOOK ON THE MOST DANGEROUS DELIVERIES...
...
PLEASE... I HAVE WORK TO DO.
YOU SHOULD LEAVE...
IT MUST BE DIFFICULT FOR YOU TO HEAR THIS. I'M SO SORRY.
I'M GLAD I GOT TO MEET YOU, LAG SEEING.
BUT...

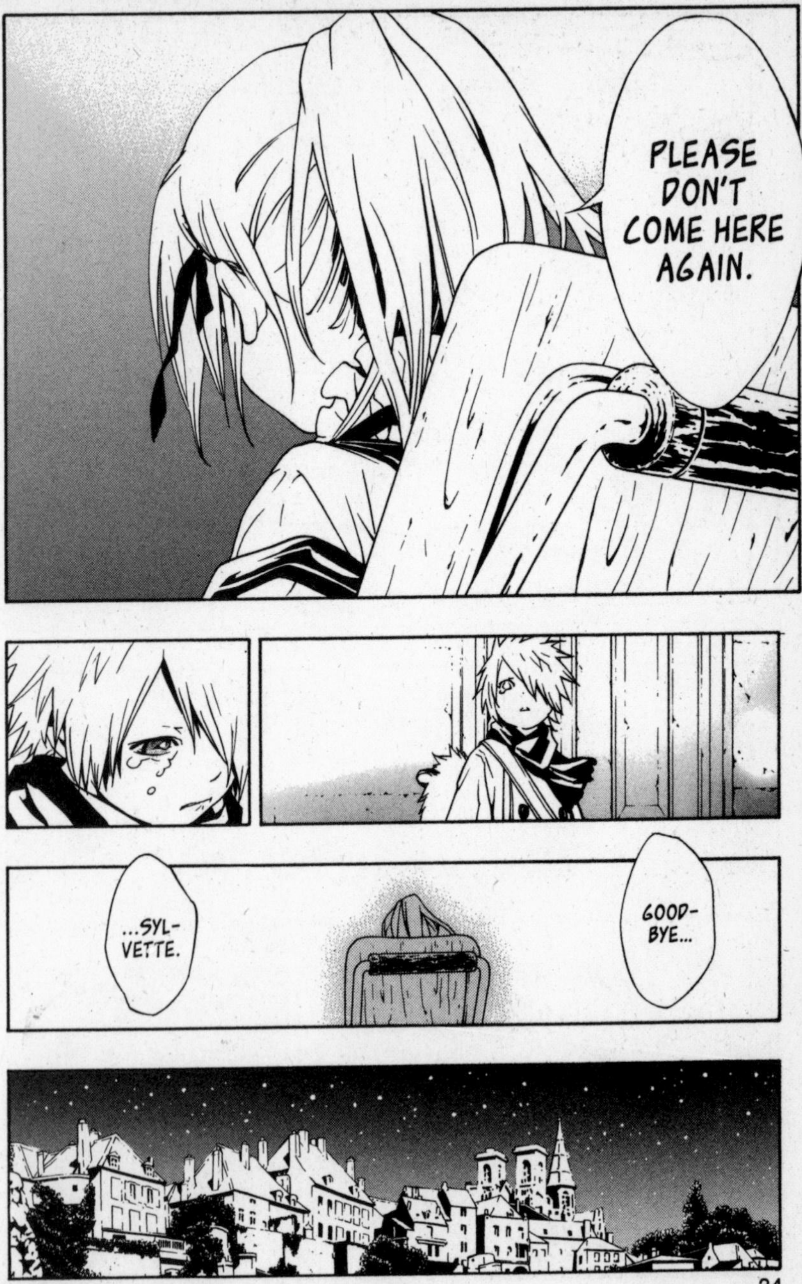
PLEASE DON'T COME HERE AGAIN.
GOOD-BYE...
...SYL-VETTE.

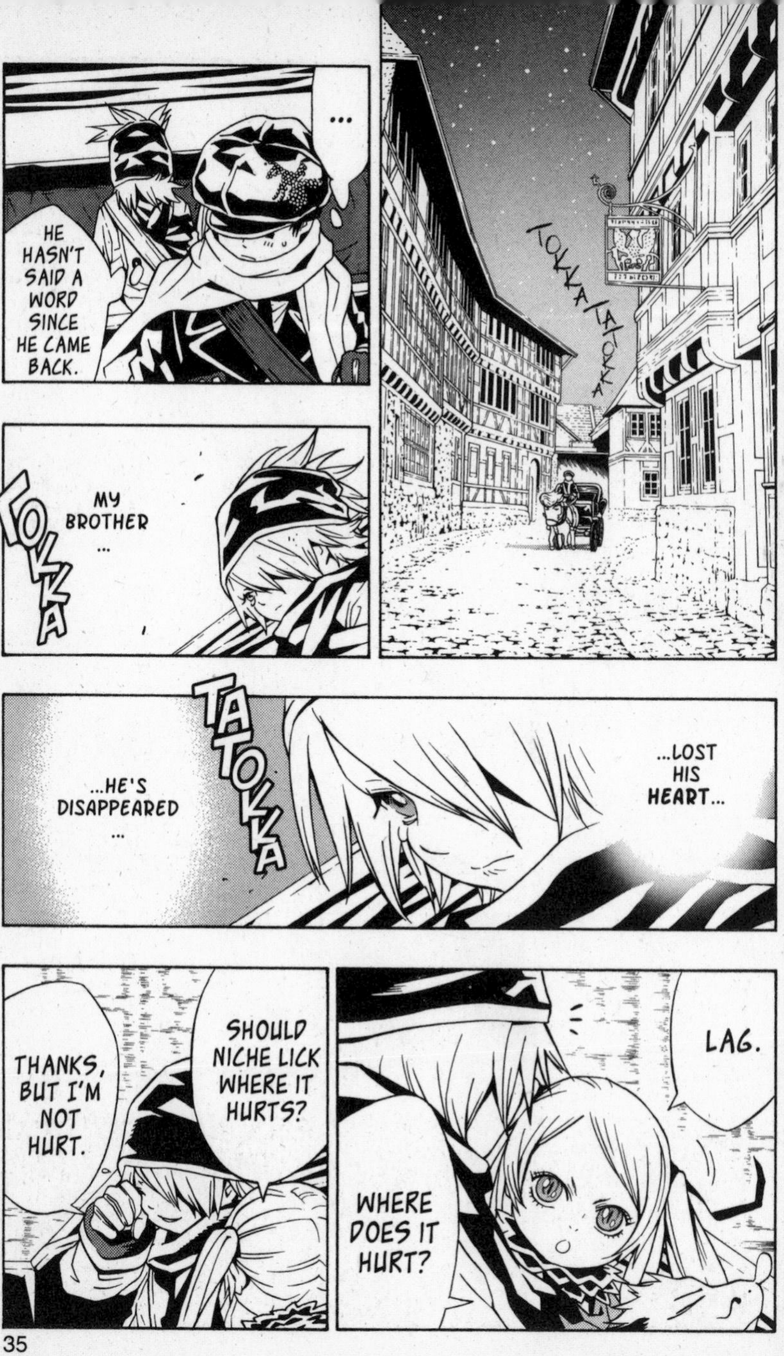
TOKKA TATOKKA
...
HE HASN'T SAID A WORD SINCE HE CAME BACK.
MY BROTHER ...
TOKKA
...LOST HIS HEART...
TATOKKA
...HE'S DISAPPEARED ...
LAG.
WHERE DOES IT HURT?
SHOULD NICHE LICK WHERE IT HURTS?
THANKS, BUT I'M NOT HURT.

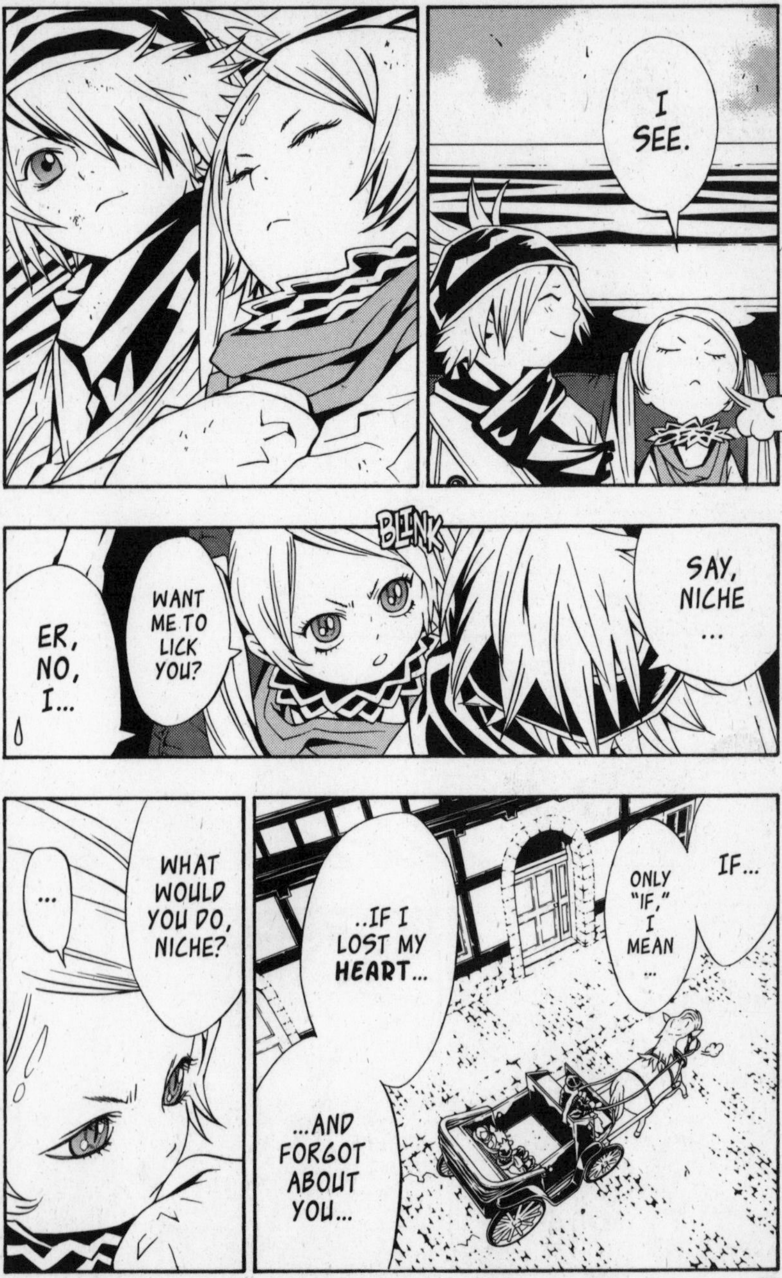
I SEE.
SAY, NICHE ...
BLINK
WANT ME TO LICK YOU?
ER, NO, I...
IF...
ONLY "IF," I MEAN ...
..IF I LOST MY HEART...
...AND FORGOT ABOUT YOU...
WHAT WOULD YOU DO, NICHE?
...

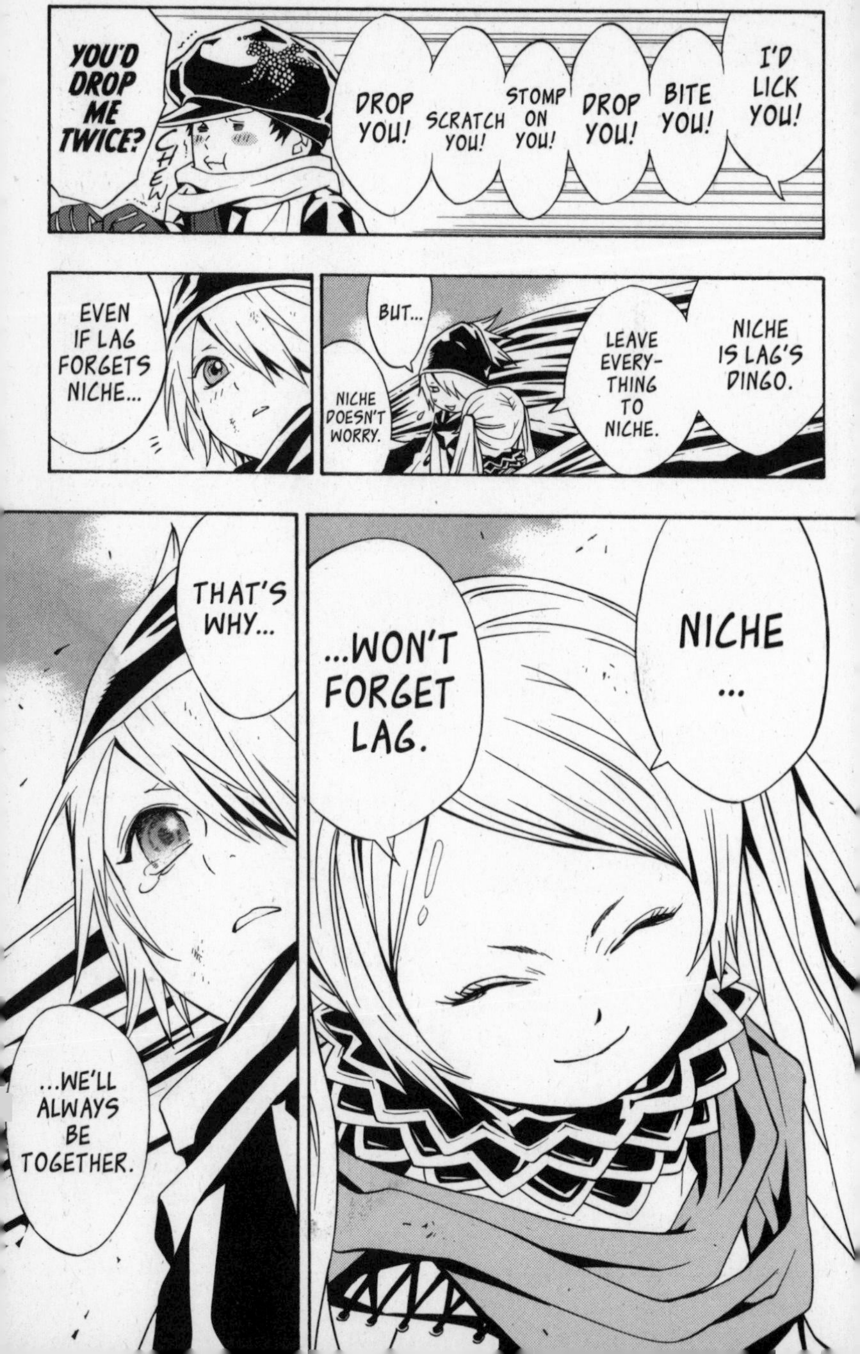
I'D LICK YOU!
BITE YOU!
DROP YOU!
STOMP ON YOU!
SCRATCH YOU!
DROP YOU!
YOU'D DROP ME TWICE?
CHEW
NICHE IS LAG'S DINGO.
LEAVE EVERY-THING TO NICHE.
BUT...
NICHE DOESN'T WORRY.
EVEN IF LAG FORGETS NICHE...
NICHE ...
...WON'T FORGET LAG.
THAT'S WHY...
...WE'LL ALWAYS BE TOGETHER.

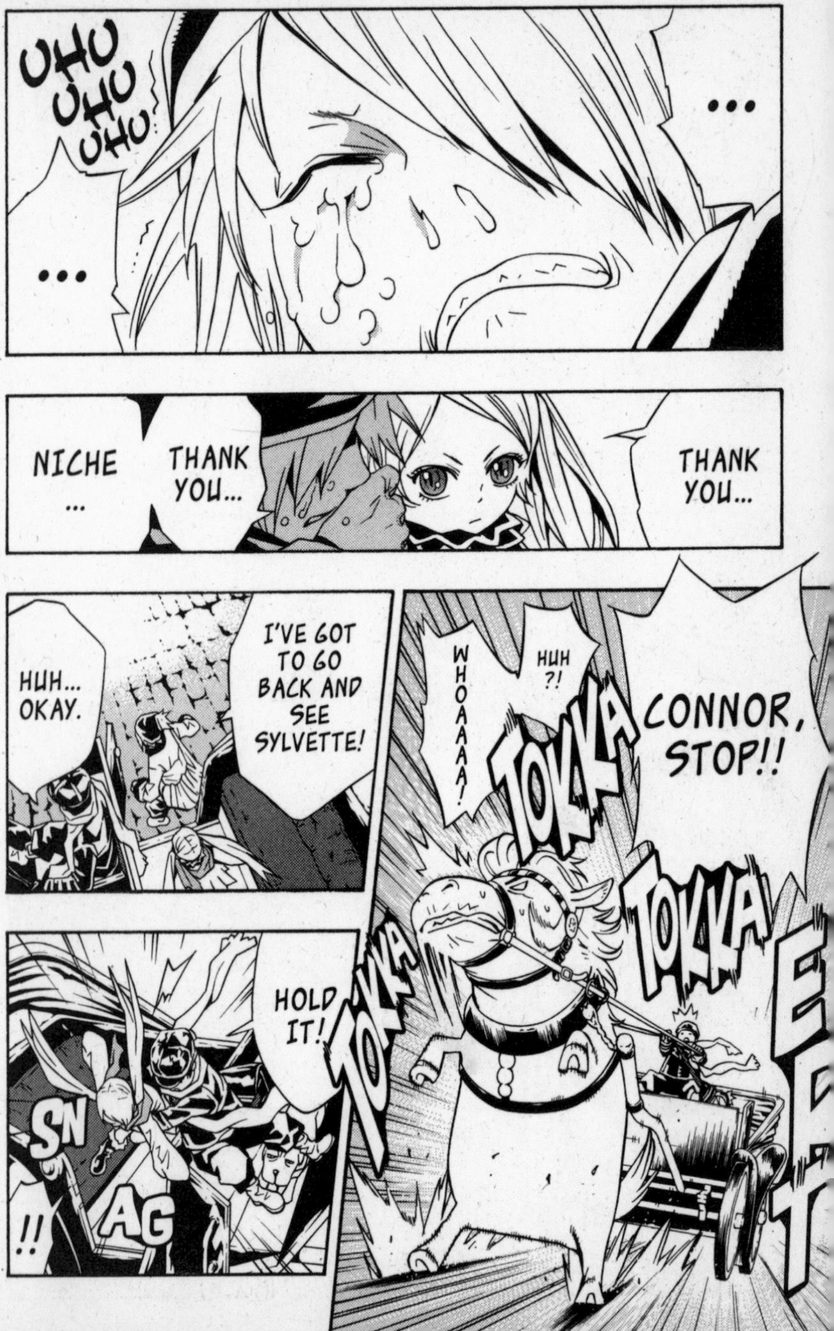
...
UHO UHO UHO
...
THANK YOU...
THANK YOU...
NICHE ...
CONNOR, STOP!!
HUH ?!
WHOAAAA!
TOKKA
TOKKA
TOKKA
EEEK
I'VE GOT TO GO BACK AND SEE SYLVETTE!
HUH... OKAY.
HOLD IT!
SNAG
!!

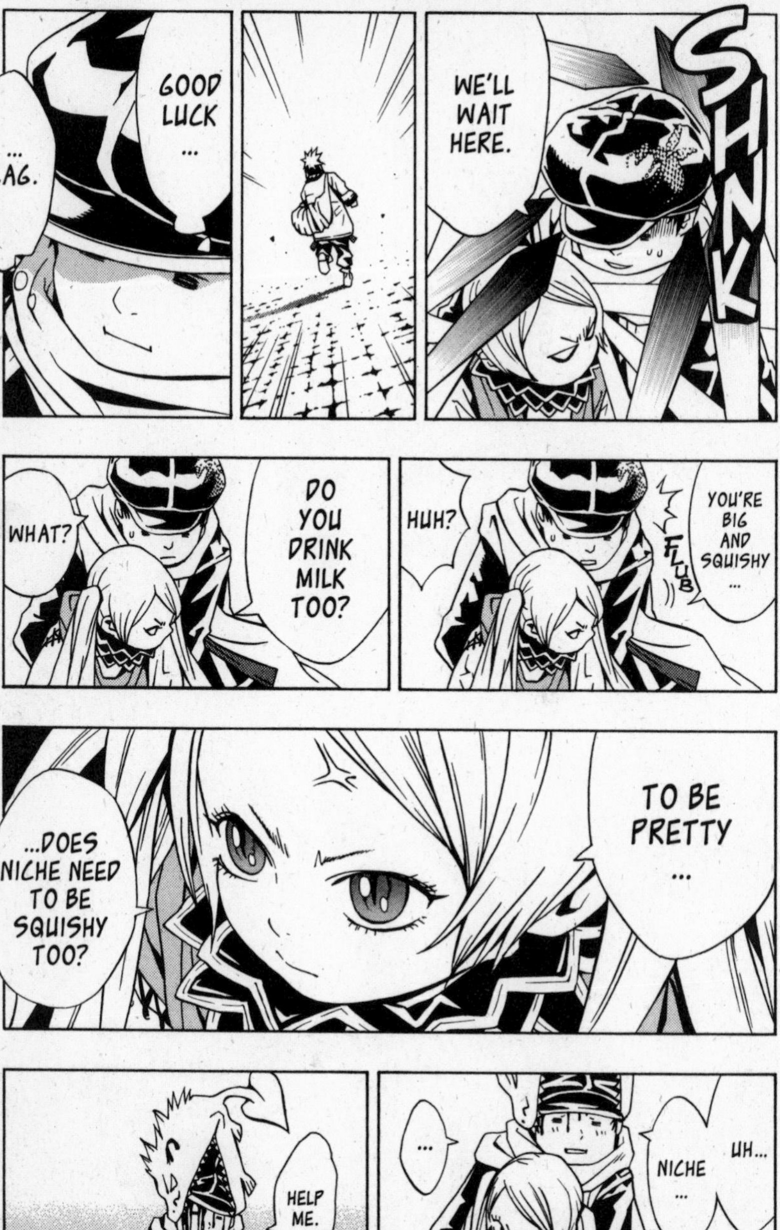
SHNK
WE'LL WAIT HERE.
GOOD LUCK ...
... LAG.
YOU'RE BIG AND SQUISHY ...
FLUB
HUH?
DO YOU DRINK MILK TOO?
WHAT?
TO BE PRETTY ...
...DOES NICHE NEED TO BE SQUISHY TOO?
UH...
NICHE ...
...
HELP ME.

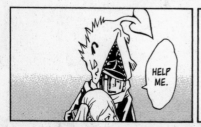

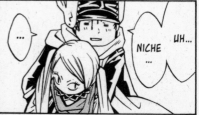

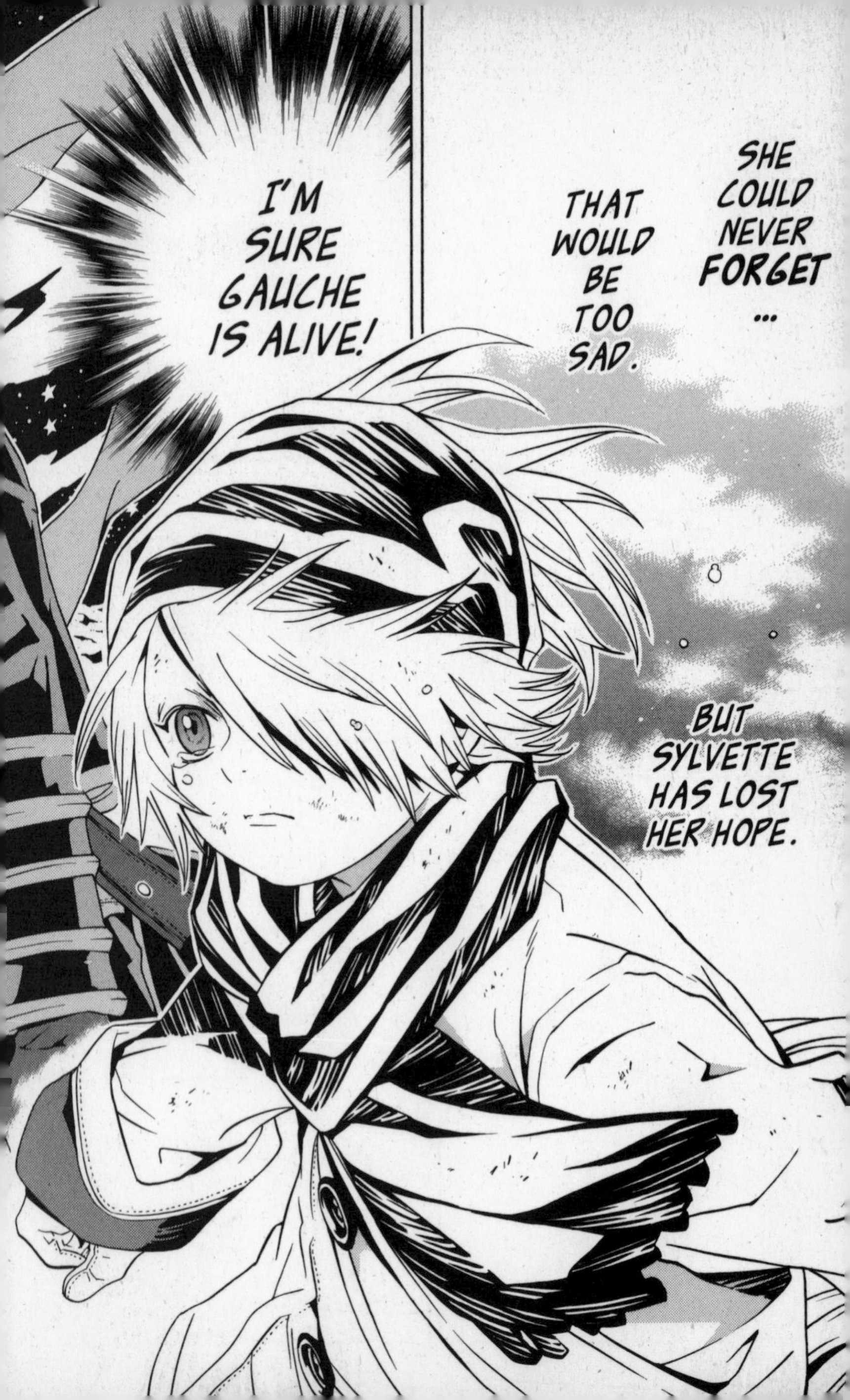
SHE COULD NEVER FORGET ...
THAT WOULD BE TOO SAD.
I'M SURE GAUCHE IS ALIVE!
BUT SYLVETTE HAS LOST HER HOPE.

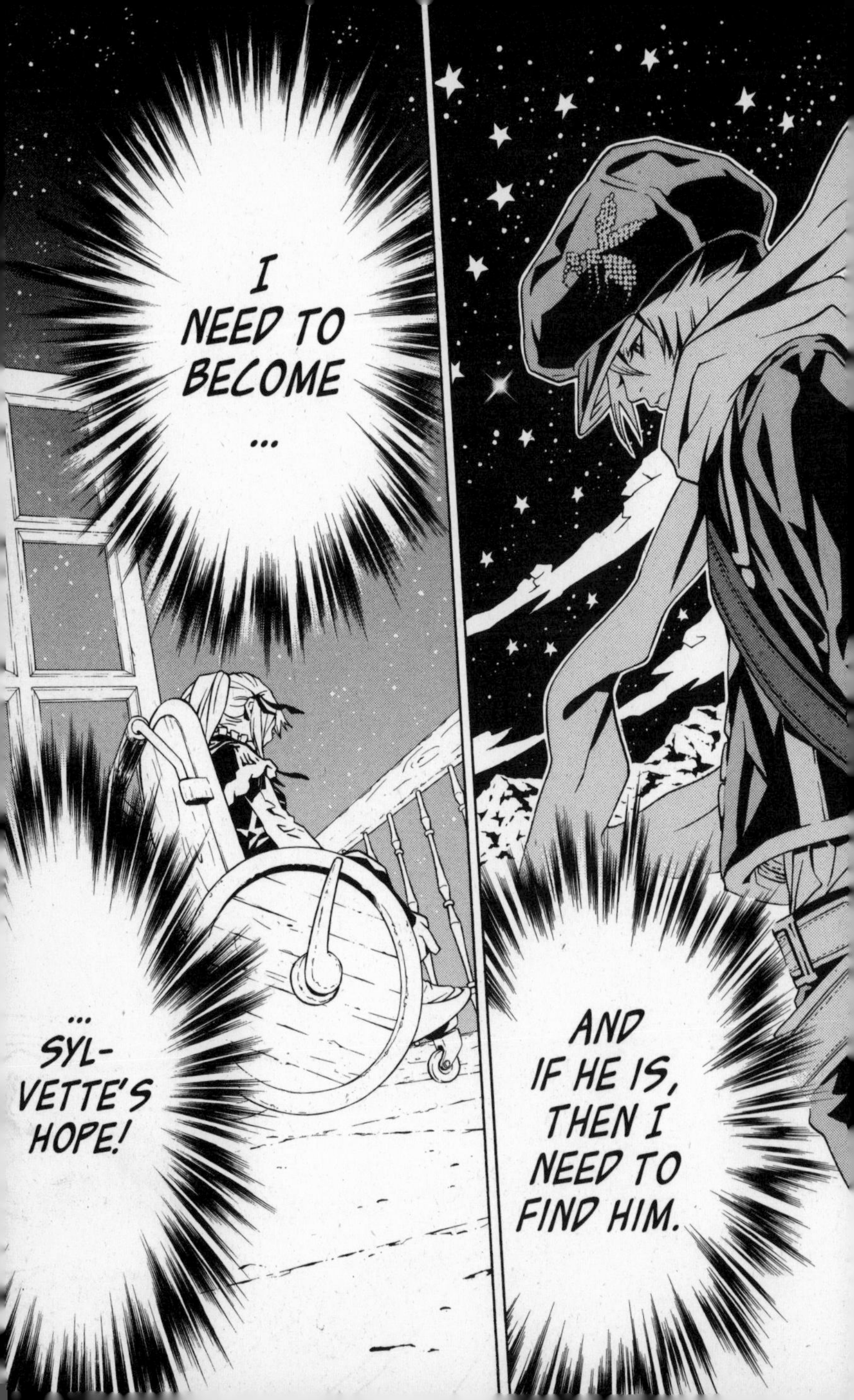
AND IF HE IS, THEN I NEED TO FIND HIM.
I NEED TO BECOME ...
... SYL-VETTE'S HOPE!

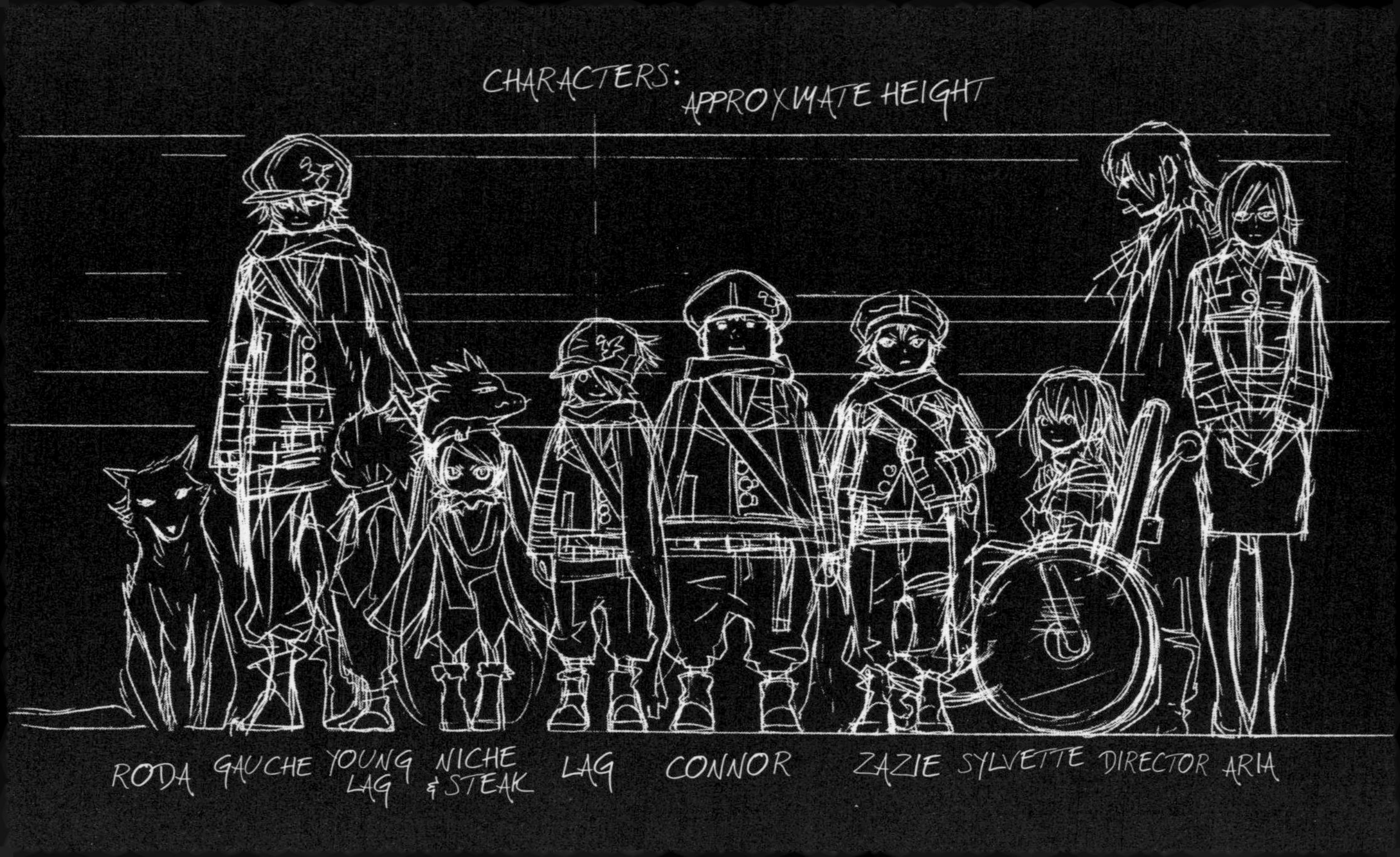
CHARACTERS: APPROXIMATE HEIGHT
RODA
GAUCHE
YOUNG LAG
NICHE & STEAK
LAG
CONNOR
ZAZIE
SYLVETTE
DIRECTOR
ARIA

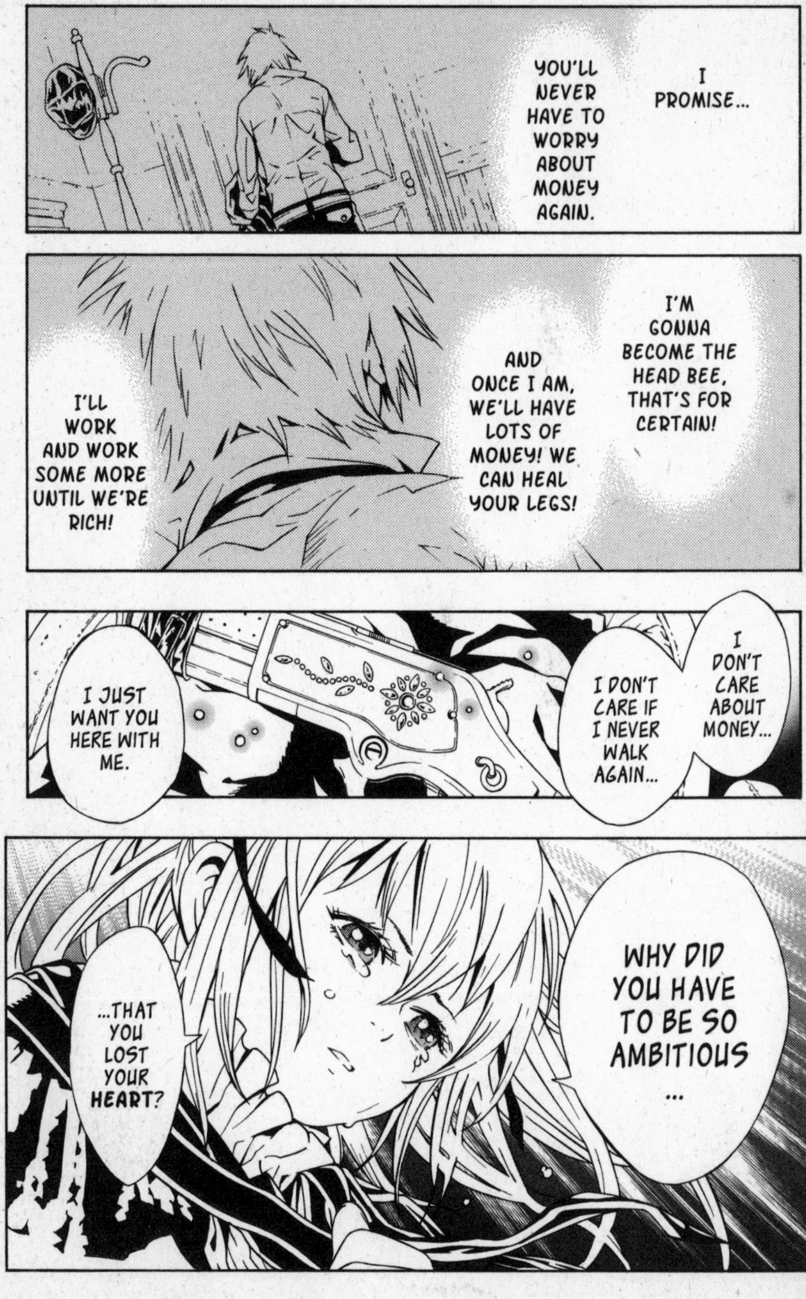
I PROMISE...
YOU'LL NEVER HAVE TO WORRY ABOUT MONEY AGAIN.
I'M GONNA BECOME THE HEAD BEE, THAT'S FOR CERTAIN!
AND ONCE I AM, WE'LL HAVE LOTS OF MONEY! WE CAN HEAL YOUR LEGS!
I'LL WORK AND WORK SOME MORE UNTIL WE'RE RICH!
I DON'T CARE ABOUT MONEY...
I DON'T CARE IF I NEVER WALK AGAIN...
I JUST WANT YOU HERE WITH ME.
WHY DID YOU HAVE TO BE SO AMBITIOUS ...
...THAT YOU LOST YOUR HEART?

Chapter 9: The Crybaby's Promise

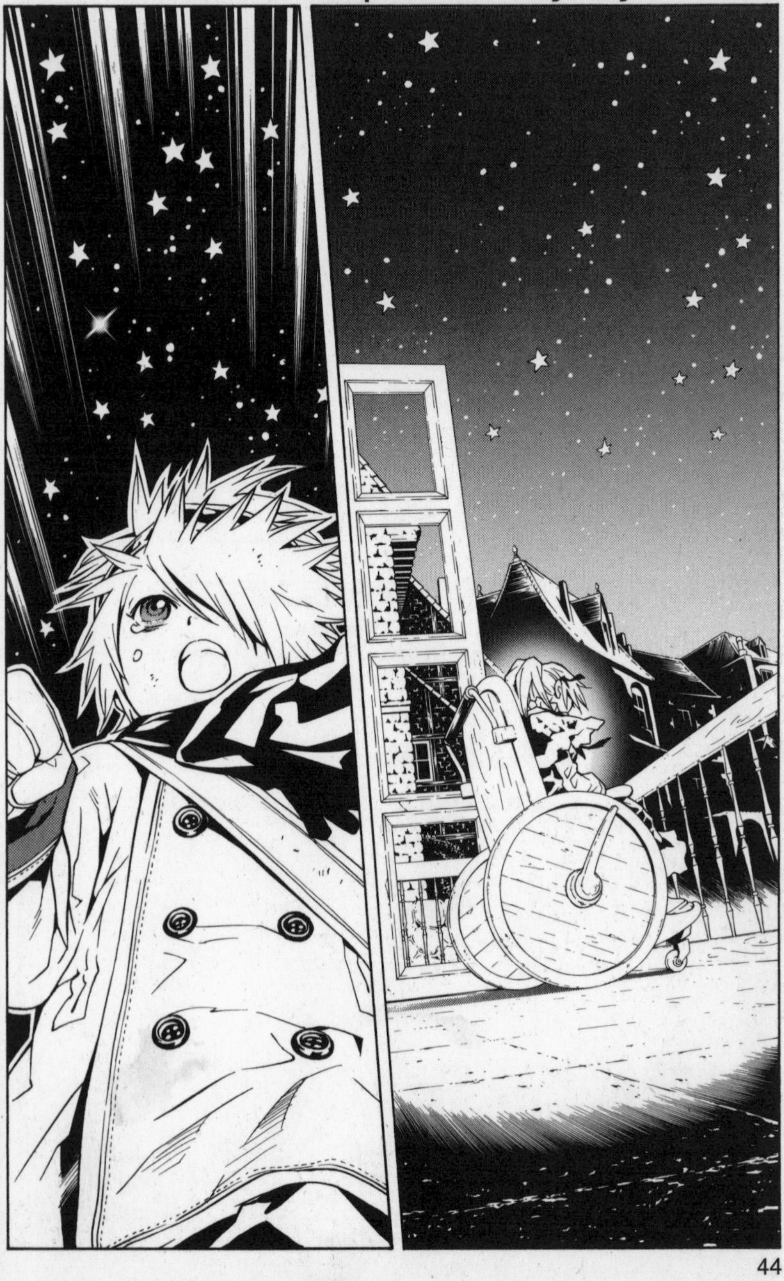

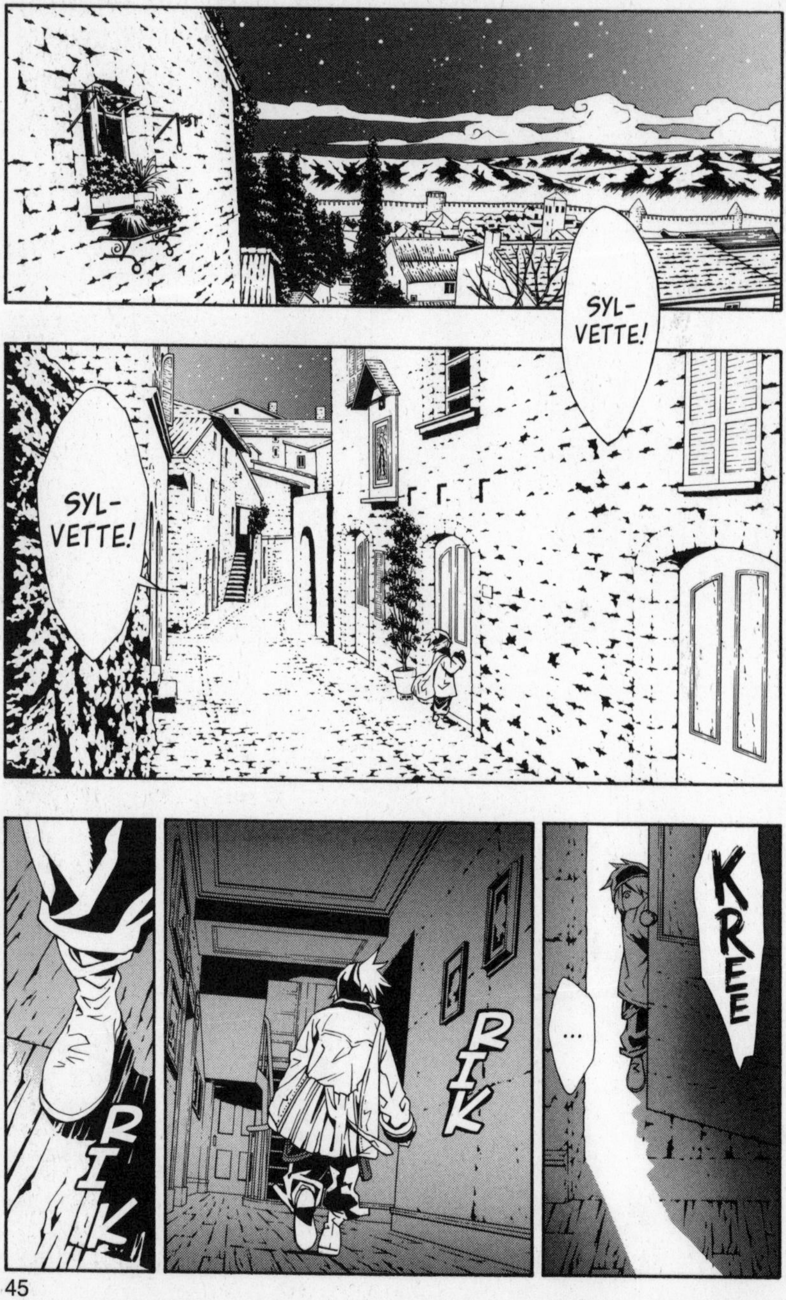
SYL-
VETTE!
SYL-
VETTE!
RIK
RIK
KREE
...

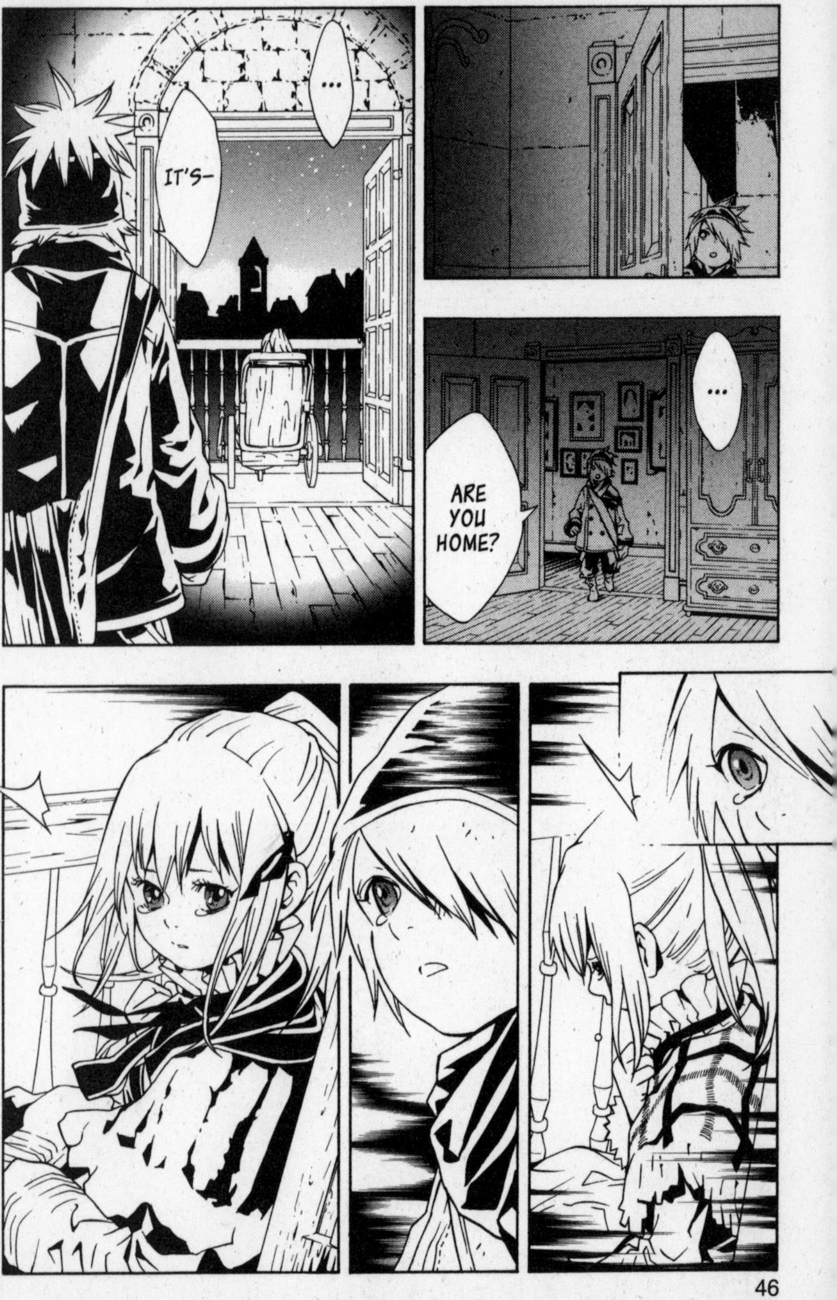
...
ARE YOU HOME?
...
IT'S—

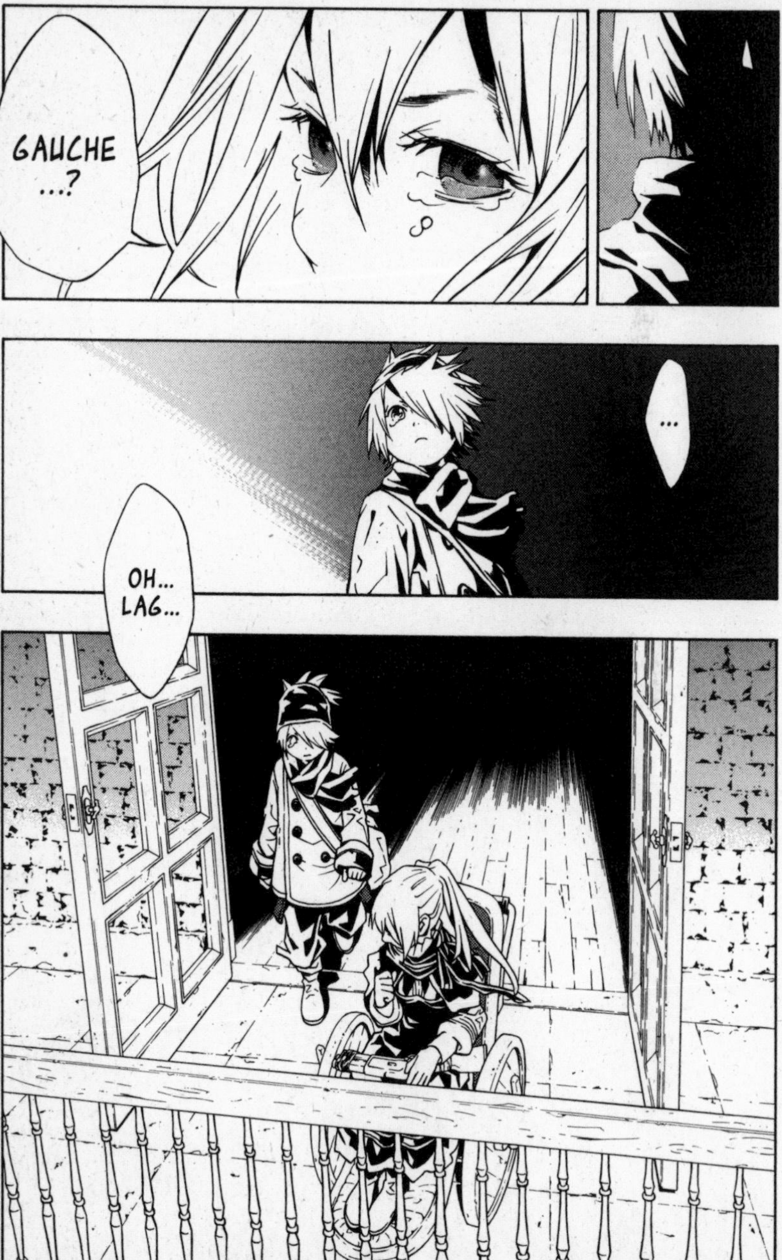
GAUCHE ...?
...
OH... LAG...

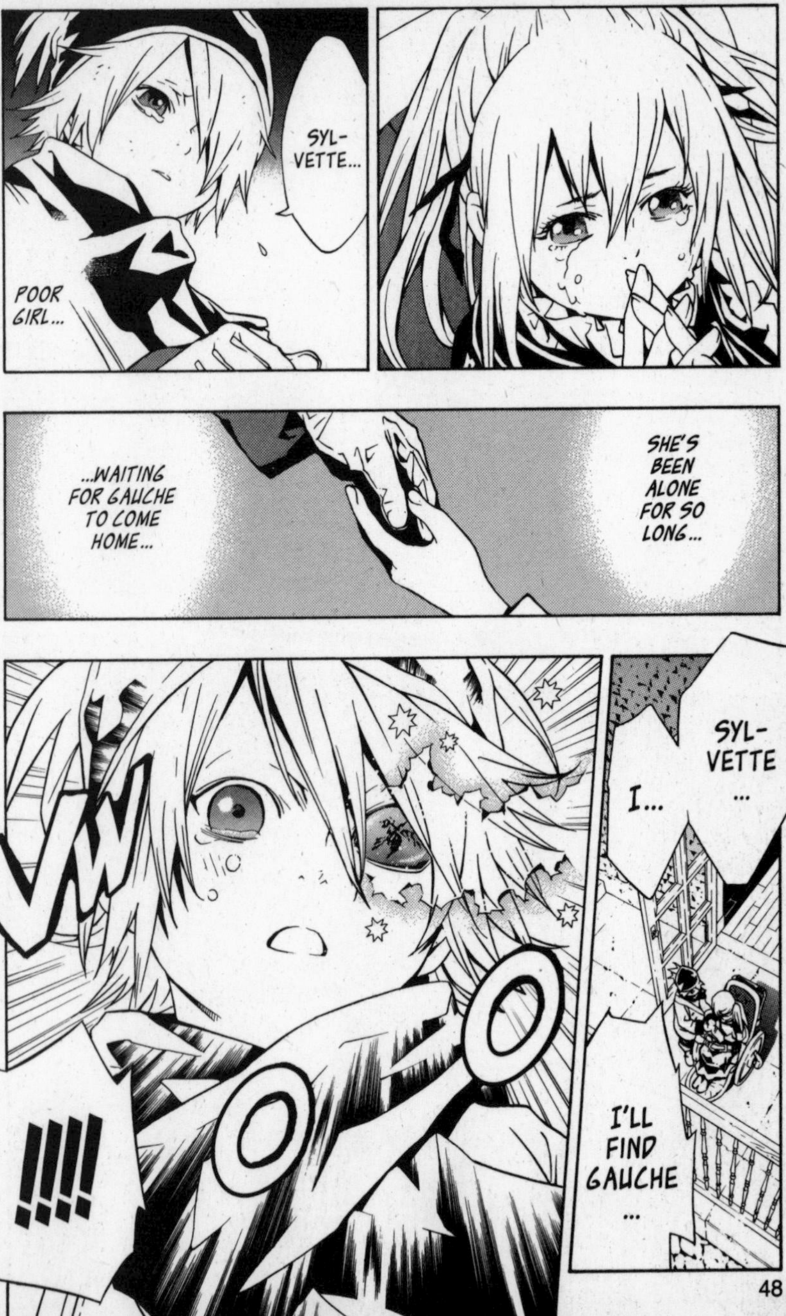
SYL-VETTE...
POOR GIRL...
SHE'S BEEN ALONE FOR SO LONG...
...WAITING FOR GAUCHE TO COME HOME...
SYL-VETTE...
I...
I'LL FIND GAUCHE...
!!!!

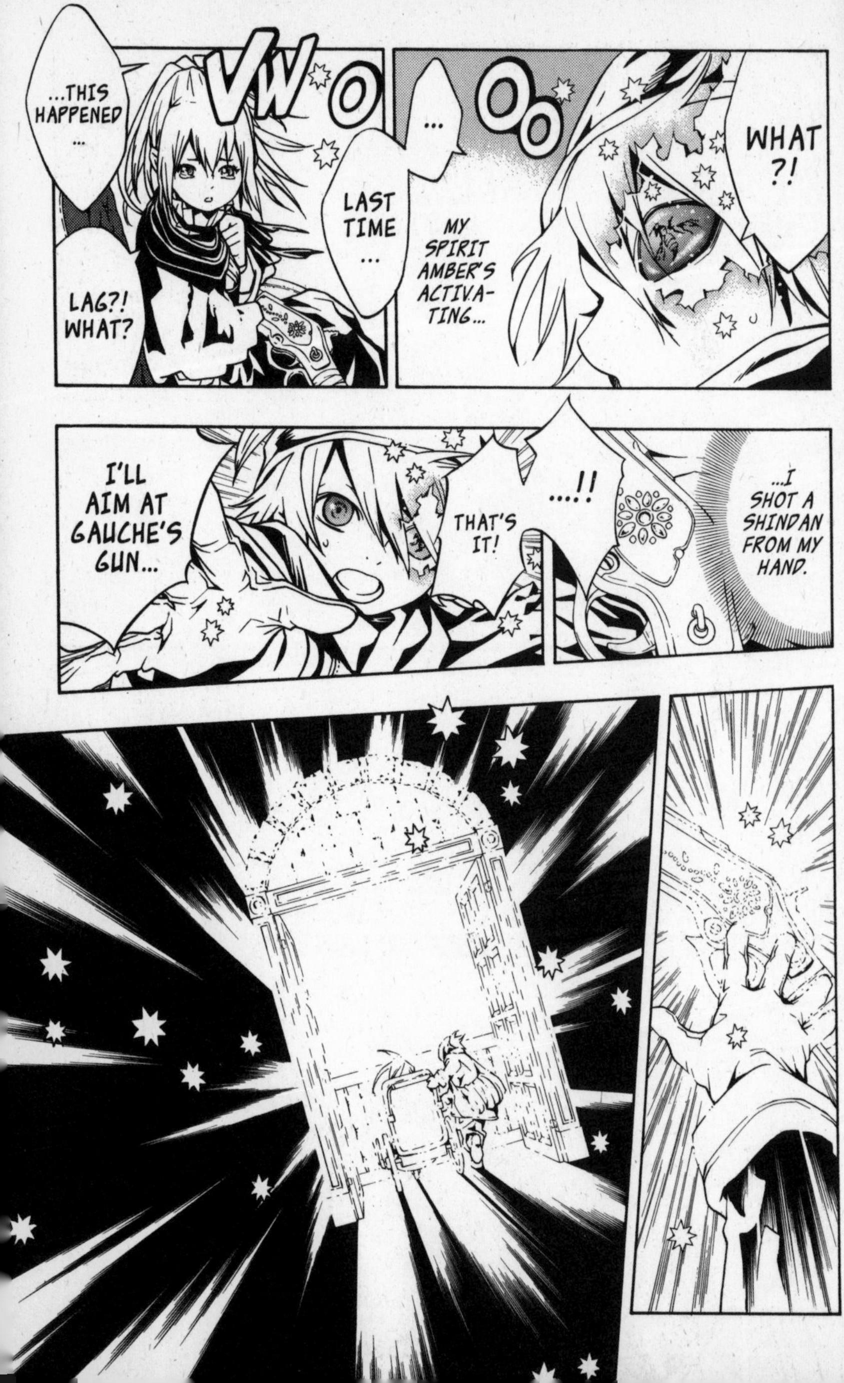
WHAT?!
MY SPIRIT AMBER'S ACTIVA-TING...
...
LAST TIME...
...THIS HAPPENED...
LAG?! WHAT?
VWOOO
...I SHOT A SHINDAN FROM MY HAND.
...!!
THAT'S IT!
I'LL AIM AT GAUCHE'S GUN...

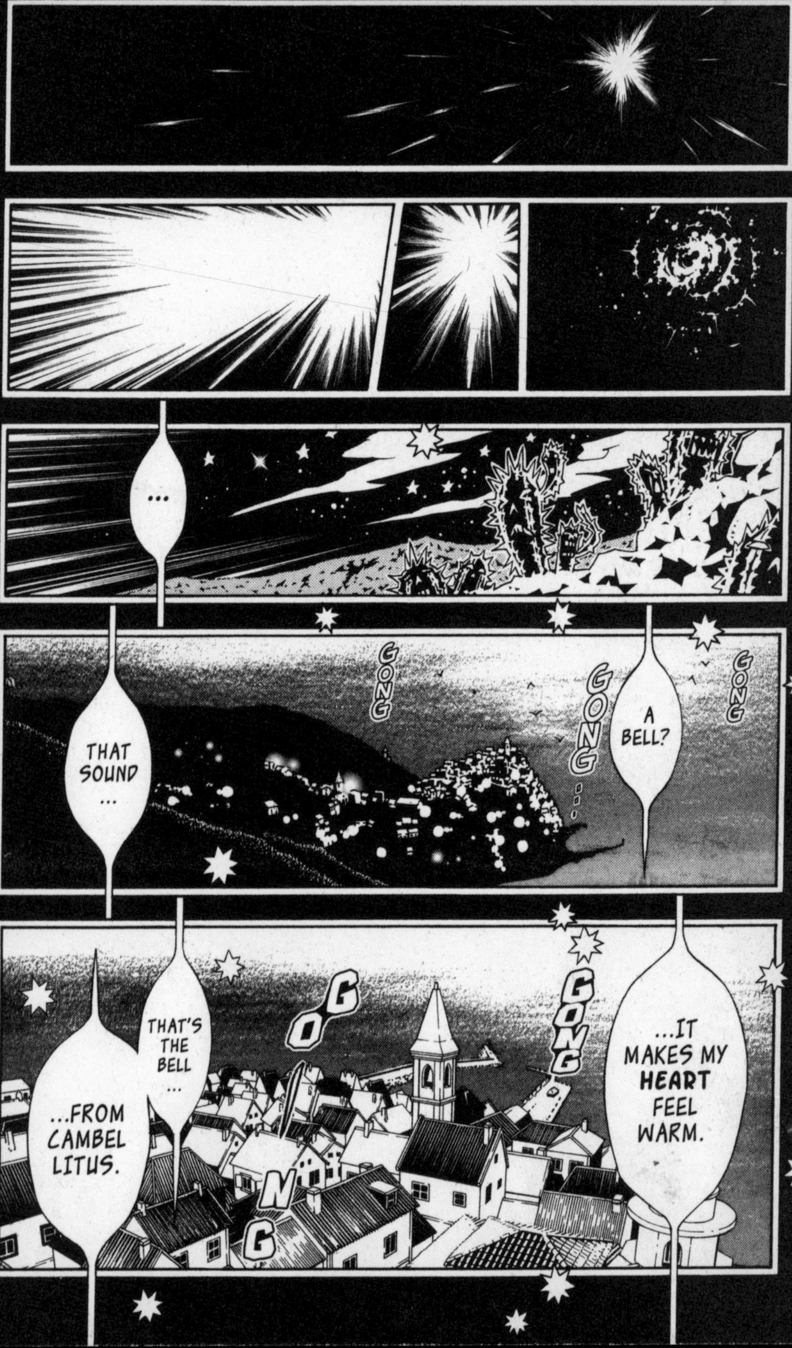
...
GONG
A BELL?
GONG...
GONG
THAT SOUND...
...IT MAKES MY HEART FEEL WARM.
GONG
GONG
THAT'S THE BELL...
...FROM CAMBEL LITUS.

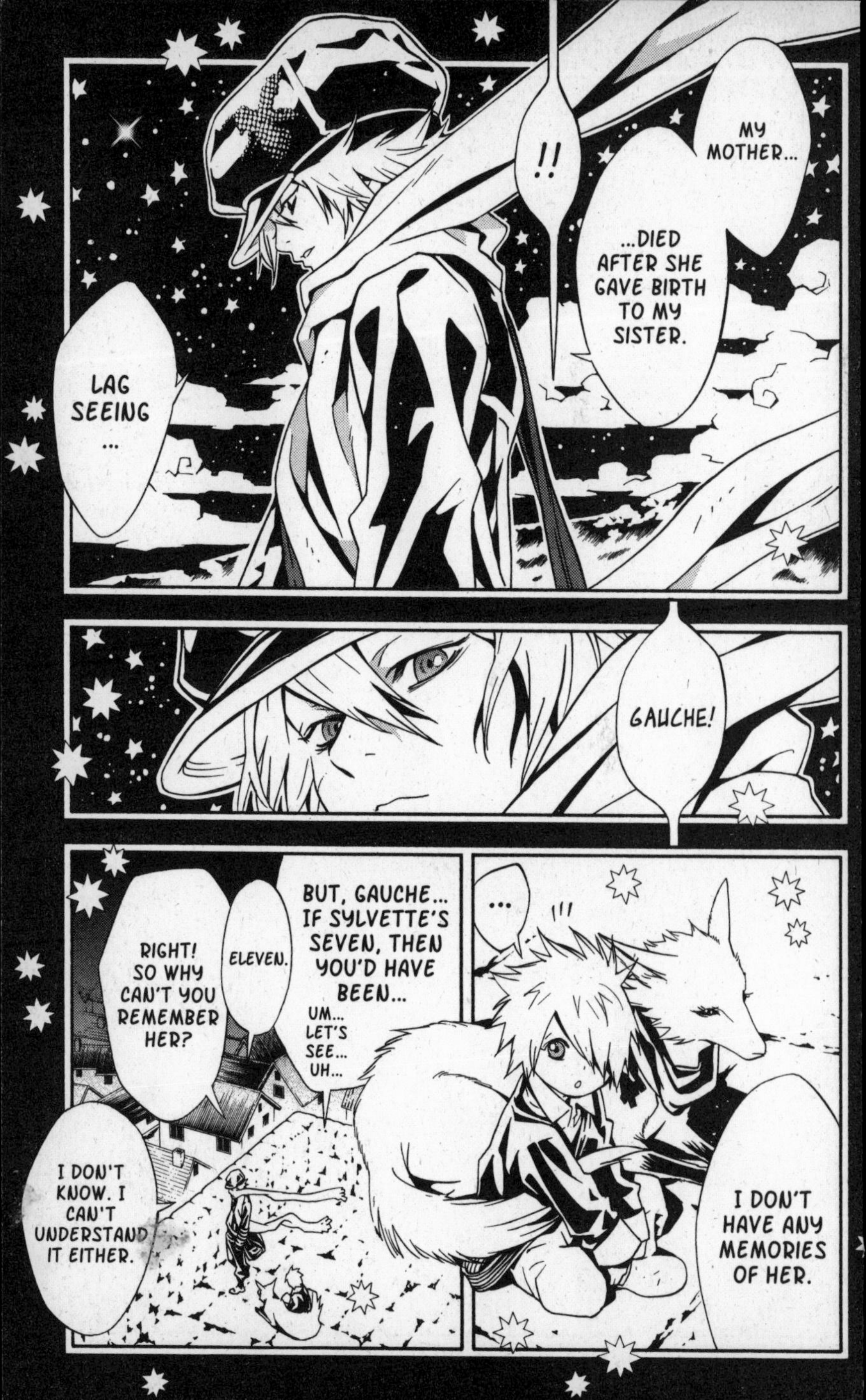
MY MOTHER...
...DIED AFTER SHE GAVE BIRTH TO MY SISTER.
!!
LAG SEEING ...
GAUCHE!
...
!!!
I DON'T HAVE ANY MEMORIES OF HER.
BUT, GAUCHE... IF SYLVETTE'S SEVEN, THEN YOU'D HAVE BEEN...
UM... LET'S SEE... UH...
ELEVEN.
RIGHT! SO WHY CAN'T YOU REMEMBER HER?
I DON'T KNOW. I CAN'T UNDERSTAND IT EITHER.

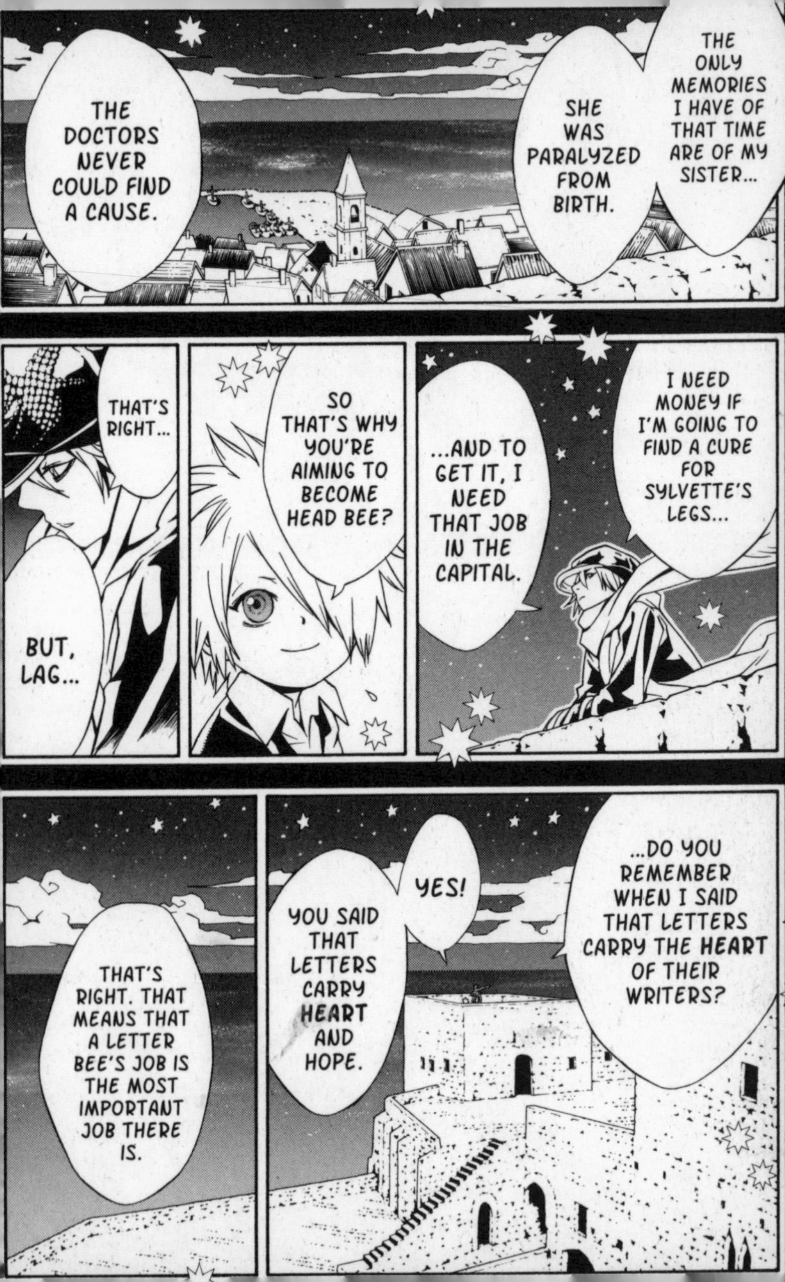
THE ONLY MEMORIES I HAVE OF THAT TIME ARE OF MY SISTER...
SHE WAS PARALYZED FROM BIRTH.
THE DOCTORS NEVER COULD FIND A CAUSE.
I NEED MONEY IF I'M GOING TO FIND A CURE FOR SYLVETTE'S LEGS...
...AND TO GET IT, I NEED THAT JOB IN THE CAPITAL.
SO THAT'S WHY YOU'RE AIMING TO BECOME HEAD BEE?
THAT'S RIGHT...
BUT, LAG...
...DO YOU REMEMBER WHEN I SAID THAT LETTERS CARRY THE HEART OF THEIR WRITERS?
YES!
YOU SAID THAT LETTERS CARRY HEART AND HOPE.
THAT'S RIGHT. THAT MEANS THAT A LETTER BEE'S JOB IS THE MOST IMPORTANT JOB THERE IS.

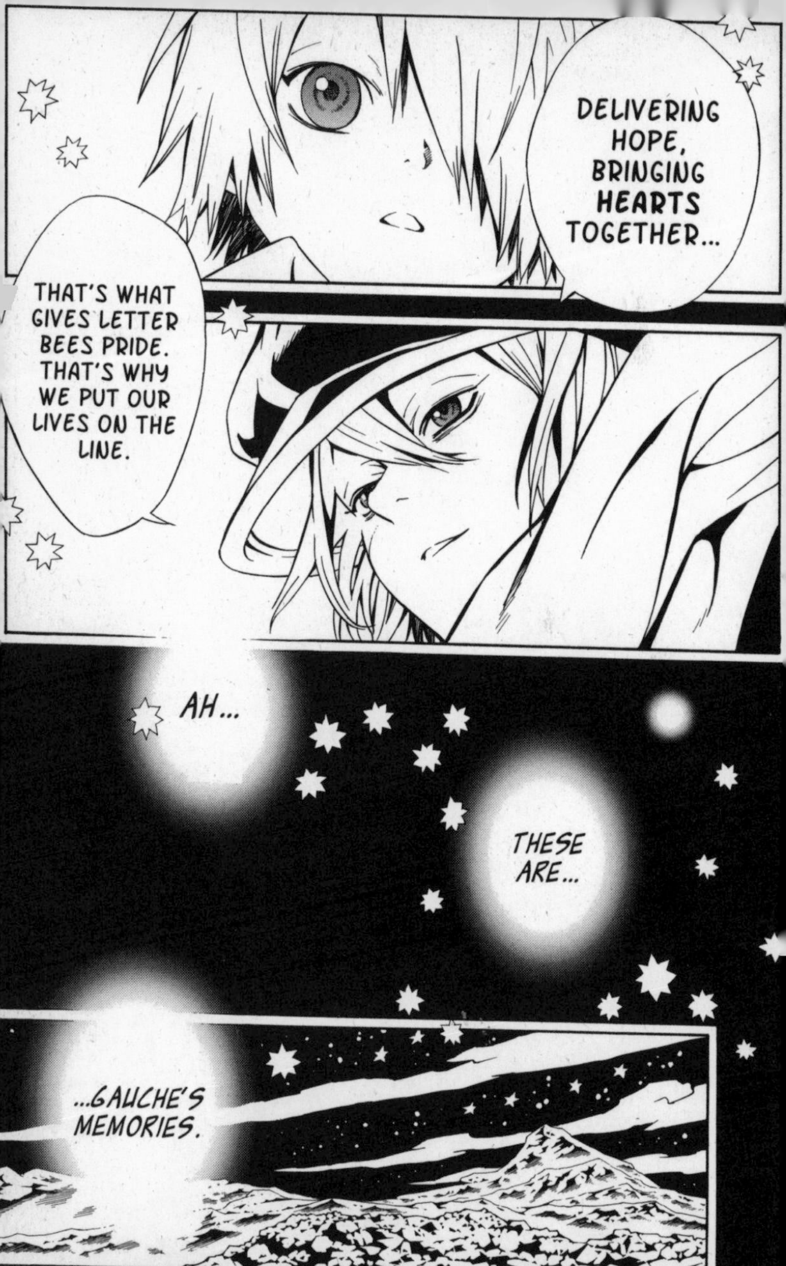
DELIVERING HOPE, BRINGING HEARTS TOGETHER...
THAT'S WHAT GIVES LETTER BEES PRIDE. THAT'S WHY WE PUT OUR LIVES ON THE LINE.
AH...
THESE ARE...
...GAUCHE'S MEMORIES.

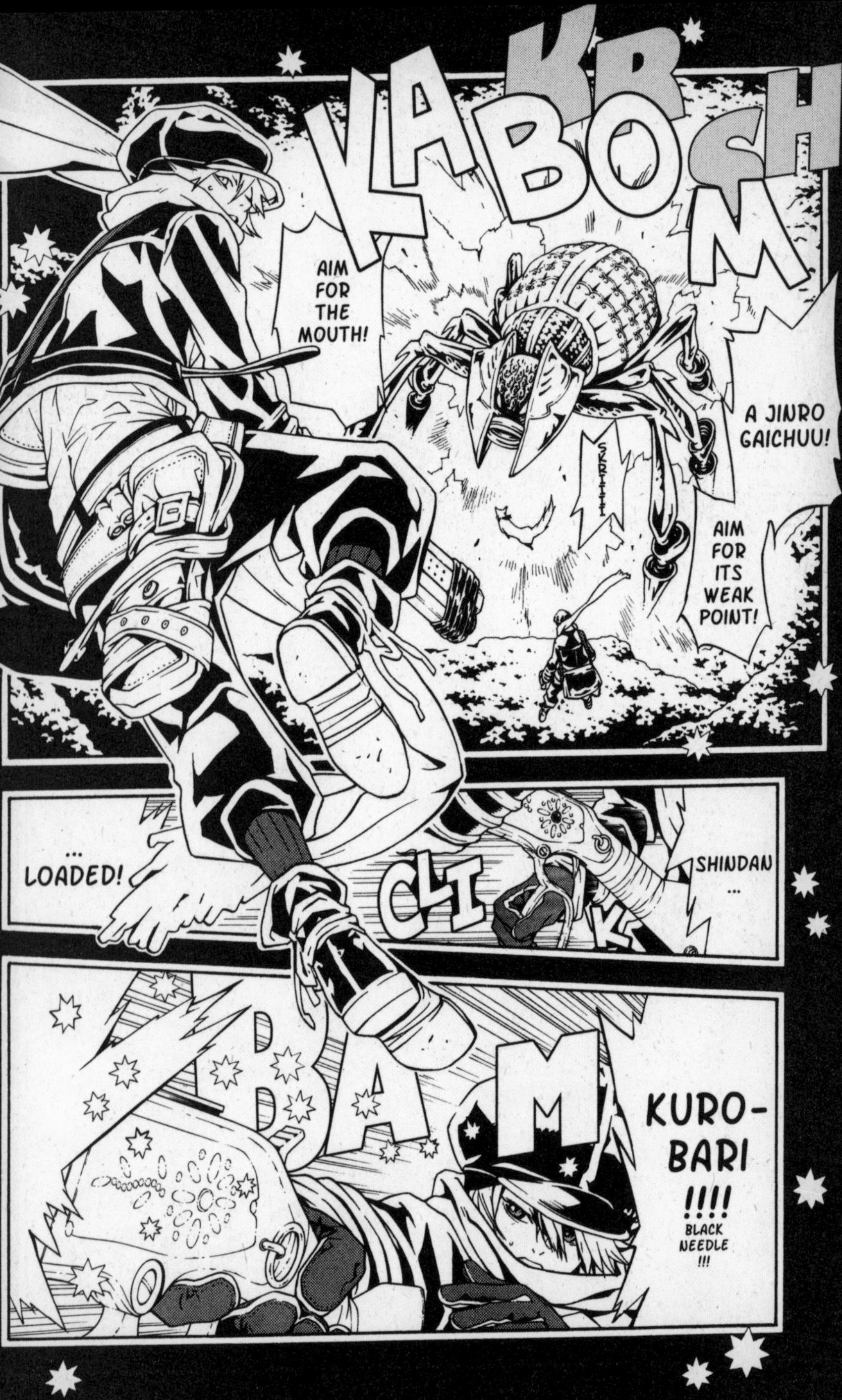

KRABOOM
KABOSH
A JINRO GAICHUU!
AIM FOR THE MOUTH!
SKRITTT
AIM FOR ITS WEAK POINT!
SHINDAN ...
CLICK
... LOADED!
BAM
KURO-BARI !!!!
BLACK NEEDLE !!!

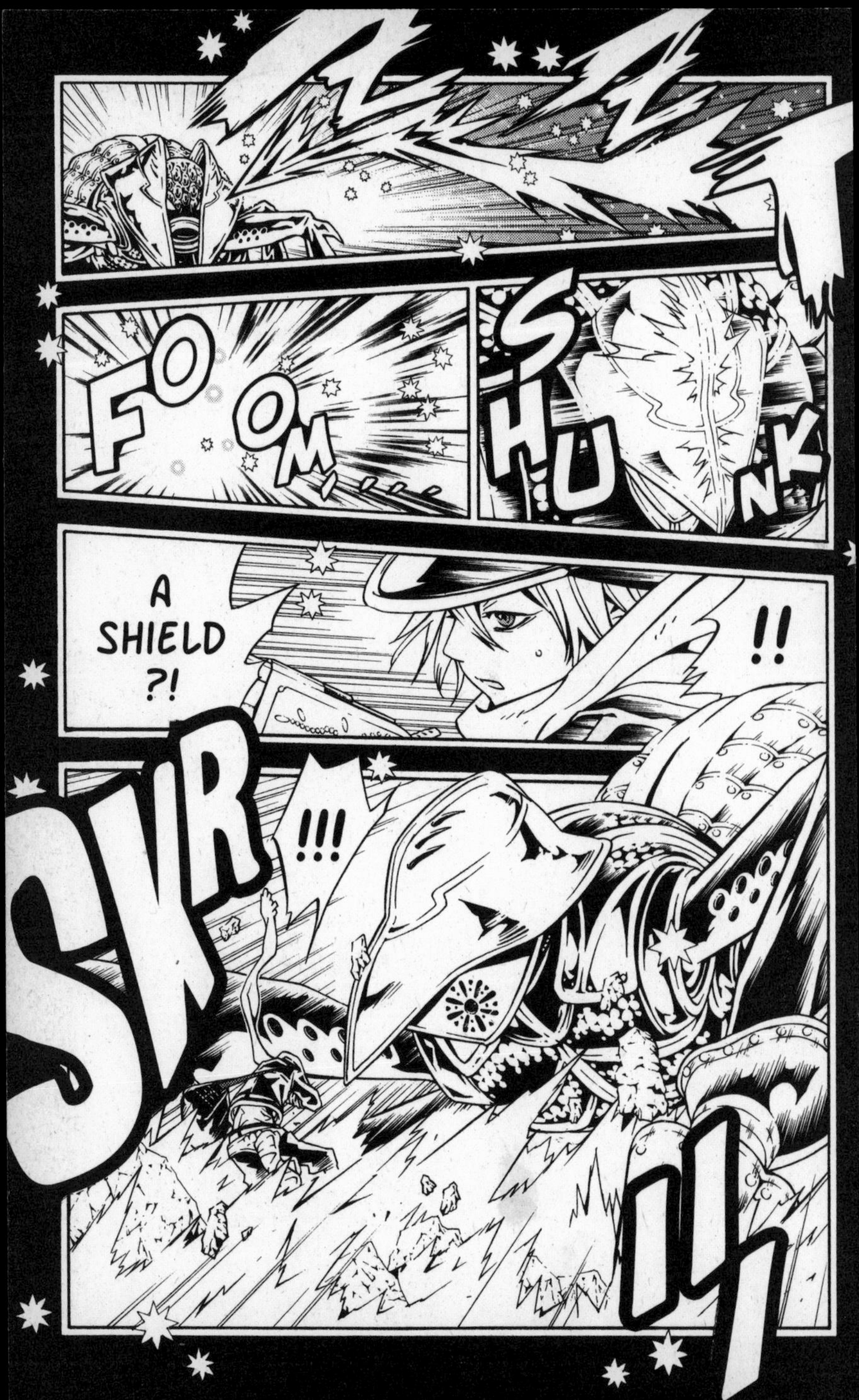
SHUNK
FOOM
A SHIELD ?!
!!
SKR
!!!

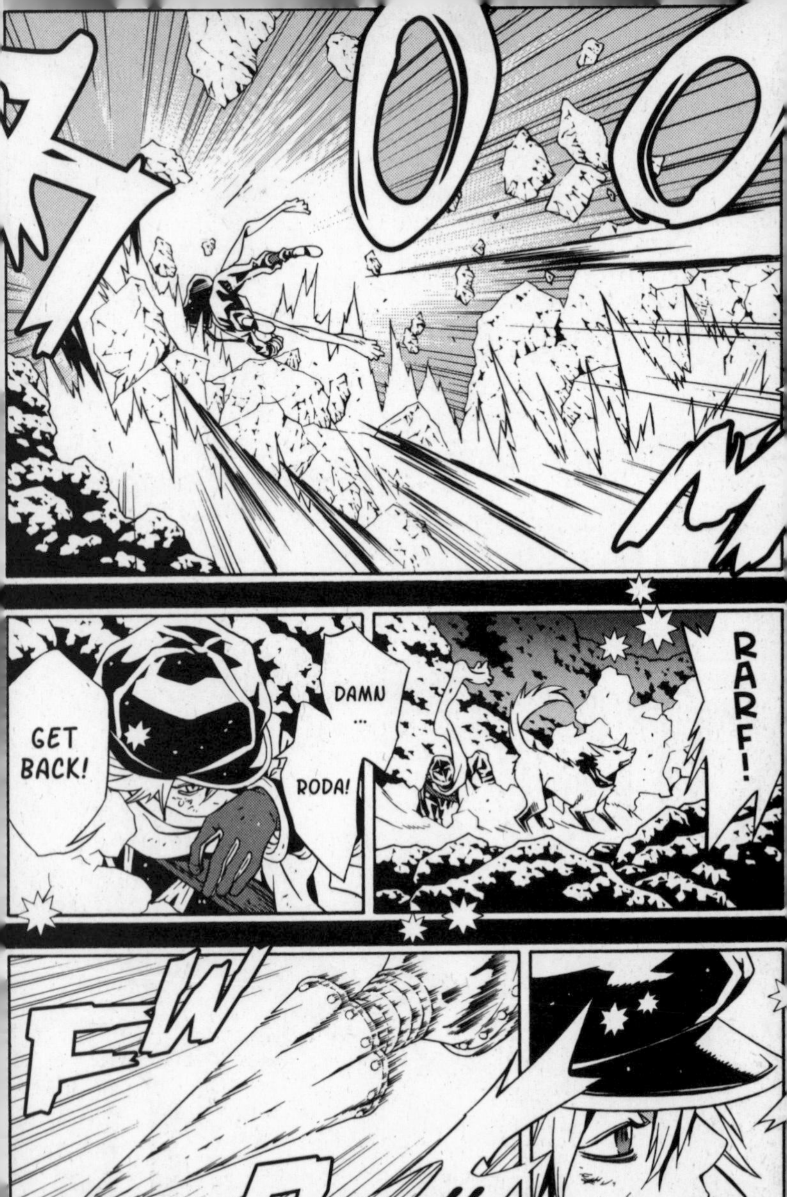

ZOOM
GET BACK!
DAMN ... RODA!
RARF!
FWA!!

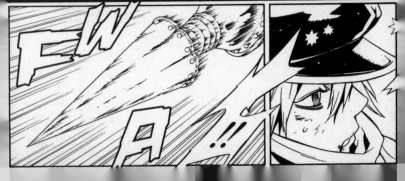

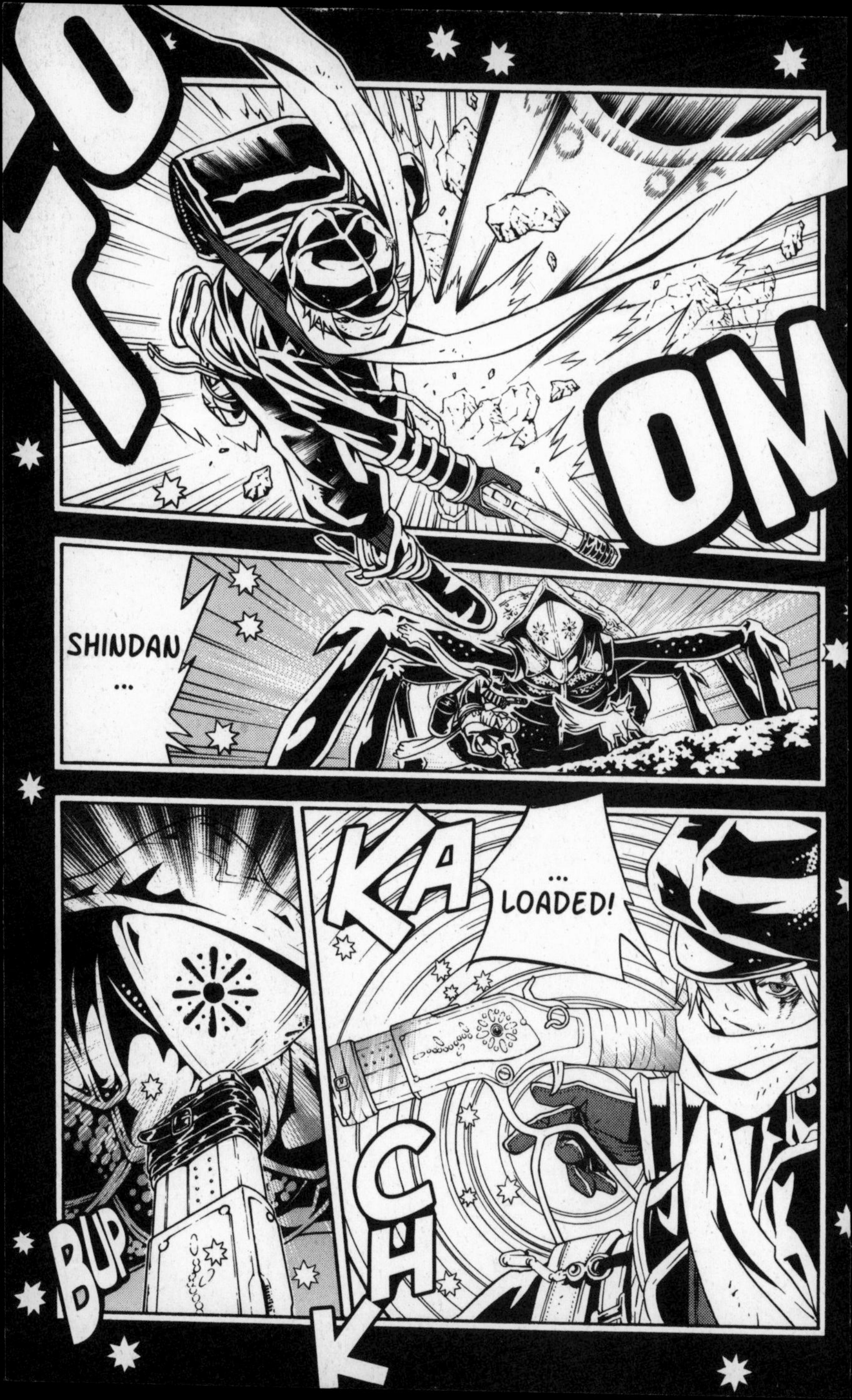
OM
SHINDAN ...
KA
... LOADED!
BUP

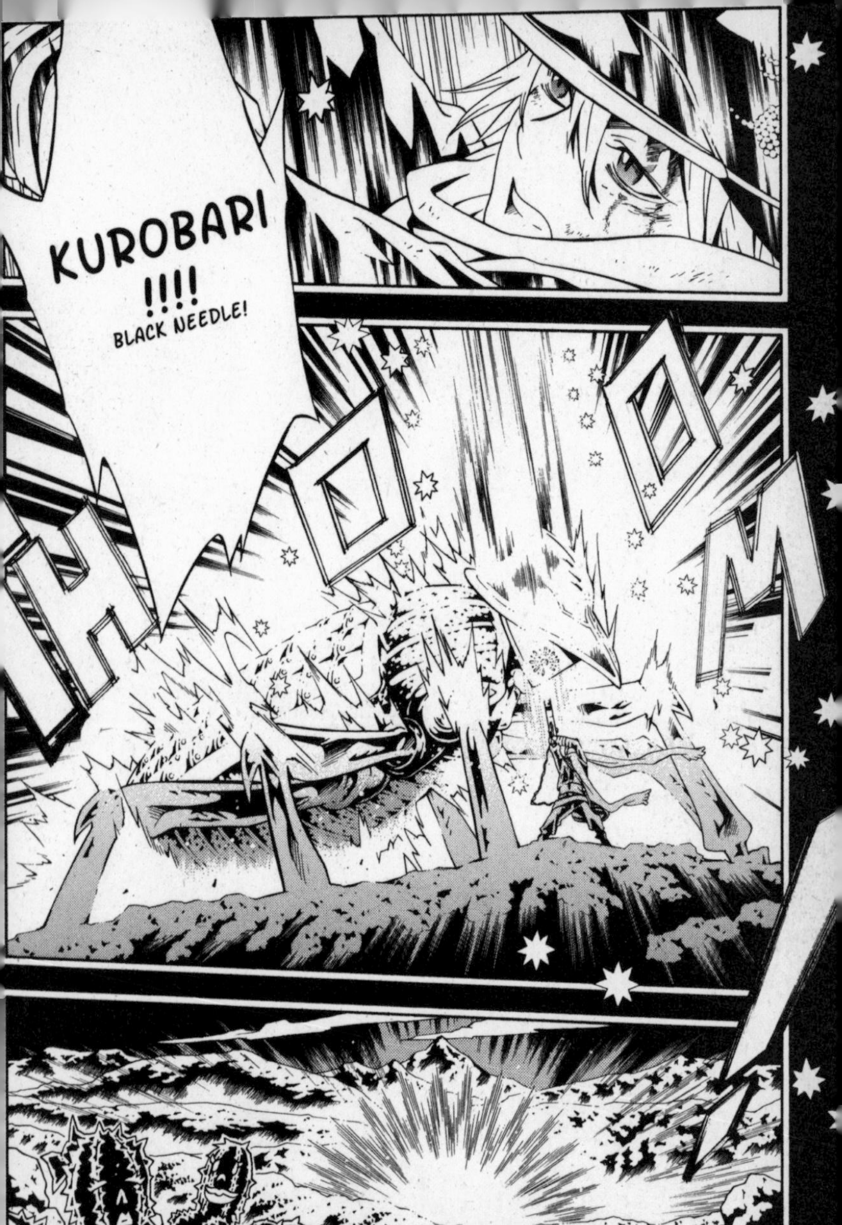
KUROBARI !!!!
BLACK NEEDLE!
CHOOOM

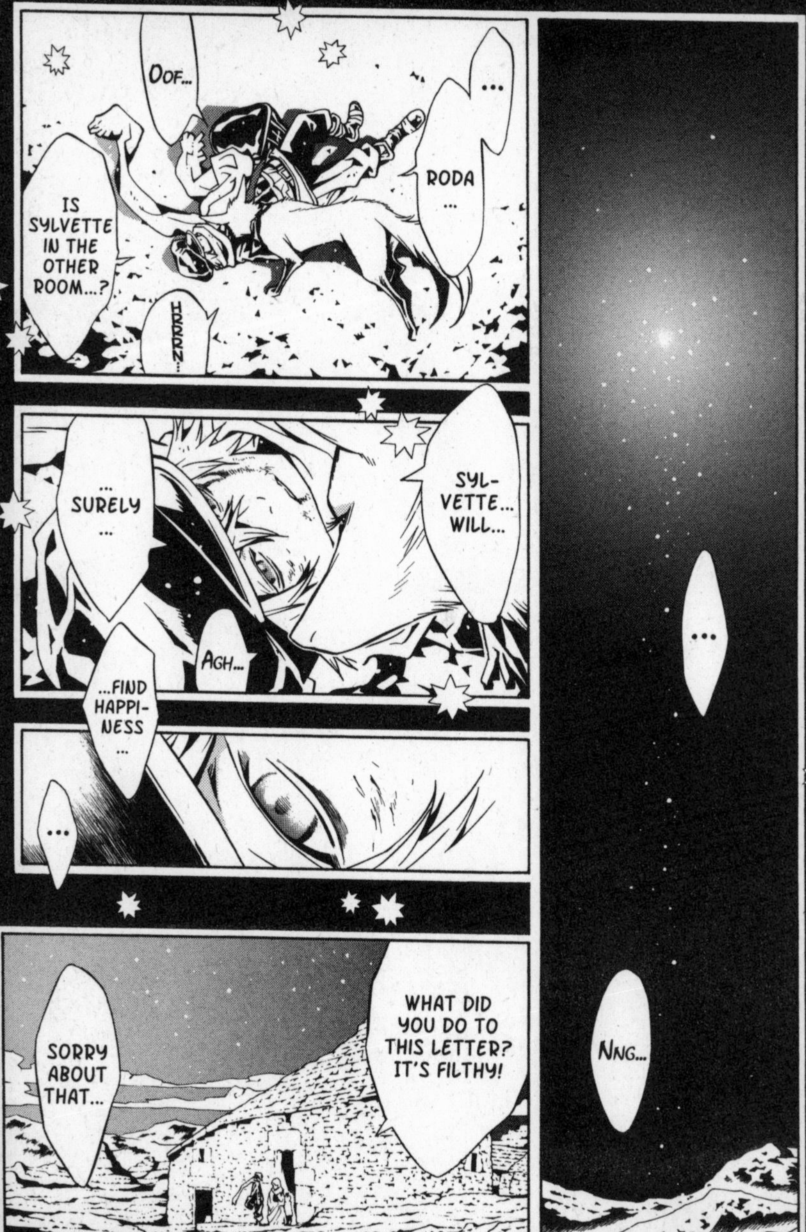
...
RODA ...
OOF...
IS SYLVETTE IN THE OTHER ROOM...?
HRRRN...
SYL-VETTE... WILL...
... SURELY ...
AGH...
...FIND HAPPI-NESS ...
...
...
NNG...
WHAT DID YOU DO TO THIS LETTER? IT'S FILTHY!
SORRY ABOUT THAT...

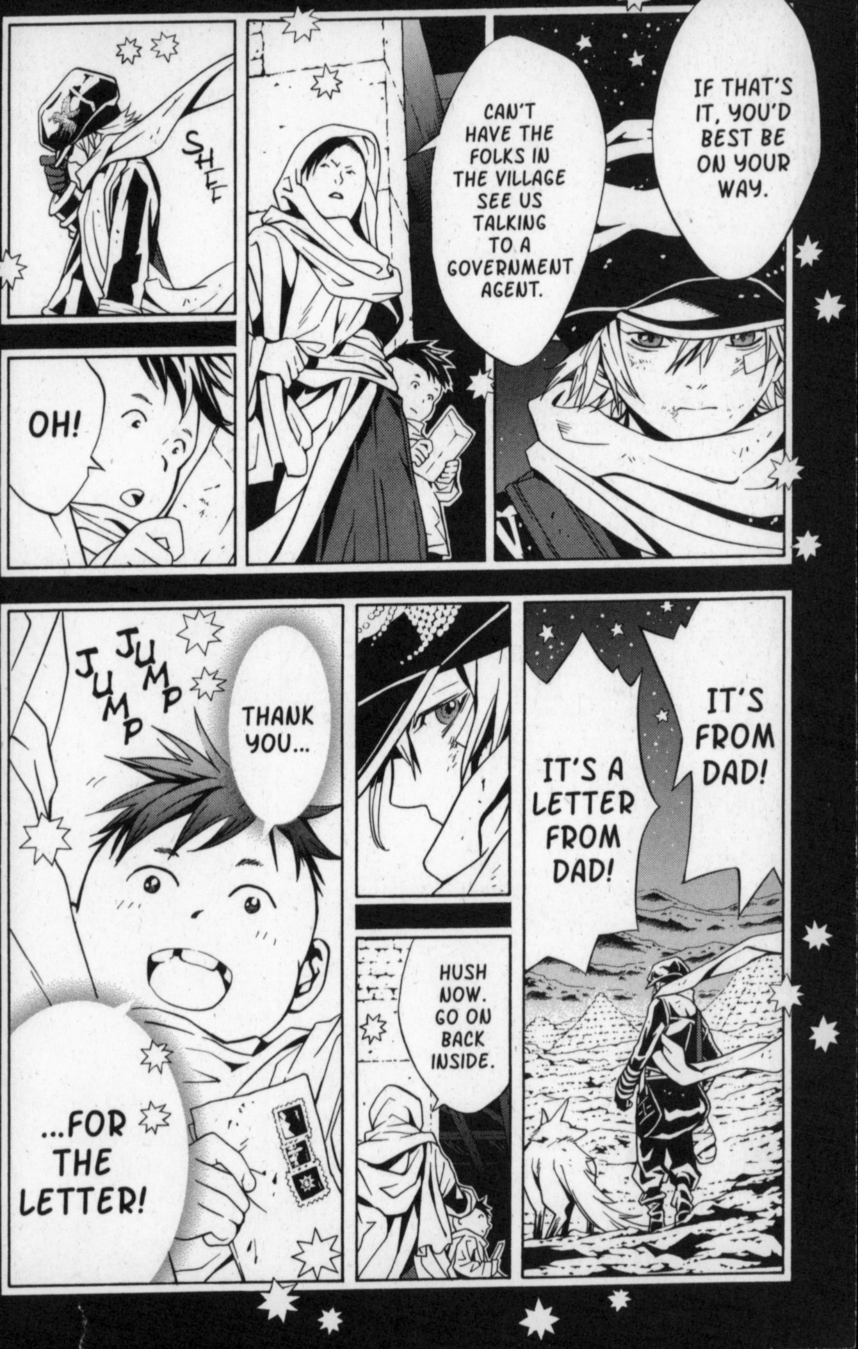
IF THAT'S IT, YOU'D BEST BE ON YOUR WAY.
CAN'T HAVE THE FOLKS IN THE VILLAGE SEE US TALKING TO A GOVERNMENT AGENT.
SHFF
OH!
IT'S FROM DAD!
IT'S A LETTER FROM DAD!
HUSH NOW. GO ON BACK INSIDE.
JUMP JUMP
THANK YOU...
...FOR THE LETTER!

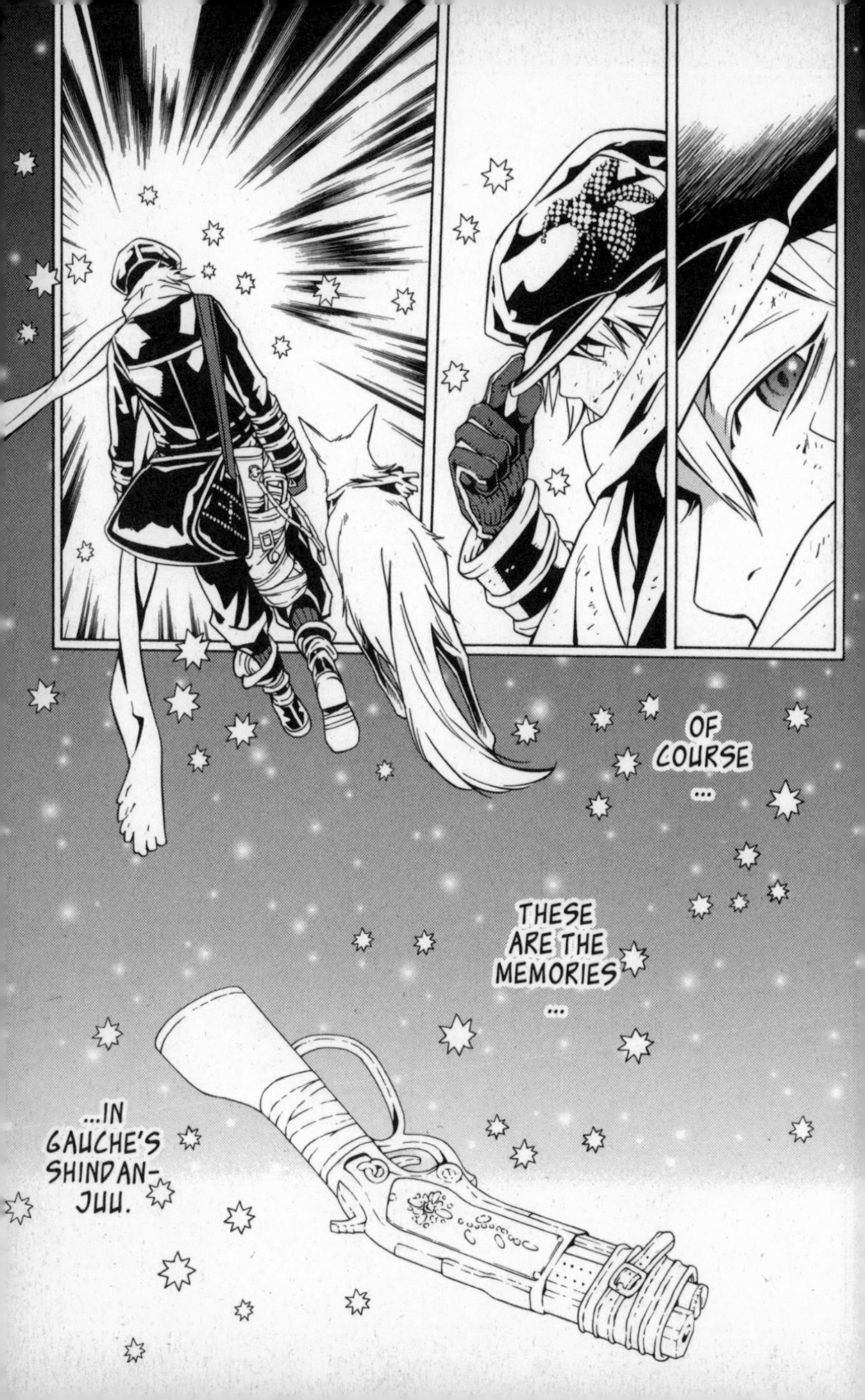
OF COURSE ...
THESE ARE THE MEMORIES ...
...IN GAUCHE'S SHINDAN-JUU.

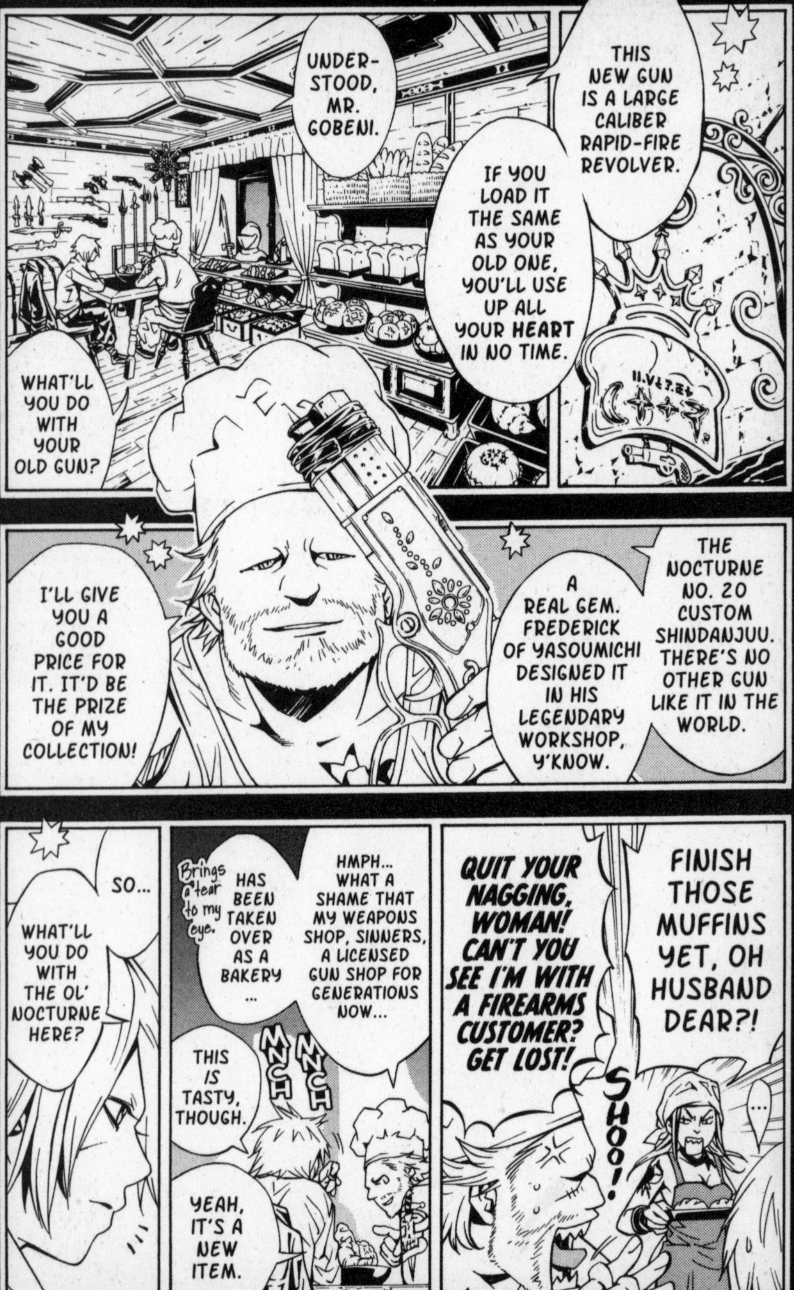
THIS NEW GUN IS A LARGE CALIBER RAPID-FIRE REVOLVER.
UNDER-STOOD, MR. GOBENI.
IF YOU LOAD IT THE SAME AS YOUR OLD ONE, YOU'LL USE UP ALL YOUR HEART IN NO TIME.
WHAT'LL YOU DO WITH YOUR OLD GUN?
THE NOCTURNE NO. 20 CUSTOM SHINDANJUU. THERE'S NO OTHER GUN LIKE IT IN THE WORLD.
A REAL GEM. FREDERICK OF YASOUMICHI DESIGNED IT IN HIS LEGENDARY WORKSHOP, Y'KNOW.
I'LL GIVE YOU A GOOD PRICE FOR IT. IT'D BE THE PRIZE OF MY COLLECTION!
FINISH THOSE MUFFINS YET, OH HUSBAND DEAR?!
QUIT YOUR NAGGING, WOMAN! CAN'T YOU SEE I'M WITH A FIREARMS CUSTOMER? GET LOST!
SHOO!
...
HMPH... WHAT A SHAME THAT MY WEAPONS SHOP, SINNERS, A LICENSED GUN SHOP FOR GENERATIONS NOW...
HAS BEEN TAKEN OVER AS A BAKERY...
Brings a tear to my eye.
MNCH MNCH
THIS IS TASTY, THOUGH.
YEAH, IT'S A NEW ITEM.
SO...
WHAT'LL YOU DO WITH THE OL' NOCTURNE HERE?

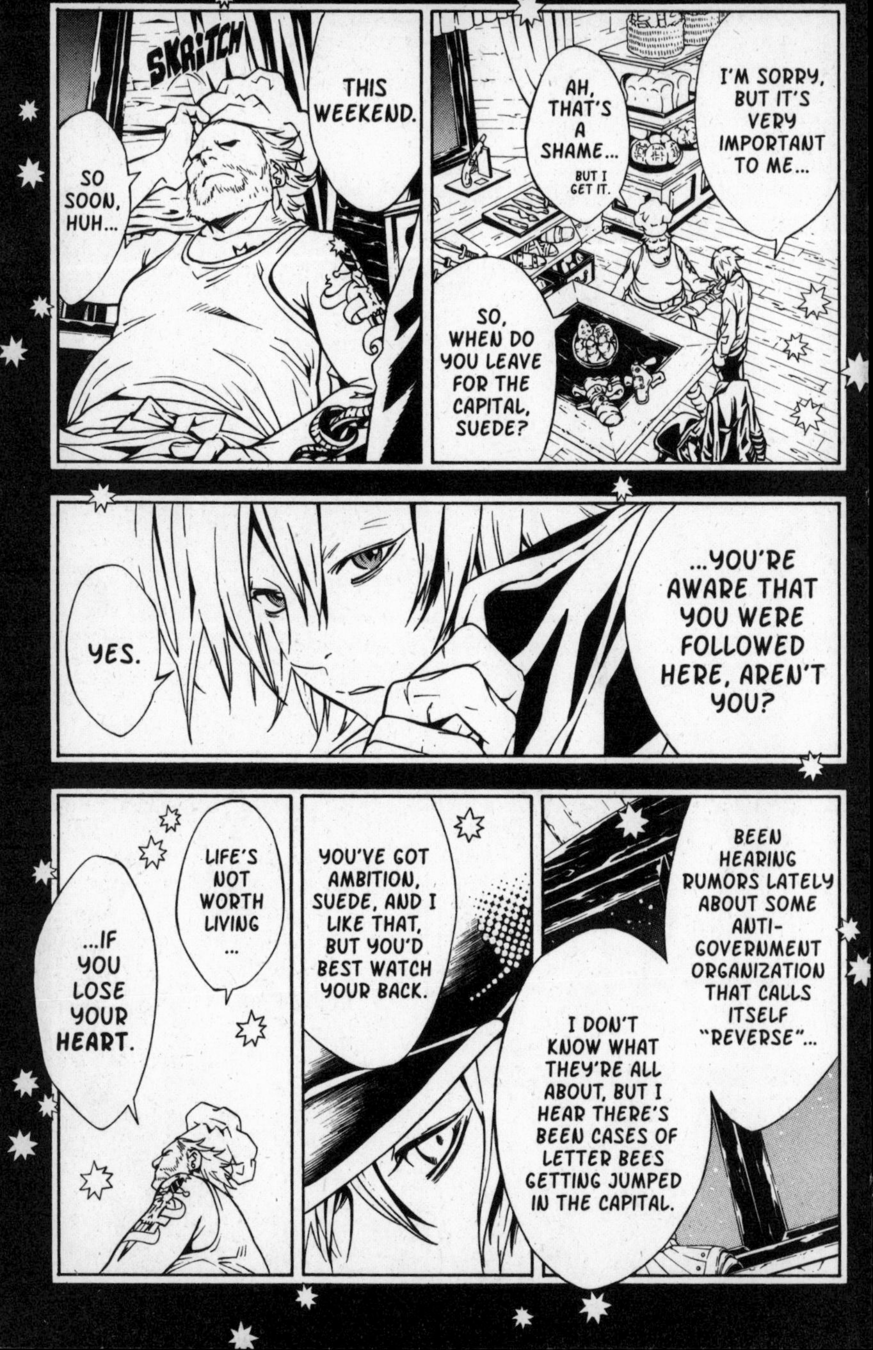
I'M SORRY, BUT IT'S VERY IMPORTANT TO ME...
AH, THAT'S A SHAME... BUT I GET IT.
SO, WHEN DO YOU LEAVE FOR THE CAPITAL, SUEDE?
THIS WEEKEND.
SKRITCH
SO SOON, HUH...
...YOU'RE AWARE THAT YOU WERE FOLLOWED HERE, AREN'T YOU?
YES.
BEEN HEARING RUMORS LATELY ABOUT SOME ANTI-GOVERNMENT ORGANIZATION THAT CALLS ITSELF "REVERSE"...
I DON'T KNOW WHAT THEY'RE ALL ABOUT, BUT I HEAR THERE'S BEEN CASES OF LETTER BEES GETTING JUMPED IN THE CAPITAL.
YOU'VE GOT AMBITION, SUEDE, AND I LIKE THAT, BUT YOU'D BEST WATCH YOUR BACK.
LIFE'S NOT WORTH LIVING ...
...IF YOU LOSE YOUR HEART.

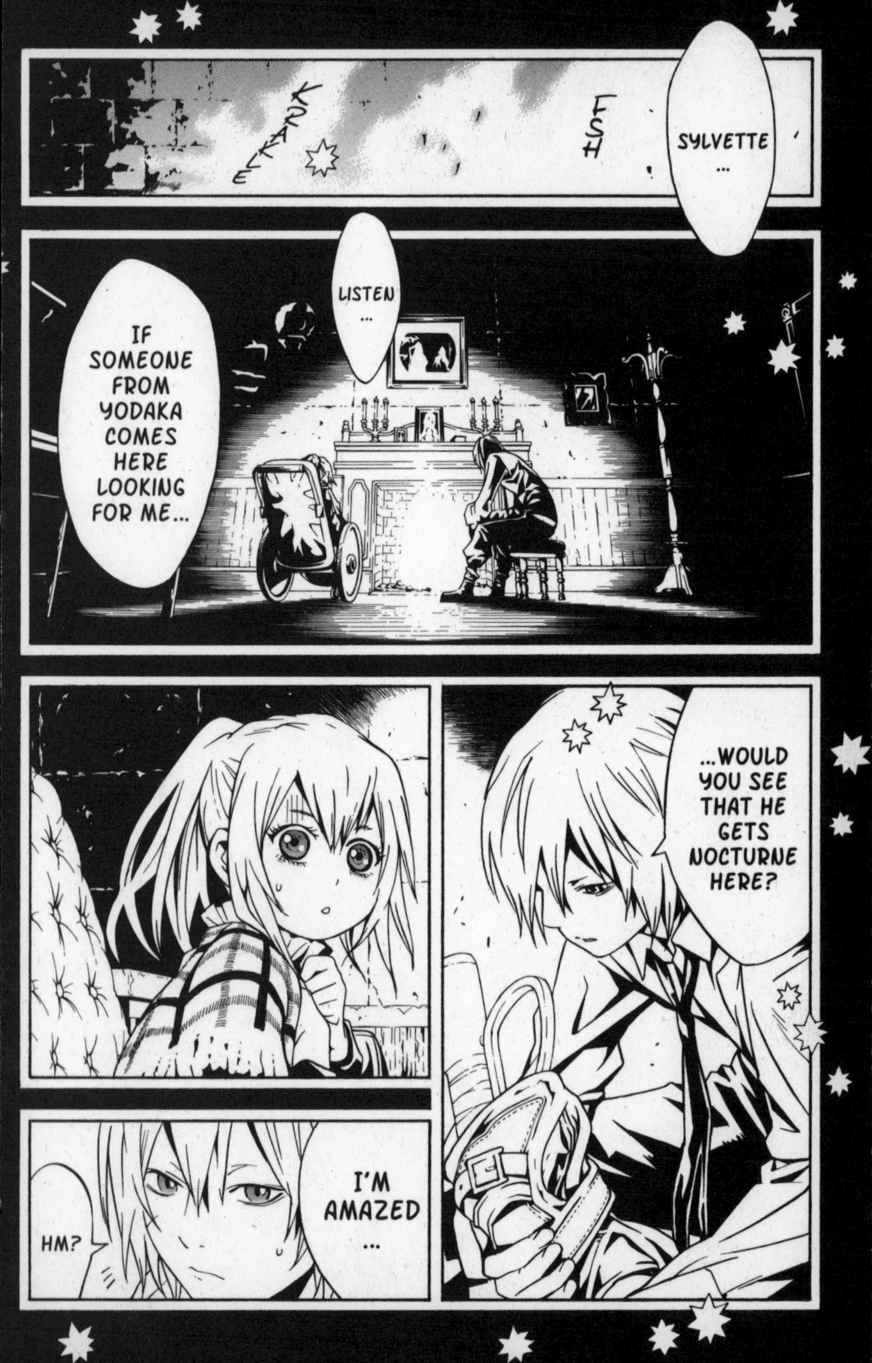

SYLVETTE ...
FSH
KRAKKLE
LISTEN ...
IF SOMEONE FROM YODAKA COMES HERE LOOKING FOR ME...
...WOULD YOU SEE THAT HE GETS NOCTURNE HERE?
I'M AMAZED ...
HM?

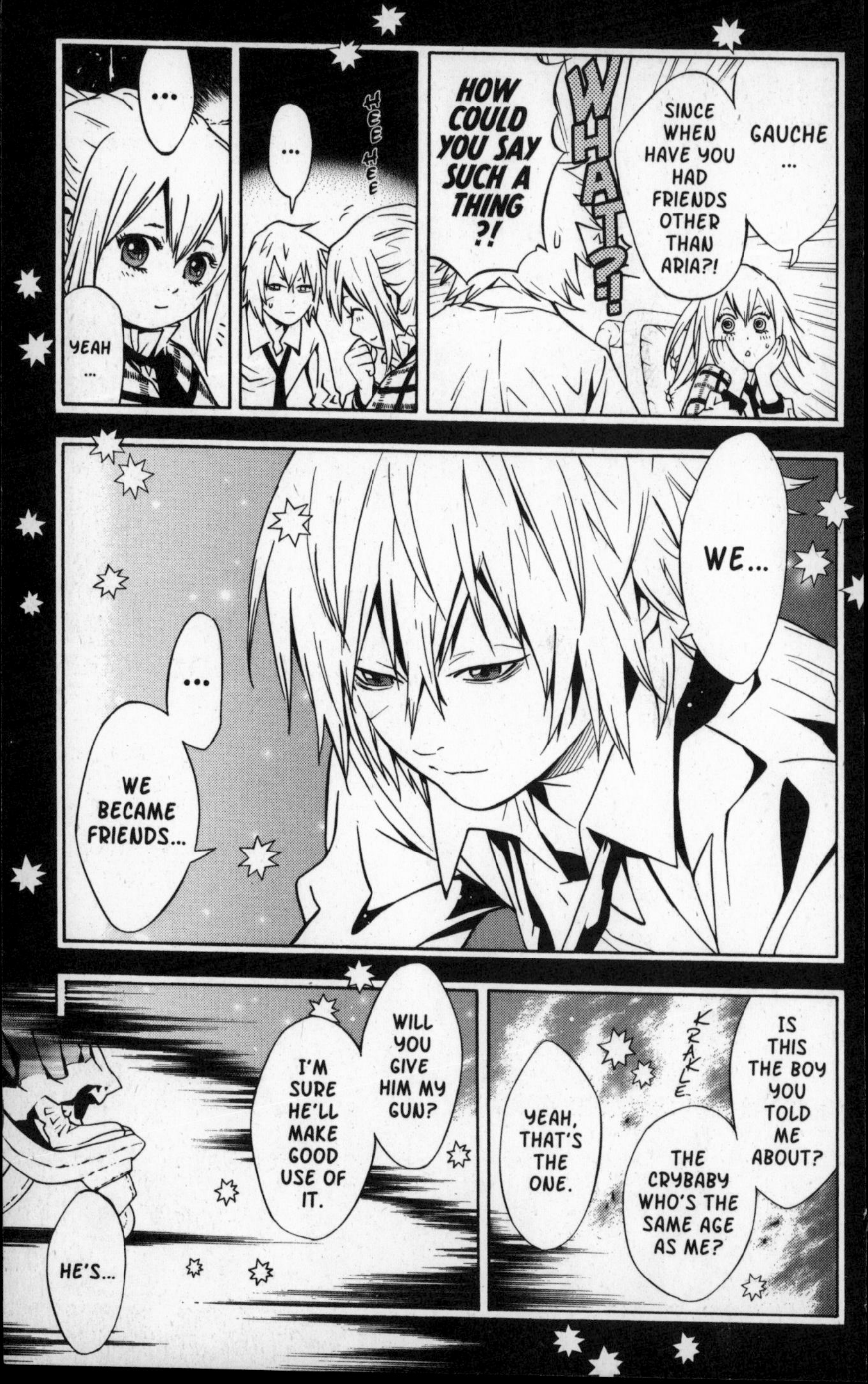
GAUCHE ...
SINCE WHEN HAVE YOU HAD FRIENDS OTHER THAN ARIA?!
WHAT?!
HOW COULD YOU SAY SUCH A THING?!
HEE HEE
...
...
YEAH ...
WE...
...
WE BECAME FRIENDS...
IS THIS THE BOY YOU TOLD ME ABOUT?
KRAKLE
THE CRYBABY WHO'S THE SAME AGE AS ME?
YEAH, THAT'S THE ONE.
WILL YOU GIVE HIM MY GUN?
I'M SURE HE'LL MAKE GOOD USE OF IT.
HE'S...

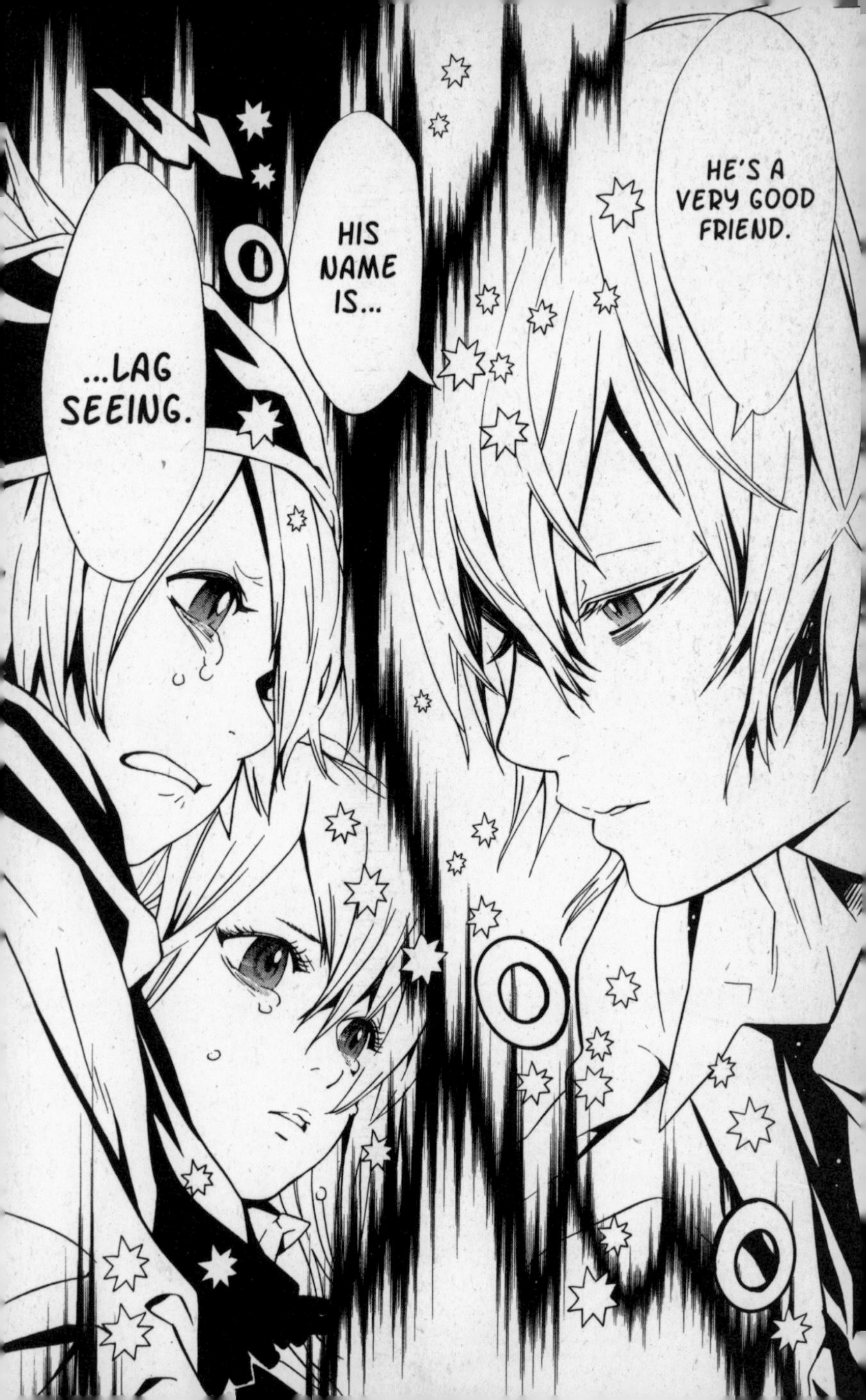
HE'S A VERY GOOD FRIEND.
HIS NAME IS...
...LAG SEEING.

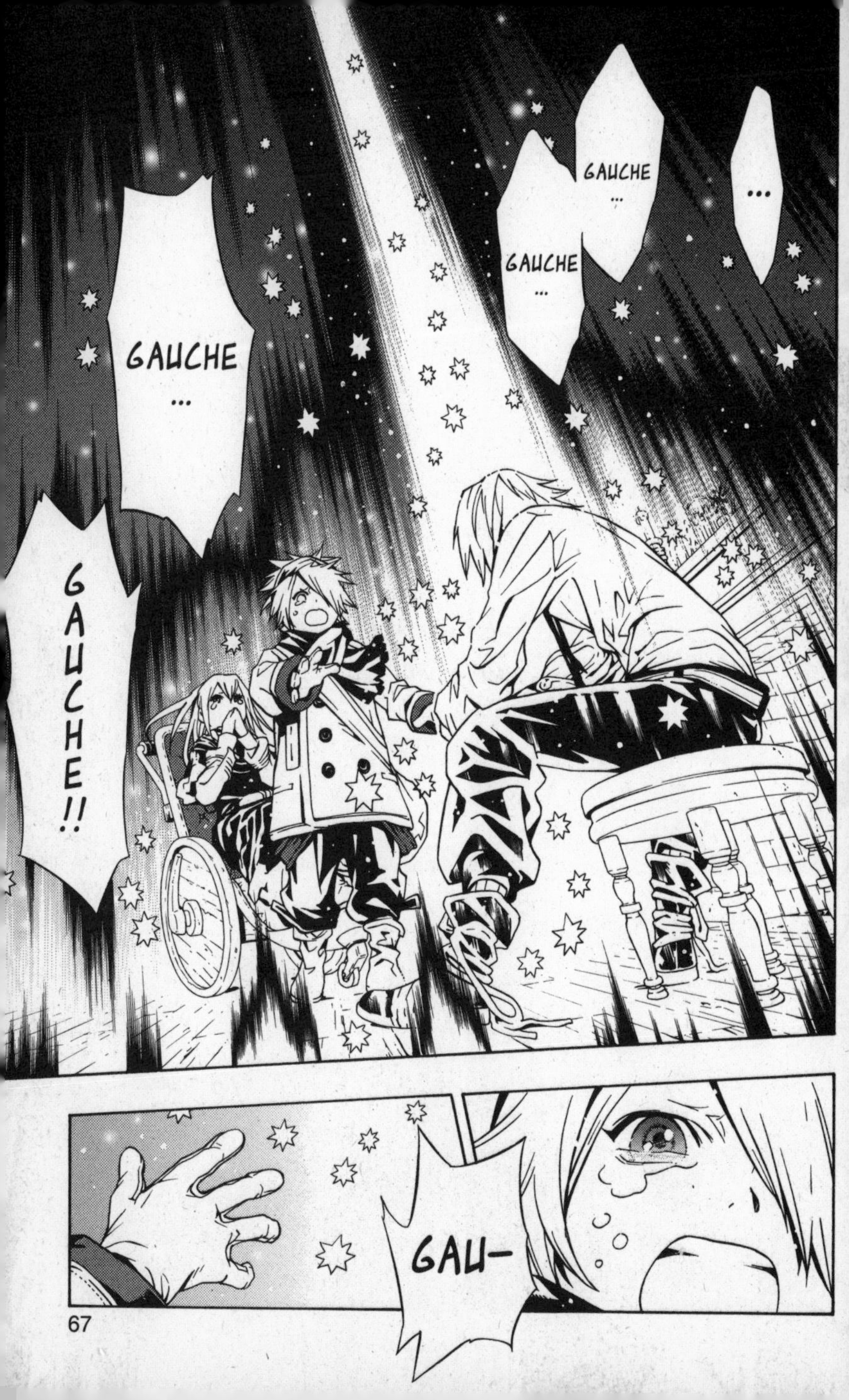
...
GAUCHE ...
GAUCHE ...
GAUCHE ...
GAUCHE!!
GAU-

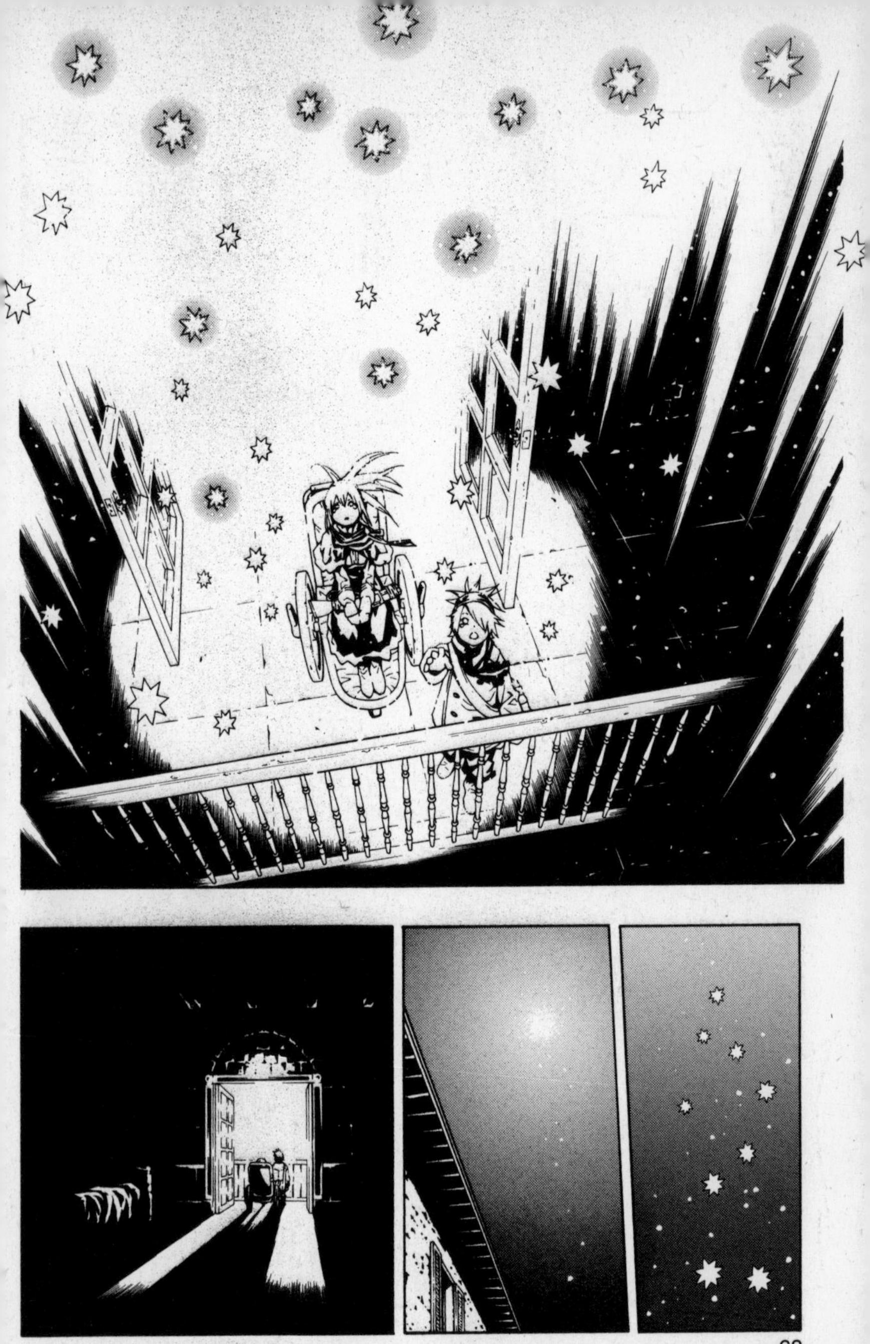

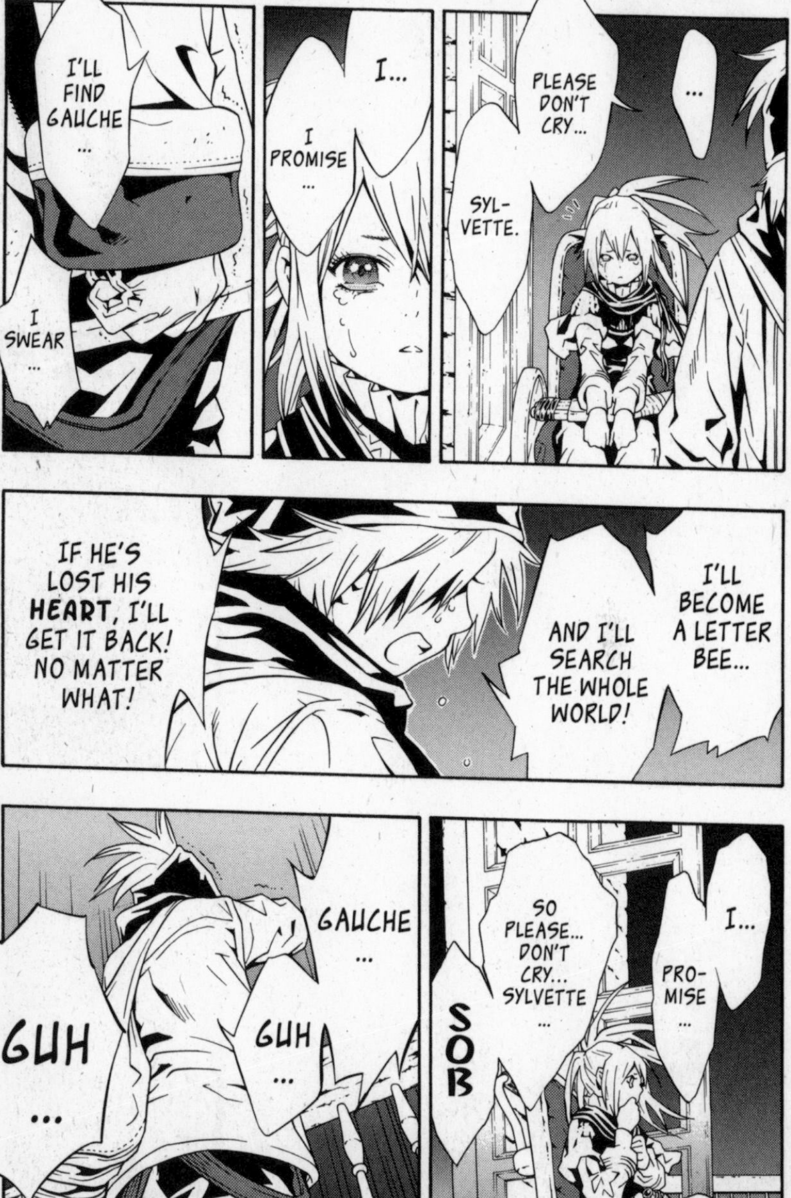
...
PLEASE DON'T CRY...
SYL-VETTE.
I...
I PROMISE ...
I'LL FIND GAUCHE ...
I SWEAR ...
I'LL BECOME A LETTER BEE...
AND I'LL SEARCH THE WHOLE WORLD!
IF HE'S LOST HIS **HEART**, I'LL GET IT BACK! NO MATTER WHAT!
I...
PRO-MISE ...
SO PLEASE... DON'T CRY... SYLVETTE ...
SOB
GAUCHE ...
GUH ...
GUH ...

BWAAHAA!!!

BWAAA!!!

I THINK YOU SHOULD HAVE IT.

I'M SORRY I COULDN'T GIVE THIS TO YOU EARLIER...

I'VE NEVER MET ANYONE WHO'S A BIGGER CRYBABY THAN ME...

OH, LAG...

...

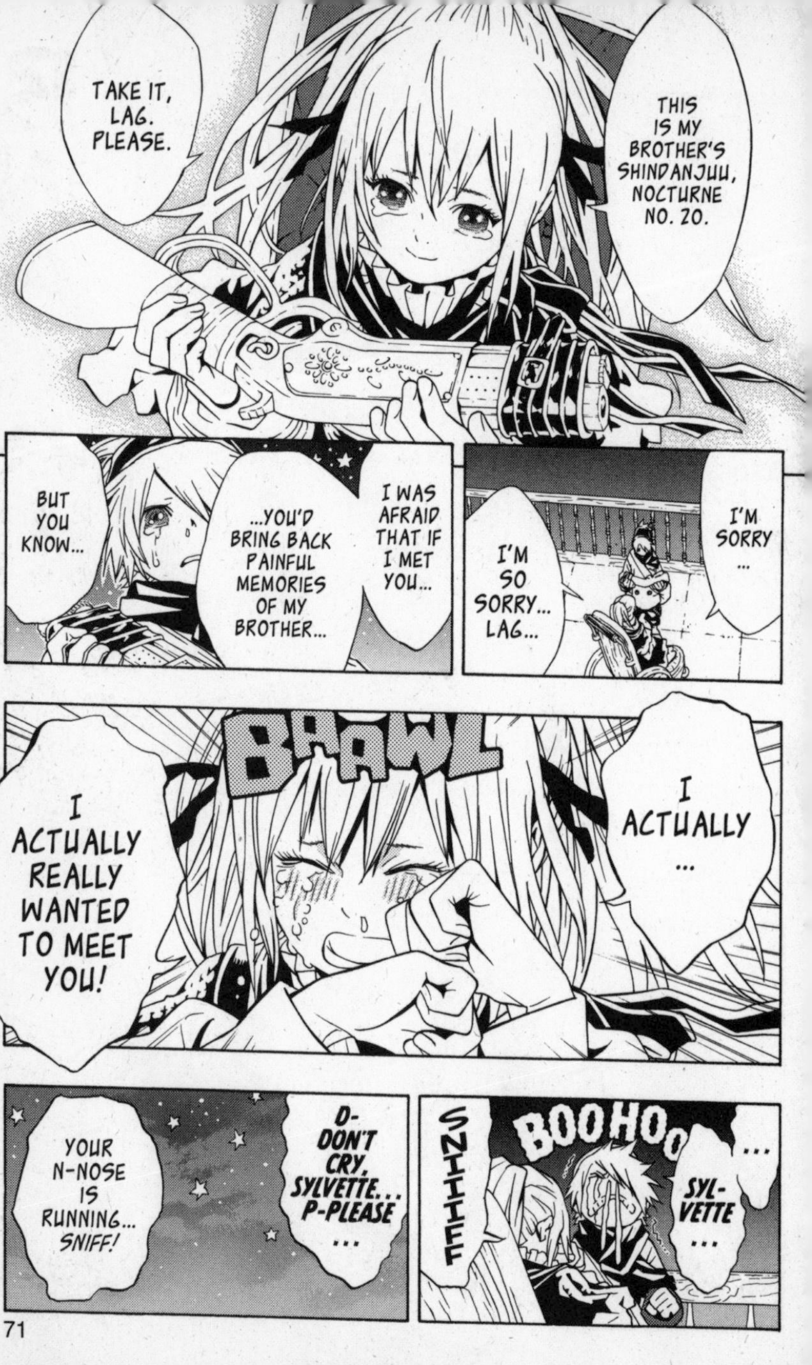
THIS IS MY BROTHER'S SHINDANJUU, NOCTURNE NO. 20.
TAKE IT, LAG. PLEASE.
I'M SORRY ...
I'M SO SORRY... LAG...
I WAS AFRAID THAT IF I MET YOU...
...YOU'D BRING BACK PAINFUL MEMORIES OF MY BROTHER...
BUT YOU KNOW...
I ACTUALLY ...
BRAWL
I ACTUALLY REALLY WANTED TO MEET YOU!
BOOHOO...
SNIIIIFF
SYL- VETTE ...
D- DON'T CRY, SYLVETTE... P-PLEASE ...
YOUR N-NOSE IS RUNNING... SNIFF!

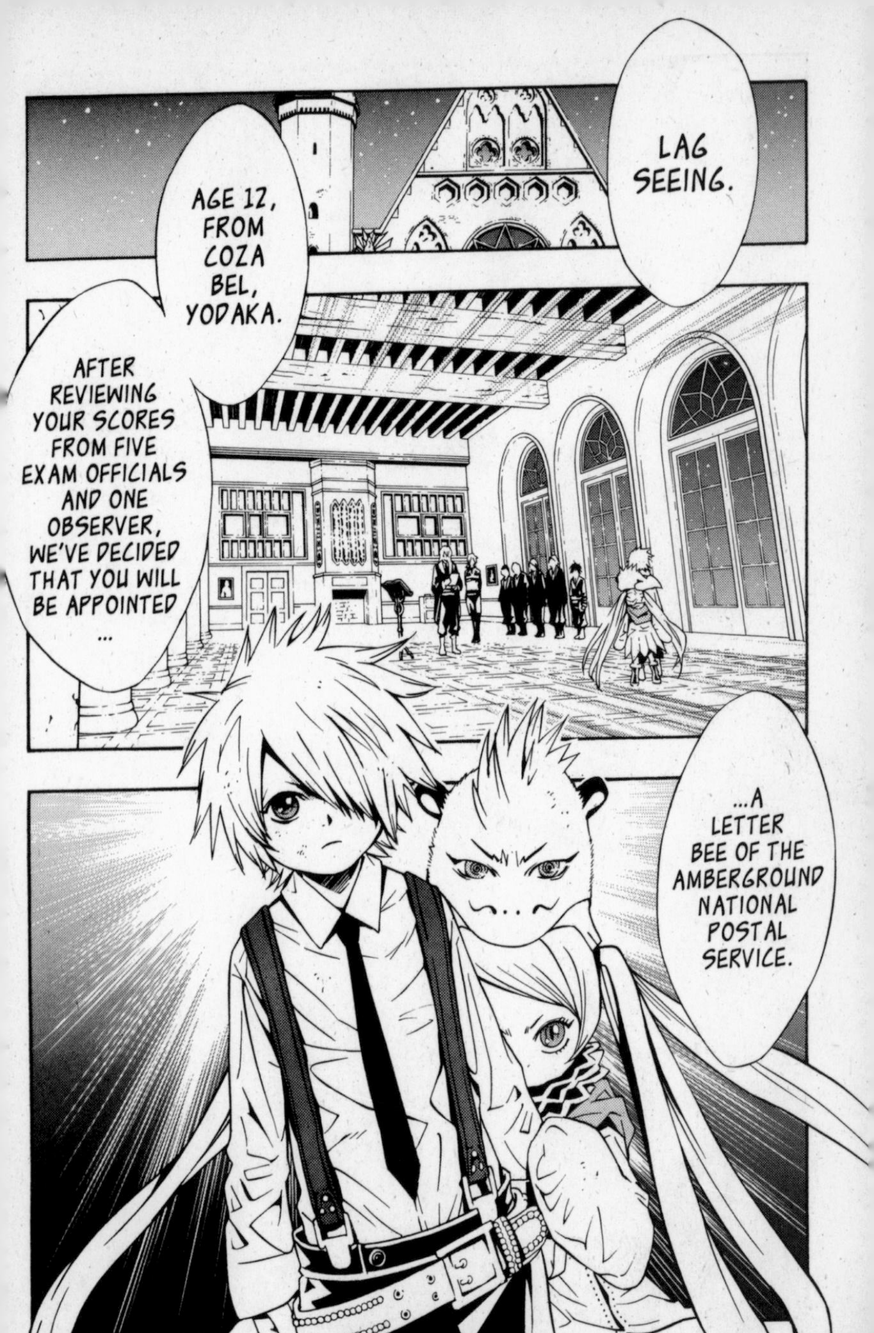
LAG SEEING.
AGE 12, FROM COZA BEL, YODAKA.
AFTER REVIEWING YOUR SCORES FROM FIVE EXAM OFFICIALS AND ONE OBSERVER, WE'VE DECIDED THAT YOU WILL BE APPOINTED ...
...A LETTER BEE OF THE AMBERGROUND NATIONAL POSTAL SERVICE.

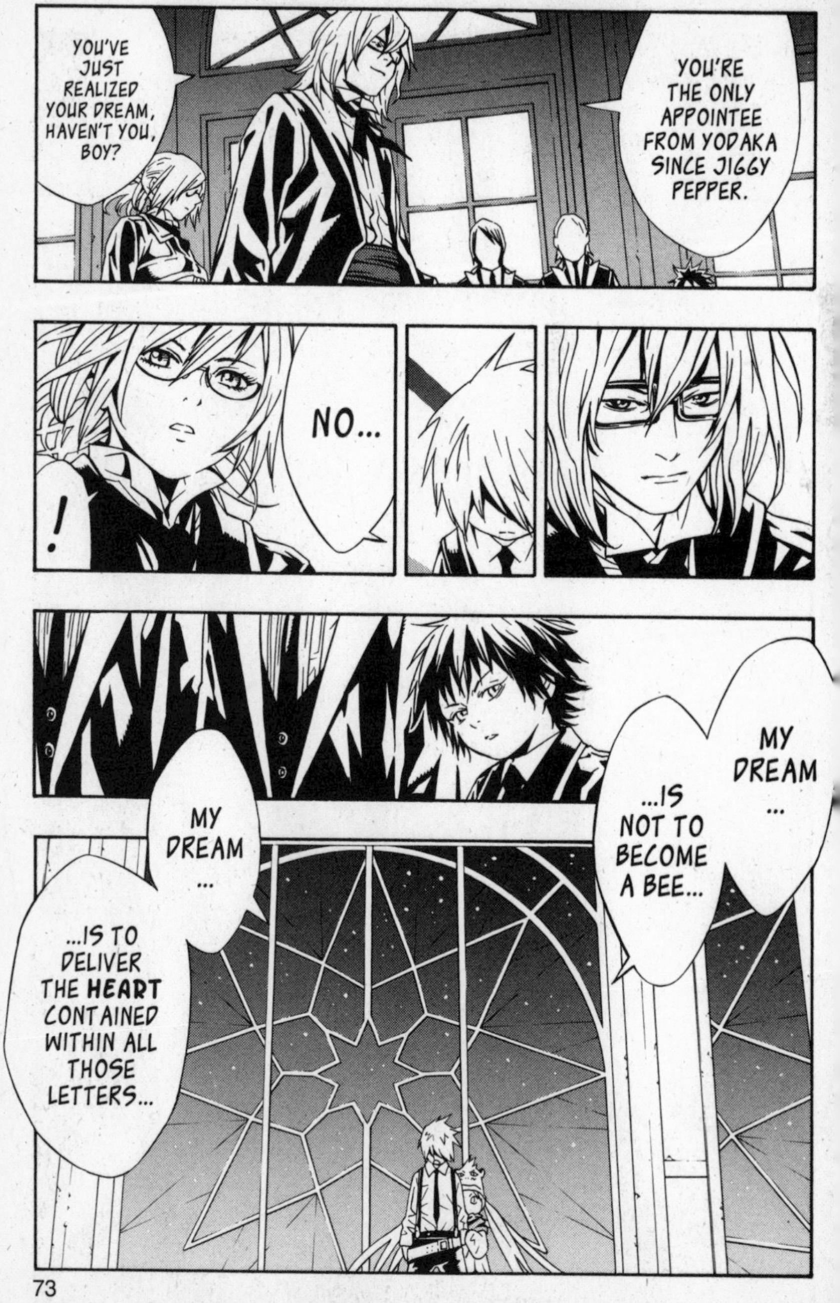
YOU'RE THE ONLY APPOINTEE FROM YODAKA SINCE JIGGY PEPPER.
YOU'VE JUST REALIZED YOUR DREAM, HAVEN'T YOU, BOY?
NO...
!
MY DREAM...
...IS NOT TO BECOME A BEE...
MY DREAM...
...IS TO DELIVER THE **HEART** CONTAINED WITHIN ALL THOSE LETTERS...

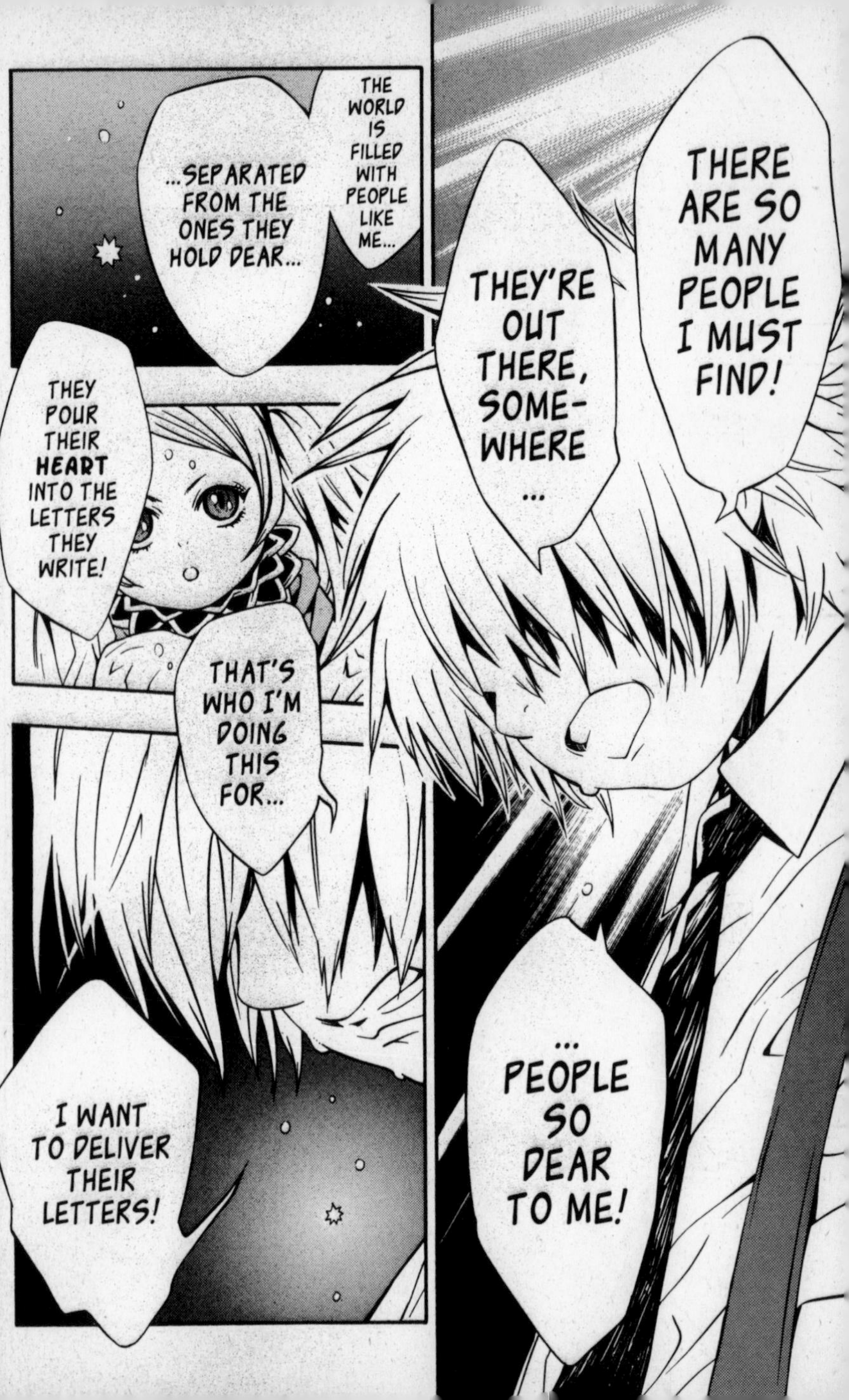
THE WORLD IS FILLED WITH PEOPLE LIKE ME...
...SEPARATED FROM THE ONES THEY HOLD DEAR...
THEY POUR THEIR HEART INTO THE LETTERS THEY WRITE!
THAT'S WHO I'M DOING THIS FOR...
I WANT TO DELIVER THEIR LETTERS!
THERE ARE SO MANY PEOPLE I MUST FIND!
THEY'RE OUT THERE, SOME-WHERE...
...PEOPLE SO DEAR TO ME!

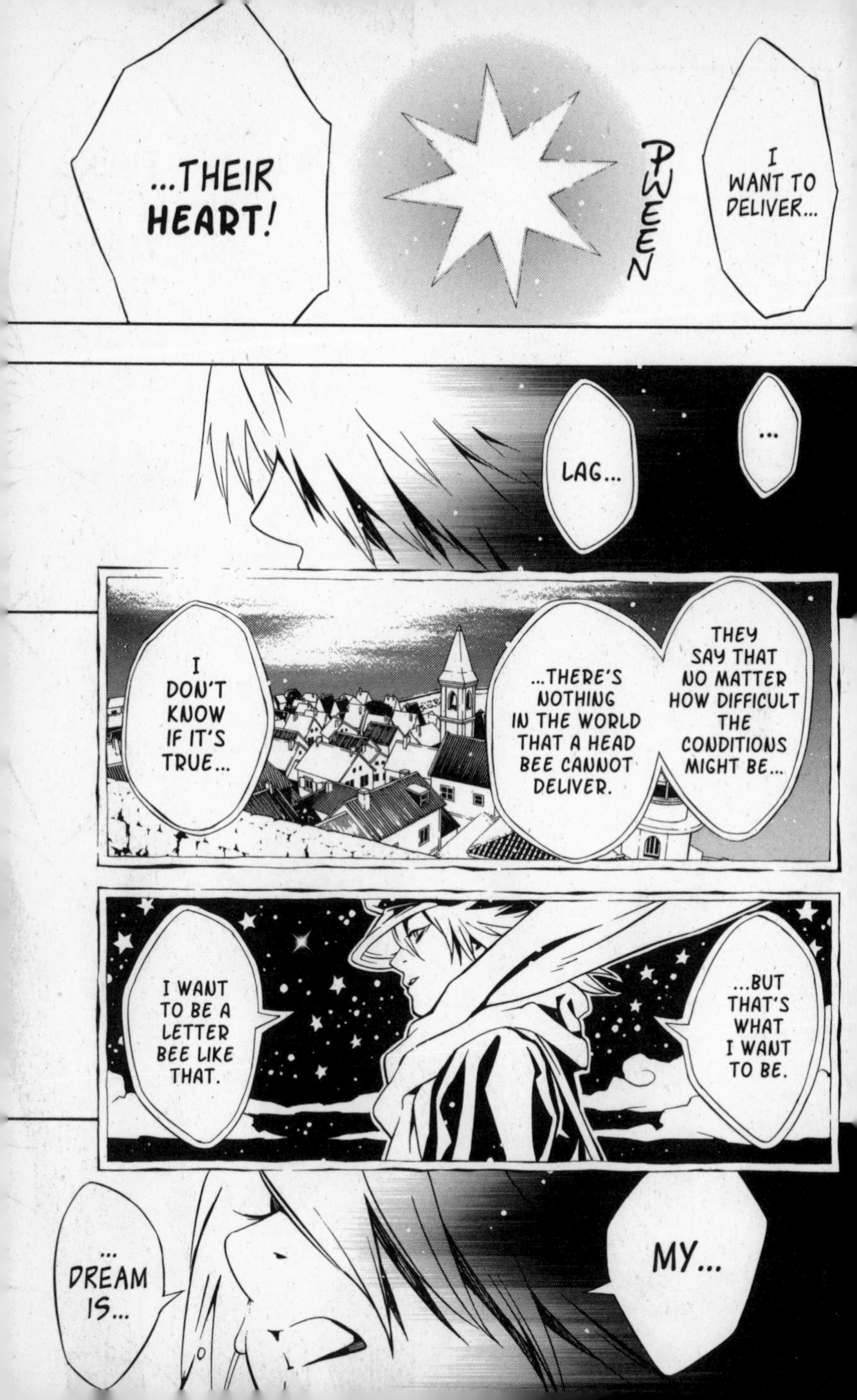
I WANT TO DELIVER...
PWEEN
...THEIR HEART!
...
LAG...
THEY SAY THAT NO MATTER HOW DIFFICULT THE CONDITIONS MIGHT BE...
...THERE'S NOTHING IN THE WORLD THAT A HEAD BEE CANNOT DELIVER.
I DON'T KNOW IF IT'S TRUE...
...BUT THAT'S WHAT I WANT TO BE.
I WANT TO BE A LETTER BEE LIKE THAT.
MY...
... DREAM IS...

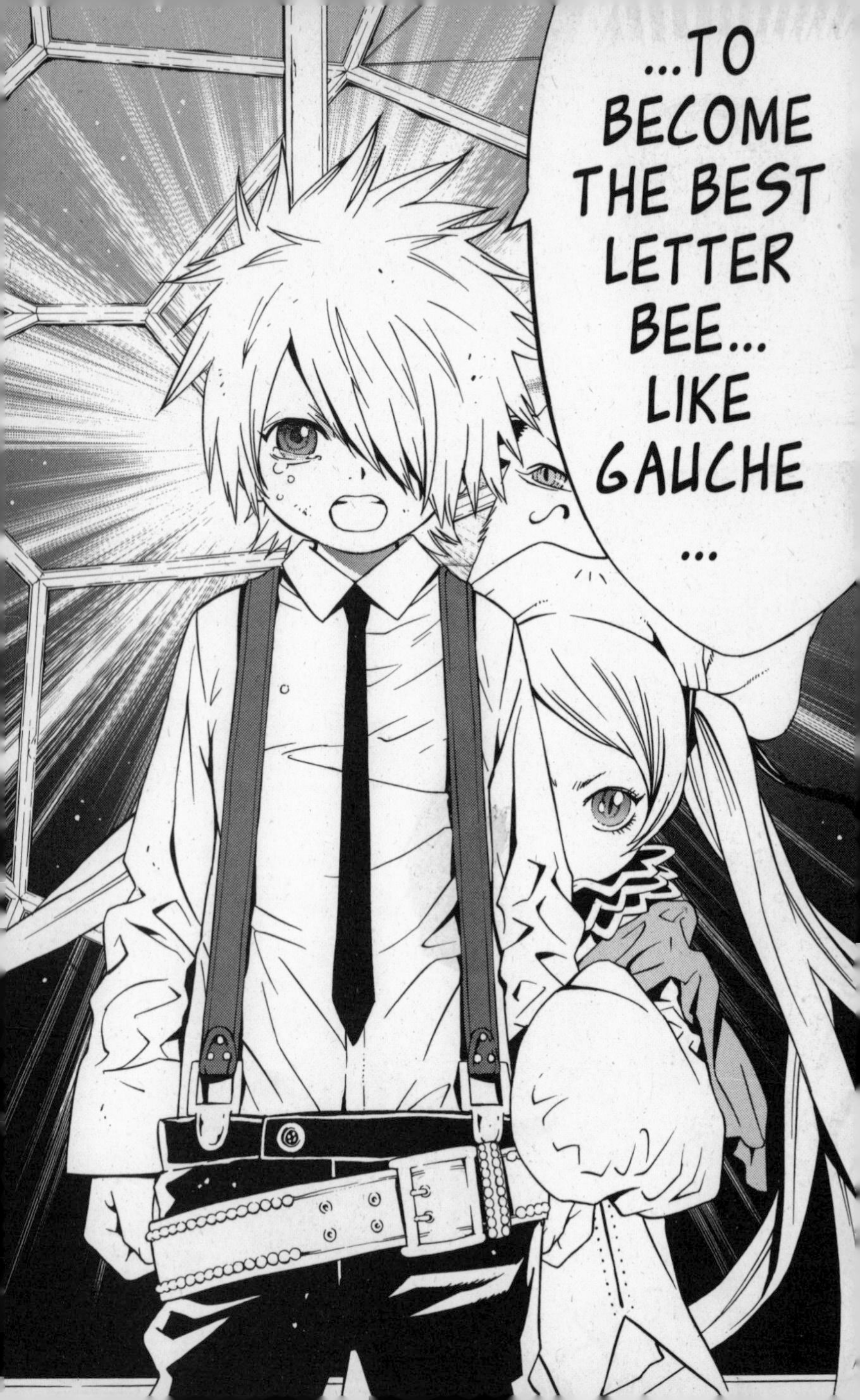
...TO BECOME THE BEST LETTER BEE... LIKE GAUCHE ...

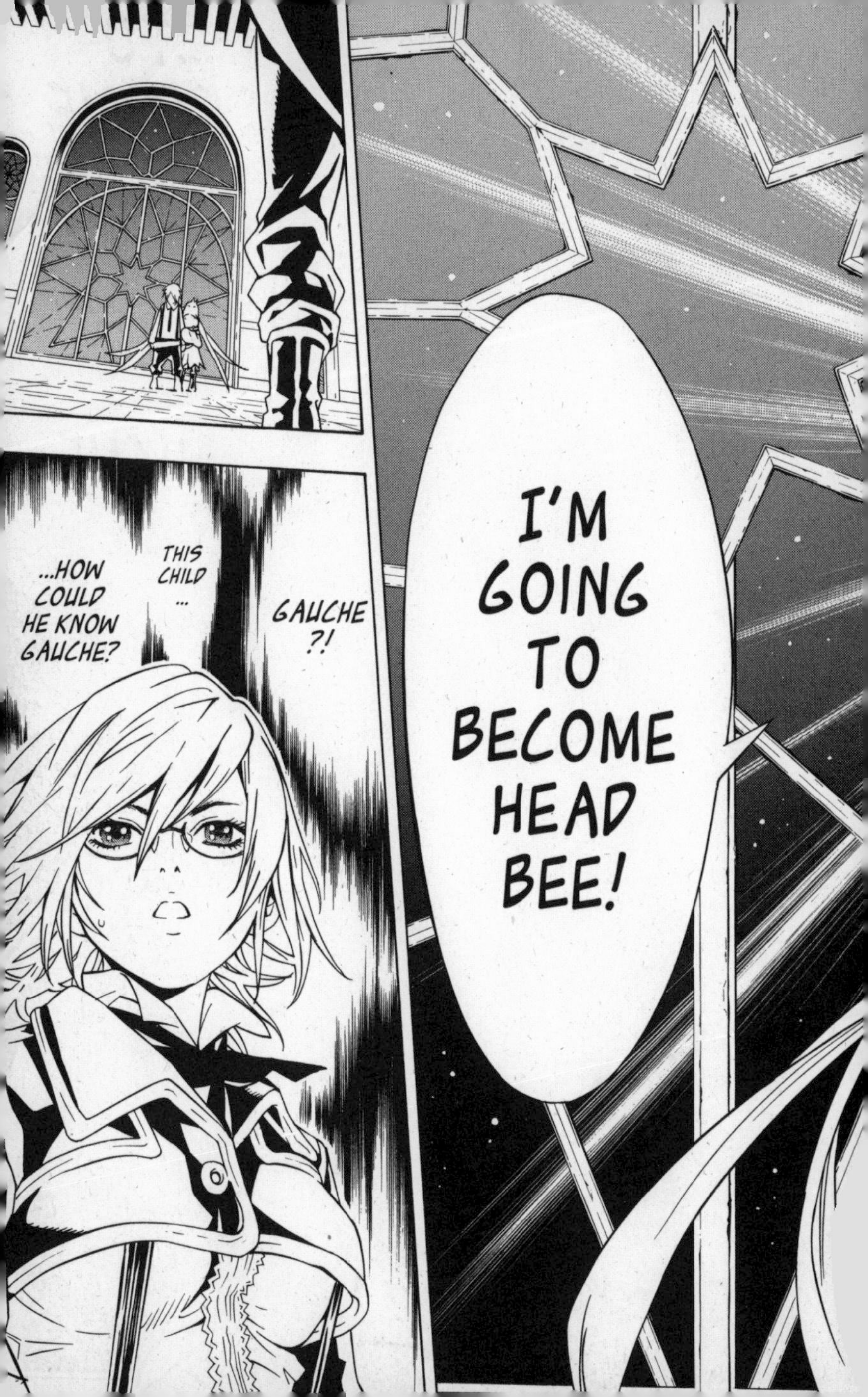
I'M GOING TO BECOME HEAD BEE!
GAUCHE?!
THIS CHILD ...
...HOW COULD HE KNOW GAUCHE?

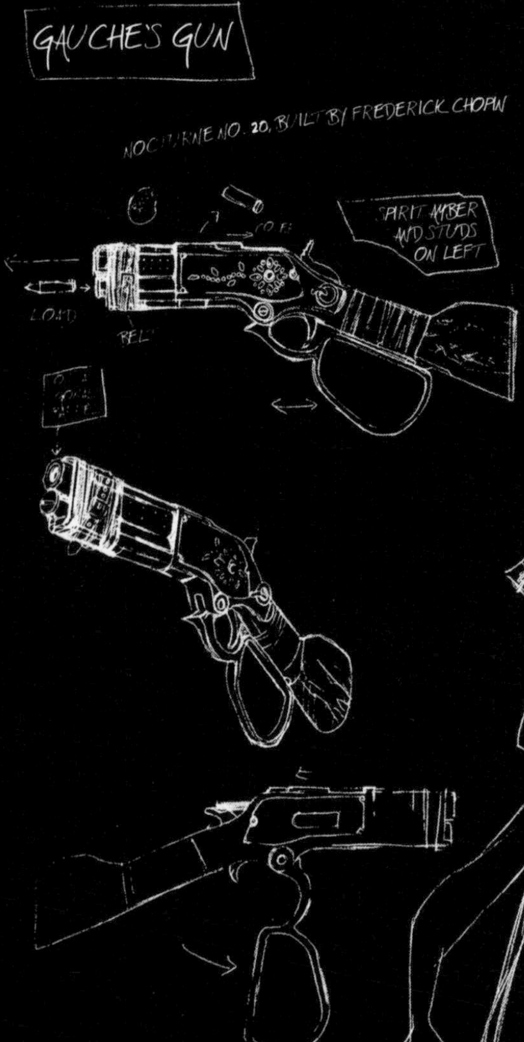
GAUCHE'S GUN
NOCTURNE NO. 20, BUILT BY FREDERICK CHOPIN
SPIRIT AMBER AND STUDS ON LEFT
LOAD

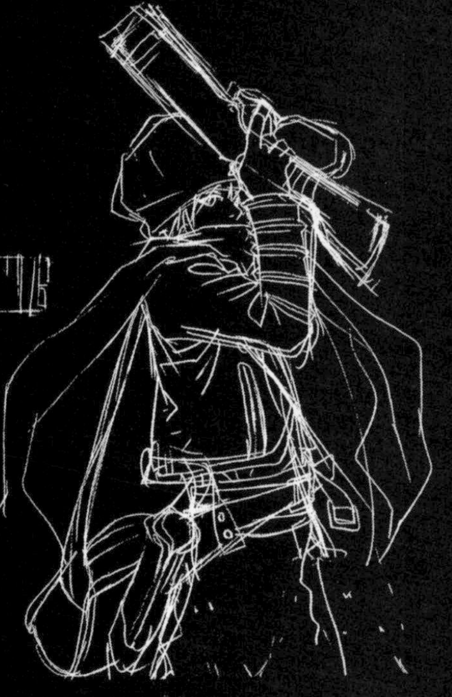

a rude sketch (nocturne)

Early rough sketch of a shindanjuu (Nocturne No. 20).

Chapter 10: Beneath the Light

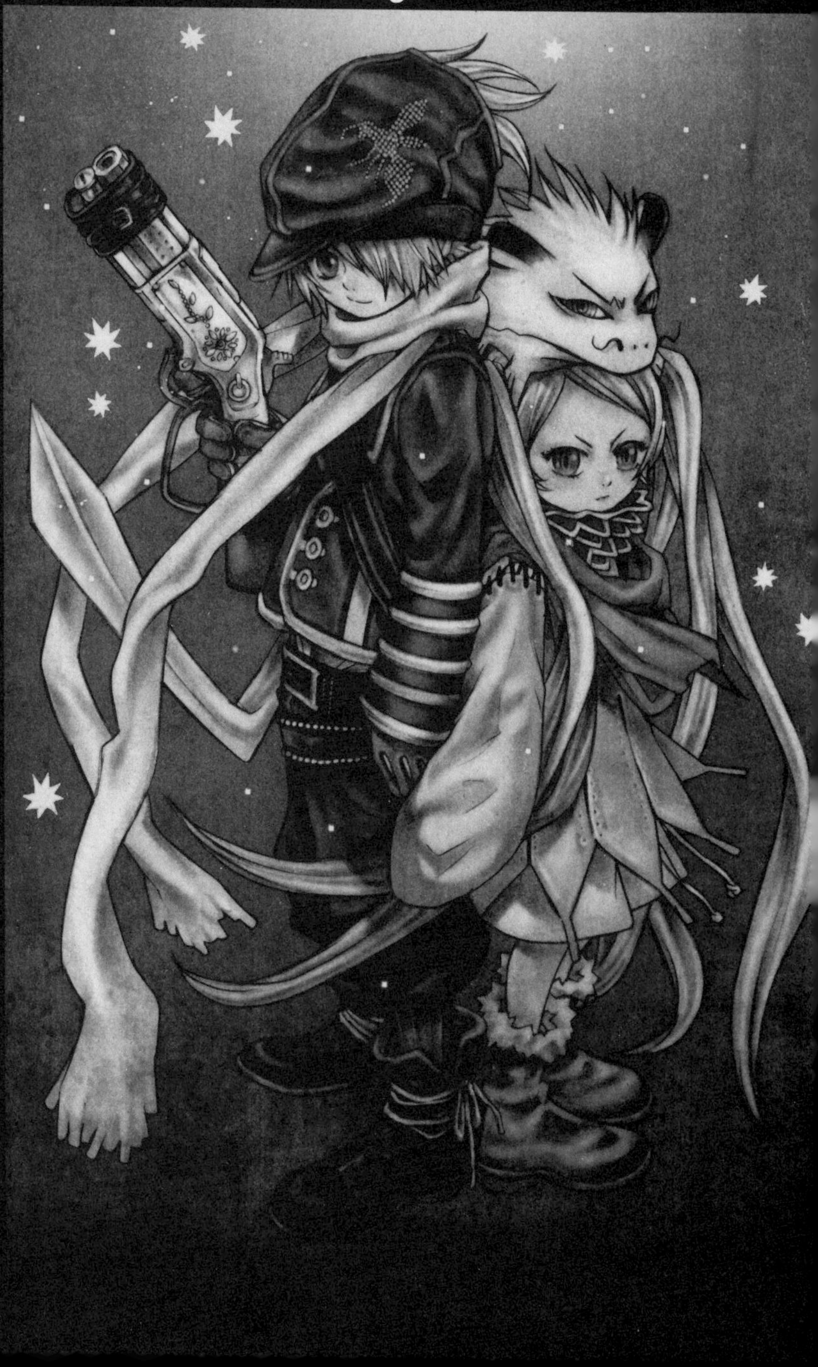

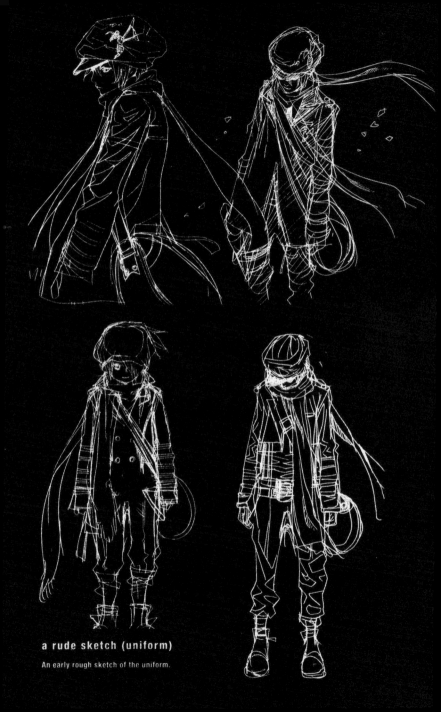

a rude sketch (uniform)

An early rough sketch of the uniform.

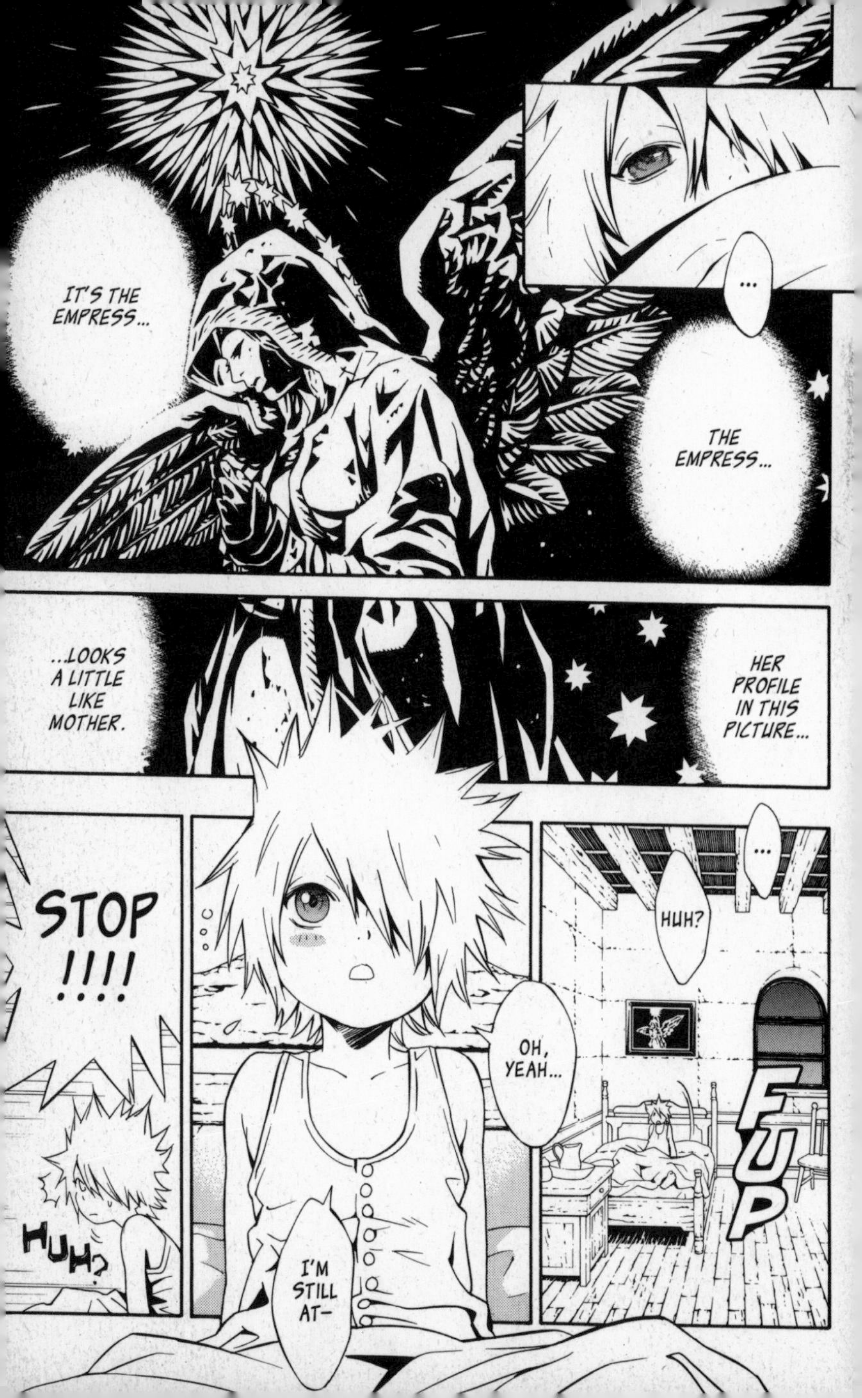
...
THE EMPRESS...
IT'S THE EMPRESS...
HER PROFILE IN THIS PICTURE...
...LOOKS A LITTLE LIKE MOTHER.
...
HUH?
FUP
OH, YEAH...
I'M STILL AT-
STOP!!!!
HUH?

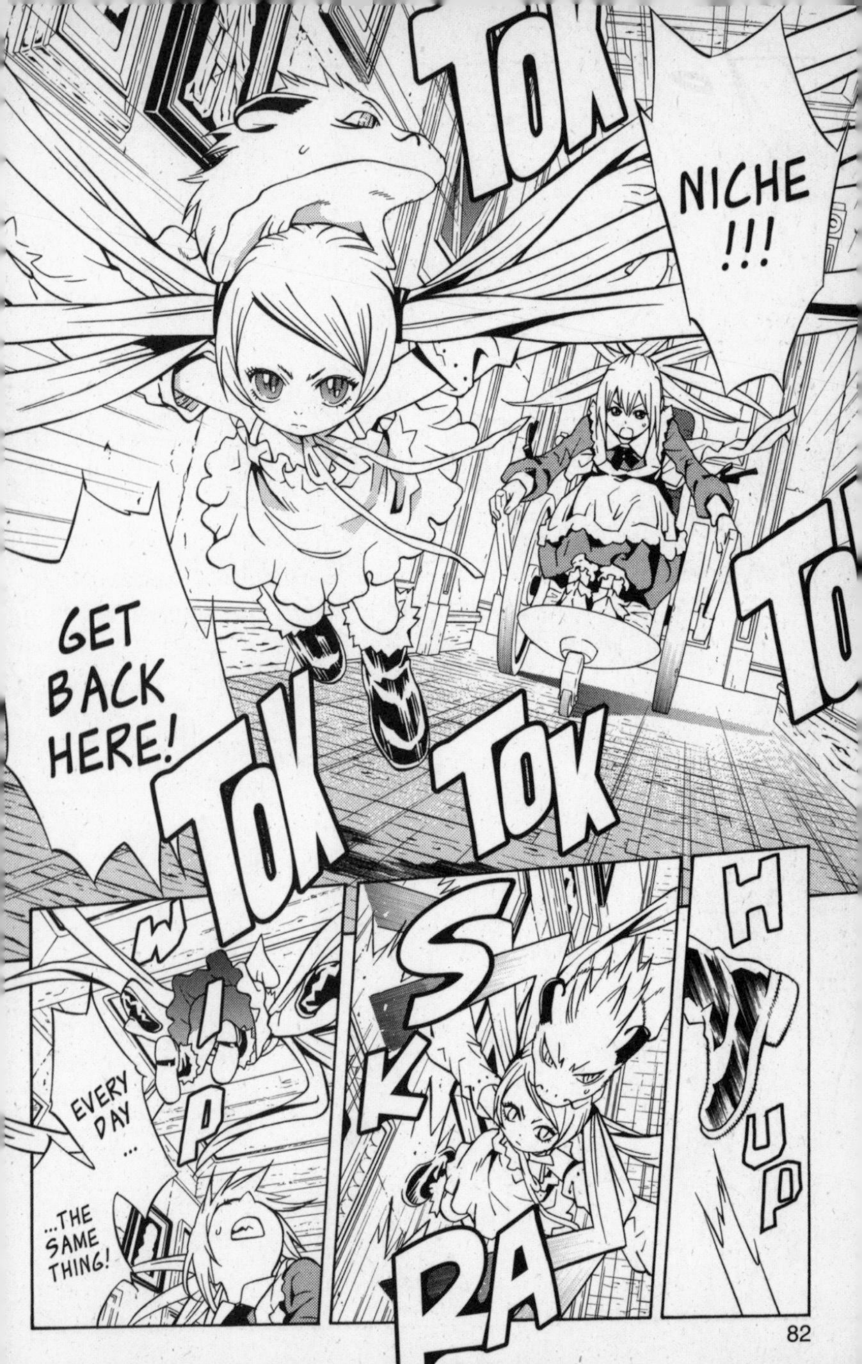
TOK
NICHE !!!
TO
TOK
TOK
GET BACK HERE!
HUP
S
K
PA
WIP
EVERY DAY ...
...THE SAME THING!

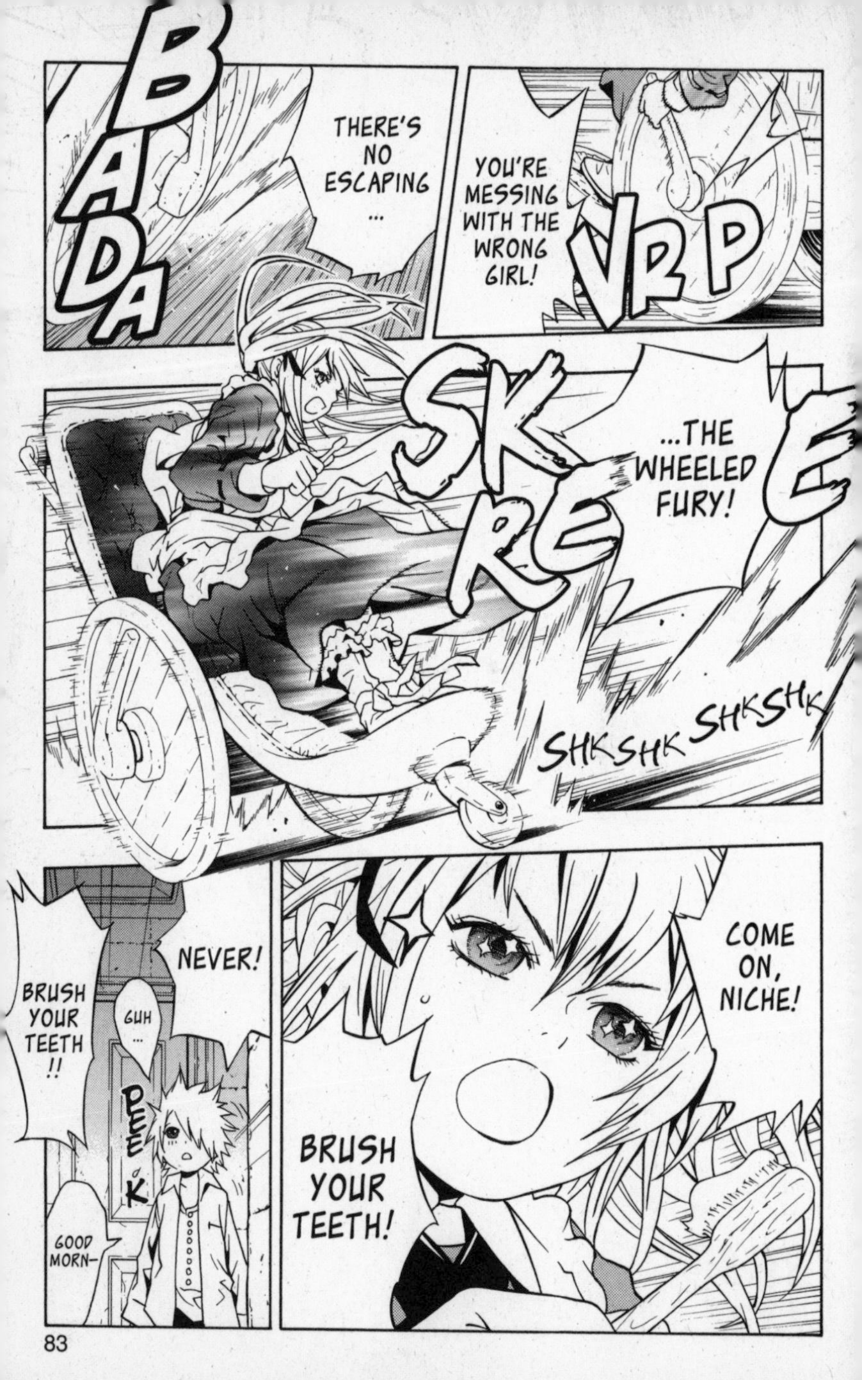
YOU'RE MESSING WITH THE WRONG GIRL!
VRP
BADA
THERE'S NO ESCAPING ...
...THE WHEELED FURY!
SKREE
SHKSHK SHKSHK
COME ON, NICHE!
BRUSH YOUR TEETH!
NEVER!
BRUSH YOUR TEETH !!
GUH ...
PEEK
GOOD MORN-

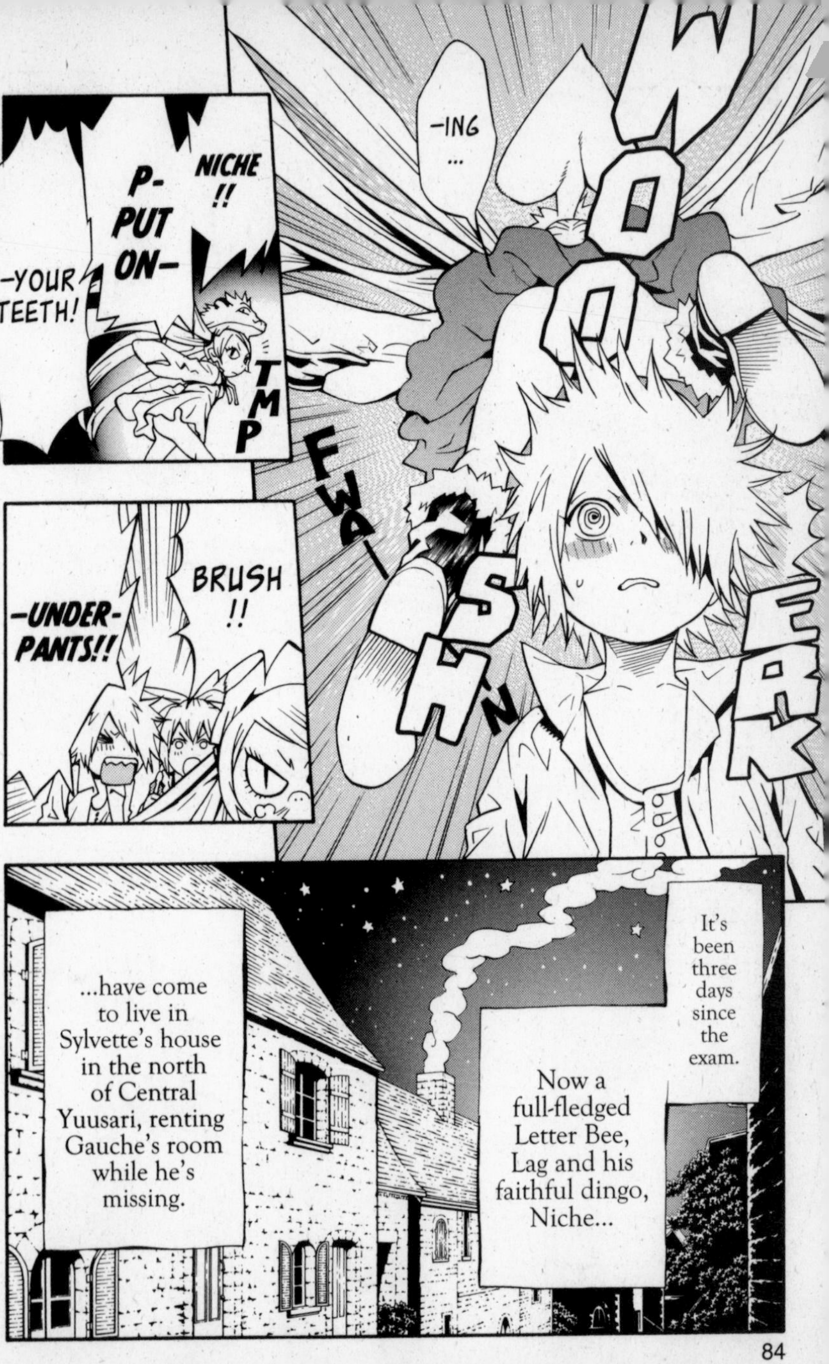
WOOO
-ING
...
FWA
SHSH
ERK
NICHE !!
P-PUT ON-
-YOUR TEETH!
TMP
BRUSH !!
-UNDER-PANTS!!
It's been three days since the exam.
Now a full-fledged Letter Bee, Lag and his faithful dingo, Niche...
...have come to live in Sylvette's house in the north of Central Yuusari, renting Gauche's room while he's missing.

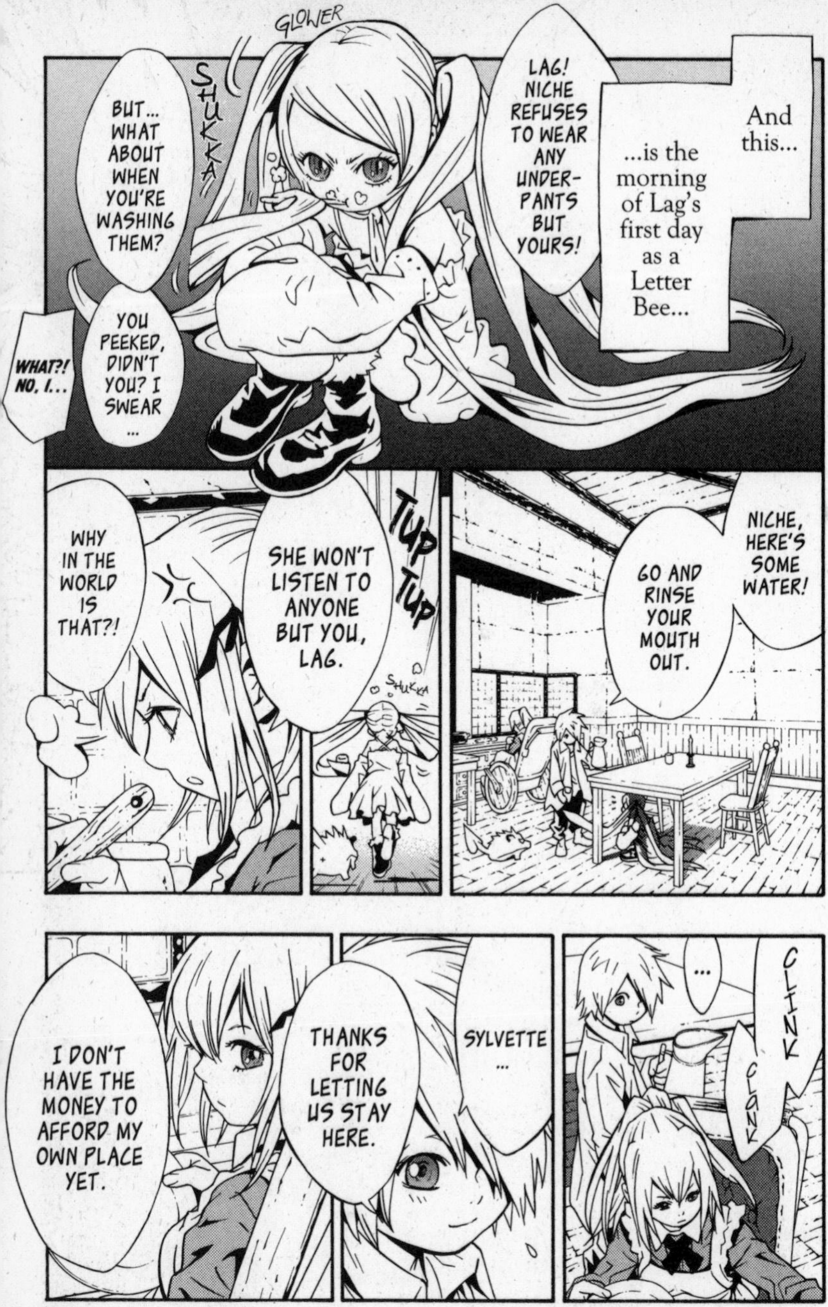
And this...
...is the morning of Lag's first day as a Letter Bee...
LAG! NICHE REFUSES TO WEAR ANY UNDER-PANTS BUT YOURS!
GLOWER
SHUKKA
BUT... WHAT ABOUT WHEN YOU'RE WASHING THEM?
YOU PEEKED, DIDN'T YOU? I SWEAR ...
WHAT?! NO, I...
NICHE, HERE'S SOME WATER!
GO AND RINSE YOUR MOUTH OUT.
TUP TUP
SHUKKA
SHE WON'T LISTEN TO ANYONE BUT YOU, LAG.
WHY IN THE WORLD IS THAT?!
CLINK
CLONK
...
SYLVETTE ...
THANKS FOR LETTING US STAY HERE.
I DON'T HAVE THE MONEY TO AFFORD MY OWN PLACE YET.

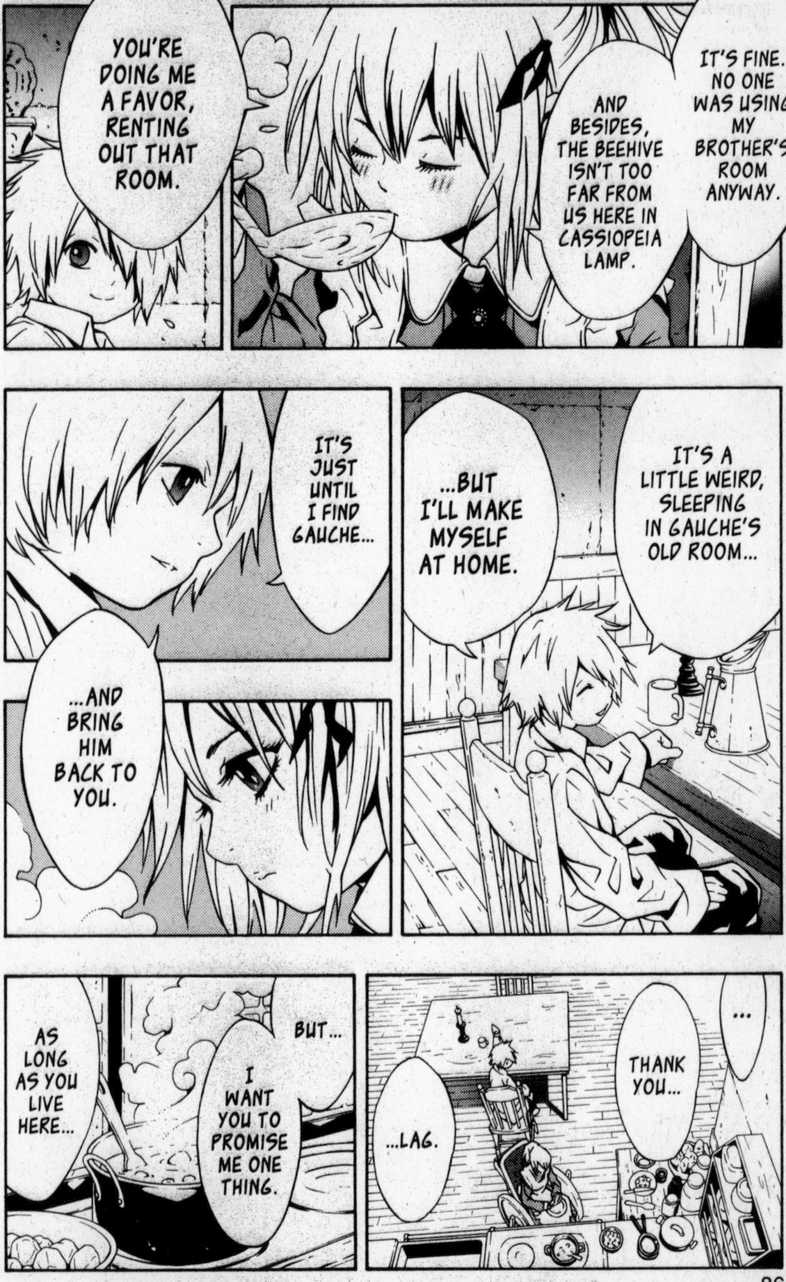
IT'S FINE. NO ONE WAS USING MY BROTHER'S ROOM ANYWAY.
AND BESIDES, THE BEEHIVE ISN'T TOO FAR FROM US HERE IN CASSIOPEIA LAMP.
YOU'RE DOING ME A FAVOR, RENTING OUT THAT ROOM.
IT'S A LITTLE WEIRD, SLEEPING IN GAUCHE'S OLD ROOM...
...BUT I'LL MAKE MYSELF AT HOME.
IT'S JUST UNTIL I FIND GAUCHE...
...AND BRING HIM BACK TO YOU.
...
THANK YOU...
...LAG.
BUT...
AS LONG AS YOU LIVE HERE...
I WANT YOU TO PROMISE ME ONE THING.

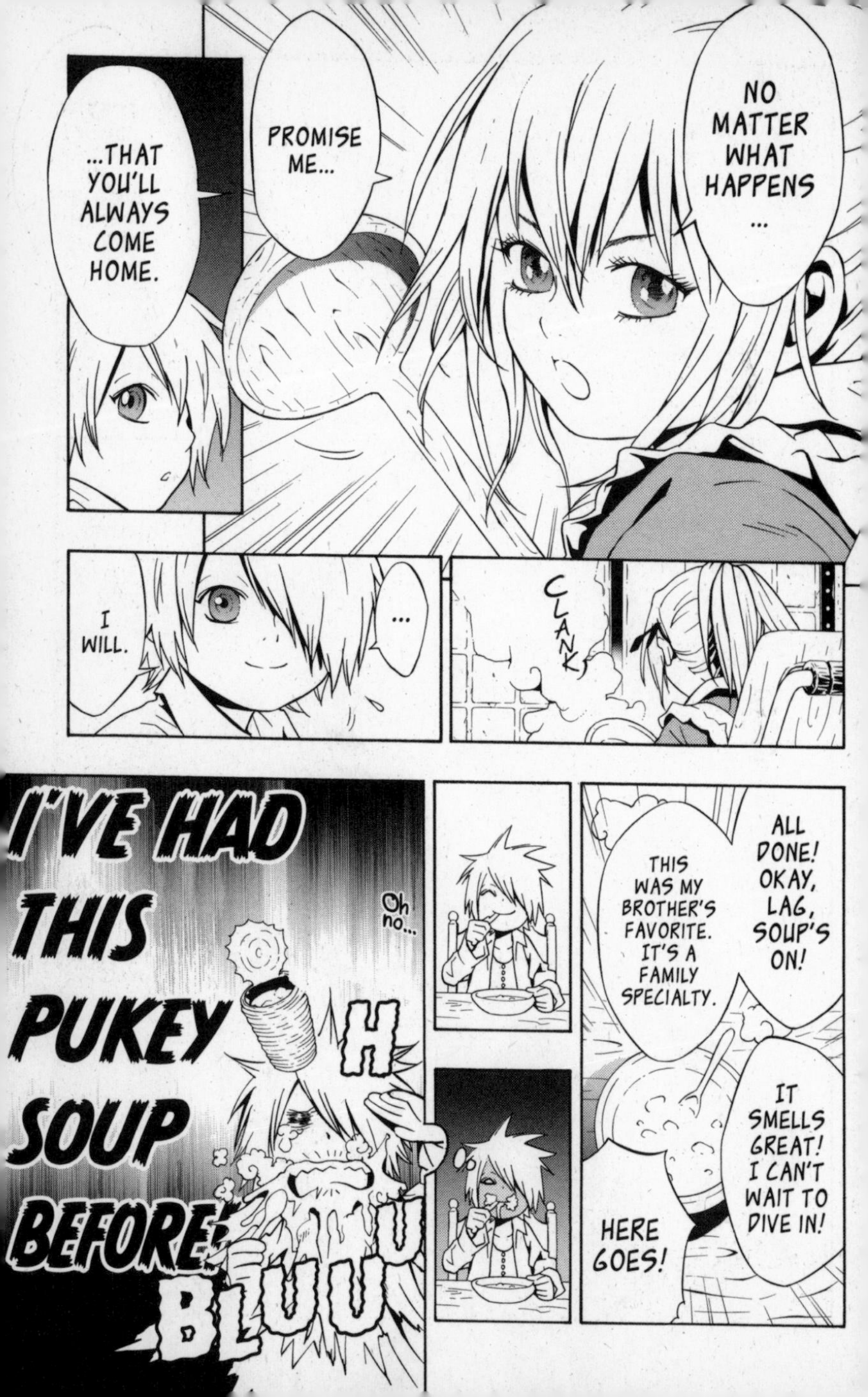
NO MATTER WHAT HAPPENS ...
PROMISE ME...
...THAT YOU'LL ALWAYS COME HOME.
CLANK
...
I WILL.
ALL DONE! OKAY, LAG, SOUP'S ON!
THIS WAS MY BROTHER'S FAVORITE. IT'S A FAMILY SPECIALTY.
IT SMELLS GREAT! I CAN'T WAIT TO DIVE IN!
HERE GOES!
Oh no...
I'VE HAD THIS PUKEY SOUP BEFORE!
BLUUUUH

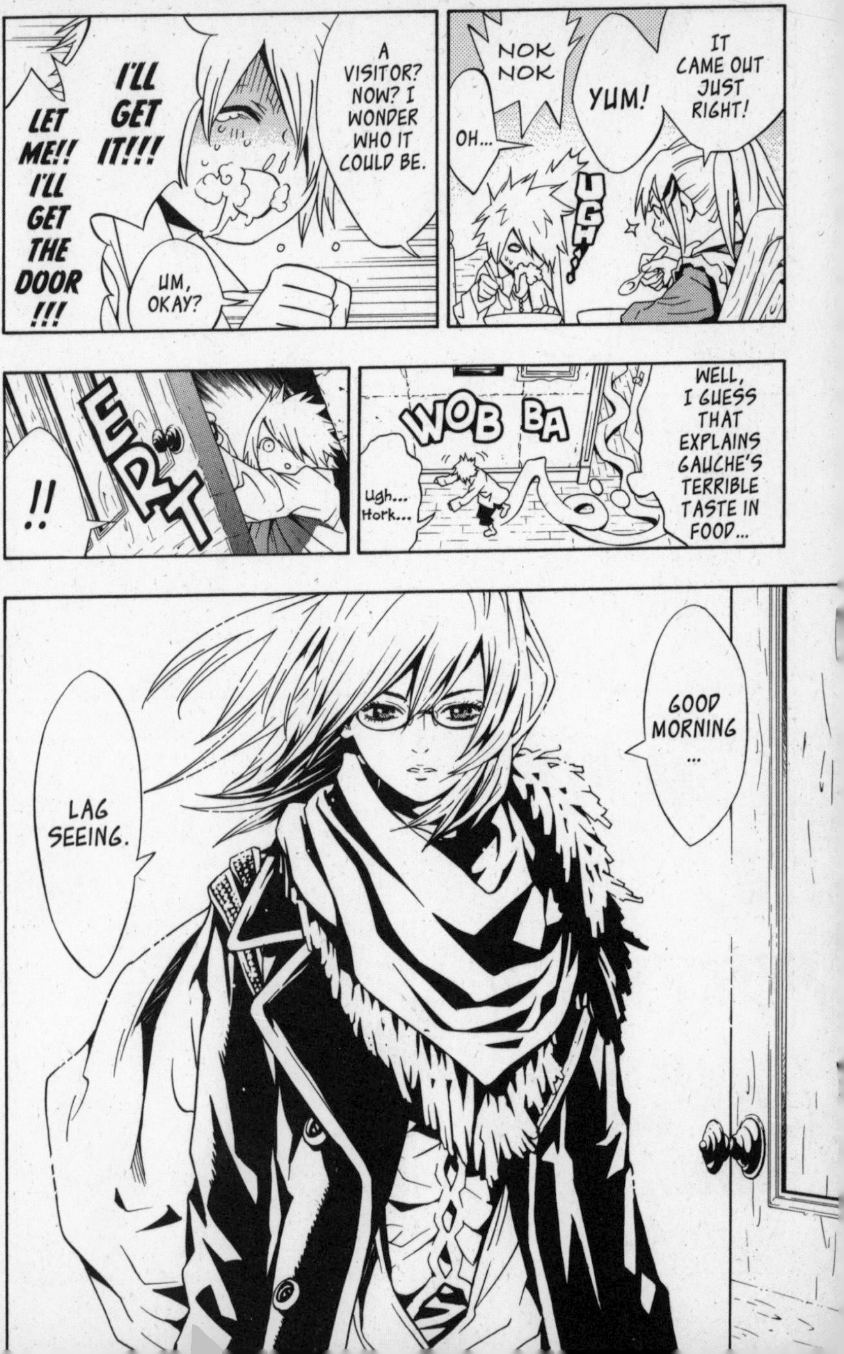

NOK NOK
IT CAME OUT JUST RIGHT!
YUM!
OH...
UGH
A VISITOR? NOW? I WONDER WHO IT COULD BE.
I'LL GET IT!!!
LET ME!! I'LL GET THE DOOR!!!
UM, OKAY?
WELL, I GUESS THAT EXPLAINS GAUCHE'S TERRIBLE TASTE IN FOOD...
WOB BA
Ugh... Hork...
!!
GOOD MORNING ...
LAG SEEING.

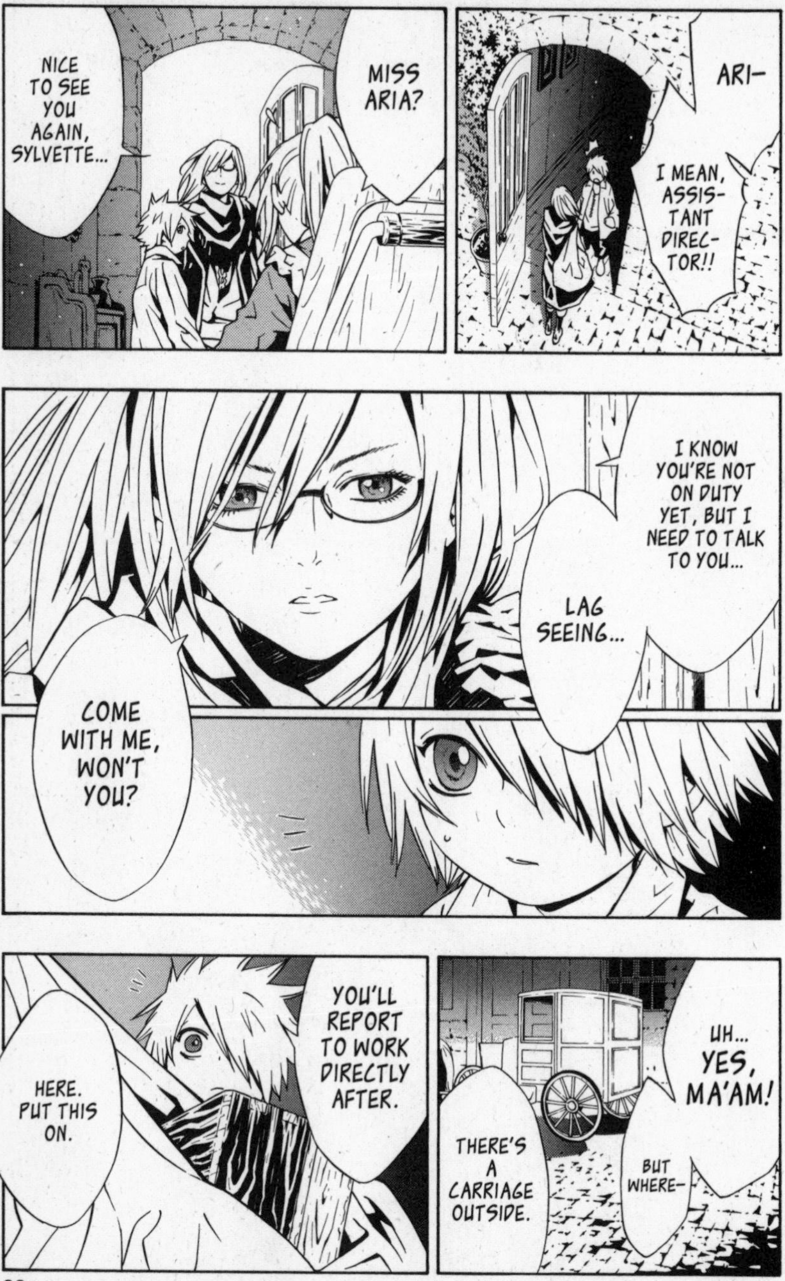
ARI-
I MEAN, ASSISTANT DIRECTOR!!
MISS ARIA?
NICE TO SEE YOU AGAIN, SYLVETTE...
I KNOW YOU'RE NOT ON DUTY YET, BUT I NEED TO TALK TO YOU...
LAG SEEING...
COME WITH ME, WON'T YOU?
THERE'S A CARRIAGE OUTSIDE.
UH... YES, MA'AM!
BUT WHERE-
YOU'LL REPORT TO WORK DIRECTLY AFTER.
HERE. PUT THIS ON.

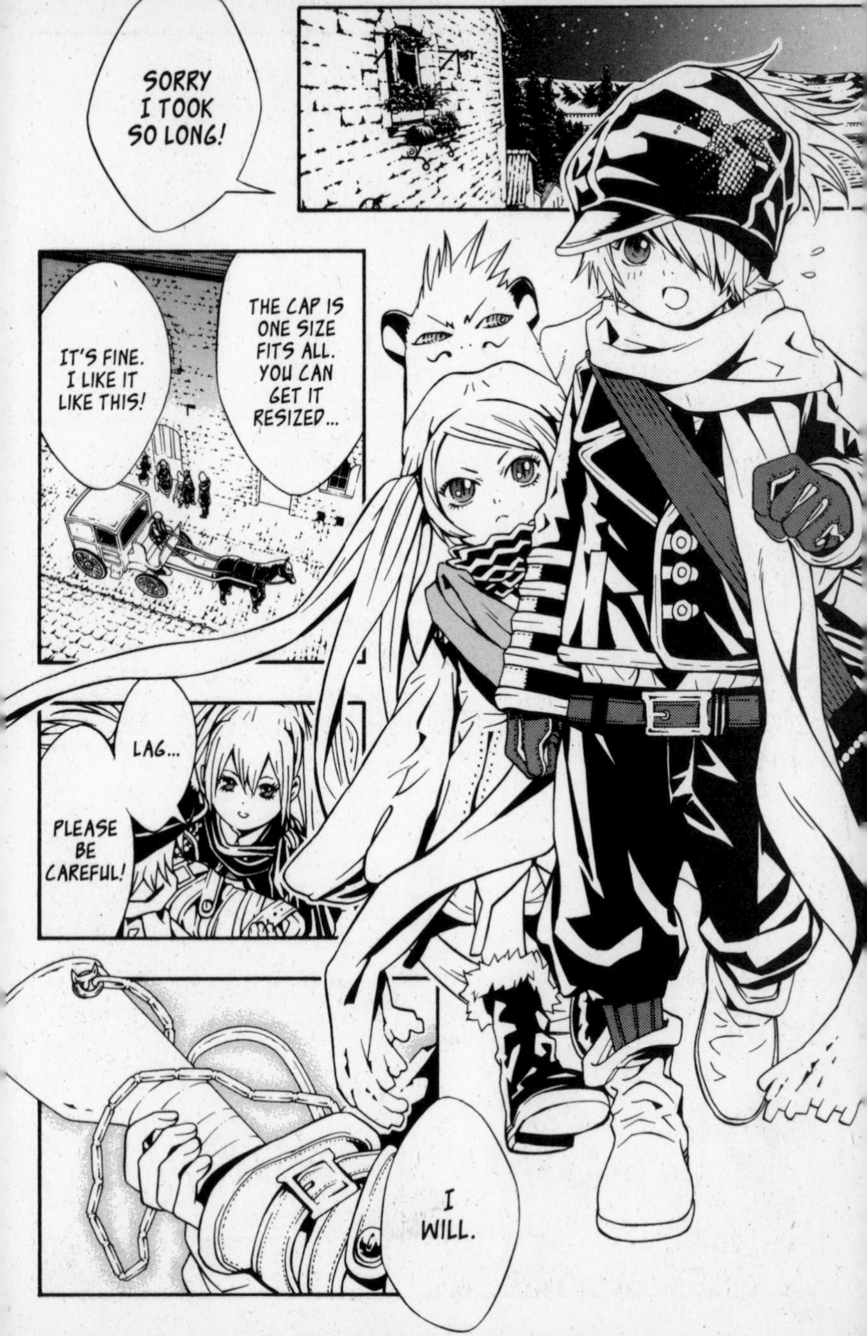
SORRY I TOOK SO LONG!
THE CAP IS ONE SIZE FITS ALL. YOU CAN GET IT RESIZED...
IT'S FINE. I LIKE IT LIKE THIS!
LAG...
PLEASE BE CAREFUL!
I WILL.

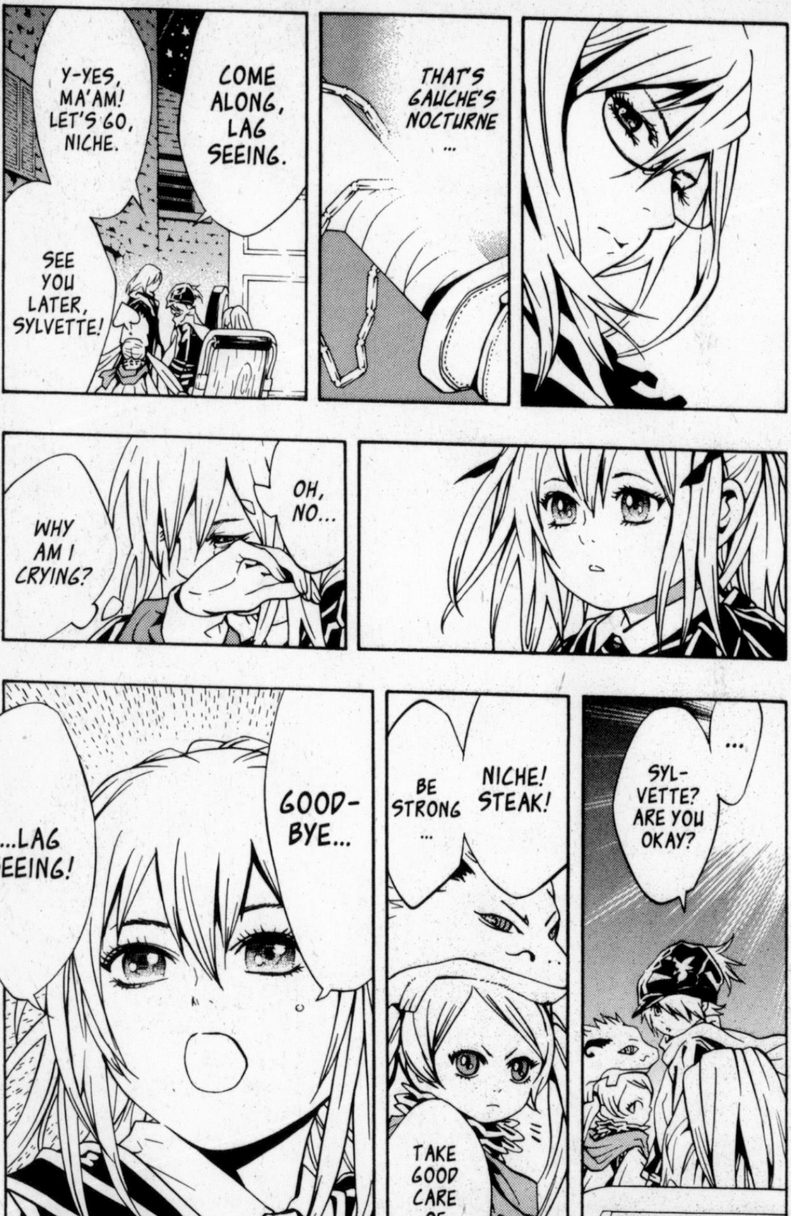
THAT'S GAUCHE'S NOCTURNE...
COME ALONG, LAG SEEING.
Y-YES, MA'AM! LET'S GO, NICHE.
SEE YOU LATER, SYLVETTE!
OH, NO...
WHY AM I CRYING?
...
SYL-VETTE? ARE YOU OKAY?
NICHE! STEAK!
BE STRONG...
TAKE GOOD CARE OF LAG...
GOOD-BYE...
...LAG SEEING!

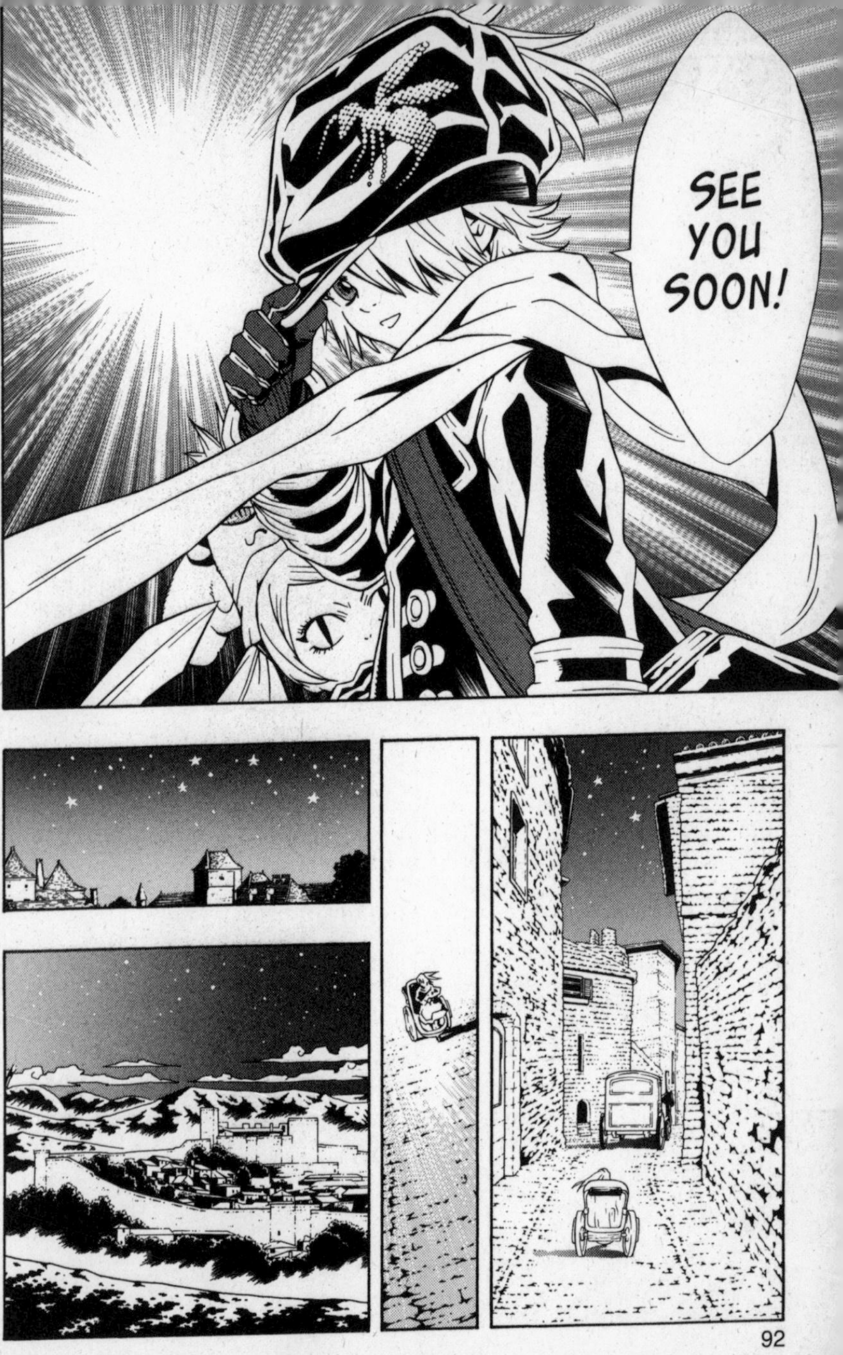
SEE YOU SOON!

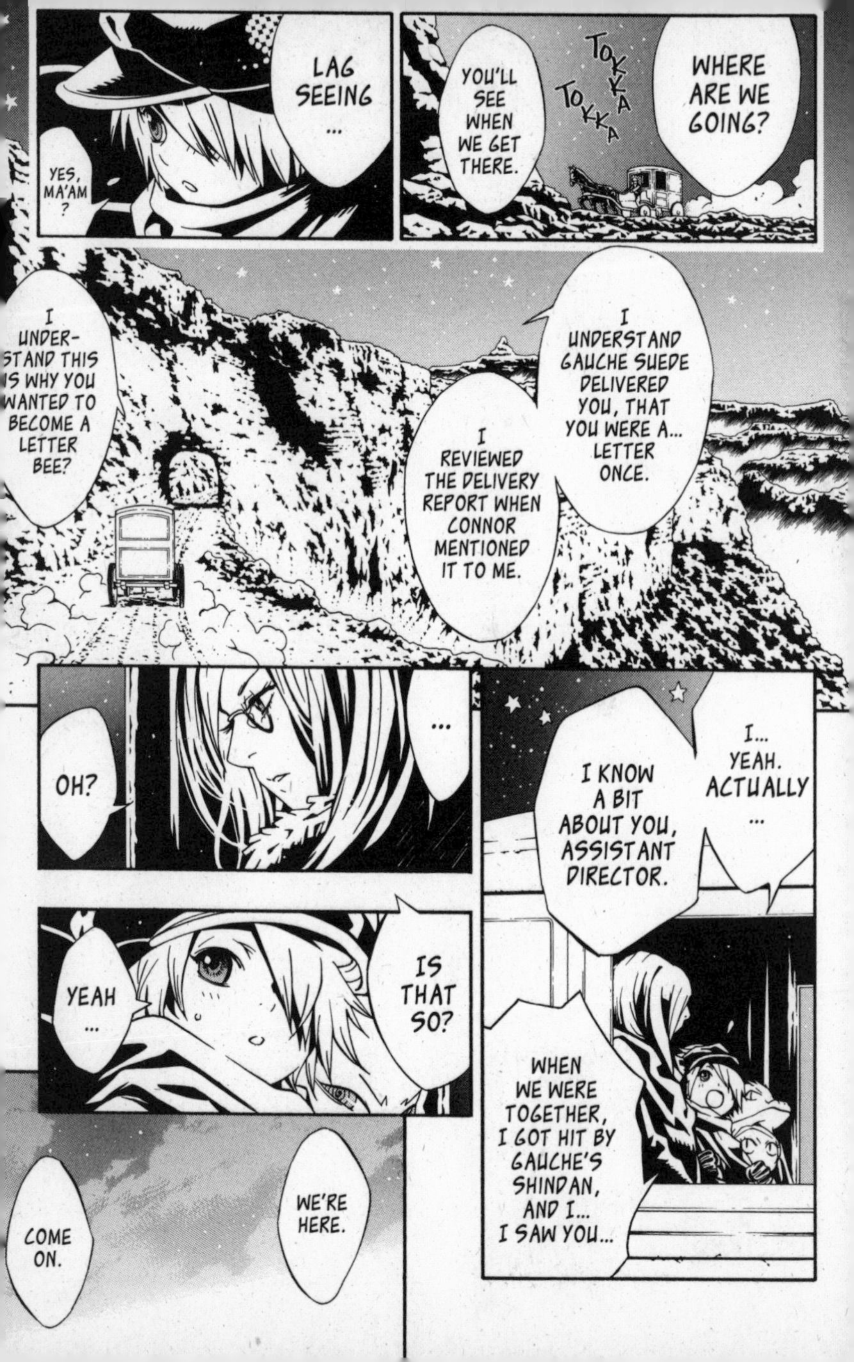
WHERE ARE WE GOING?
TOKKA TOKKA
YOU'LL SEE WHEN WE GET THERE.
LAG SEEING ...
YES, MA'AM?
I UNDERSTAND GAUCHE SUEDE DELIVERED YOU, THAT YOU WERE A... LETTER ONCE.
I REVIEWED THE DELIVERY REPORT WHEN CONNOR MENTIONED IT TO ME.
I UNDER-STAND THIS IS WHY YOU WANTED TO BECOME A LETTER BEE?
I... YEAH. ACTUALLY ...
I KNOW A BIT ABOUT YOU, ASSISTANT DIRECTOR.
WHEN WE WERE TOGETHER, I GOT HIT BY GAUCHE'S SHINDAN, AND I... I SAW YOU...
...
OH?
IS THAT SO?
YEAH ...
WE'RE HERE.
COME ON.

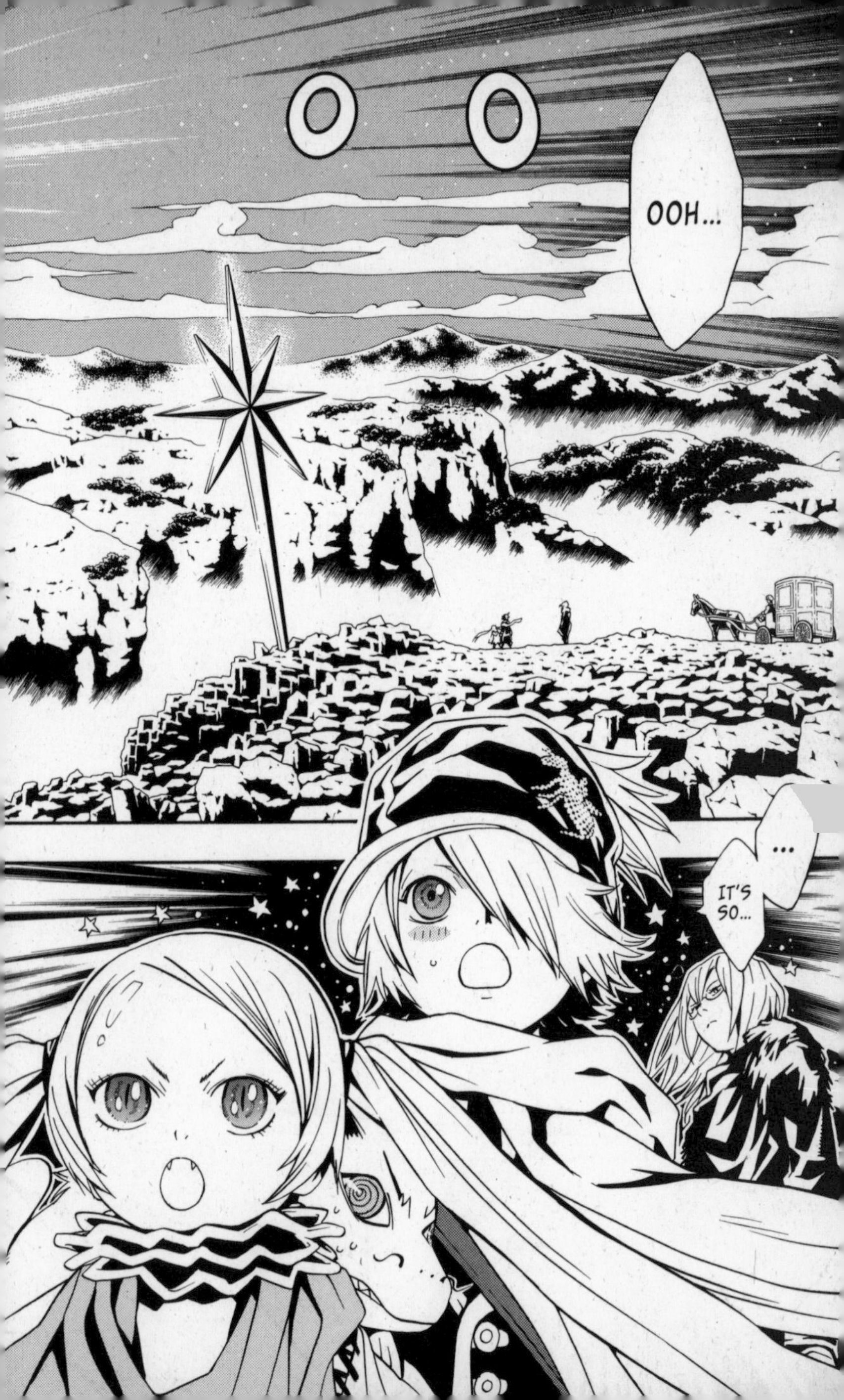
OOH...
...
IT'S SO...

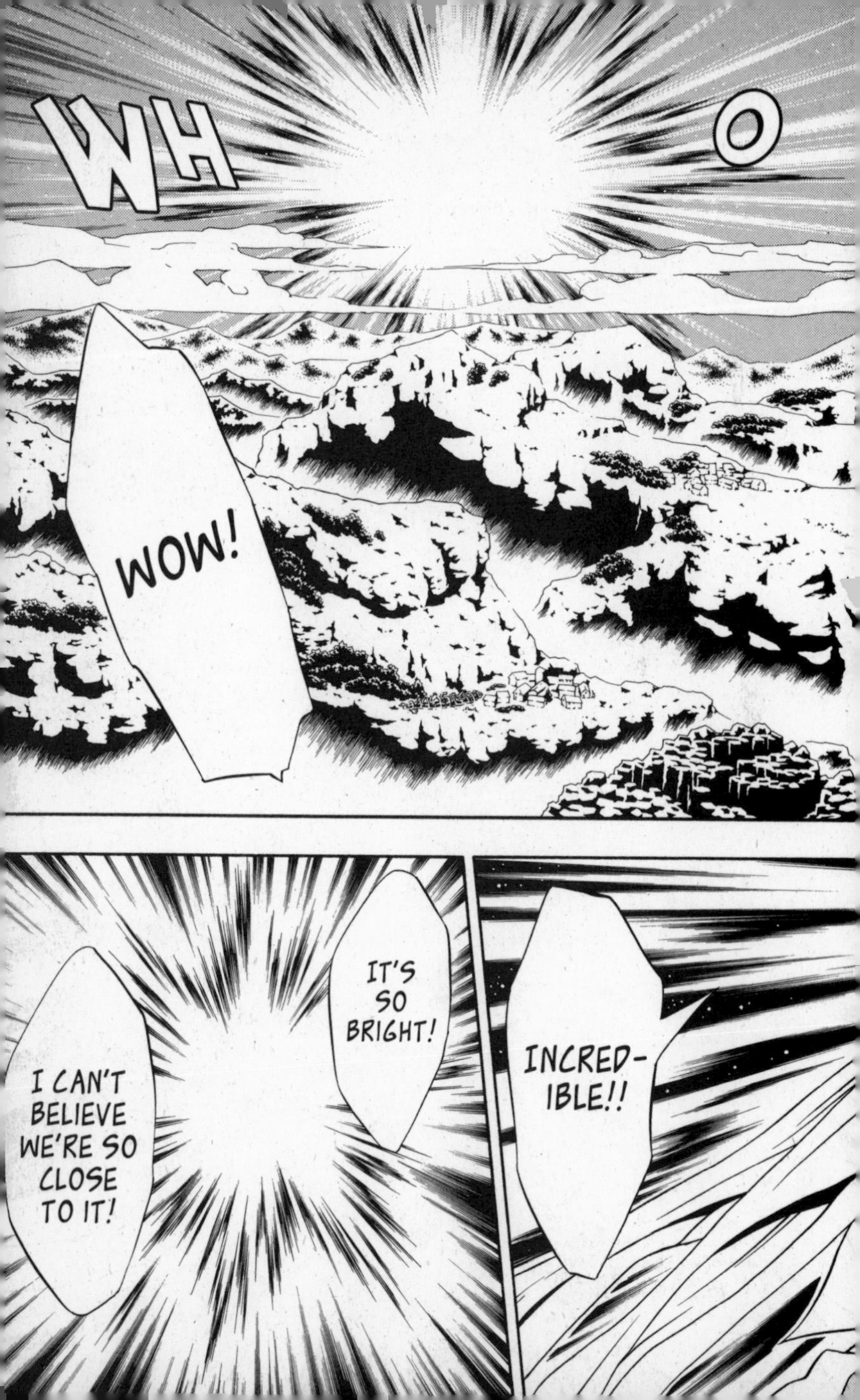
WHOO
WOW!
INCRED-IBLE!!
IT'S SO BRIGHT!
I CAN'T BELIEVE WE'RE SO CLOSE TO IT!

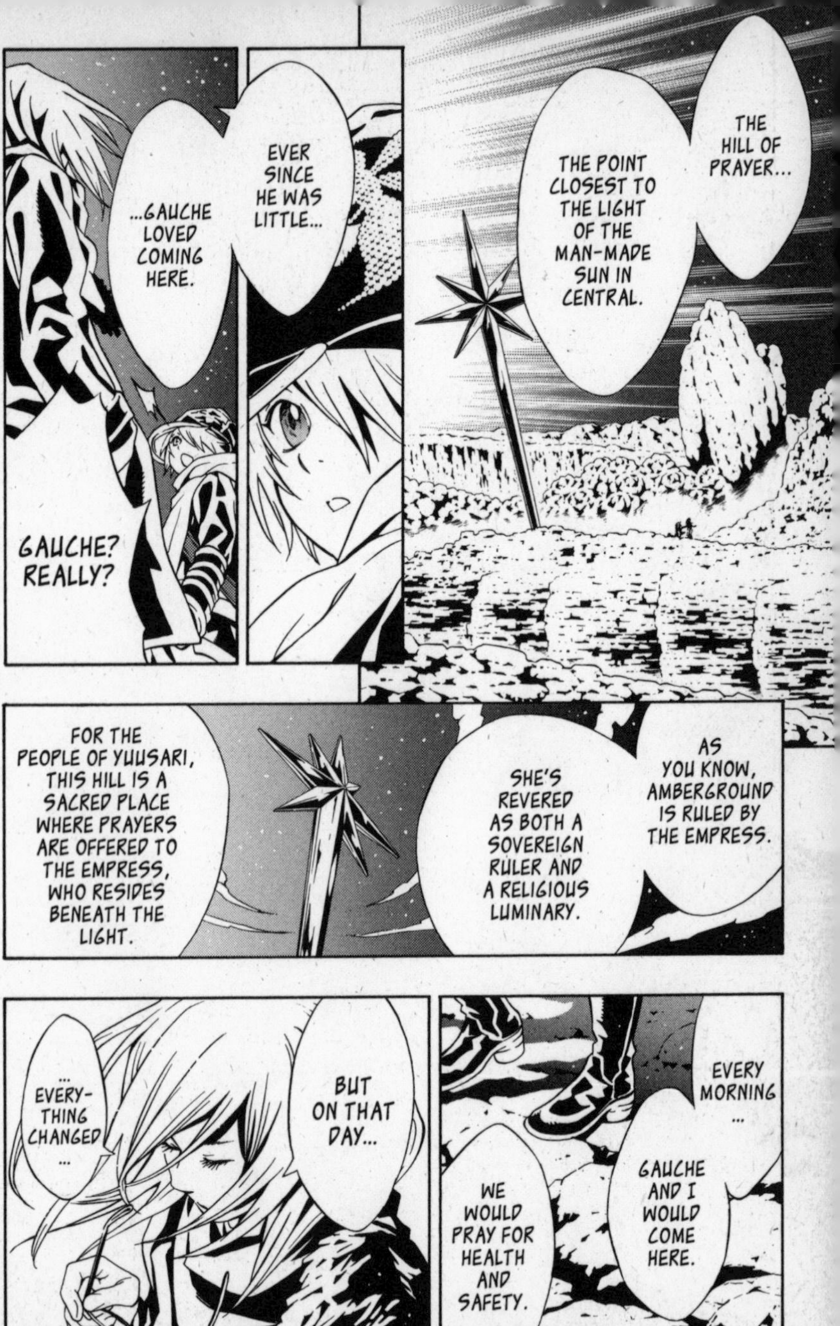
THE HILL OF PRAYER...
THE POINT CLOSEST TO THE LIGHT OF THE MAN-MADE SUN IN CENTRAL.
EVER SINCE HE WAS LITTLE...
...GAUCHE LOVED COMING HERE.
GAUCHE? REALLY?
AS YOU KNOW, AMBERGROUND IS RULED BY THE EMPRESS.
SHE'S REVERED AS BOTH A SOVEREIGN RULER AND A RELIGIOUS LUMINARY.
FOR THE PEOPLE OF YUUSARI, THIS HILL IS A SACRED PLACE WHERE PRAYERS ARE OFFERED TO THE EMPRESS, WHO RESIDES BENEATH THE LIGHT.
EVERY MORNING...
GAUCHE AND I WOULD COME HERE.
WE WOULD PRAY FOR HEALTH AND SAFETY.
BUT ON THAT DAY...
...EVERYTHING CHANGED...

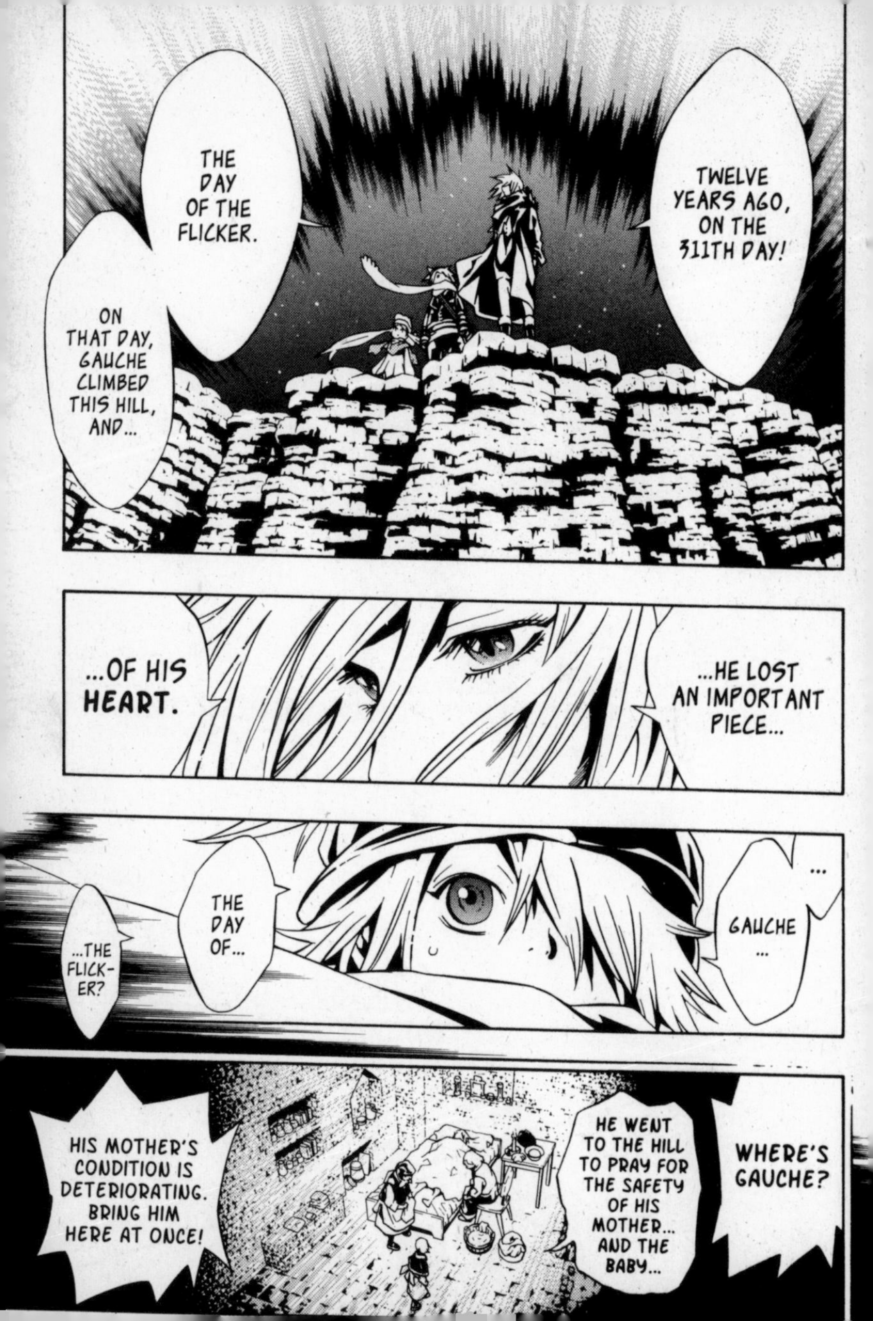
TWELVE YEARS AGO, ON THE 311TH DAY!
THE DAY OF THE FLICKER.
ON THAT DAY, GAUCHE CLIMBED THIS HILL, AND...
...HE LOST AN IMPORTANT PIECE...
...OF HIS HEART.
... GAUCHE ...
THE DAY OF...
...THE FLICKER?
WHERE'S GAUCHE?
HE WENT TO THE HILL TO PRAY FOR THE SAFETY OF HIS MOTHER... AND THE BABY...
HIS MOTHER'S CONDITION IS DETERIORATING. BRING HIM HERE AT ONCE!

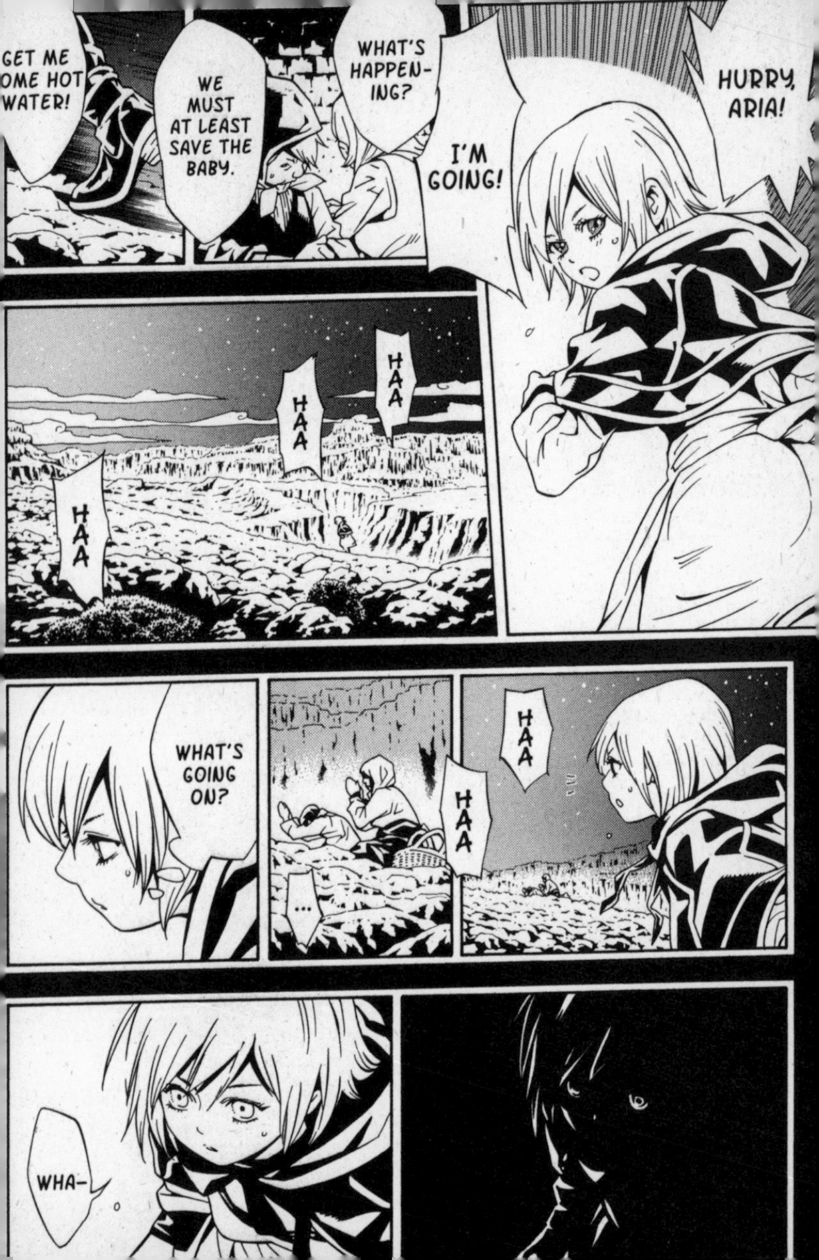
HURRY, ARIA!
I'M GOING!
WHAT'S HAPPEN-ING?
WE MUST AT LEAST SAVE THE BABY.
GET ME OME HOT WATER!
HAA
HAA
HAA
HAA
HAA
...
WHAT'S GOING ON?
WHA-

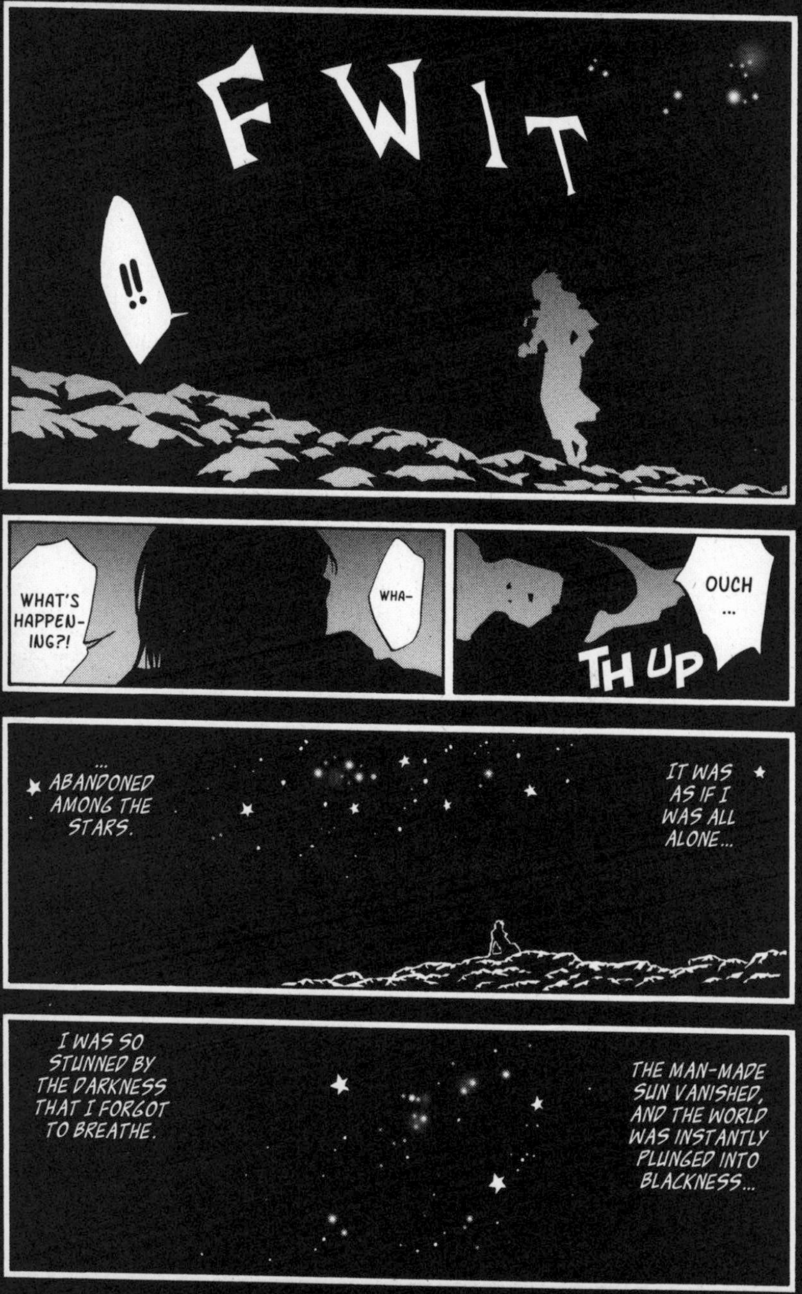
FWIT
!!
WHAT'S HAPPENING?!
WHA-
OUCH ...
THUP
IT WAS AS IF I WAS ALL ALONE...
... ABANDONED AMONG THE STARS.
THE MAN-MADE SUN VANISHED, AND THE WORLD WAS INSTANTLY PLUNGED INTO BLACKNESS...
I WAS SO STUNNED BY THE DARKNESS THAT I FORGOT TO BREATHE.

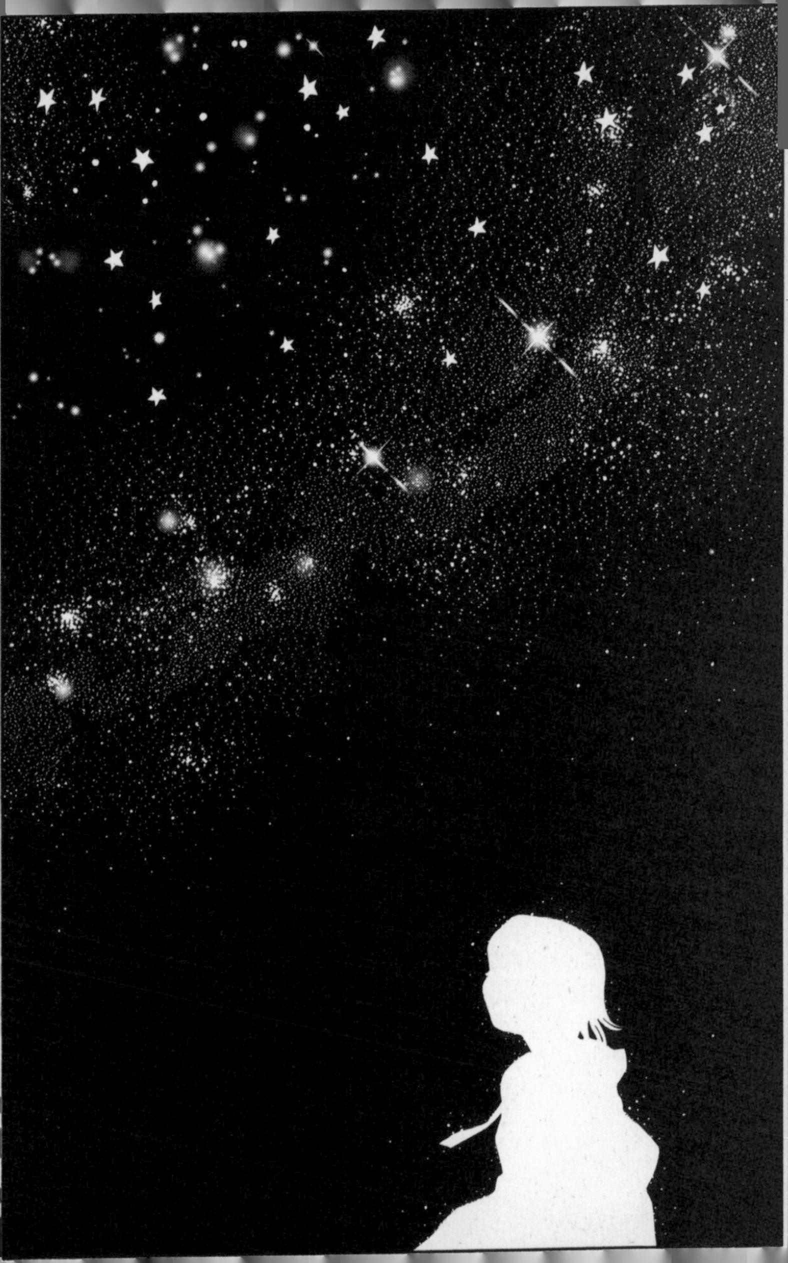

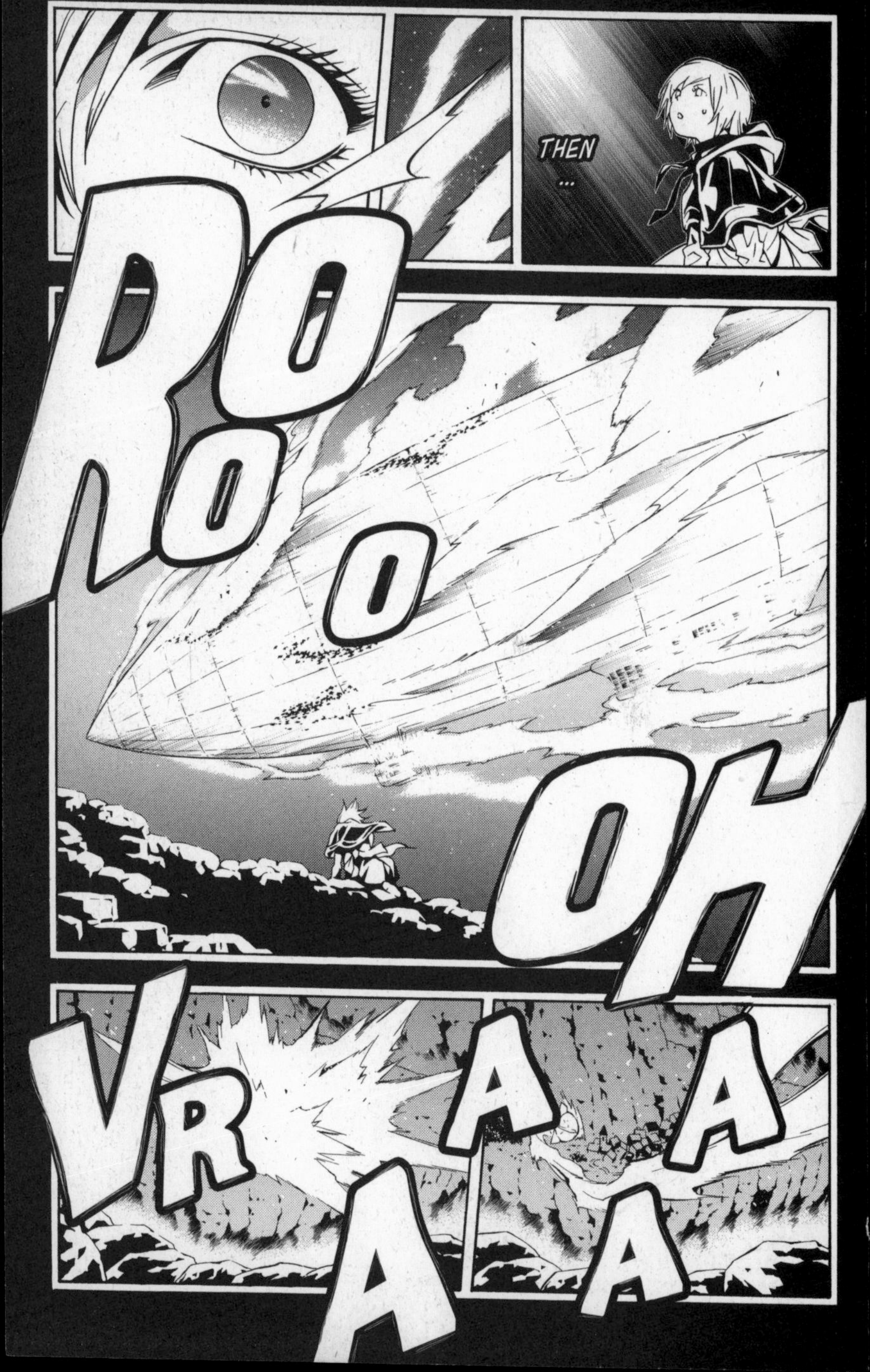
THEN
...
DOOOOOH
VRAAAA

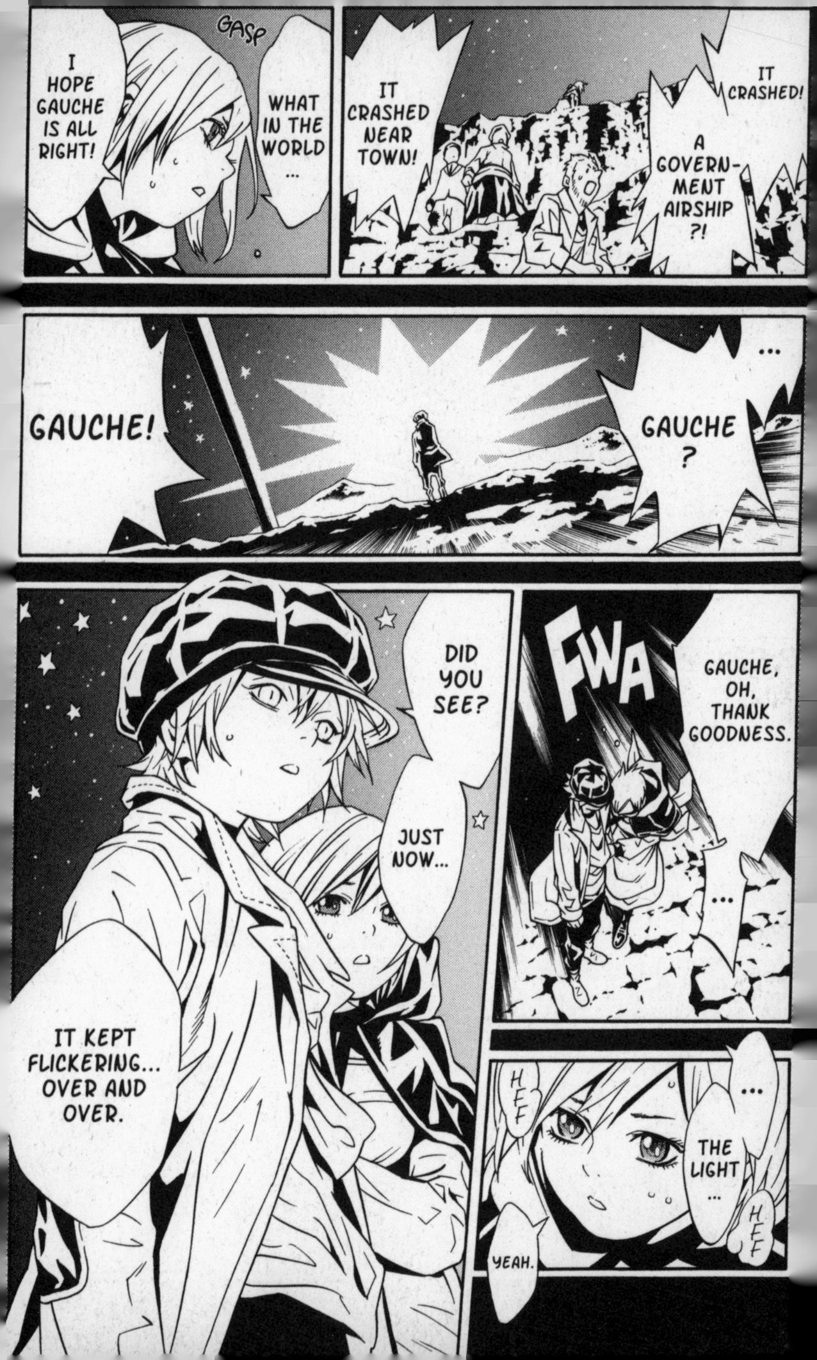
IT CRASHED!
A GOVERNMENT AIRSHIP ?!
IT CRASHED NEAR TOWN!
WHAT IN THE WORLD ...
GASP
I HOPE GAUCHE IS ALL RIGHT!
...
GAUCHE ?
GAUCHE!
GAUCHE, OH, THANK GOODNESS.
FWA
...
...
THE LIGHT ...
HEF
HEF
DID YOU SEE?
JUST NOW...
IT KEPT FLICKERING... OVER AND OVER.
YEAH.

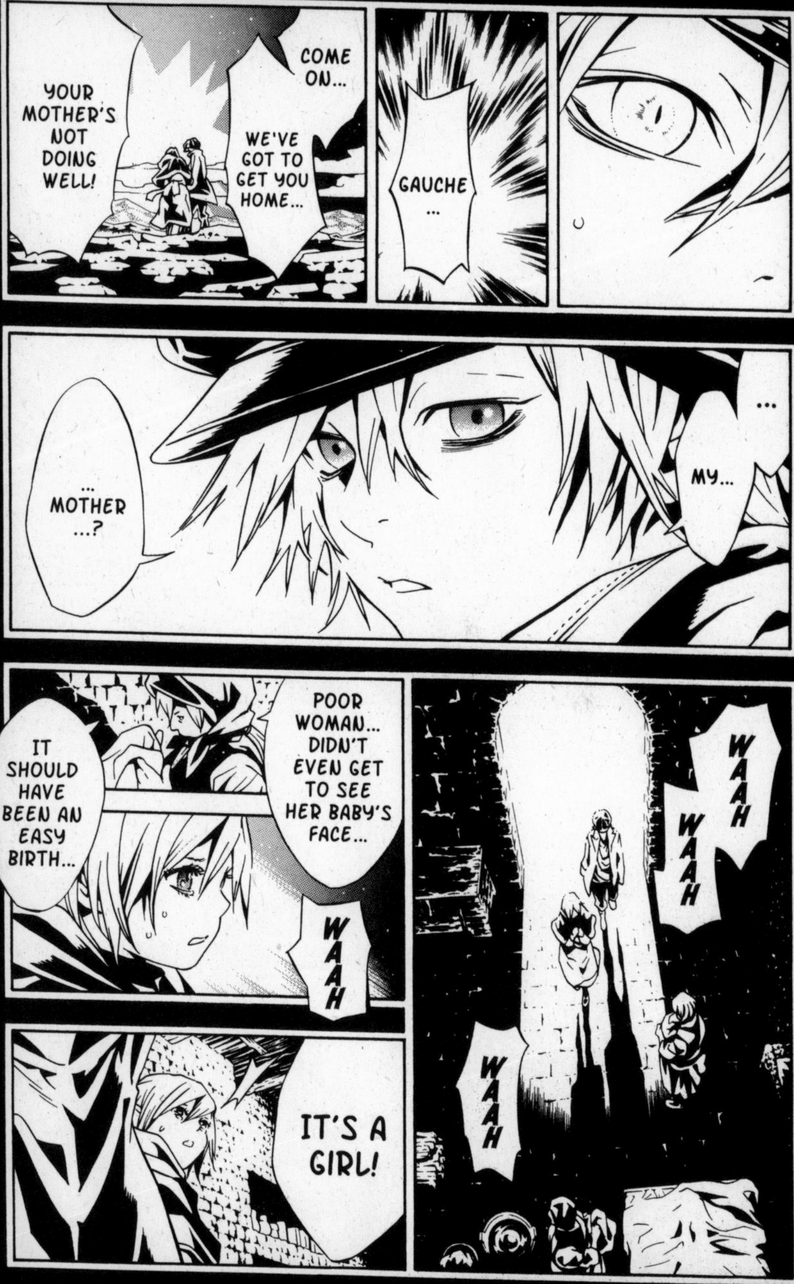
GAUCHE ...
COME ON...
WE'VE GOT TO GET YOU HOME...
YOUR MOTHER'S NOT DOING WELL!
... MY...
... MOTHER ...?
WAAH WAAH
WAAH
POOR WOMAN... DIDN'T EVEN GET TO SEE HER BABY'S FACE...
IT SHOULD HAVE BEEN AN EASY BIRTH...
WAAH
IT'S A GIRL!

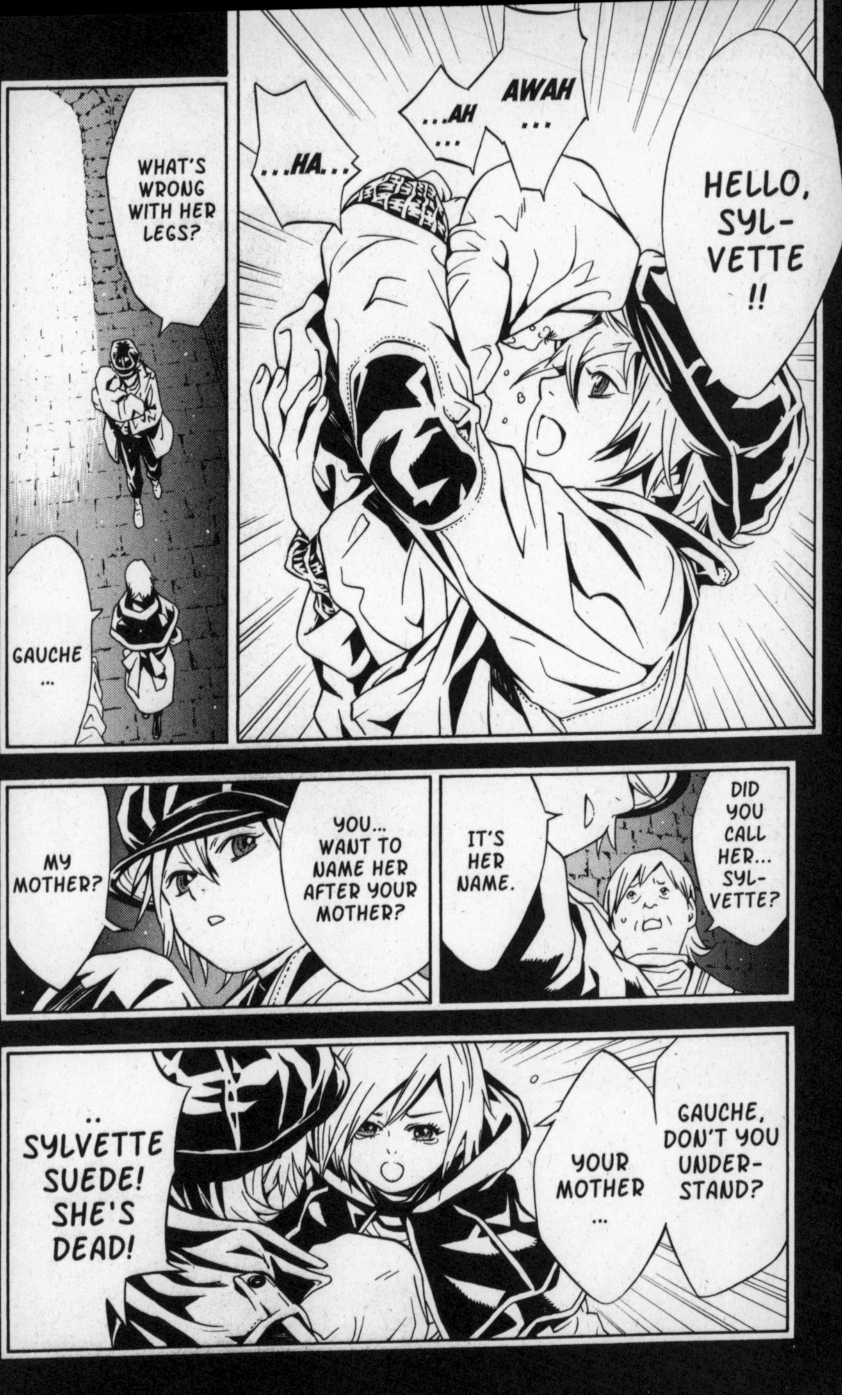
HELLO, SYL-VETTE!!
AWAH...
...AH...
...HA...
WHAT'S WRONG WITH HER LEGS?
GAUCHE...
DID YOU CALL HER... SYL-VETTE?
IT'S HER NAME.
YOU... WANT TO NAME HER AFTER YOUR MOTHER?
MY MOTHER?
GAUCHE, DON'T YOU UNDER-STAND?
YOUR MOTHER...
.. SYLVETTE SUEDE! SHE'S DEAD!

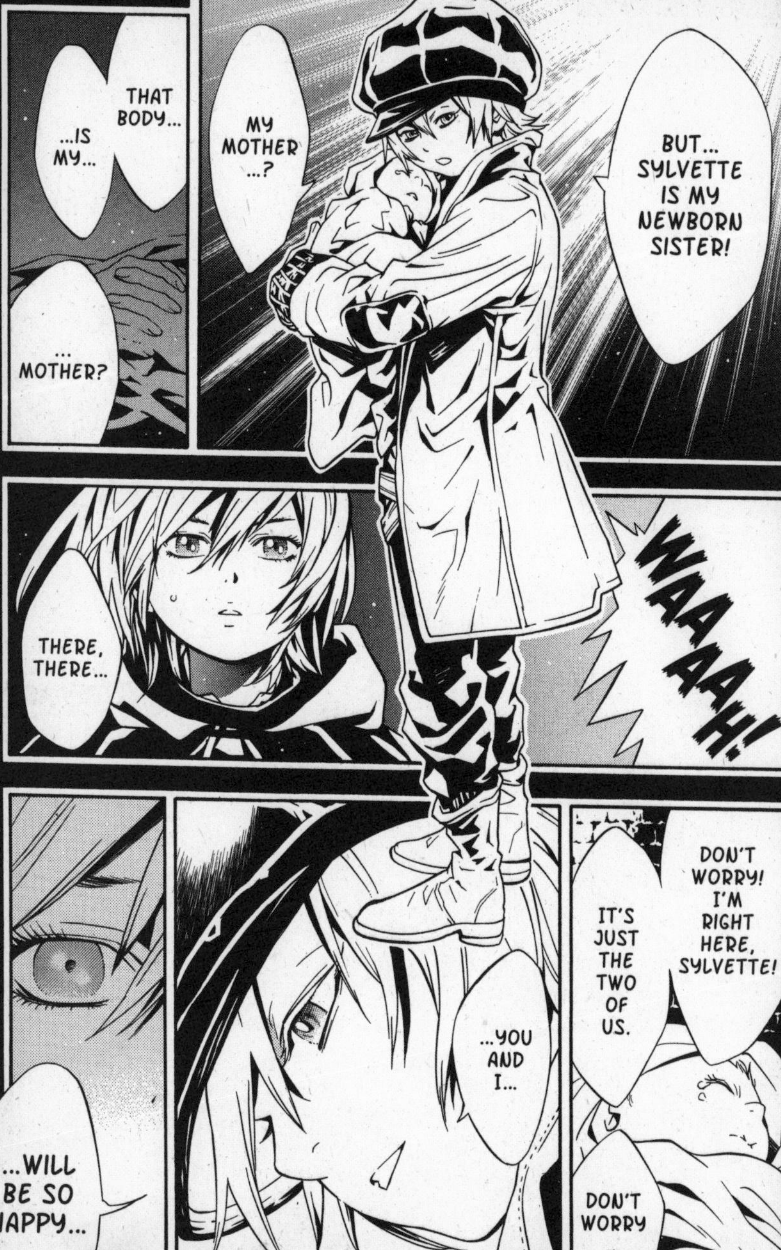
BUT... SYLVETTE IS MY NEWBORN SISTER!
MY MOTHER ...?
THAT BODY...
...IS MY...
... MOTHER?
WAAAAH!
THERE, THERE...
DON'T WORRY! I'M RIGHT HERE, SYLVETTE!
IT'S JUST THE TWO OF US.
DON'T WORRY ...
...YOU AND I...
...WILL BE SO HAPPY...

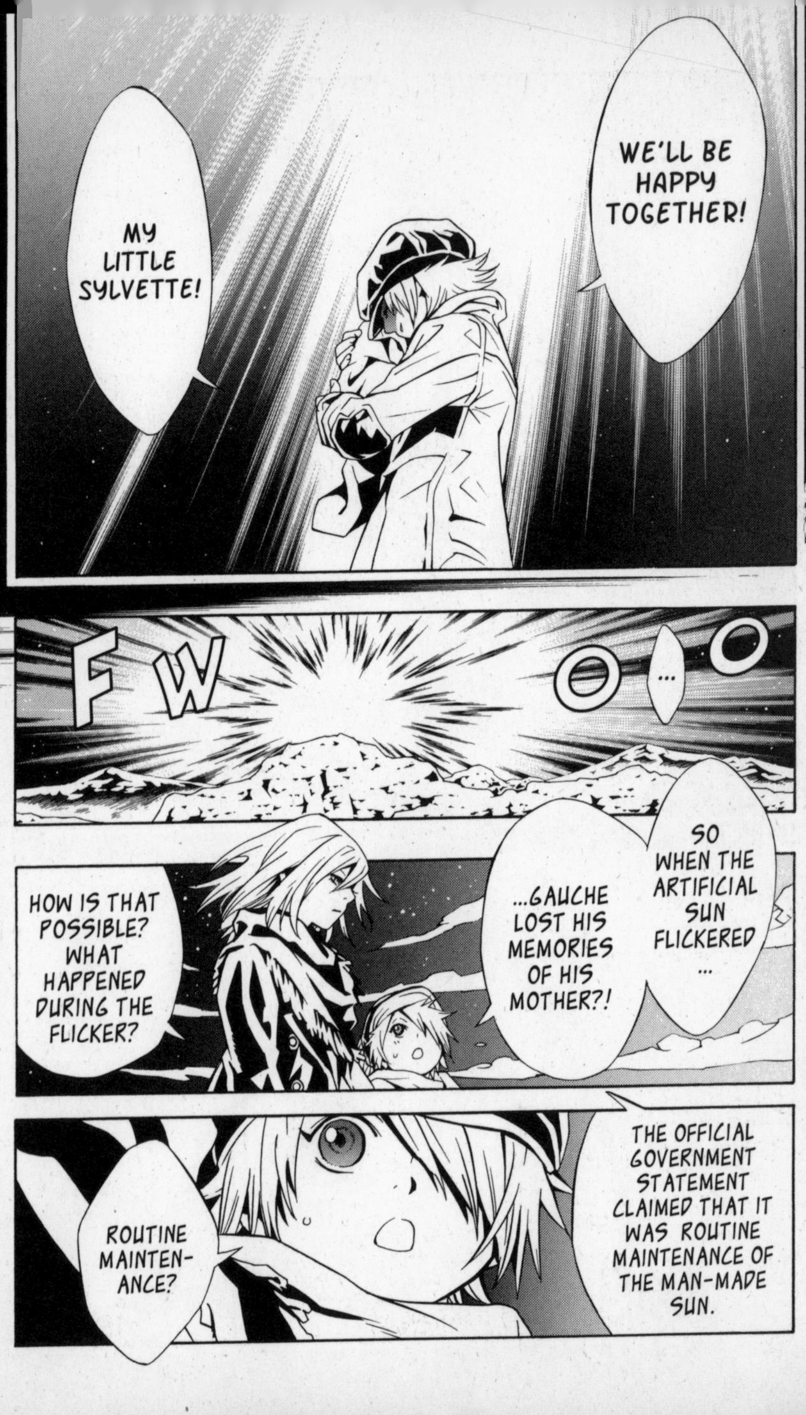
WE'LL BE HAPPY TOGETHER!
MY LITTLE SYLVETTE!
FWOO
...
SO WHEN THE ARTIFICIAL SUN FLICKERED...
...GAUCHE LOST HIS MEMORIES OF HIS MOTHER?!
HOW IS THAT POSSIBLE? WHAT HAPPENED DURING THE FLICKER?
THE OFFICIAL GOVERNMENT STATEMENT CLAIMED THAT IT WAS ROUTINE MAINTENANCE OF THE MAN-MADE SUN.
ROUTINE MAINTEN-ANCE?

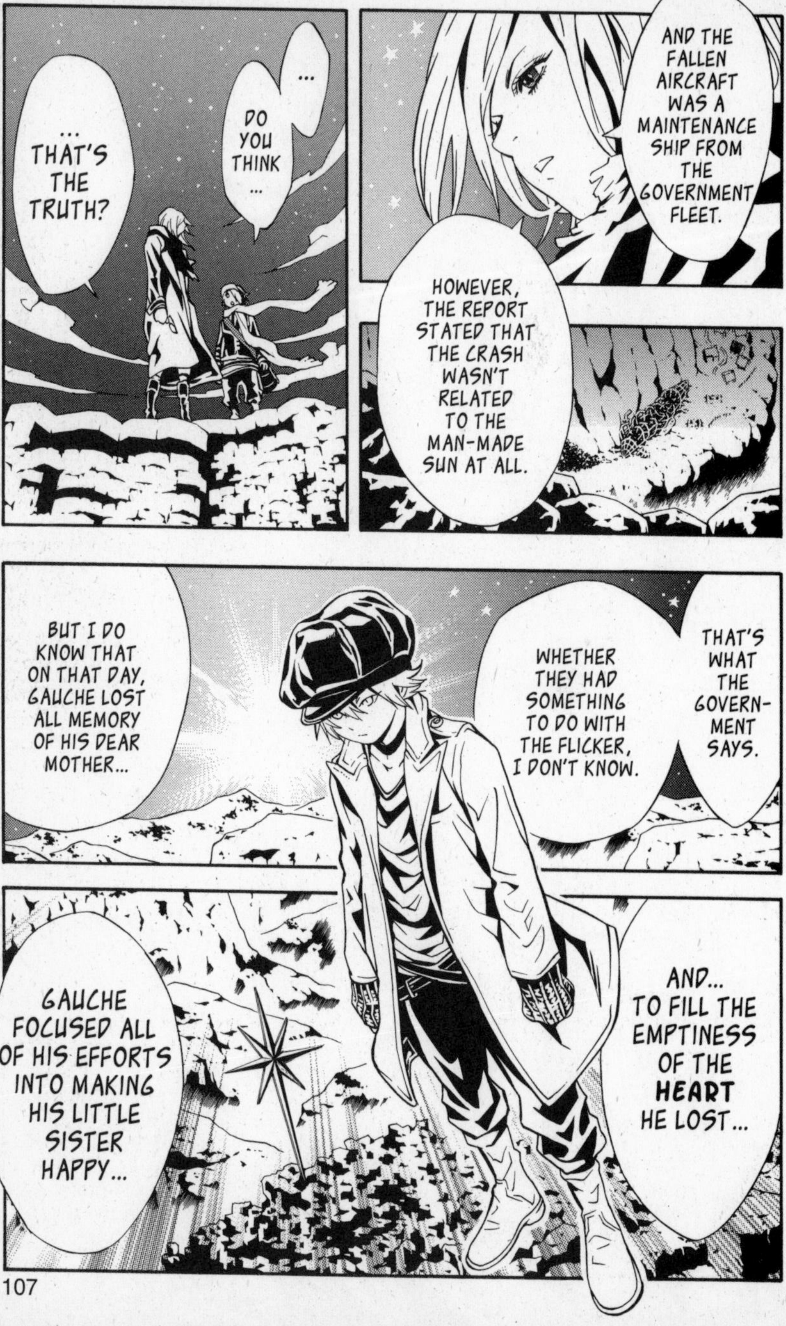
AND THE FALLEN AIRCRAFT WAS A MAINTENANCE SHIP FROM THE GOVERNMENT FLEET.
HOWEVER, THE REPORT STATED THAT THE CRASH WASN'T RELATED TO THE MAN-MADE SUN AT ALL.
...
DO YOU THINK ...
... THAT'S THE TRUTH?
THAT'S WHAT THE GOVERN-MENT SAYS.
WHETHER THEY HAD SOMETHING TO DO WITH THE FLICKER, I DON'T KNOW.
BUT I DO KNOW THAT ON THAT DAY, GAUCHE LOST ALL MEMORY OF HIS DEAR MOTHER...
AND... TO FILL THE EMPTINESS OF THE **HEART** HE LOST...
GAUCHE FOCUSED ALL OF HIS EFFORTS INTO MAKING HIS LITTLE SISTER HAPPY...

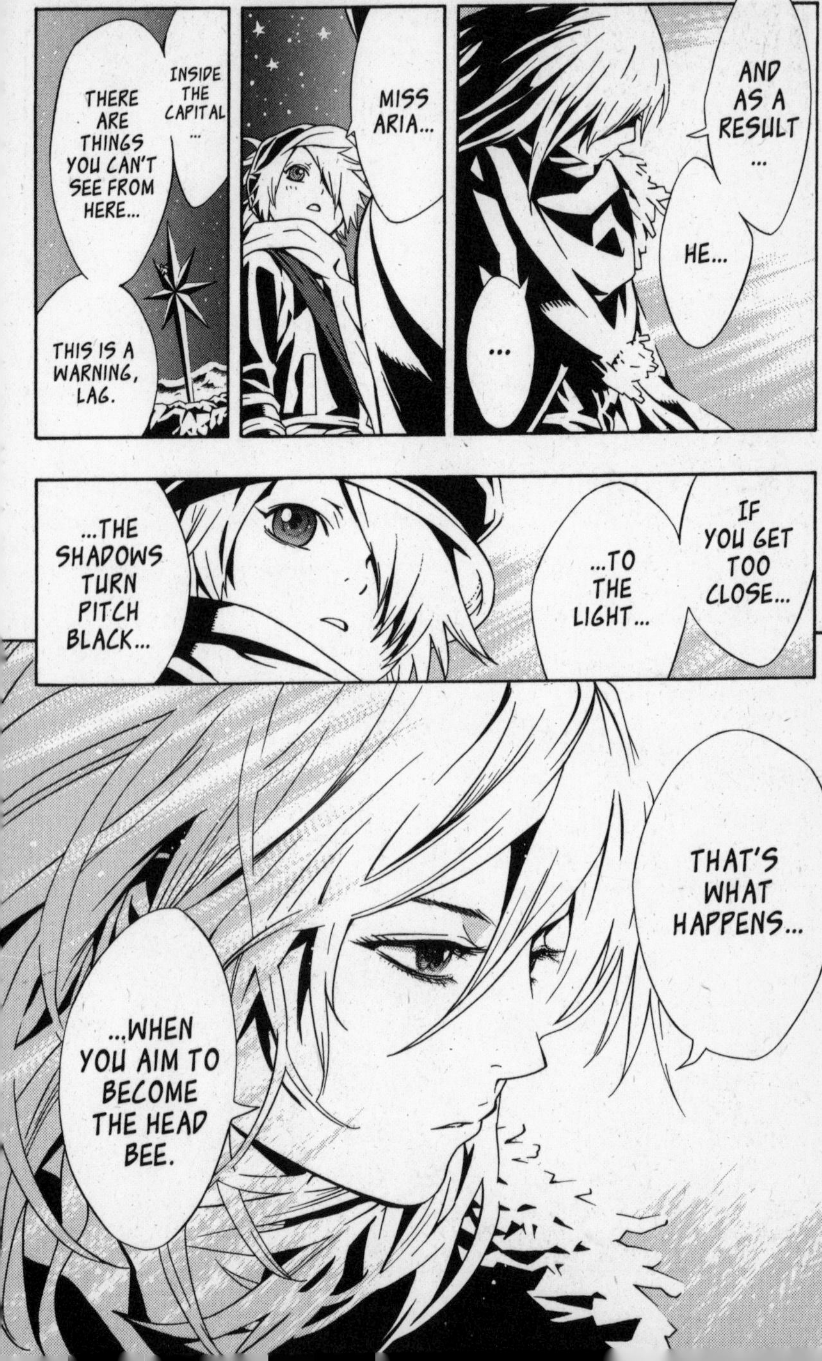
AND AS A RESULT...
HE...
...
MISS ARIA...
INSIDE THE CAPITAL...
THERE ARE THINGS YOU CAN'T SEE FROM HERE...
THIS IS A WARNING, LAG.
IF YOU GET TOO CLOSE...
...TO THE LIGHT...
...THE SHADOWS TURN PITCH BLACK...
THAT'S WHAT HAPPENS...
...WHEN YOU AIM TO BECOME THE HEAD BEE.

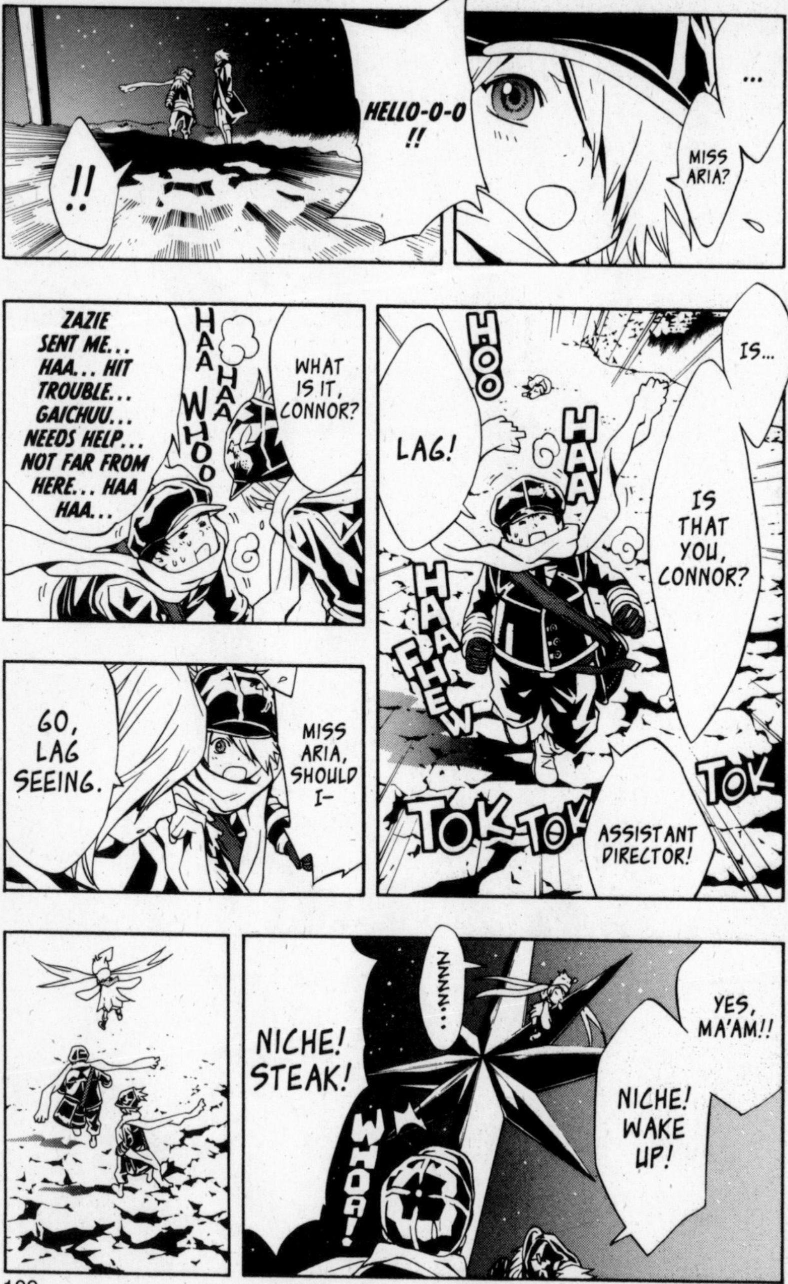
...
MISS ARIA?
HELLO-O-O !!
!!
IS...
IS THAT YOU, CONNOR?
HOO
HAA
LAG!
HAA HAA FHEW
TOK
TOK TOK
ASSISTANT DIRECTOR!
WHAT IS IT, CONNOR?
HAA HAA WHOO
ZAZIE SENT ME... HAA... HIT TROUBLE... GAICHUU... NEEDS HELP... NOT FAR FROM HERE... HAA HAA...
MISS ARIA, SHOULD I–
GO, LAG SEEING.
YES, MA'AM!!
NICHE! WAKE UP!
ZNNN...
NICHE! STEAK!
WHOA!

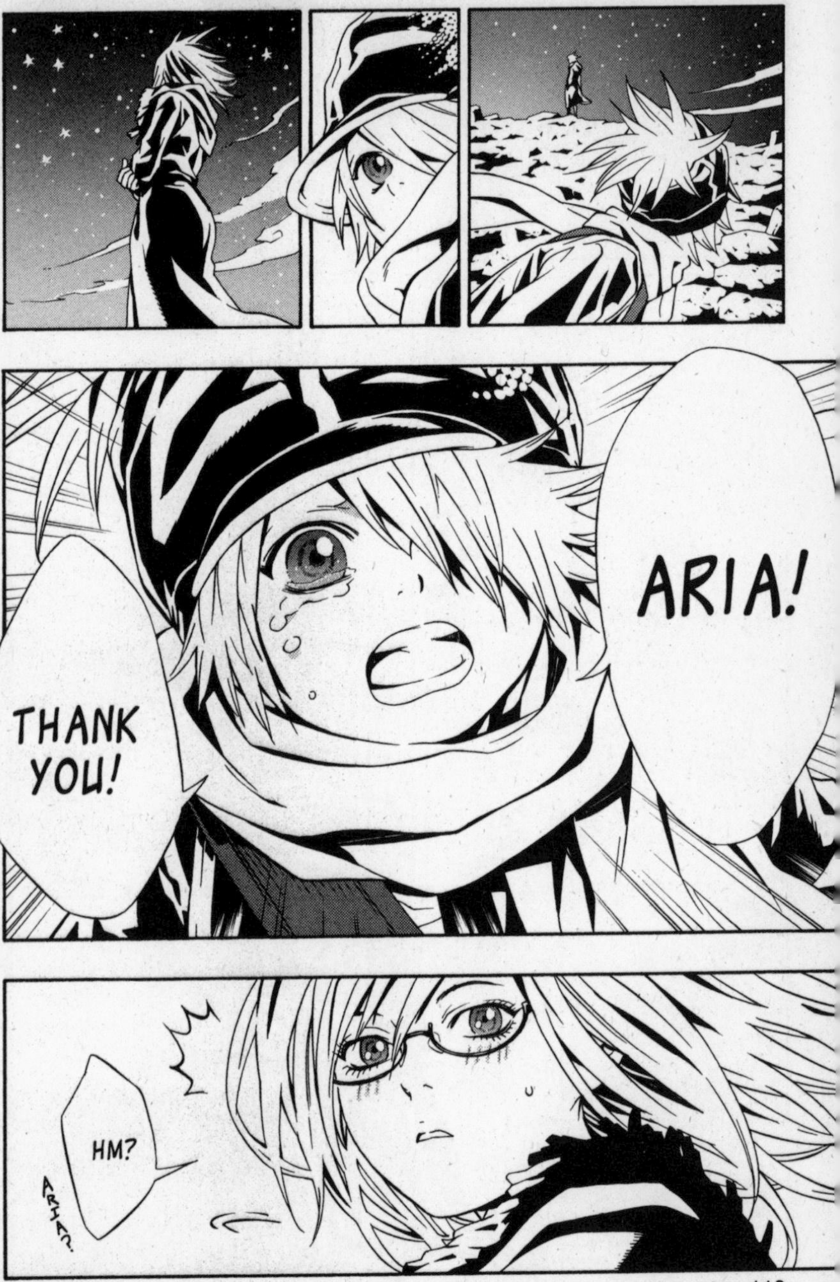
ARIA!
THANK YOU!
HM?
ARIA?

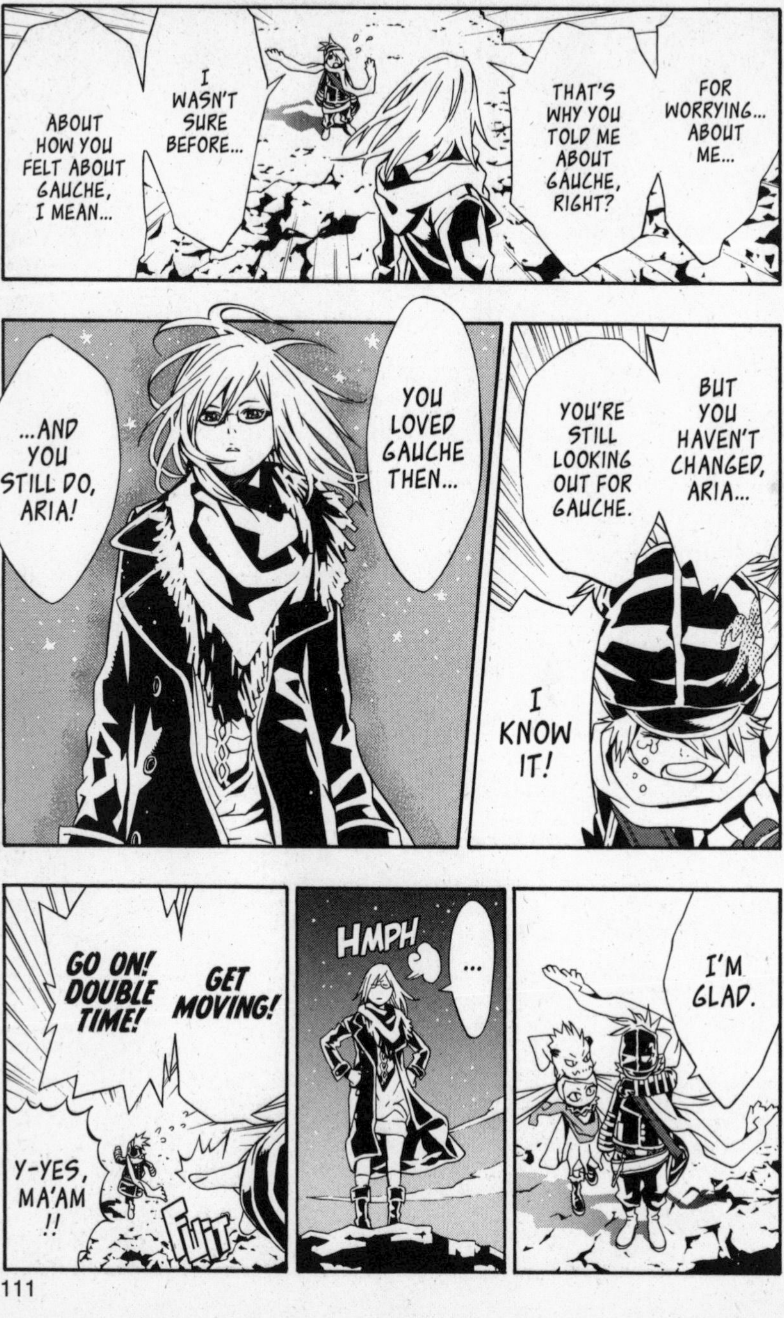
FOR WORRYING... ABOUT ME...
THAT'S WHY YOU TOLD ME ABOUT GAUCHE, RIGHT?
I WASN'T SURE BEFORE...
ABOUT HOW YOU FELT ABOUT GAUCHE, I MEAN...
BUT YOU HAVEN'T CHANGED, ARIA...
YOU'RE STILL LOOKING OUT FOR GAUCHE.
I KNOW IT!
YOU LOVED GAUCHE THEN...
...AND YOU STILL DO, ARIA!
I'M GLAD.
...
HMPH
GET MOVING!
GO ON! DOUBLE TIME!
Y-YES, MA'AM!!
FLIT

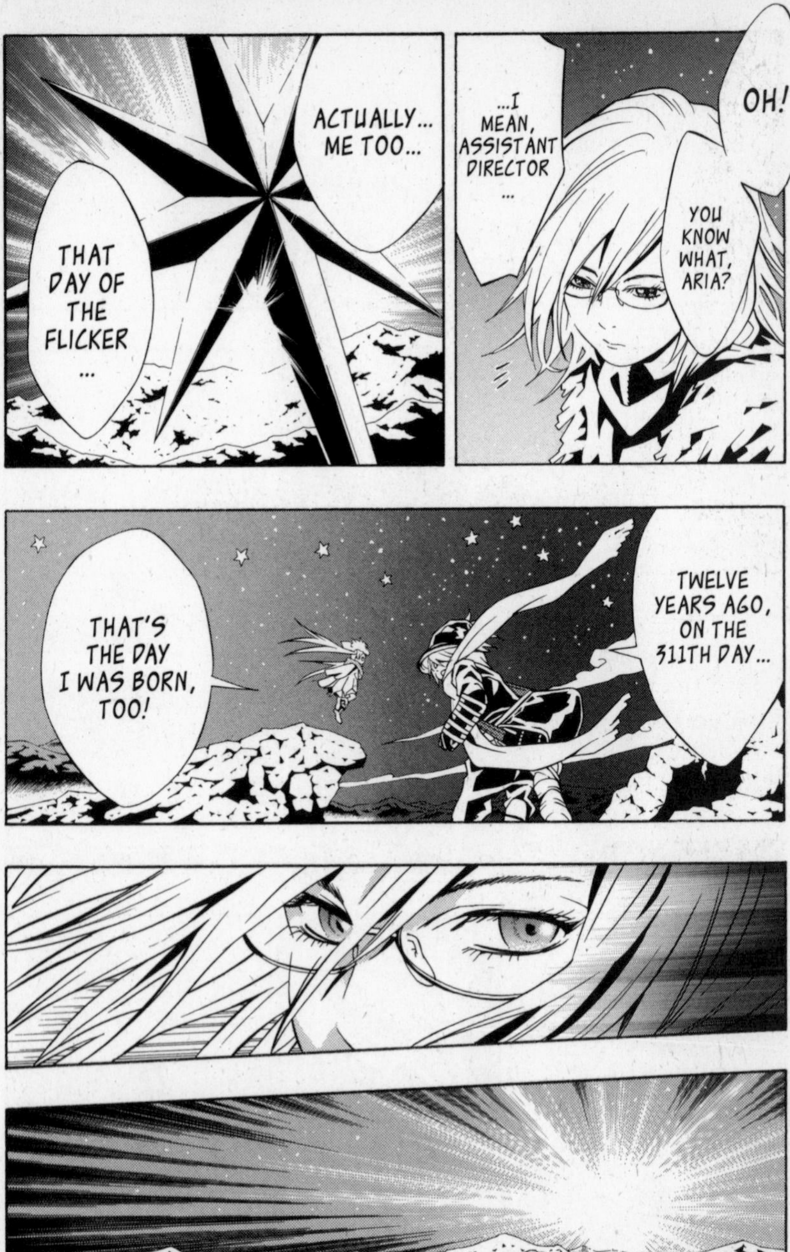
OH!
YOU KNOW WHAT, ARIA?
...I MEAN, ASSISTANT DIRECTOR ...
ACTUALLY... ME TOO...
THAT DAY OF THE FLICKER ...
TWELVE YEARS AGO, ON THE 311TH DAY...
THAT'S THE DAY I WAS BORN, TOO!

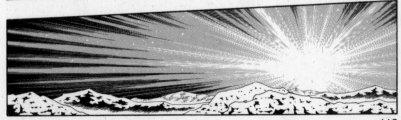

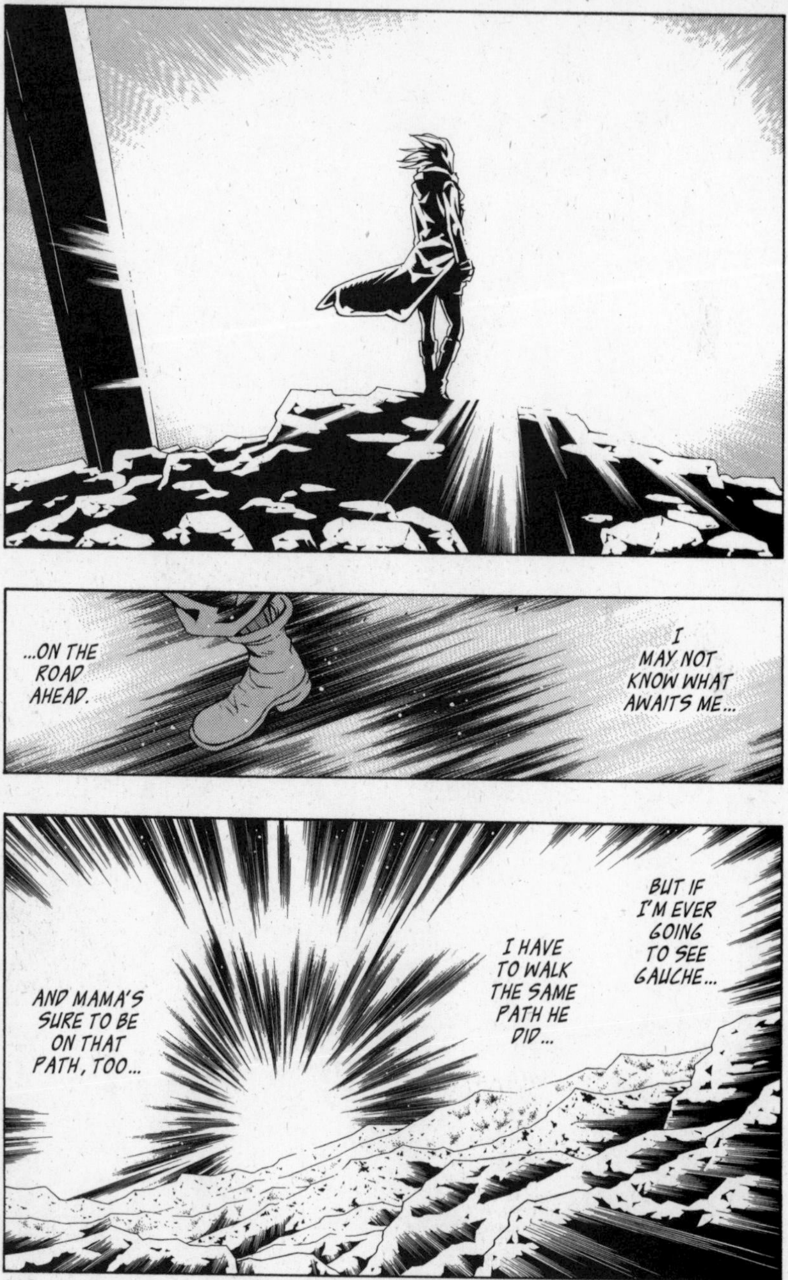
I MAY NOT KNOW WHAT AWAITS ME...
...ON THE ROAD AHEAD.
BUT IF I'M EVER GOING TO SEE GAUCHE...
I HAVE TO WALK THE SAME PATH HE DID...
AND MAMA'S SURE TO BE ON THAT PATH, TOO...

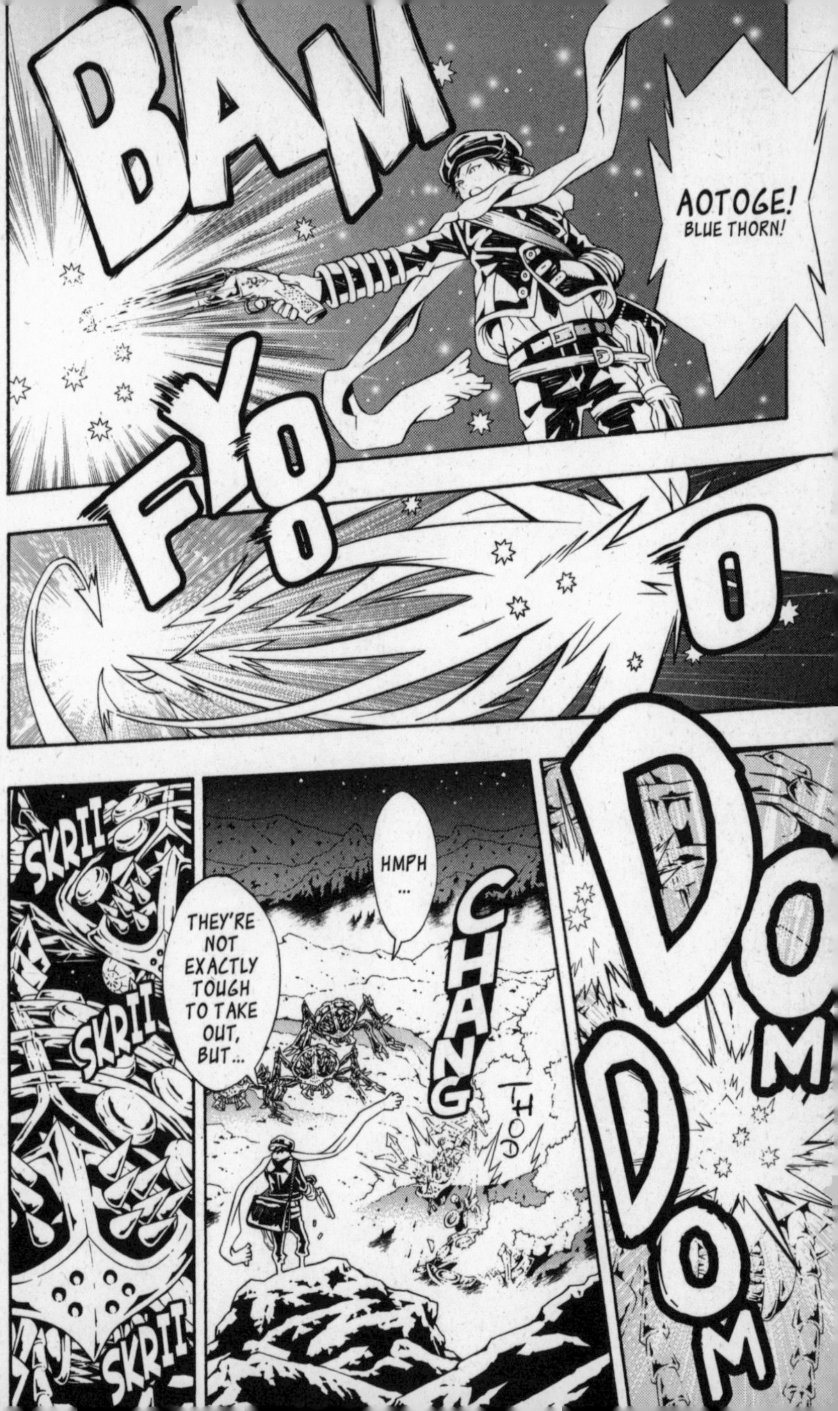

AOTOGE!
BLUE THORN!
BAM
FYOO
DO
DOM
DOM
HMPH ...
THEY'RE NOT EXACTLY TOUGH TO TAKE OUT, BUT...
CHANG
THOD
SKRII
SKRII
SKRII

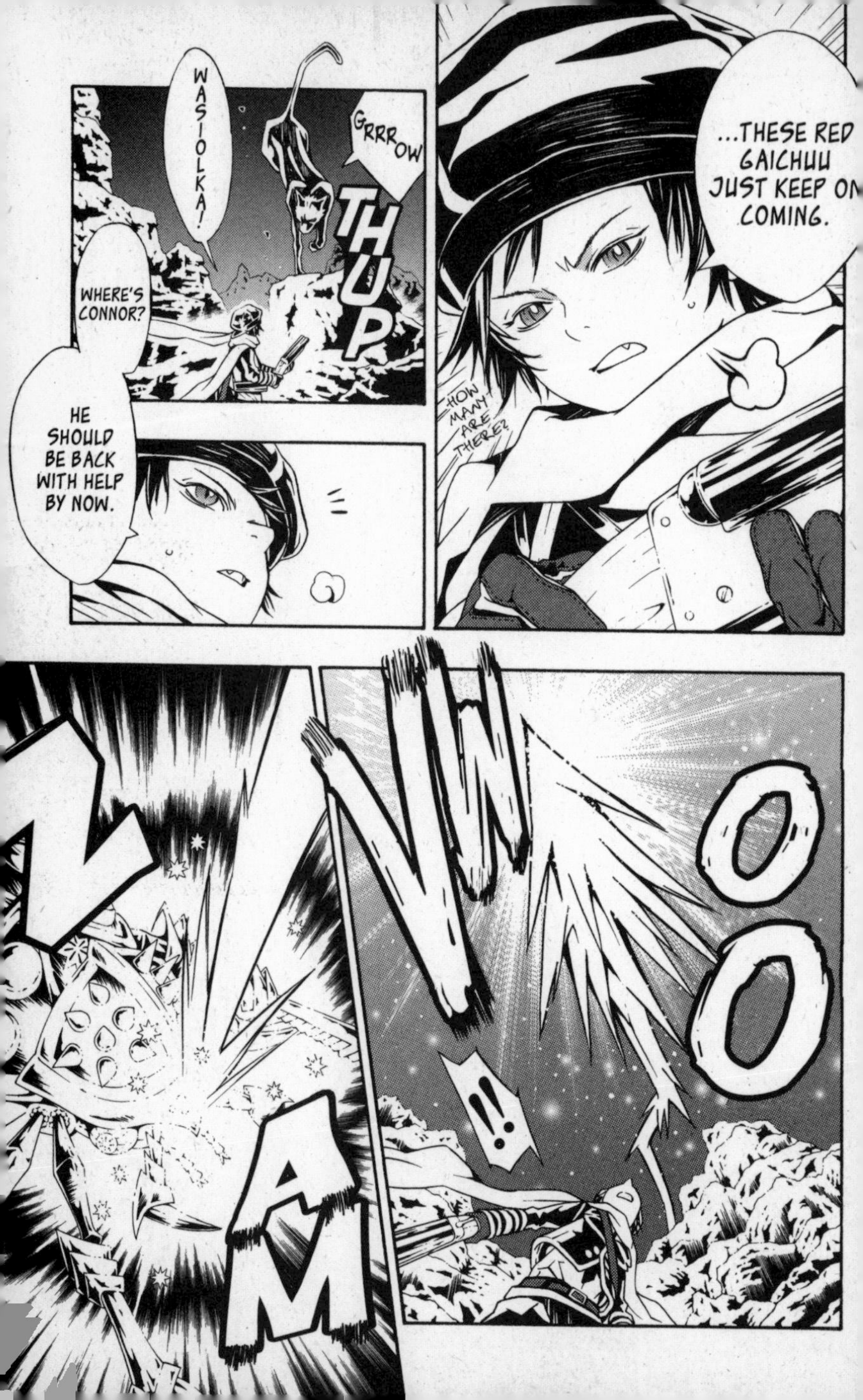
...THESE RED GAICHUU JUST KEEP ON COMING.
HOW MANY ARE THERE?
GRRROW
THUP
WASIOLKA!
WHERE'S CONNOR?
HE SHOULD BE BACK WITH HELP BY NOW.
!!
WOO
ZAM

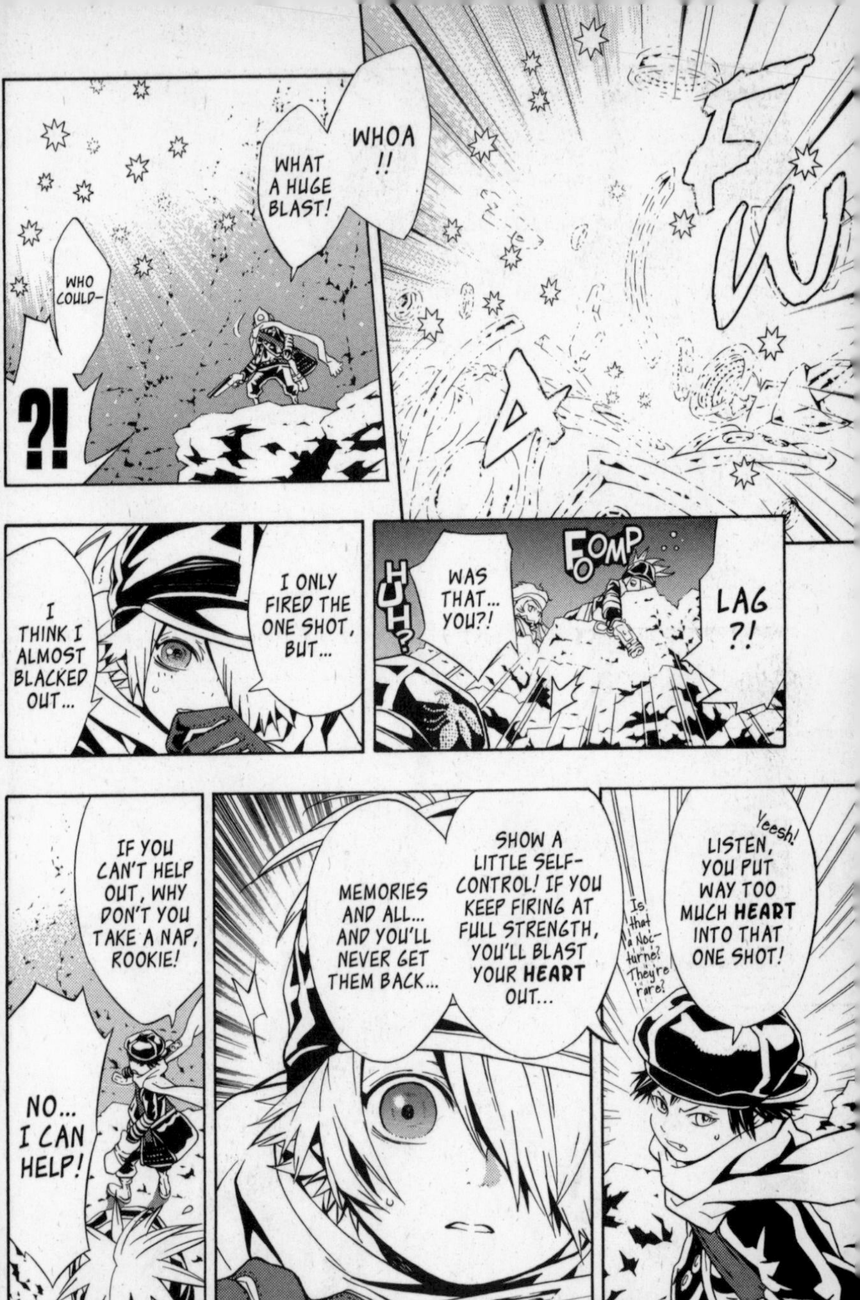
WHOA !!
WHAT A HUGE BLAST!
WHO COULD—
?!
LAG ?!
WAS THAT... YOU?!
HUH?
FOOMP
I ONLY FIRED THE ONE SHOT, BUT...
I THINK I ALMOST BLACKED OUT...
Yeesh!
LISTEN, YOU PUT WAY TOO MUCH HEART INTO THAT ONE SHOT!
Is that a Noc-turne? They're rare?
SHOW A LITTLE SELF-CONTROL! IF YOU KEEP FIRING AT FULL STRENGTH, YOU'LL BLAST YOUR HEART OUT...
MEMORIES AND ALL... AND YOU'LL NEVER GET THEM BACK...
IF YOU CAN'T HELP OUT, WHY DON'T YOU TAKE A NAP, ROOKIE!
NO... I CAN HELP!

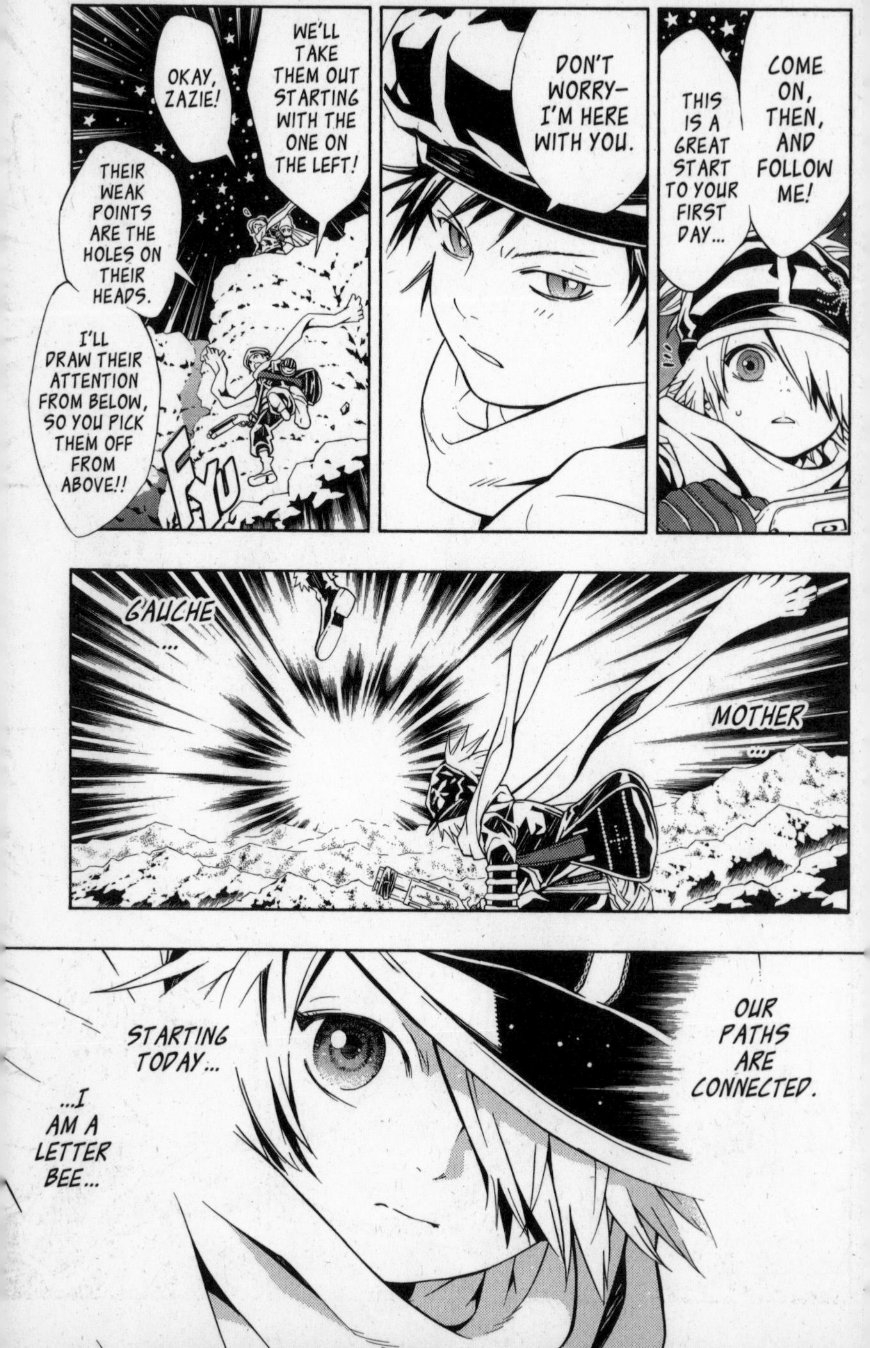
COME ON, THEN, AND FOLLOW ME!
THIS IS A GREAT START TO YOUR FIRST DAY...
DON'T WORRY— I'M HERE WITH YOU.
WE'LL TAKE THEM OUT STARTING WITH THE ONE ON THE LEFT!
OKAY, ZAZIE!
THEIR WEAK POINTS ARE THE HOLES ON THEIR HEADS.
I'LL DRAW THEIR ATTENTION FROM BELOW, SO YOU PICK THEM OFF FROM ABOVE!!
FYU
MOTHER...
GAUCHE...
OUR PATHS ARE CONNECTED.
STARTING TODAY...
...I AM A LETTER BEE...

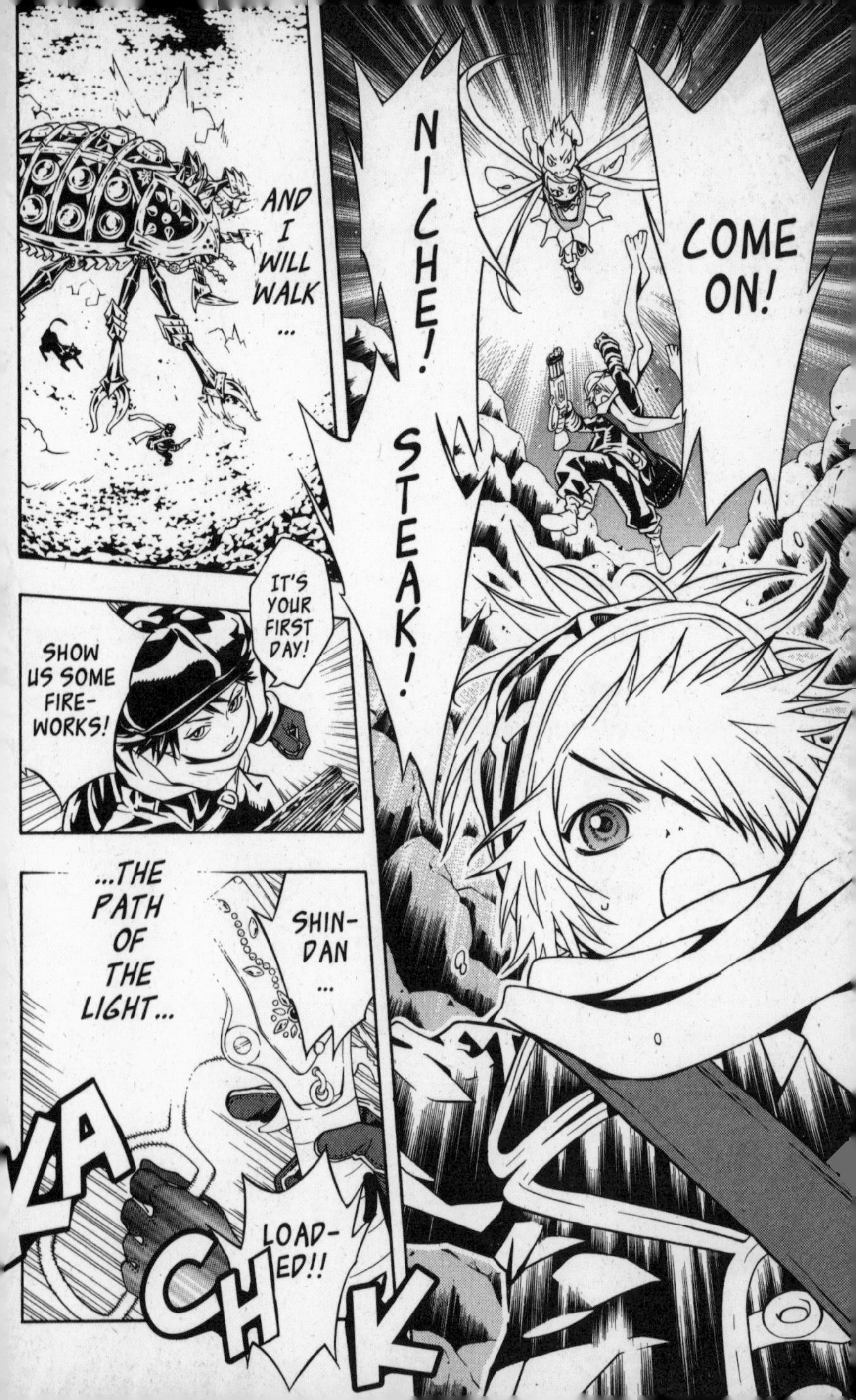
COME ON!
NICHE! STEAK!
AND I WILL WALK ...
IT'S YOUR FIRST DAY!
SHOW US SOME FIRE-WORKS!
...THE PATH OF THE LIGHT...
SHIN-DAN ...
LOADED!!
ACHK

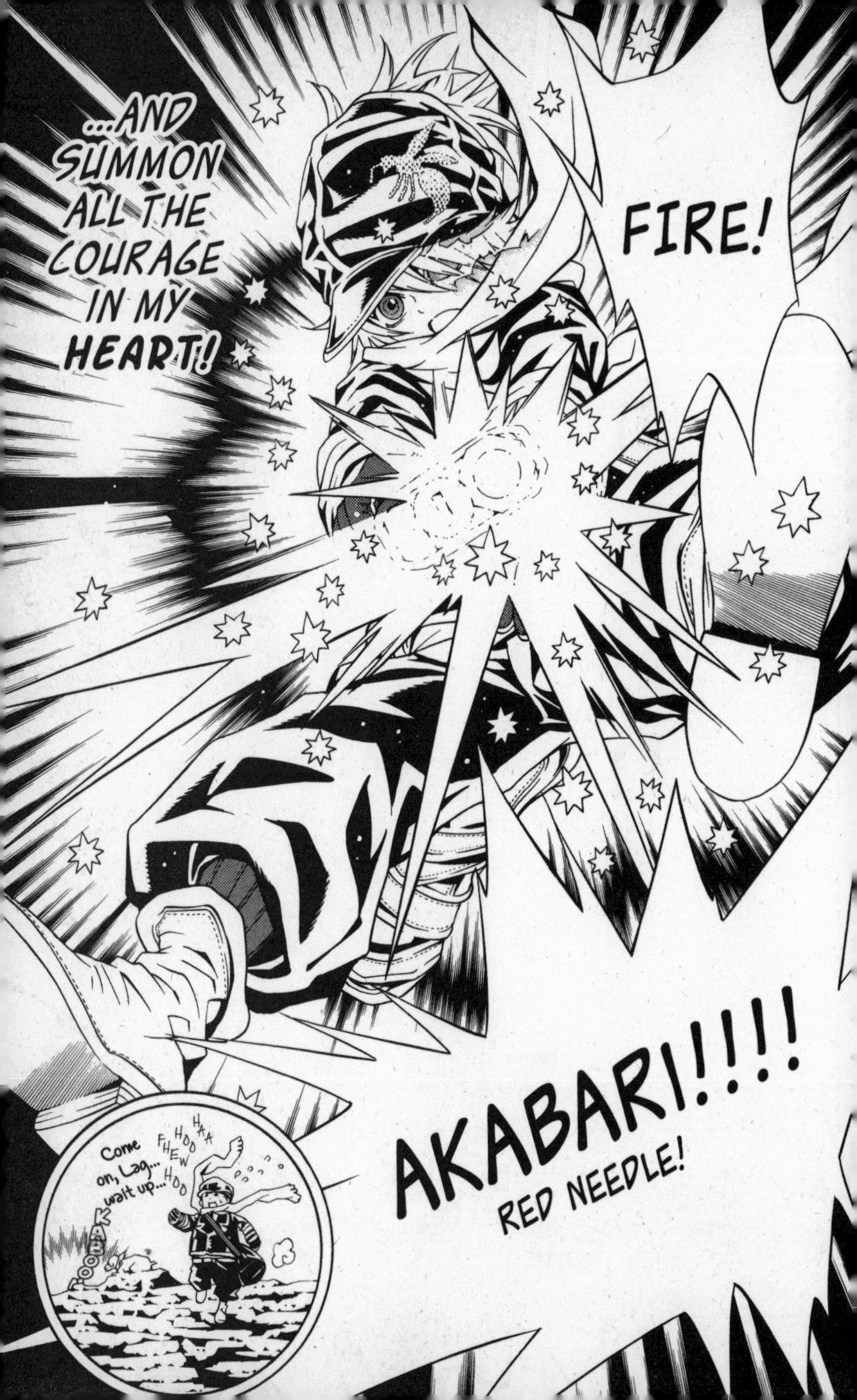
FIRE!
...AND SUMMON ALL THE COURAGE IN MY HEART!
AKABARI!!!!
RED NEEDLE!
Come on, Lag... wait up...
HAA HOO FHEW HOO

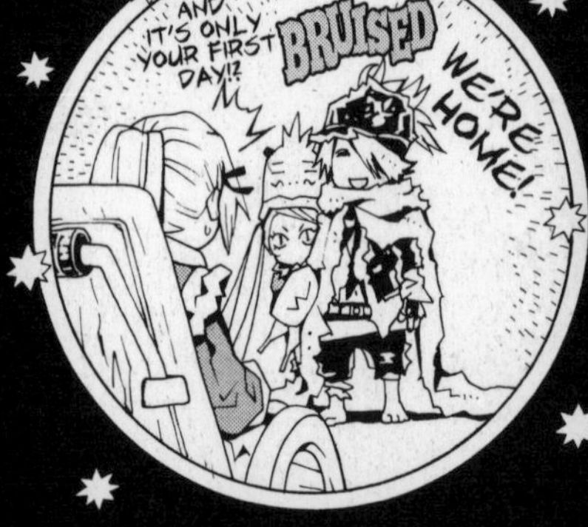AND IT'S ONLY YOUR FIRST DAY!?
BRUISED
WE'RE HOME!

SPECIAL CHAPTER: A Bee and His Dingo

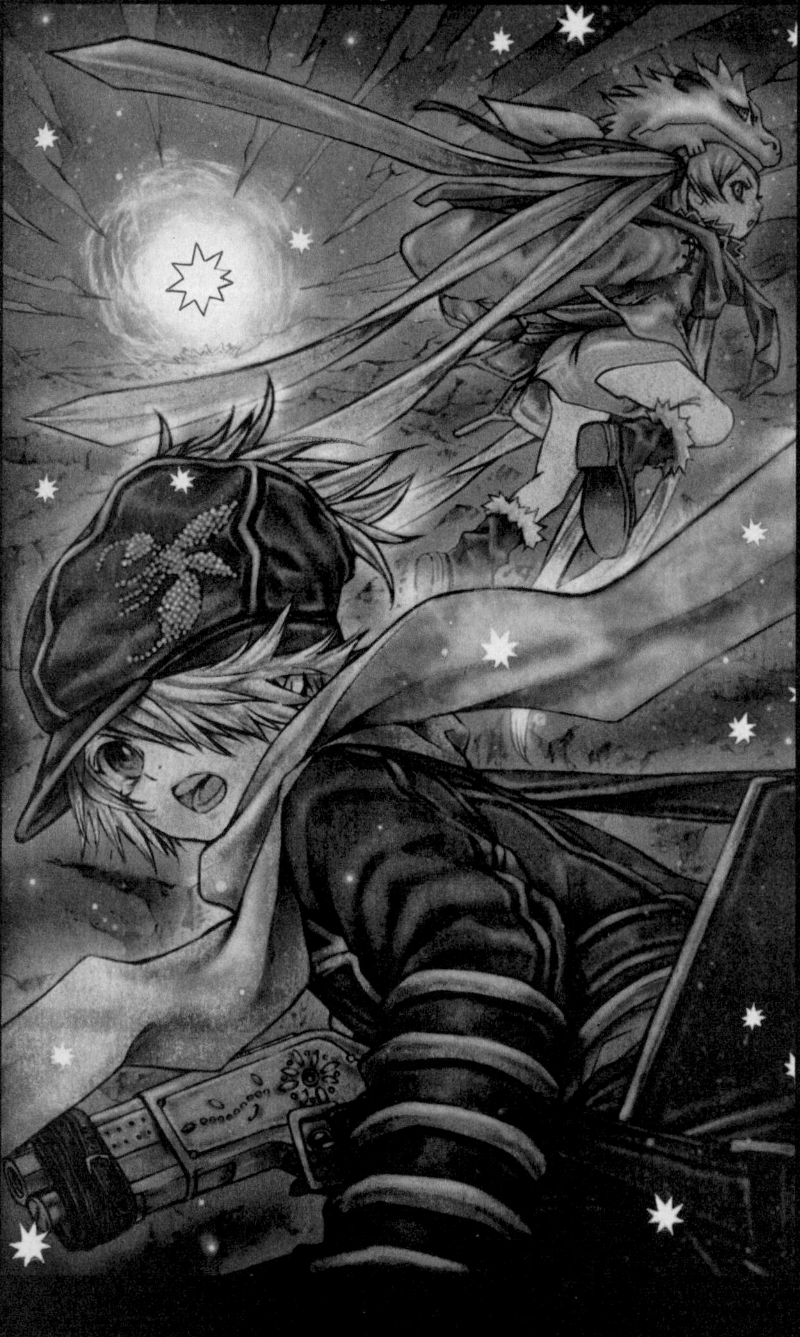

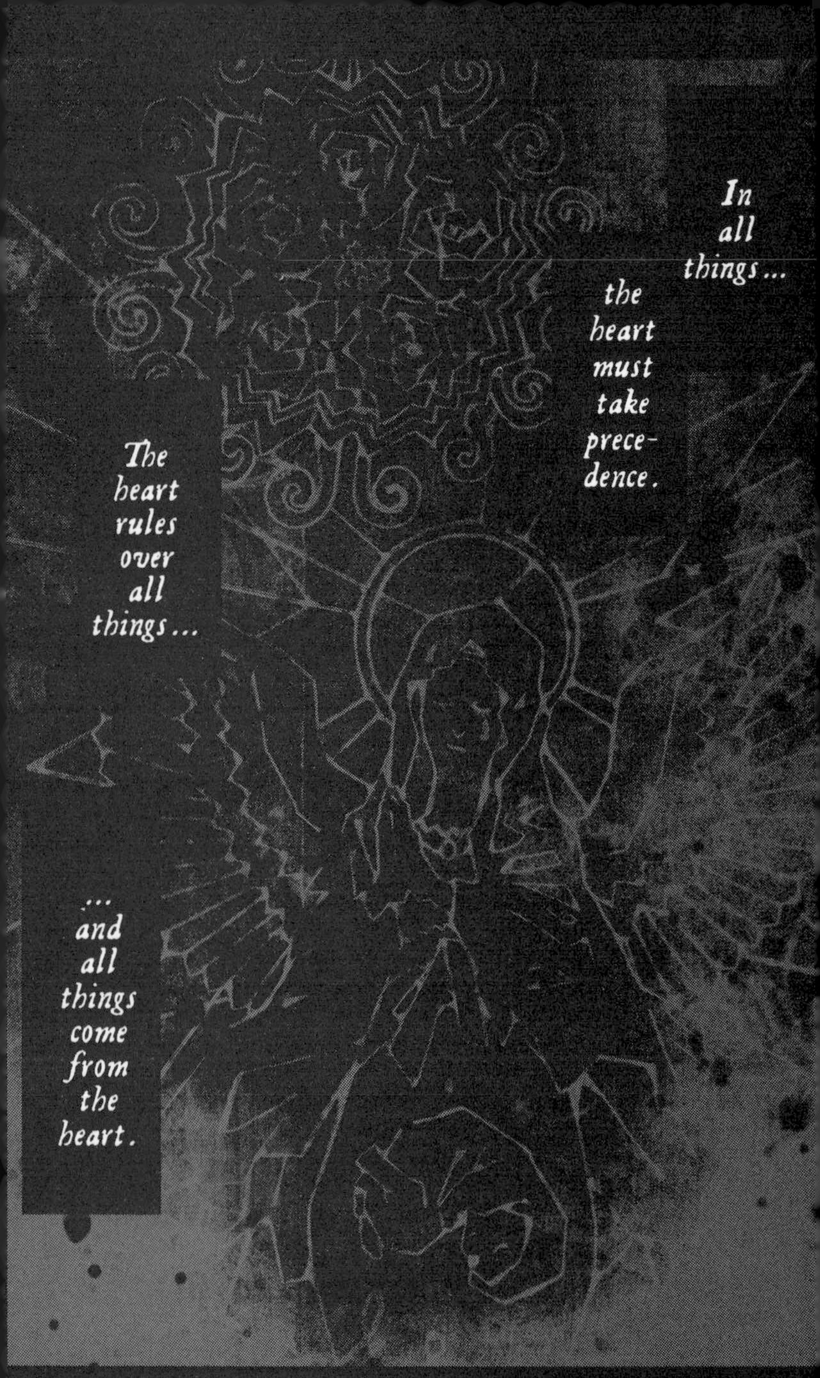
In all things...
the heart must take precedence.
The heart rules over all things...
... and all things come from the heart.

–THE SCRIPTURES OF AMBERGROUND, 1st verse

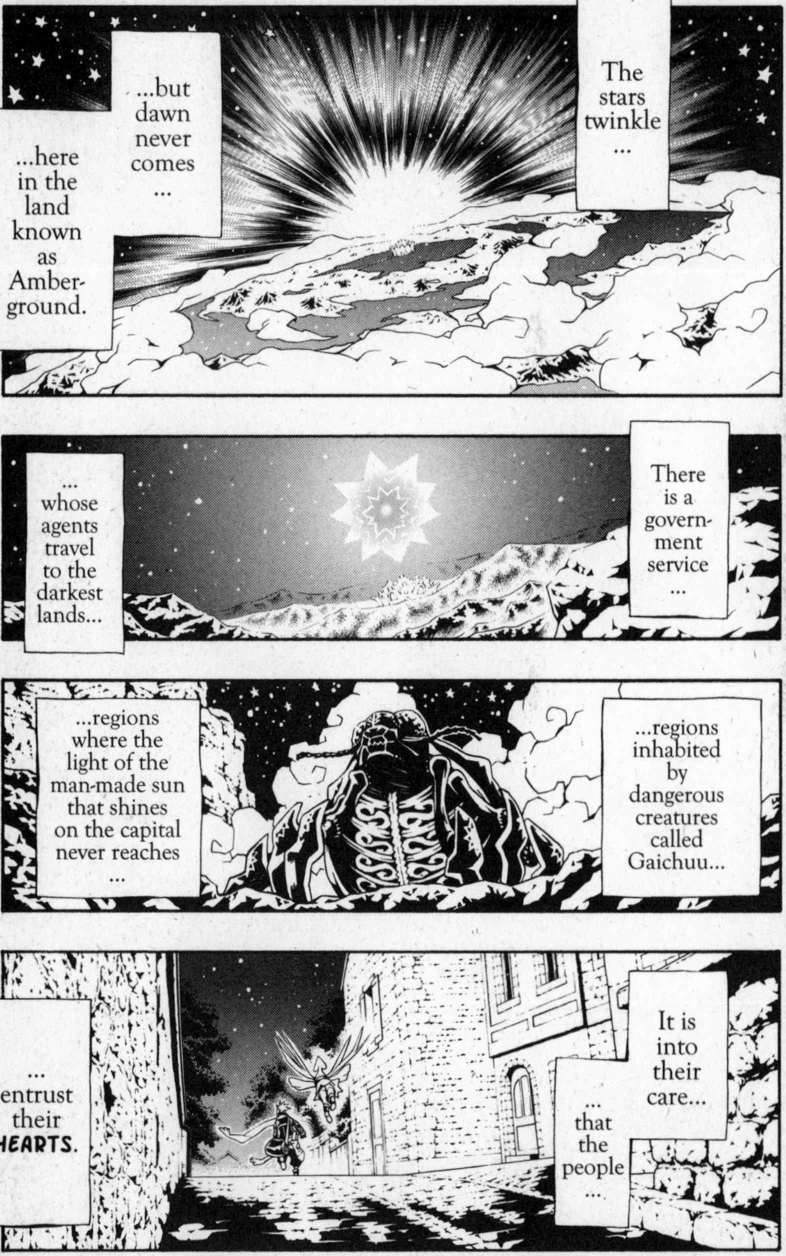
The stars twinkle...
...but dawn never comes...
...here in the land known as Amber-ground.
There is a government service...
...whose agents travel to the darkest lands...
...regions inhabited by dangerous creatures called Gaichuu...
...regions where the light of the man-made sun that shines on the capital never reaches...
It is into their care...
...that the people...
...entrust their HEARTS.

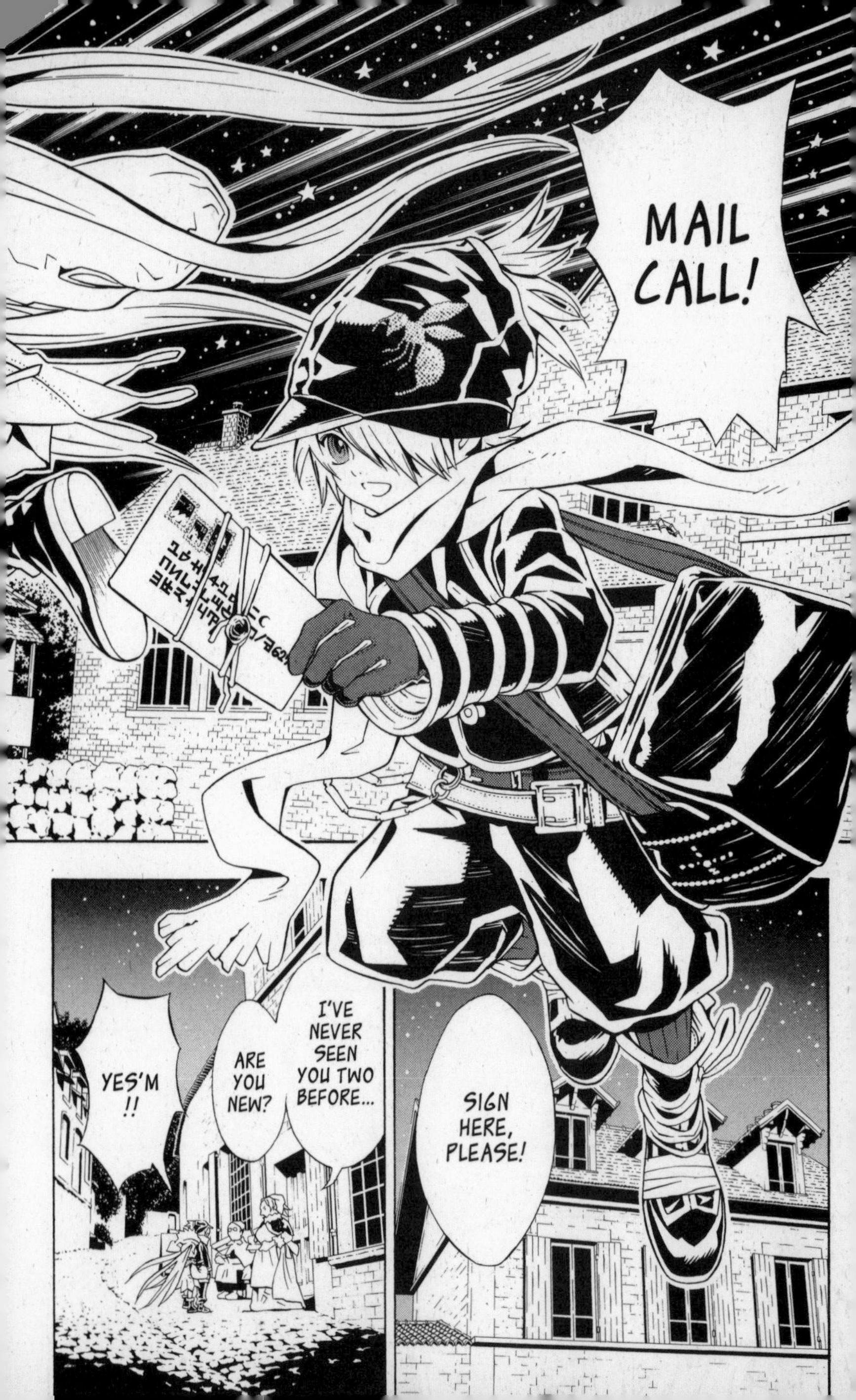
MAIL CALL!
SIGN HERE, PLEASE!
I'VE NEVER SEEN YOU TWO BEFORE...
ARE YOU NEW?
YES'M !!

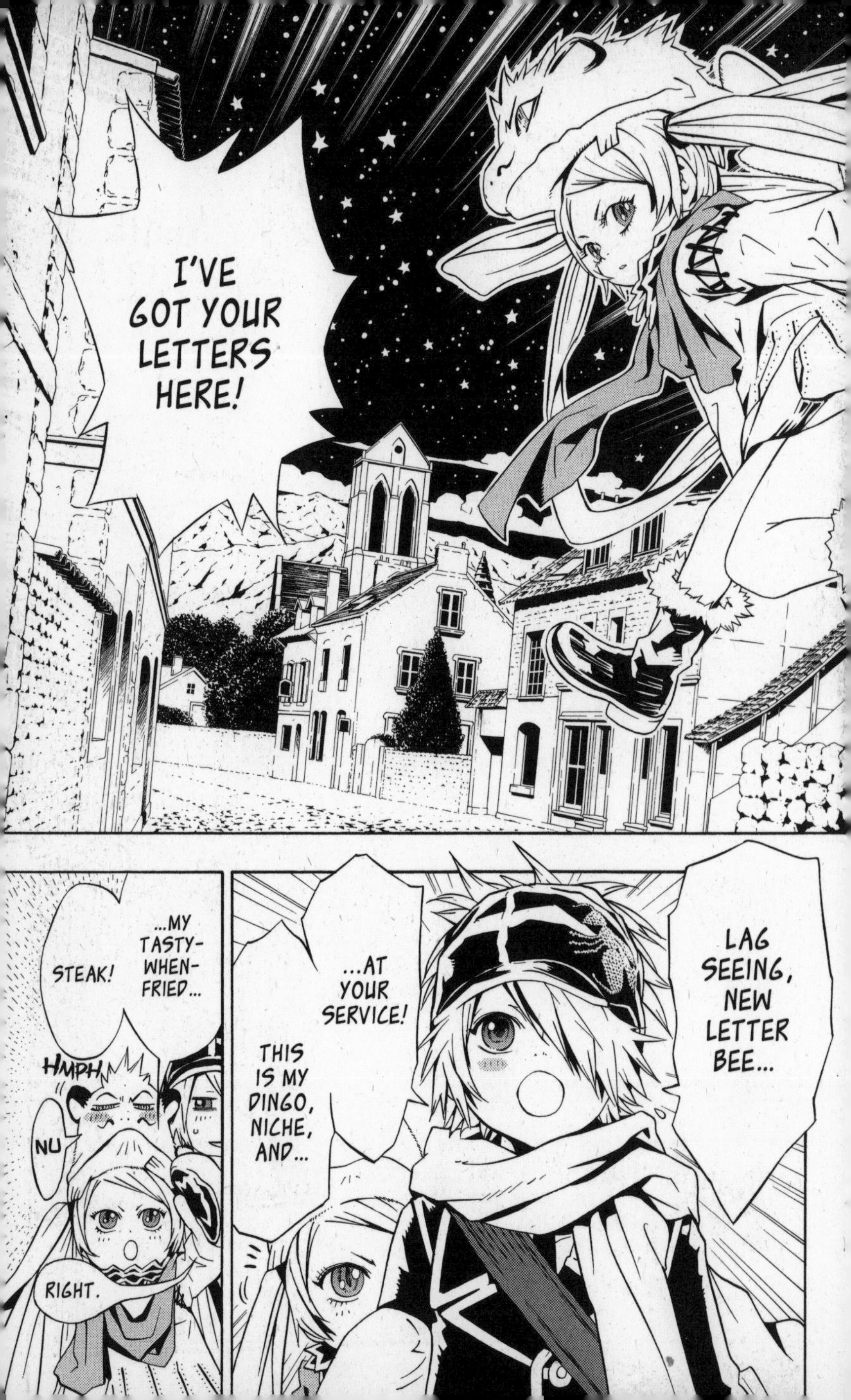
I'VE GOT YOUR LETTERS HERE!
LAG SEEING, NEW LETTER BEE...
...AT YOUR SERVICE!
THIS IS MY DINGO, NICHE, AND...
...MY TASTY-WHEN-FRIED...
STEAK!
HMPH
NU
RIGHT.

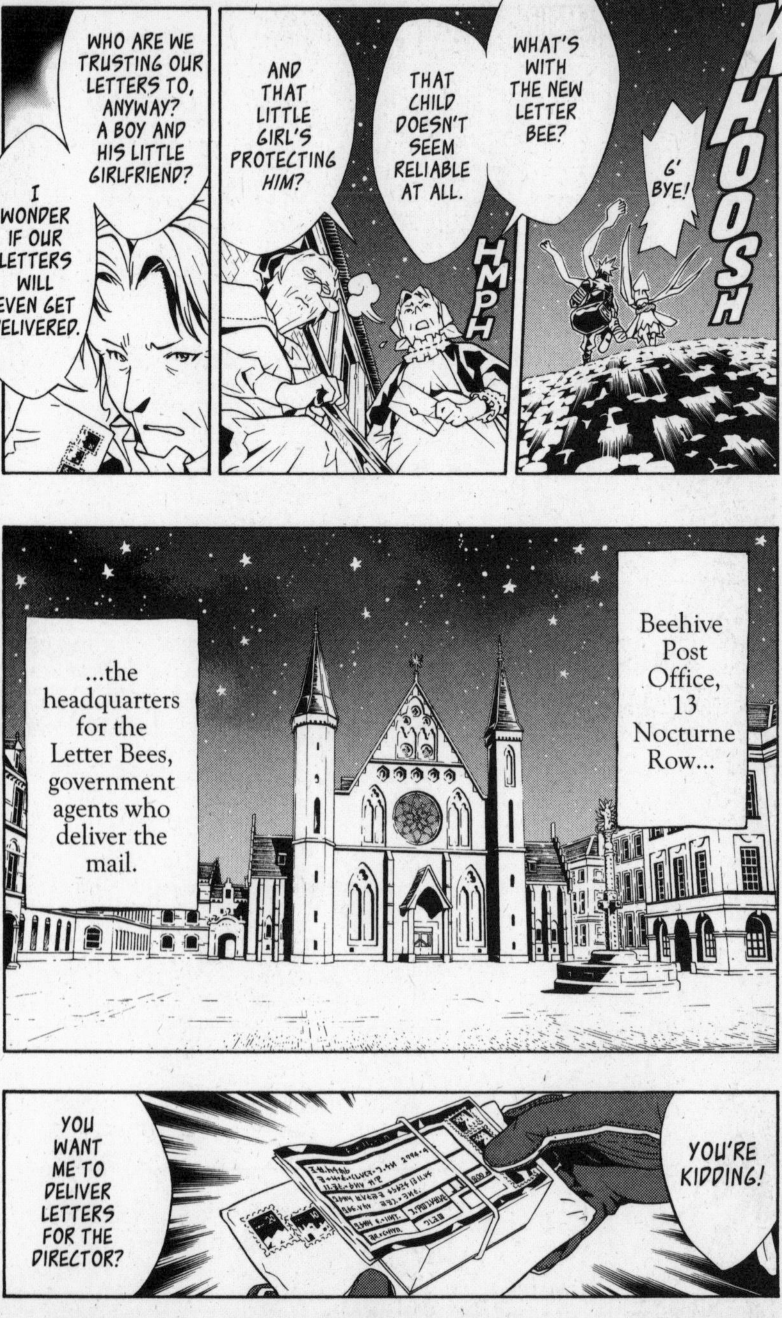
WHOOSH
G' BYE!
WHAT'S WITH THE NEW LETTER BEE?
THAT CHILD DOESN'T SEEM RELIABLE AT ALL.
HMPH
AND THAT LITTLE GIRL'S PROTECTING HIM?
WHO ARE WE TRUSTING OUR LETTERS TO, ANYWAY? A BOY AND HIS LITTLE GIRLFRIEND?
I WONDER IF OUR LETTERS WILL EVEN GET DELIVERED.
Beehive Post Office, 13 Nocturne Row...
...the headquarters for the Letter Bees, government agents who deliver the mail.
YOU'RE KIDDING!
YOU WANT ME TO DELIVER LETTERS FOR THE DIRECTOR?

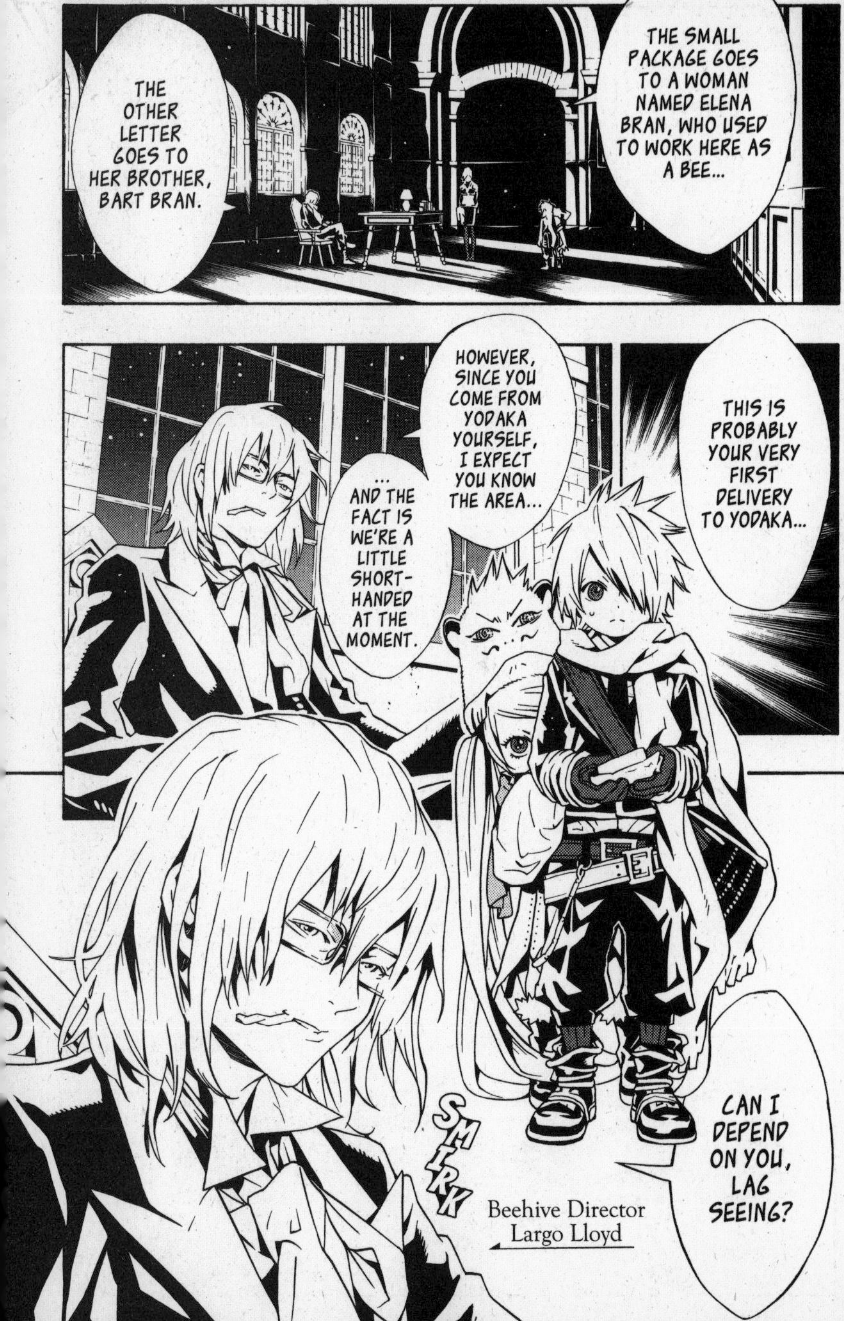
THE SMALL PACKAGE GOES TO A WOMAN NAMED ELENA BRAN, WHO USED TO WORK HERE AS A BEE...
THE OTHER LETTER GOES TO HER BROTHER, BART BRAN.
THIS IS PROBABLY YOUR VERY FIRST DELIVERY TO YODAKA...
HOWEVER, SINCE YOU COME FROM YODAKA YOURSELF, I EXPECT YOU KNOW THE AREA...
... AND THE FACT IS WE'RE A LITTLE SHORT-HANDED AT THE MOMENT.
SMIRK
Beehive Director Largo Lloyd
CAN I DEPEND ON YOU, LAG SEEING?

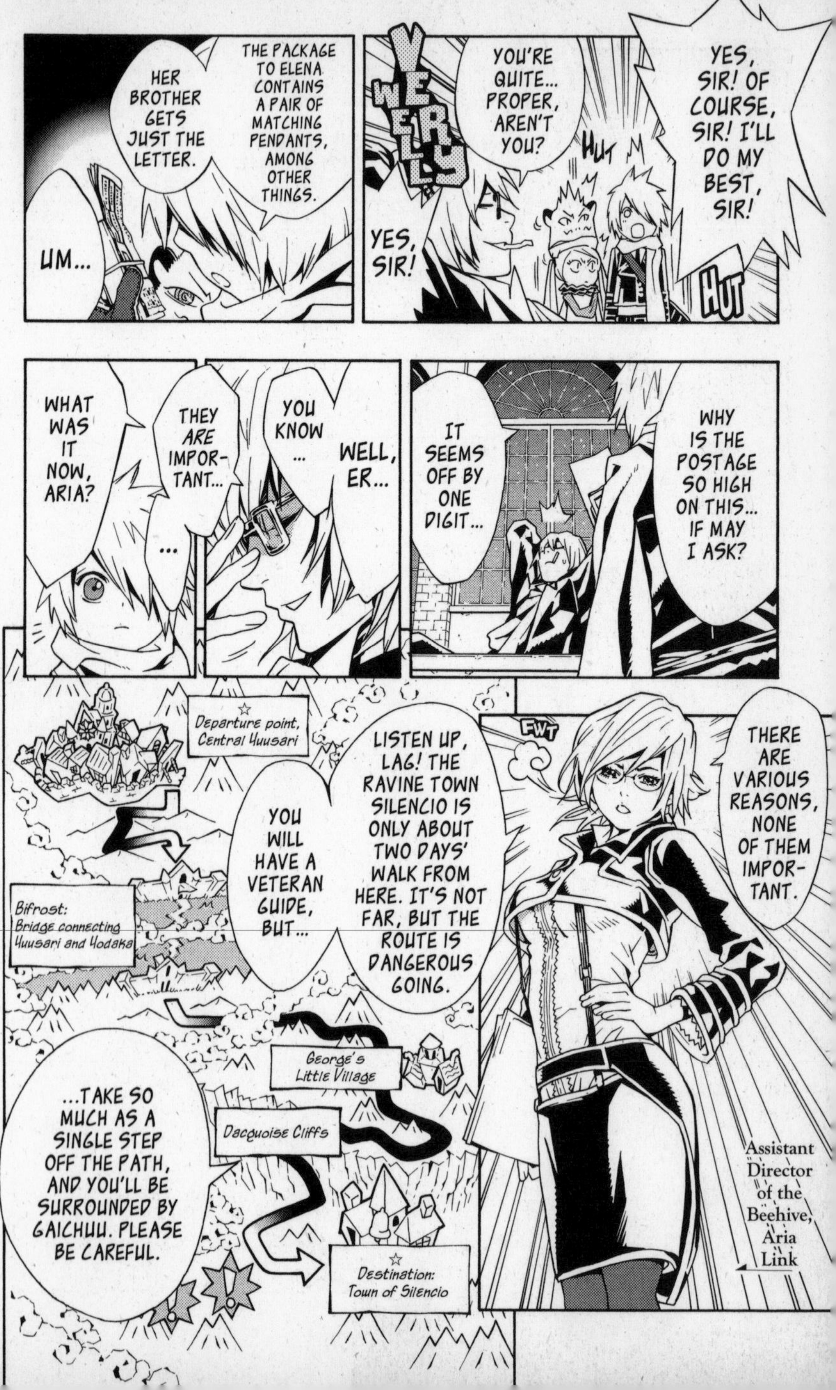
YES, SIR! OF COURSE, SIR! I'LL DO MY BEST, SIR!
HUT
HUT
YOU'RE QUITE... PROPER, AREN'T YOU?
VERY WELL
YES, SIR!
THE PACKAGE TO ELENA CONTAINS A PAIR OF MATCHING PENDANTS, AMONG OTHER THINGS.
HER BROTHER GETS JUST THE LETTER.
UM...
WHY IS THE POSTAGE SO HIGH ON THIS... IF MAY I ASK?
IT SEEMS OFF BY ONE DIGIT...
WELL, ER...
YOU KNOW ...
THEY ARE IMPORTANT...
WHAT WAS IT NOW, ARIA?
...
FWT
THERE ARE VARIOUS REASONS, NONE OF THEM IMPORTANT.
Assistant Director of the Beehive, Aria Link
LISTEN UP, LAG! THE RAVINE TOWN SILENCIO IS ONLY ABOUT TWO DAYS' WALK FROM HERE. IT'S NOT FAR, BUT THE ROUTE IS DANGEROUS GOING.
YOU WILL HAVE A VETERAN GUIDE, BUT...
...TAKE SO MUCH AS A SINGLE STEP OFF THE PATH, AND YOU'LL BE SURROUNDED BY GAICHUU. PLEASE BE CAREFUL.
☆ Departure point, Central Yuusari
Bifrost: Bridge connecting Yuusari and Yodaka
George's Little Village
Dacquoise Cliffs
☆ Destination: Town of Silencio

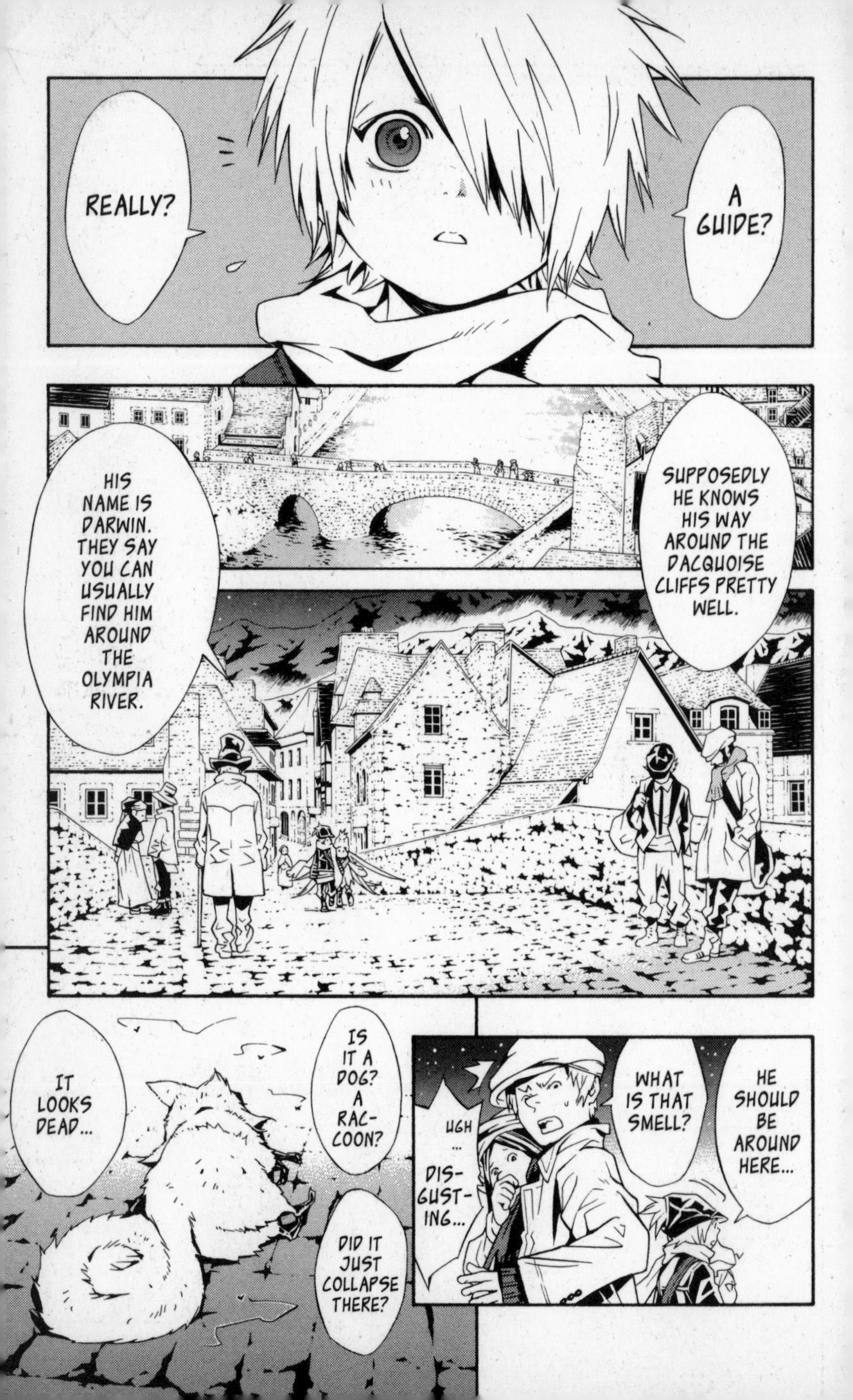
A GUIDE?
REALLY?
SUPPOSEDLY HE KNOWS HIS WAY AROUND THE DACQUOISE CLIFFS PRETTY WELL.
HIS NAME IS DARWIN. THEY SAY YOU CAN USUALLY FIND HIM AROUND THE OLYMPIA RIVER.
HE SHOULD BE AROUND HERE...
WHAT IS THAT SMELL?
UGH... DIS-GUST-ING...
IS IT A DOG? A RAC-COON?
IT LOOKS DEAD...
DID IT JUST COLLAPSE THERE?

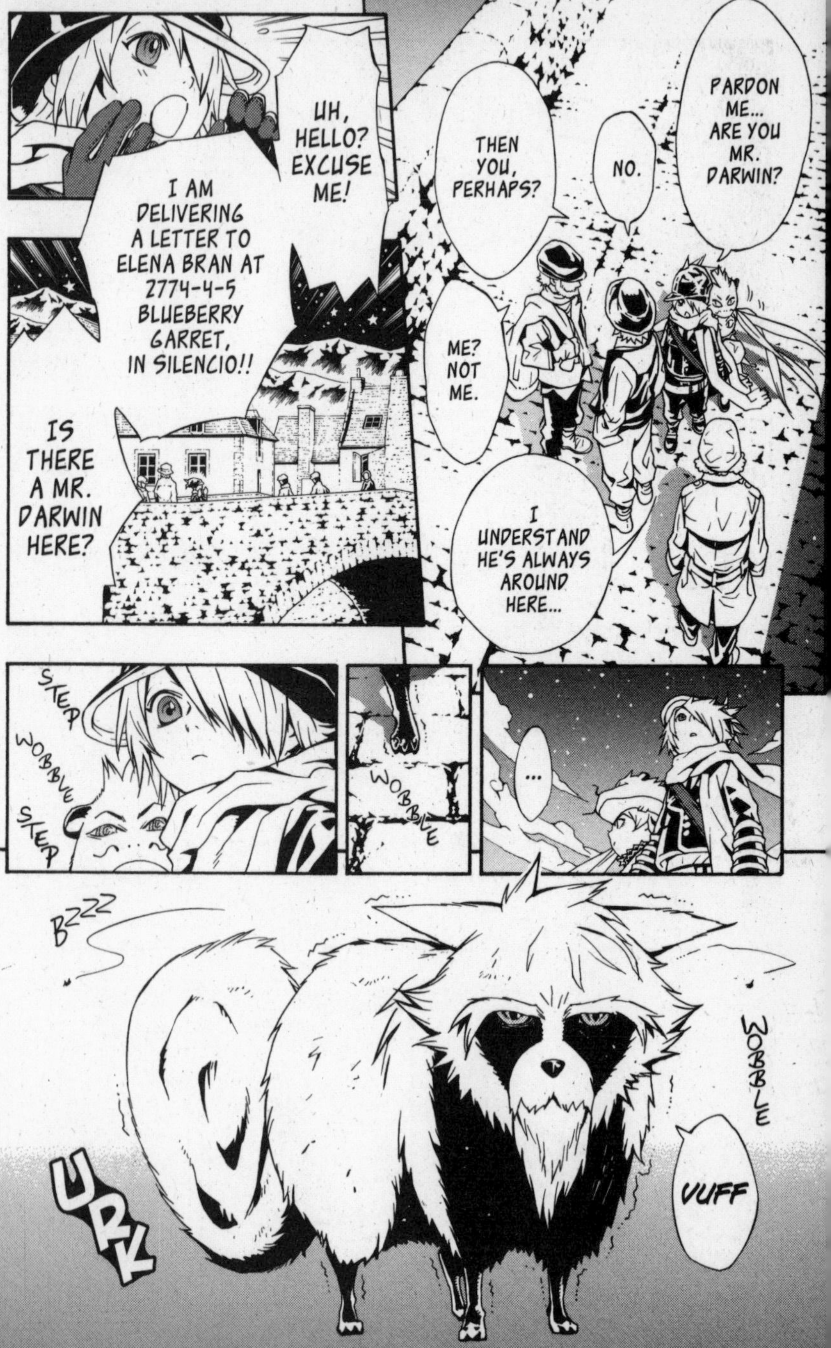
PARDON ME... ARE YOU MR. DARWIN?
NO.
THEN YOU, PERHAPS?
ME? NOT ME.
I UNDERSTAND HE'S ALWAYS AROUND HERE...
UH, HELLO? EXCUSE ME!
I AM DELIVERING A LETTER TO ELENA BRAN AT 2774-4-5 BLUEBERRY GARRET, IN SILENCIO!!
IS THERE A MR. DARWIN HERE?
...
WOBBLE
STEP
WOBBLE
STEP
BZZZ
WOBBLE
VUFF
URK

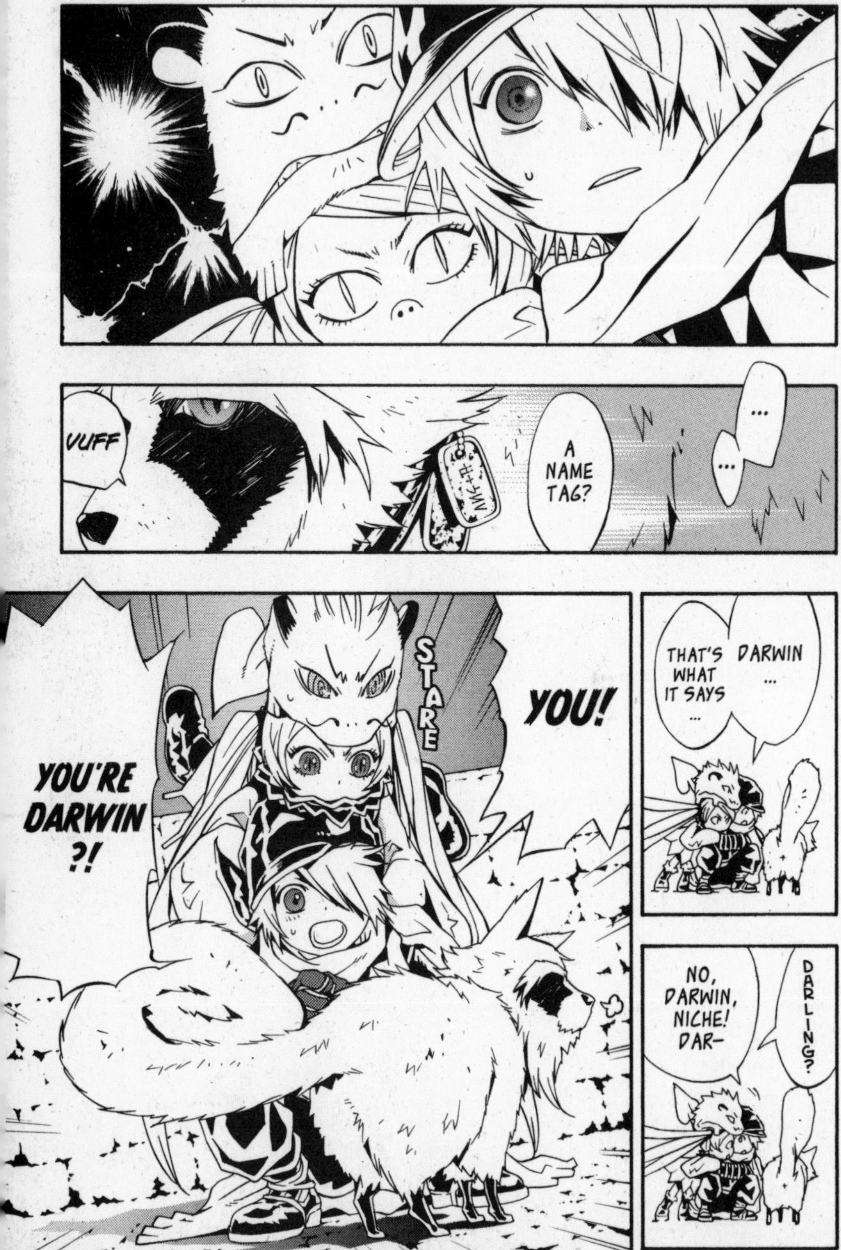
...
...
A NAME TAG?
VUFF
DARWIN ...
THAT'S WHAT IT SAYS ...
DARLING?
NO, DARWIN, NICHE! DAR—
STARE
YOU!
YOU'RE DARWIN ?!

WOBBLE STEP WOBBLE STEP WOBBLE STEP

HOW DO YOU DO?

I'M LAG SEEING—

HMPH

OH...

WOBBLE

I WONDER IF HE WANTS US TO FOLLOW HIM...

...

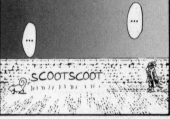

W-WAIT, DARWIN!!

I HAVE A FEELING HE DOESN'T, BUT LET'S GO, NICHE!

TOK TOK TOK

...

...

...

SCOOT SCOOT

DIRECTOR ...

WHY DIDN'T YOU TELL LAG SEEING THE TRUTH?

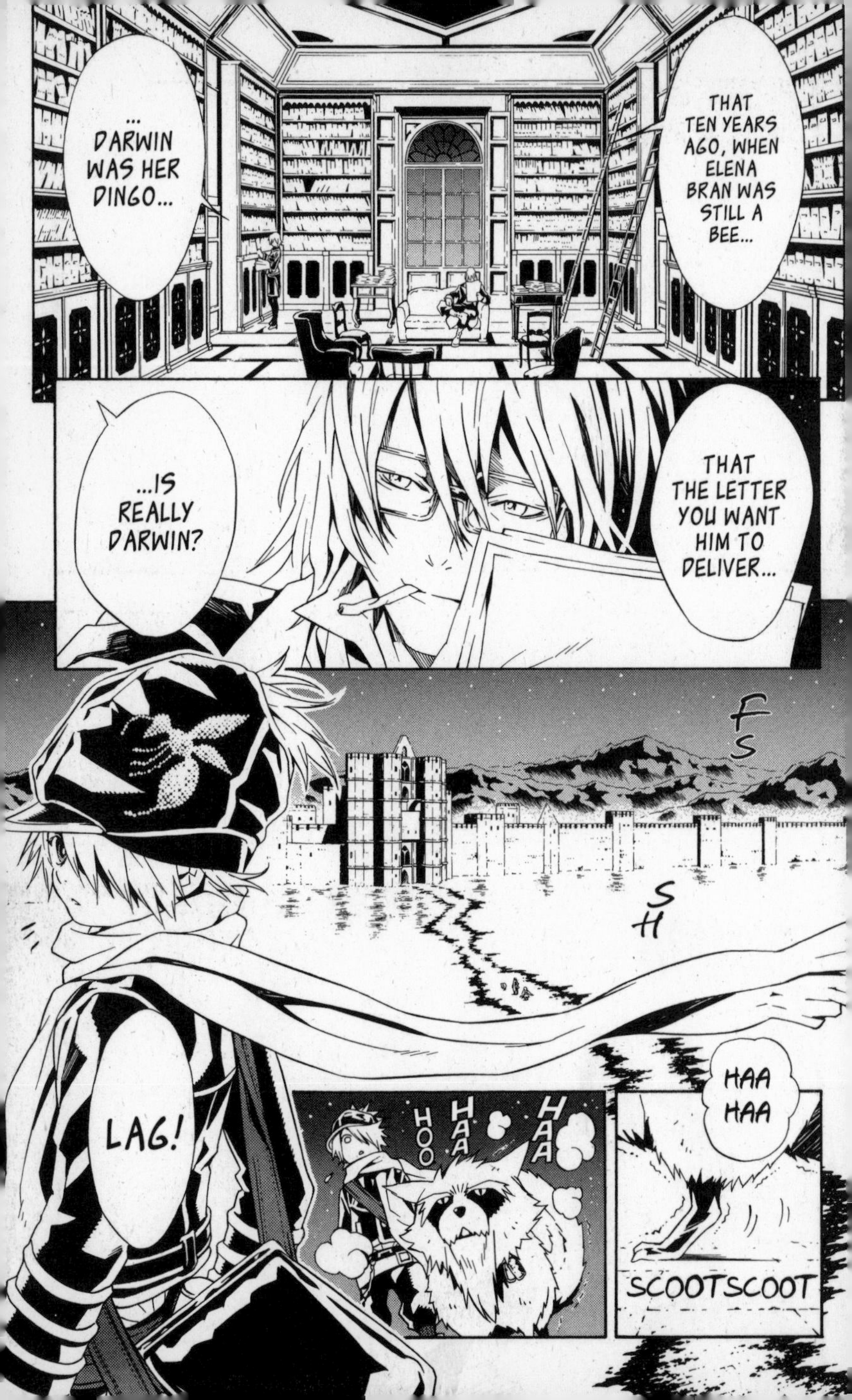
THAT TEN YEARS AGO, WHEN ELENA BRAN WAS STILL A BEE...
... DARWIN WAS HER DINGO...
THAT THE LETTER YOU WANT HIM TO DELIVER...
...IS REALLY DARWIN?
FSSH
LAG!
HAA HAA
SCOOTSCOOT
HAA HAA HOO

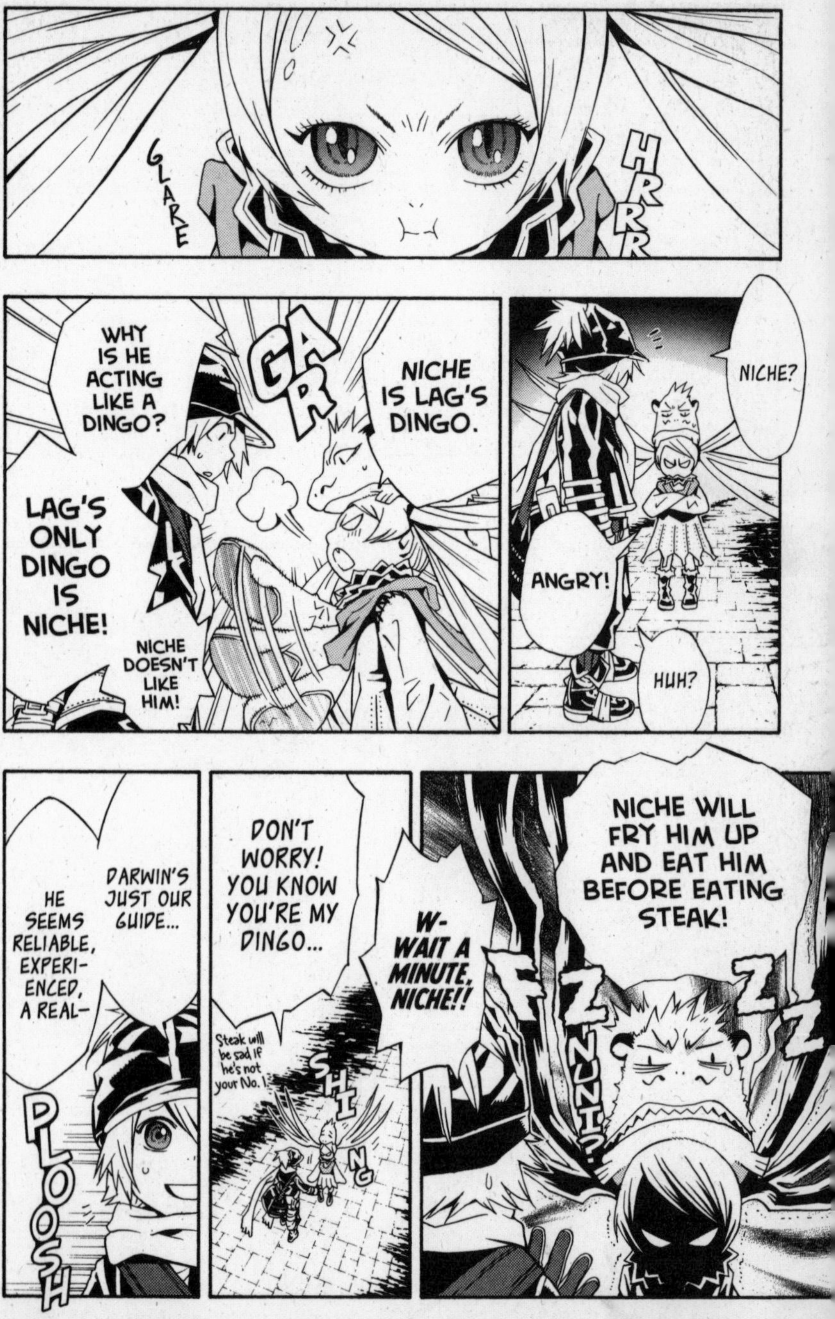
HRRR
GLARE
NICHE?
ANGRY!
HUH?
NICHE IS LAG'S DINGO.
GAR
WHY IS HE ACTING LIKE A DINGO?
LAG'S ONLY DINGO IS NICHE!
NICHE DOESN'T LIKE HIM!
NICHE WILL FRY HIM UP AND EAT HIM BEFORE EATING STEAK!
FZZZ
NUNI?
W-WAIT A MINUTE, NICHE!!
DON'T WORRY! YOU KNOW YOU'RE MY DINGO...
Steak will be sad if he's not your No. 1.
SHING
DARWIN'S JUST OUR GUIDE...
HE SEEMS RELIABLE, EXPERIENCED, A REAL-
PLOOSH

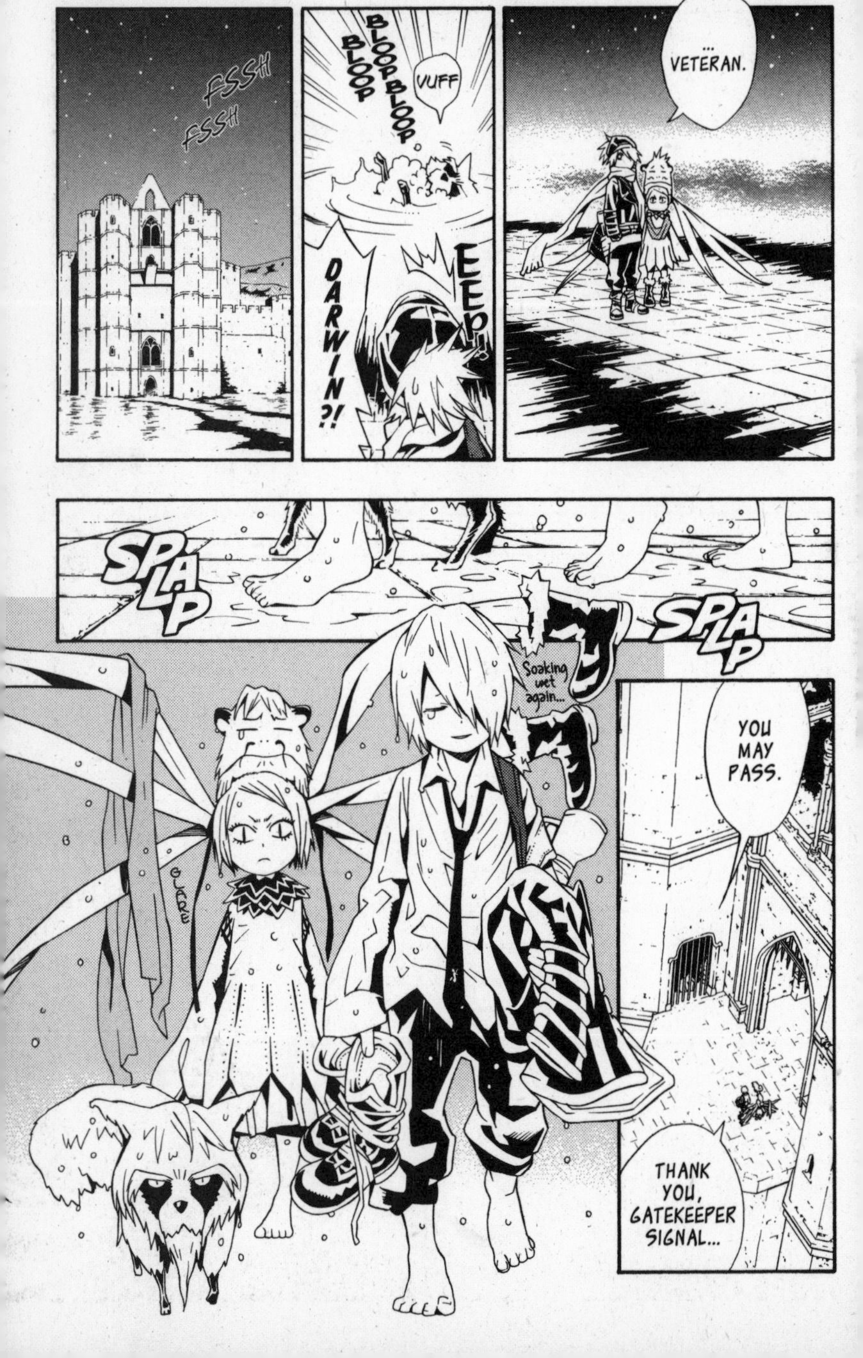

... VETERAN.
BLOOP BLOOP BLOOP BLOOP
VUFF
EEP!!
DARWIN?!
FSSH FSSH
SPLAP
SPLAP
YOU MAY PASS.
THANK YOU, GATEKEEPER SIGNAL...
Soaking wet again...
GLARE

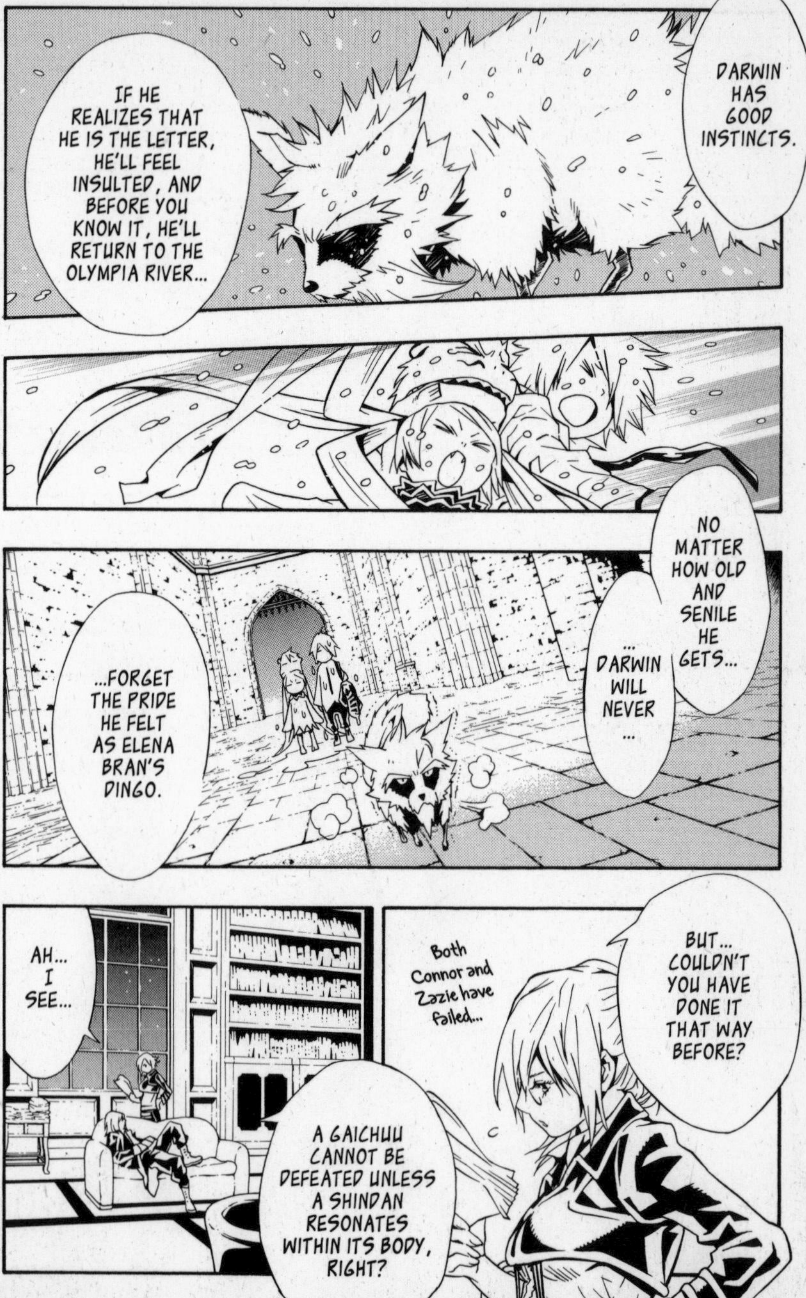
DARWIN HAS GOOD INSTINCTS.
IF HE REALIZES THAT HE IS THE LETTER, HE'LL FEEL INSULTED, AND BEFORE YOU KNOW IT, HE'LL RETURN TO THE OLYMPIA RIVER...
NO MATTER HOW OLD AND SENILE HE GETS...
...DARWIN WILL NEVER...
...FORGET THE PRIDE HE FELT AS ELENA BRAN'S DINGO.
BUT... COULDN'T YOU HAVE DONE IT THAT WAY BEFORE?
Both Connor and Zazie have failed...
A GAICHUU CANNOT BE DEFEATED UNLESS A SHINDAN RESONATES WITHIN ITS BODY, RIGHT?
AH... I SEE...

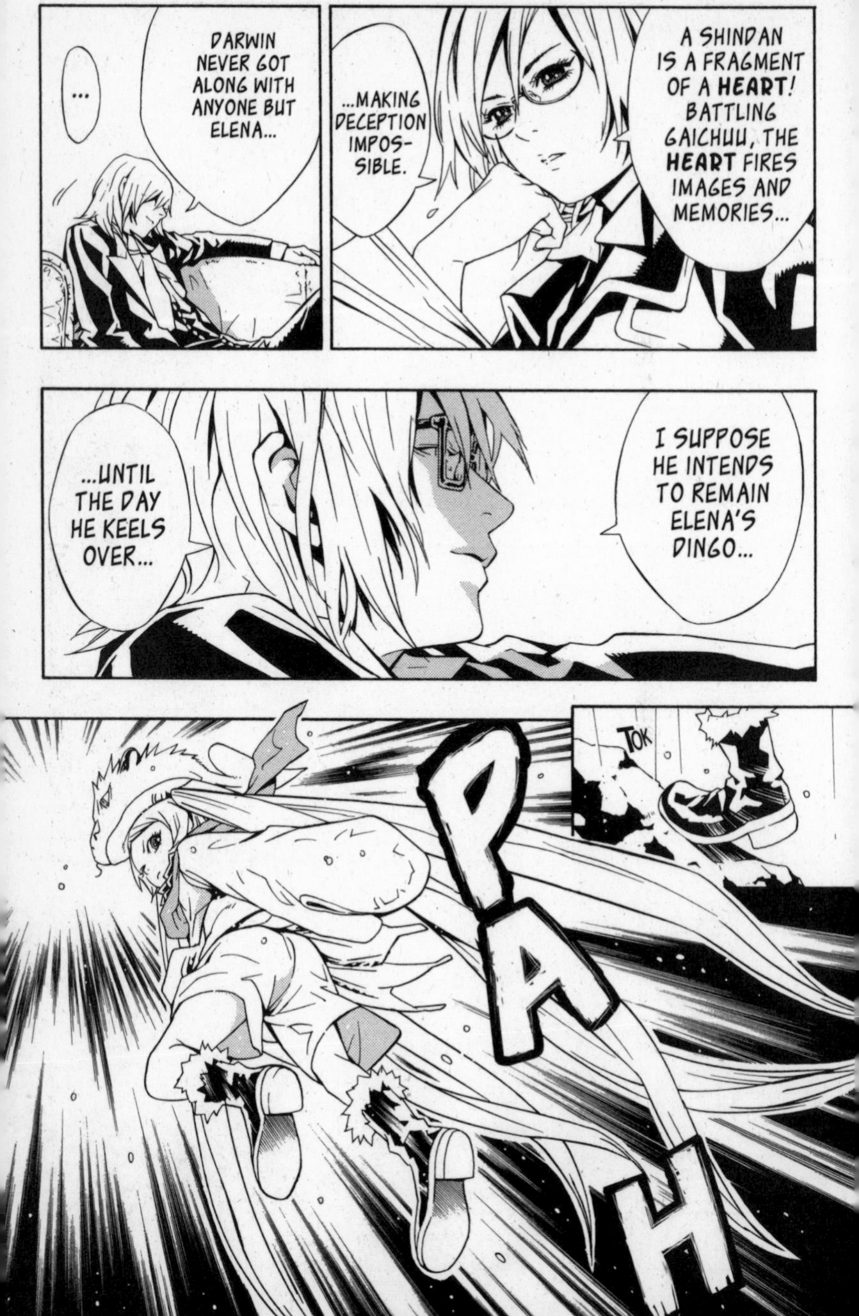
A SHINDAN IS A FRAGMENT OF A **HEART**! BATTLING GAICHUU, THE **HEART** FIRES IMAGES AND MEMORIES...
...MAKING DECEPTION IMPOSSIBLE.
DARWIN NEVER GOT ALONG WITH ANYONE BUT ELENA...
...
I SUPPOSE HE INTENDS TO REMAIN ELENA'S DINGO...
...UNTIL THE DAY HE KEELS OVER...
TOK
PAH

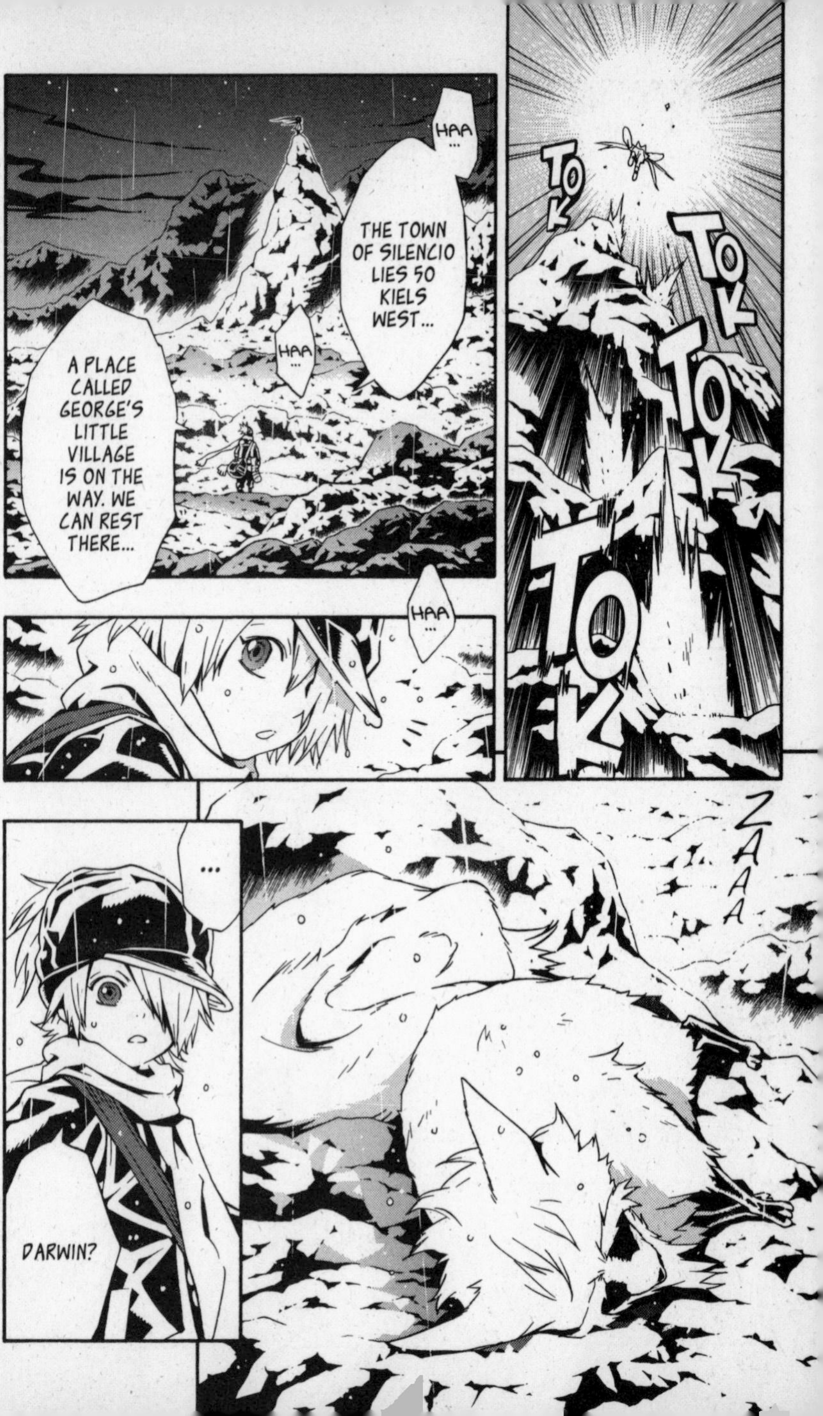
TOK
TOK
TOK
TOK
HAA...
THE TOWN OF SILENCIO LIES 50 KIELS WEST...
HAA...
A PLACE CALLED GEORGE'S LITTLE VILLAGE IS ON THE WAY. WE CAN REST THERE...
HAA...
ZAAA
...
DARWIN?

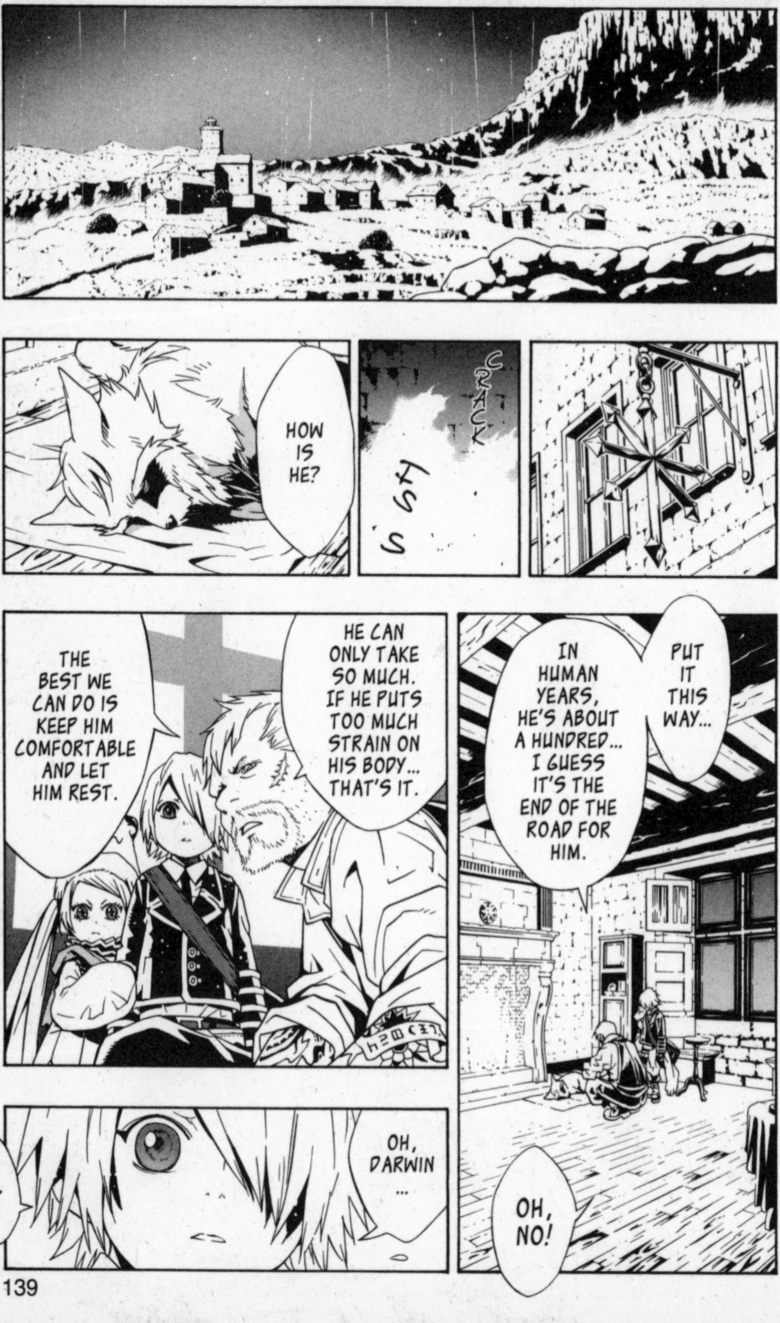
CRACK
HOW IS HE?
PUT IT THIS WAY...
IN HUMAN YEARS, HE'S ABOUT A HUNDRED... I GUESS IT'S THE END OF THE ROAD FOR HIM.
HE CAN ONLY TAKE SO MUCH. IF HE PUTS TOO MUCH STRAIN ON HIS BODY... THAT'S IT.
THE BEST WE CAN DO IS KEEP HIM COMFORTABLE AND LET HIM REST.
OH, NO!
OH, DARWIN...
...

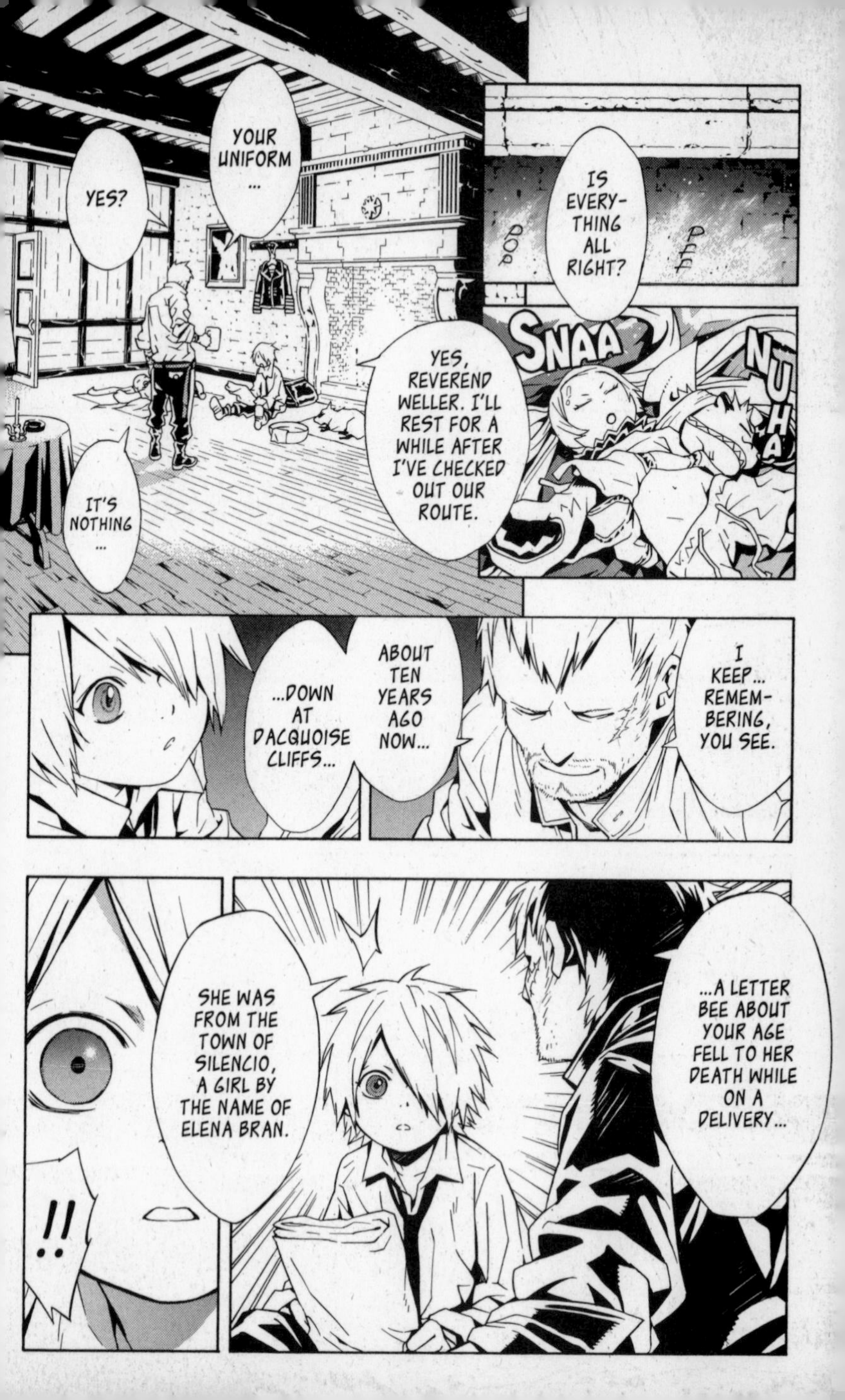

IS EVERY-THING ALL RIGHT?
POP
PFF
SNAA
NUHA
YES, REVEREND WELLER. I'LL REST FOR A WHILE AFTER I'VE CHECKED OUT OUR ROUTE.
YOUR UNIFORM ...
YES?
IT'S NOTHING ...
I KEEP... REMEM-BERING, YOU SEE.
ABOUT TEN YEARS AGO NOW...
...DOWN AT DACQUOISE CLIFFS...
...A LETTER BEE ABOUT YOUR AGE FELL TO HER DEATH WHILE ON A DELIVERY...
SHE WAS FROM THE TOWN OF SILENCIO, A GIRL BY THE NAME OF ELENA BRAN.
!!

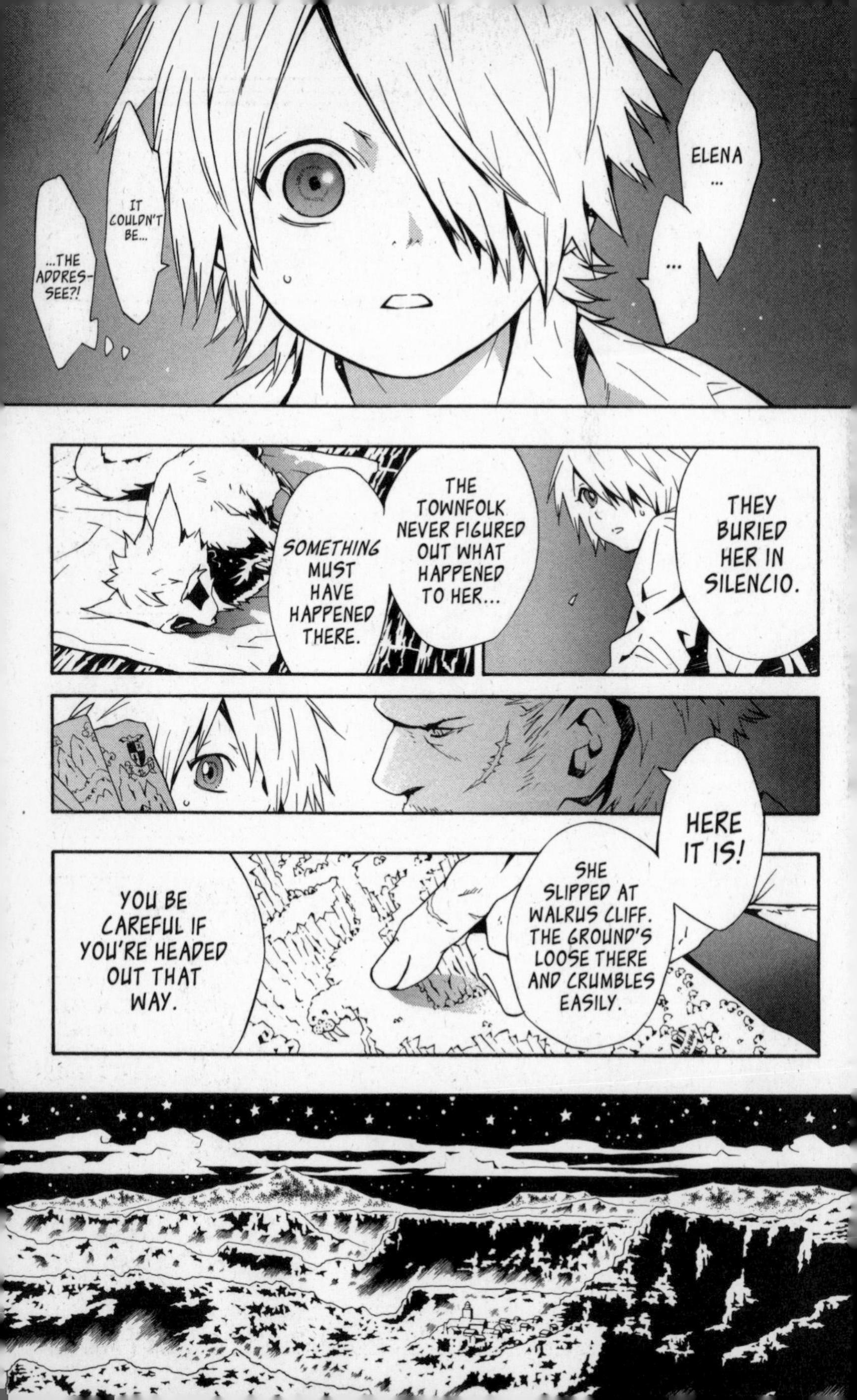
ELENA ... ...
IT COULDN'T BE...
...THE ADDRES-SEE?!
THEY BURIED HER IN SILENCIO.
THE TOWNFOLK NEVER FIGURED OUT WHAT HAPPENED TO HER...
SOMETHING MUST HAVE HAPPENED THERE.
HERE IT IS!
SHE SLIPPED AT WALRUS CLIFF. THE GROUND'S LOOSE THERE AND CRUMBLES EASILY.
YOU BE CAREFUL IF YOU'RE HEADED OUT THAT WAY.

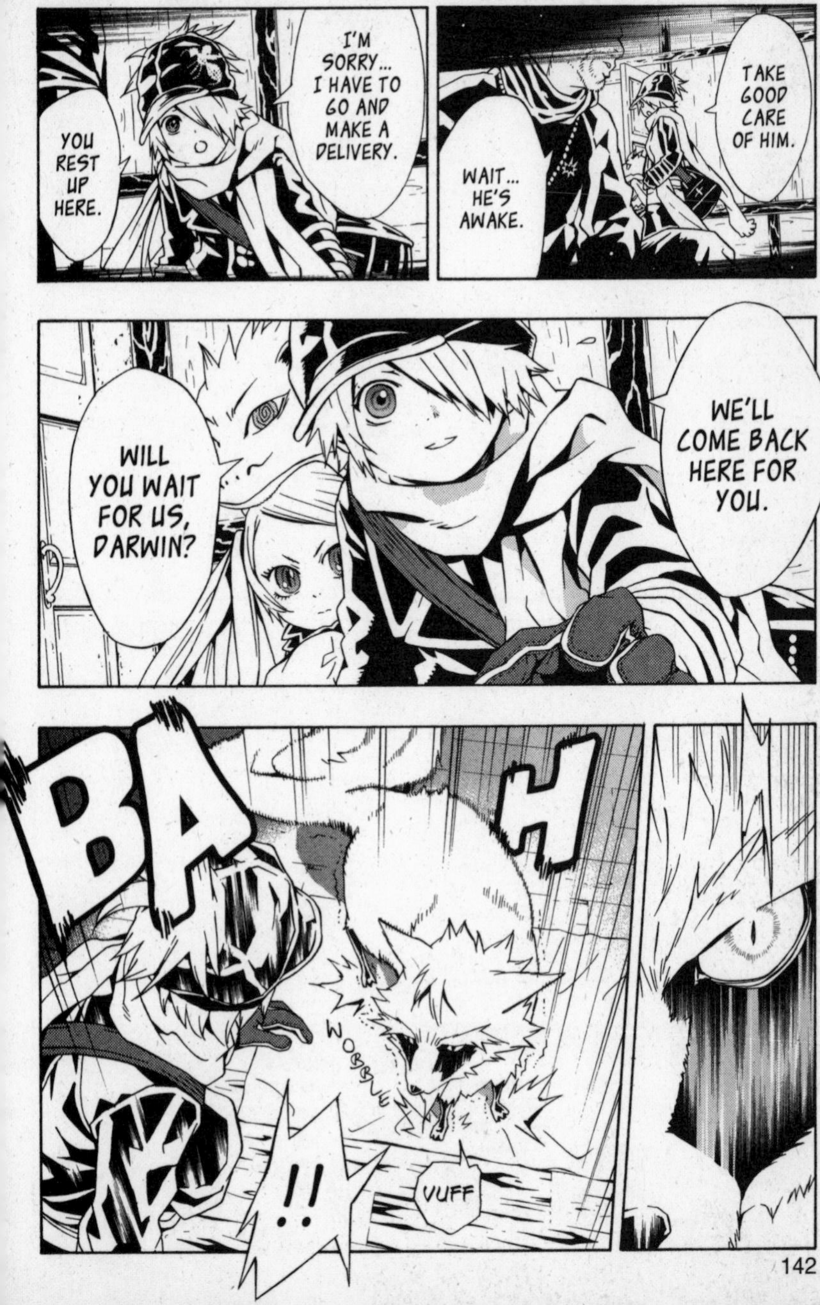
TAKE GOOD CARE OF HIM.
WAIT... HE'S AWAKE.
I'M SORRY... I HAVE TO GO AND MAKE A DELIVERY.
YOU REST UP HERE.
WE'LL COME BACK HERE FOR YOU.
WILL YOU WAIT FOR US, DARWIN?
BAH
WOBBLE
VUFF
!!

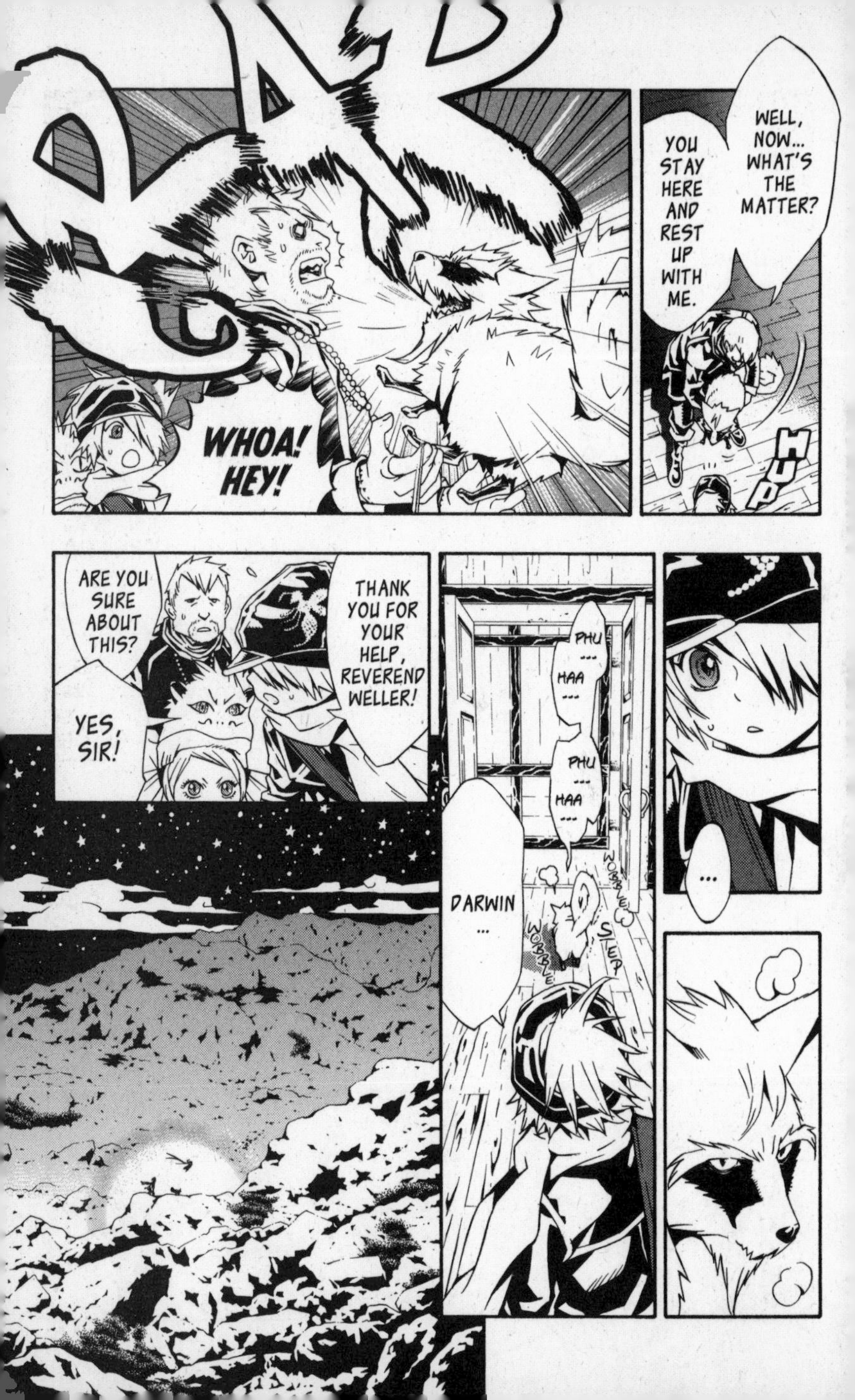

WELL, NOW... WHAT'S THE MATTER?
YOU STAY HERE AND REST UP WITH ME.
HUP
WHOA! HEY!
...
PHU... HAA...
PHU... HAA...
WOBBLE
STEP
WOBBLE
DARWIN...
THANK YOU FOR YOUR HELP, REVEREND WELLER!
ARE YOU SURE ABOUT THIS?
YES, SIR!

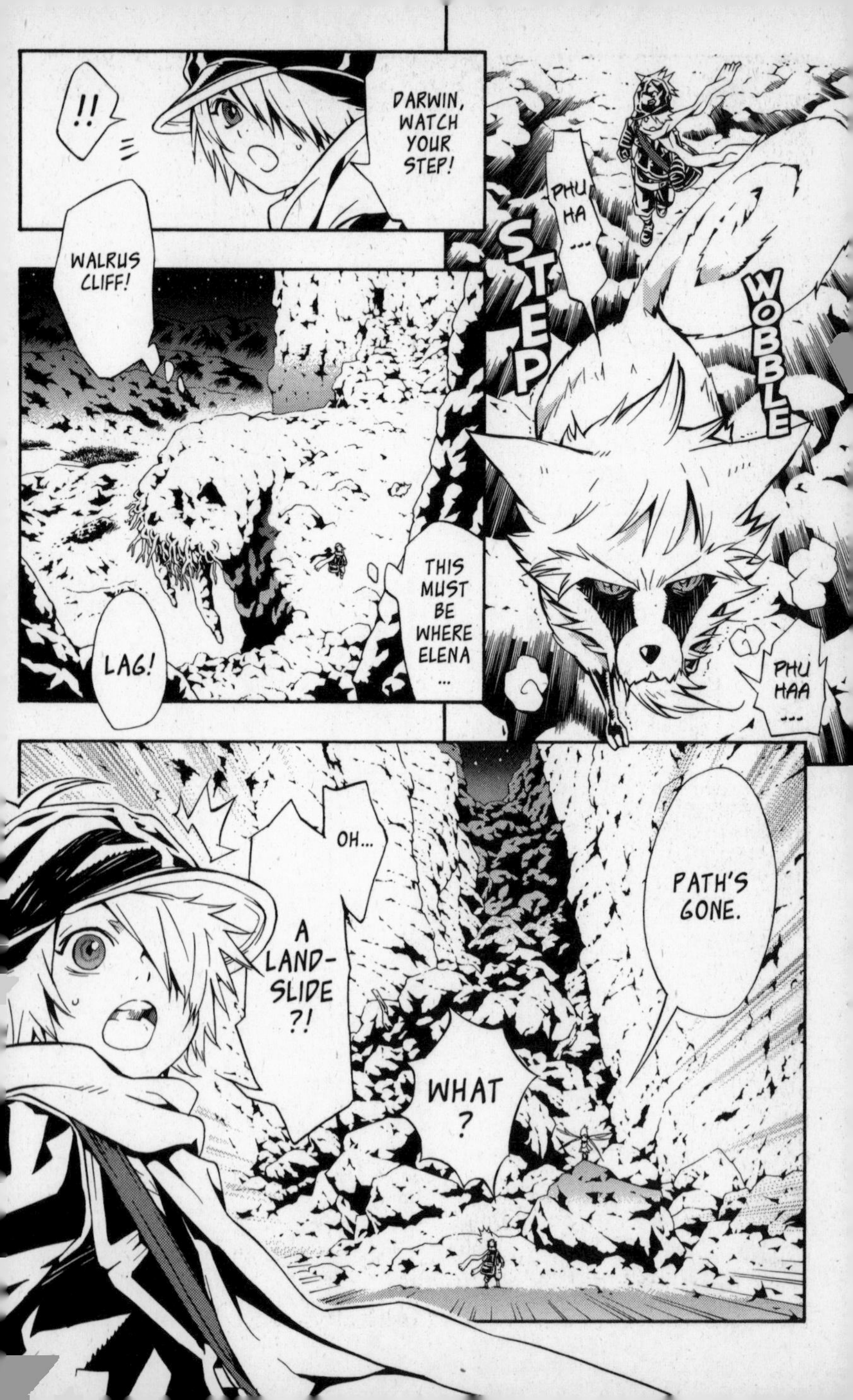

PHU HA ...
STEP
STEP
WOBBLE
...
PHU HAA ...
DARWIN, WATCH YOUR STEP!
!!
WALRUS CLIFF!
THIS MUST BE WHERE ELENA ...
LAG!
PATH'S GONE.
WHAT?
OH...
A LAND-SLIDE?!

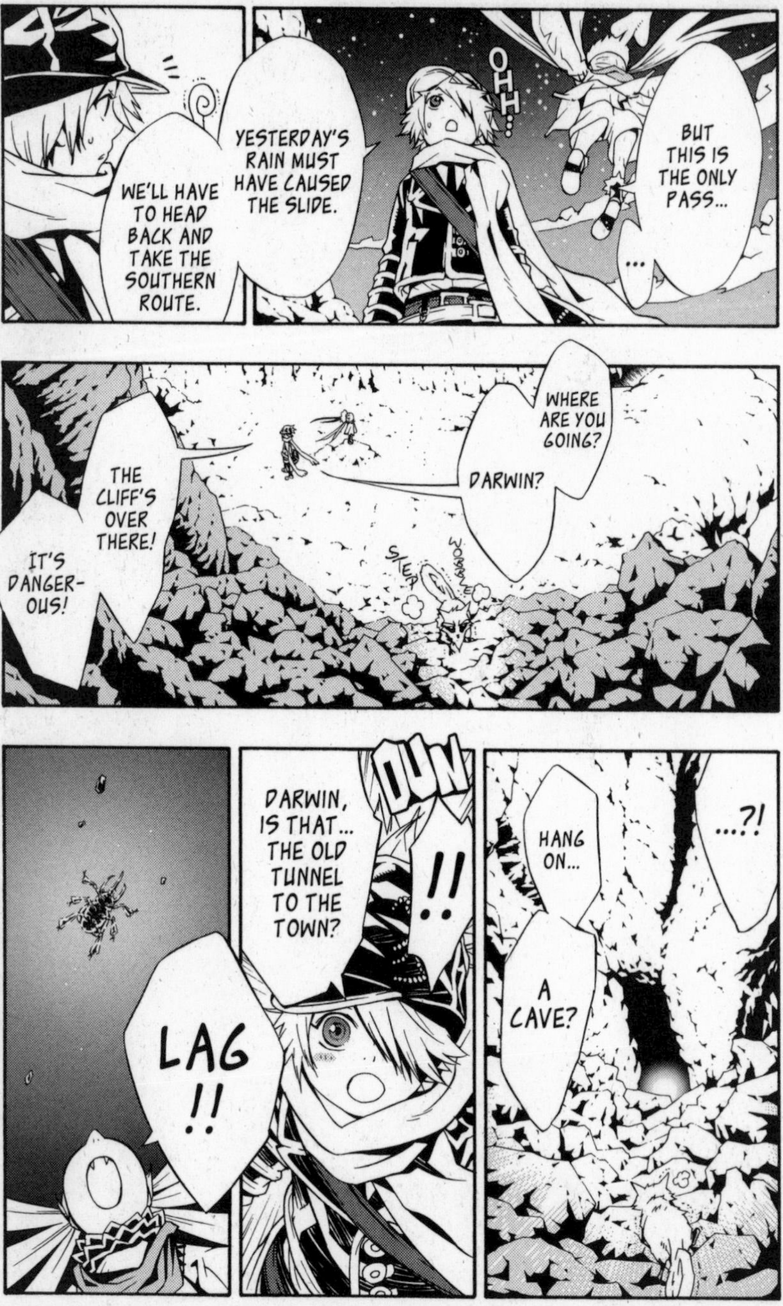
BUT THIS IS THE ONLY PASS...
OHH...
...
YESTERDAY'S RAIN MUST HAVE CAUSED THE SLIDE.
WE'LL HAVE TO HEAD BACK AND TAKE THE SOUTHERN ROUTE.
WHERE ARE YOU GOING?
DARWIN?
SKIP
WOBBLE
THE CLIFF'S OVER THERE!
IT'S DANGER-OUS!
...?!
HANG ON...
A CAVE?
DUN
DARWIN, IS THAT... THE OLD TUNNEL TO THE TOWN?
!!
LAG !!

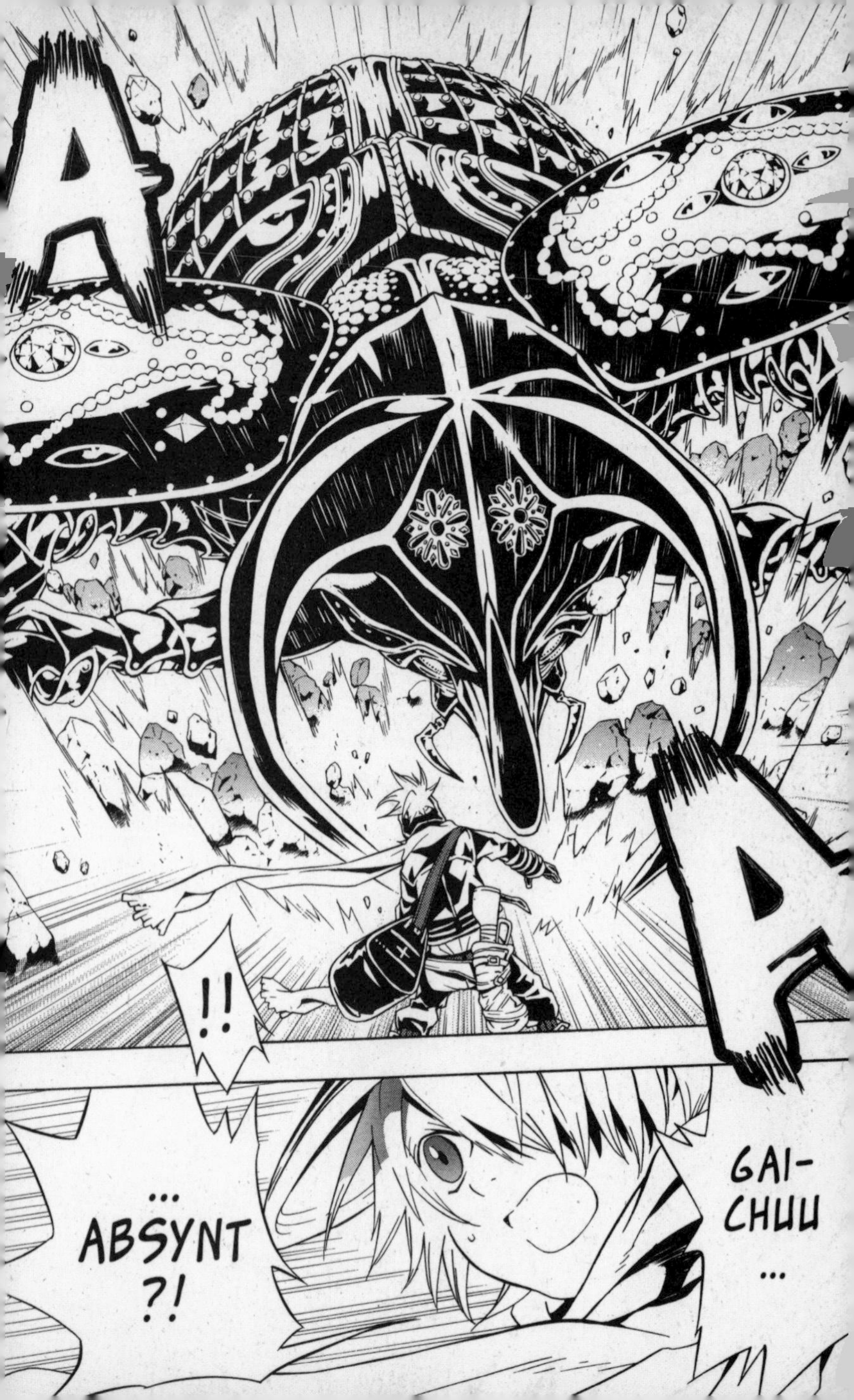

A
A
!!
GAI-
CHUU
...
...
ABSYNT
?!

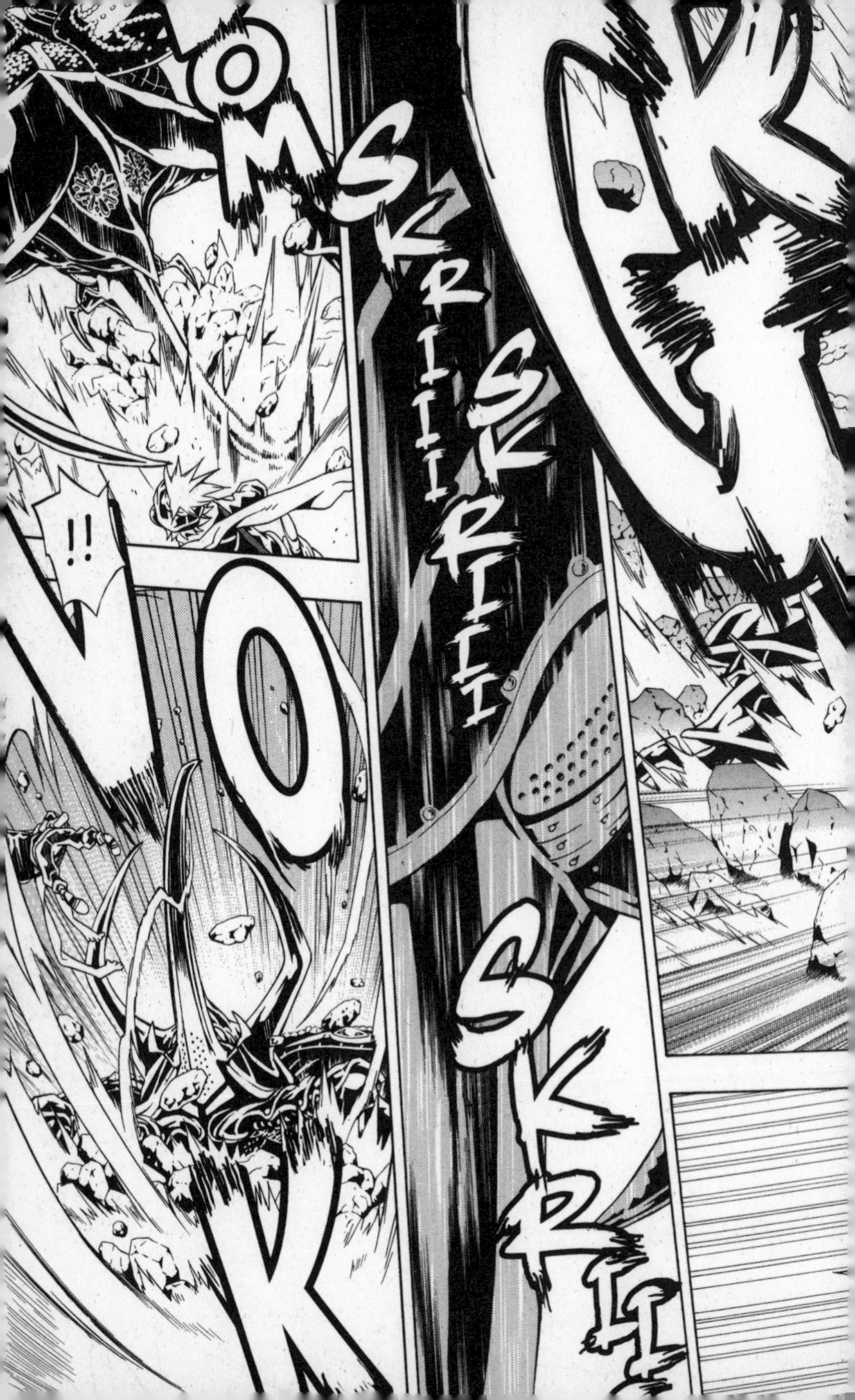
SKRIIII
SKRIII
!!
SKRII

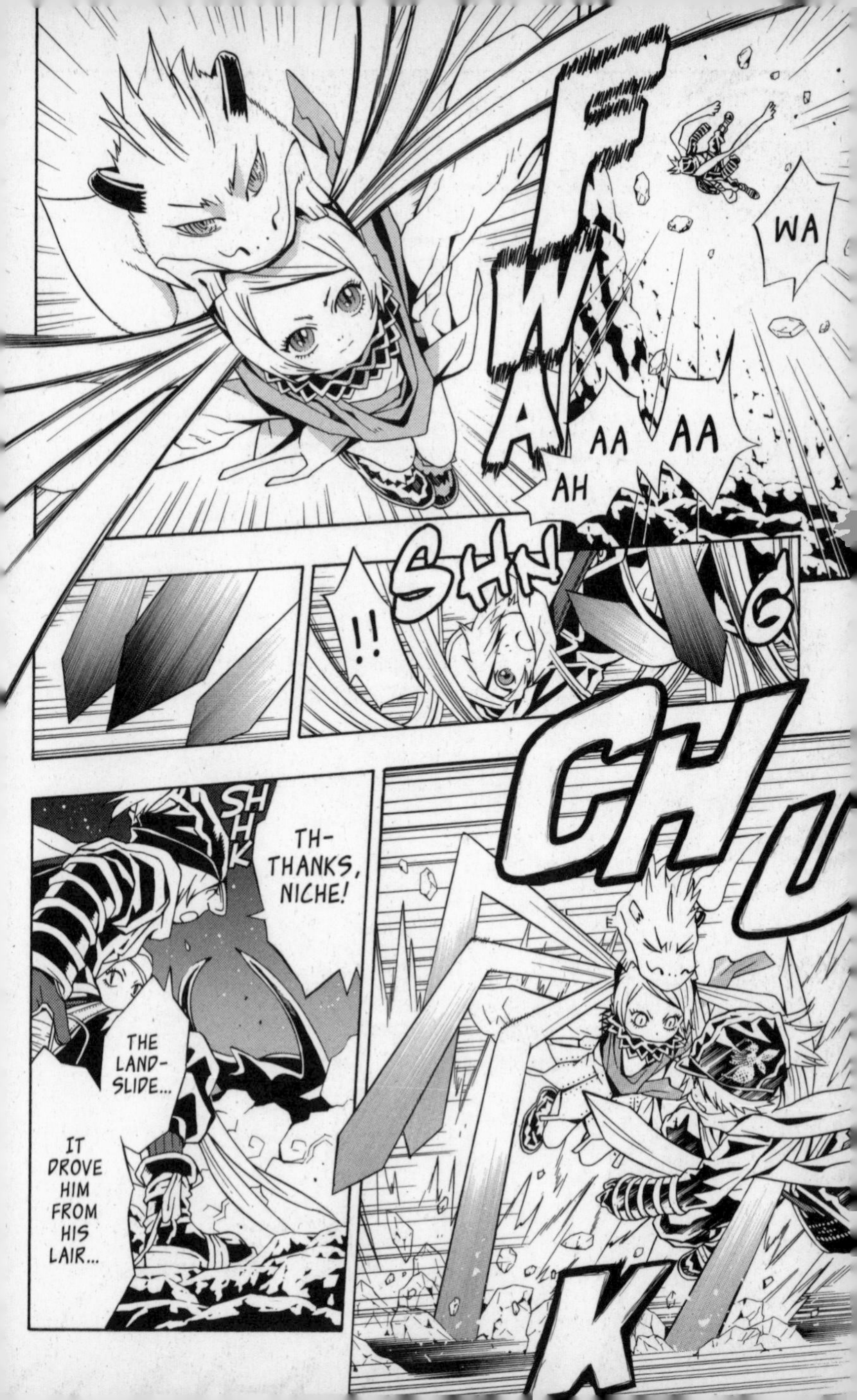
WA
FWA AA AA AH
SHN G
!!
CH
K
SHHK
TH-THANKS, NICHE!
THE LAND-SLIDE...
IT DROVE HIM FROM HIS LAIR...

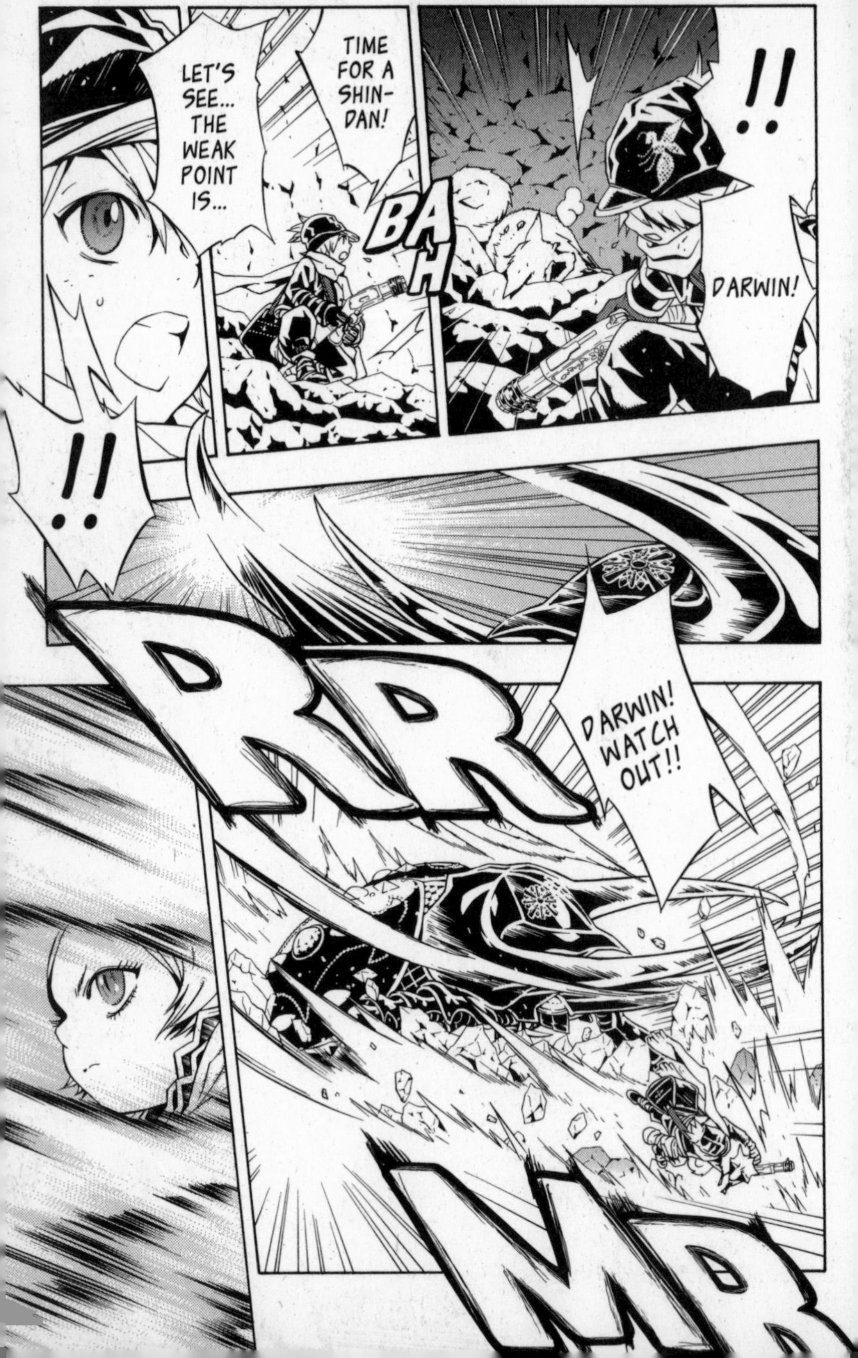
!!
DARWIN!
TIME FOR A SHIN-DAN!
BAH
LET'S SEE... THE WEAK POINT IS...
!!
DARWIN! WATCH OUT!!

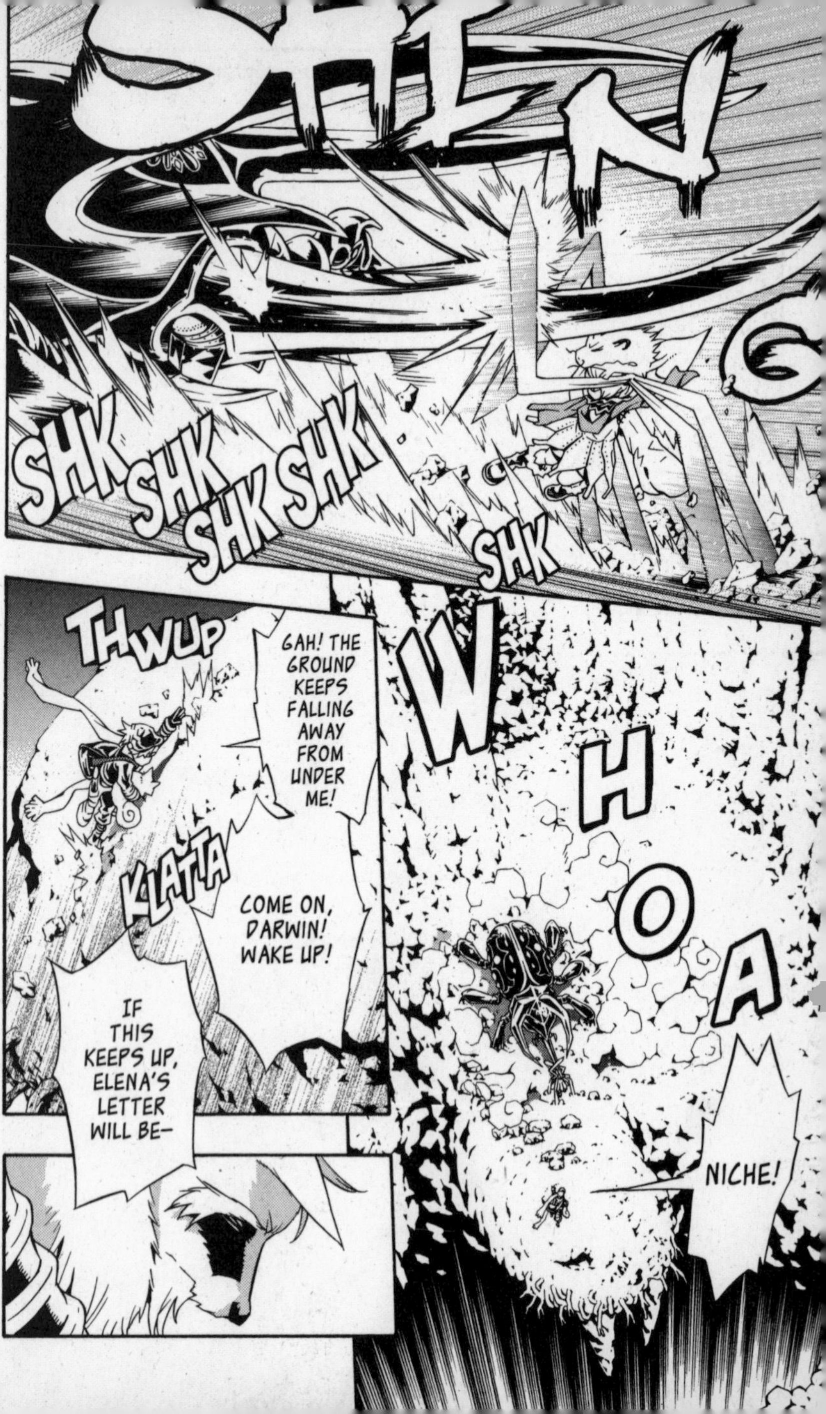
SHING
SHK SHK SHK SHK
SHK
WHOA
NICHE!
THWUP
GAH! THE GROUND KEEPS FALLING AWAY FROM UNDER ME!
KLATTA
COME ON, DARWIN! WAKE UP!
IF THIS KEEPS UP, ELENA'S LETTER WILL BE—

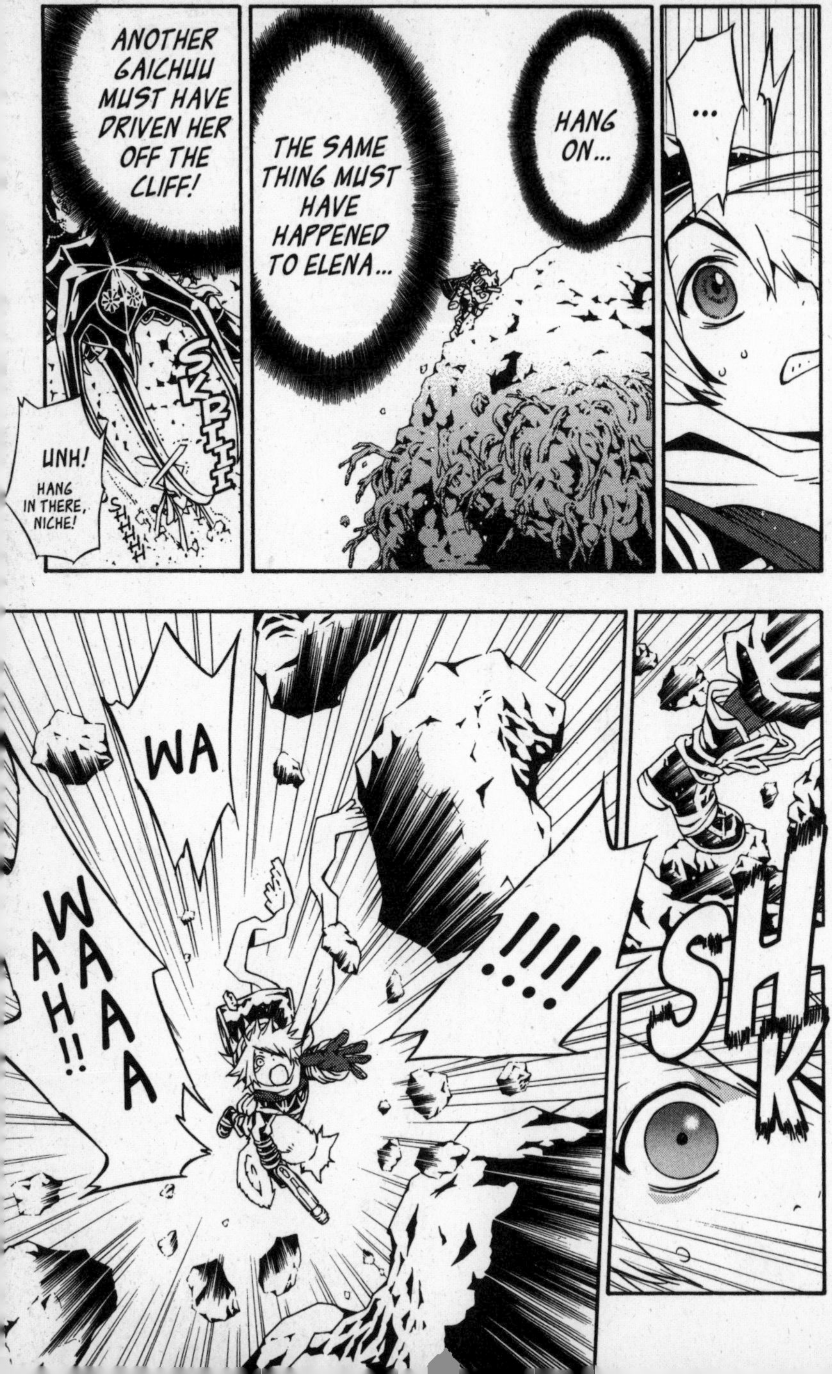
...
HANG ON...
THE SAME THING MUST HAVE HAPPENED TO ELENA...
ANOTHER GAICHUU MUST HAVE DRIVEN HER OFF THE CLIFF!
SKRIII
UNH!
HANG IN THERE, NICHE!
SHHHHH
SHK
!!!!
WA
WAAAAA
AAH!!

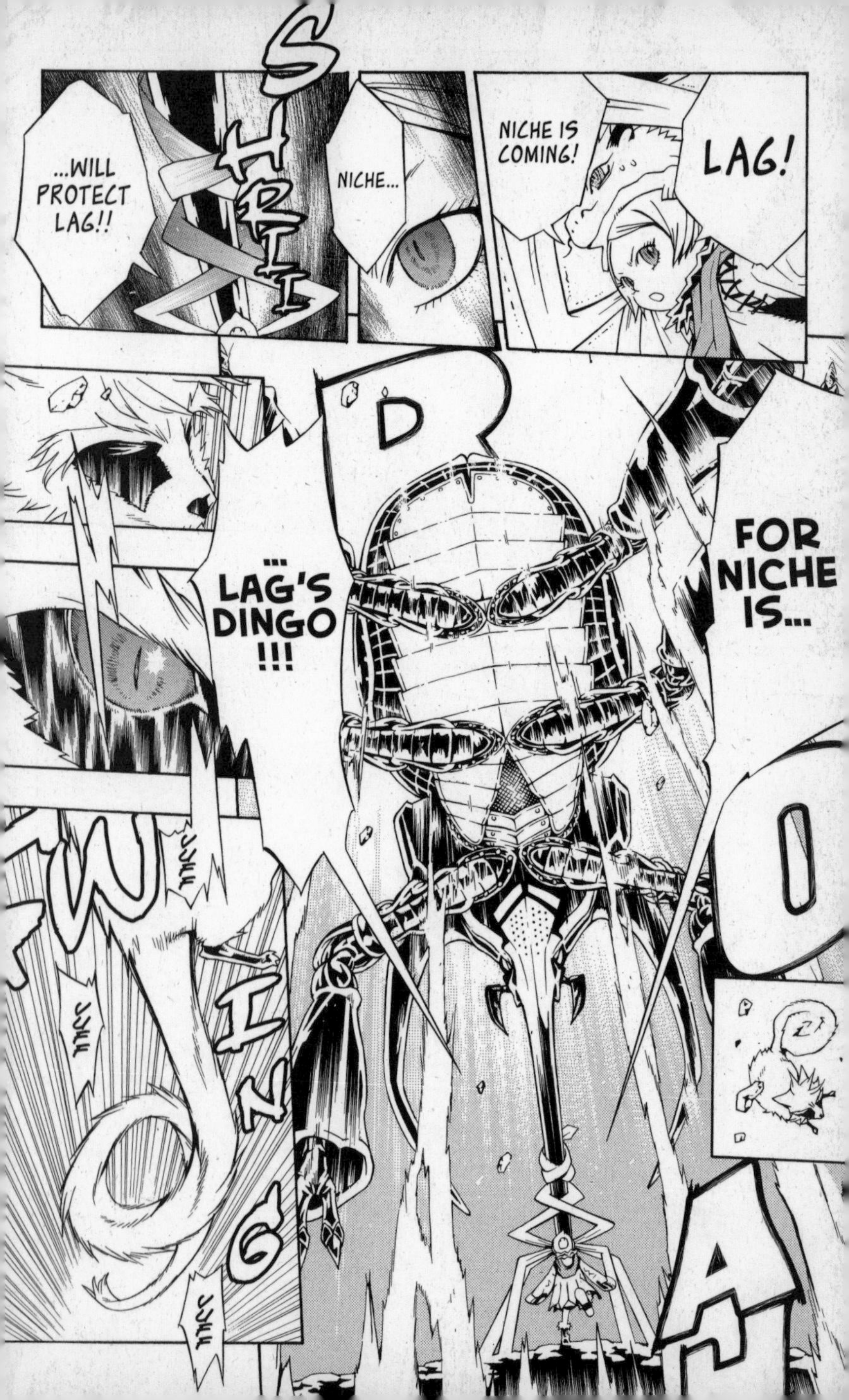
LAG!
NICHE IS COMING!
NICHE...
...WILL PROTECT LAG!!
SHRII
FOR NICHE IS...
...LAG'S DINGO!!!

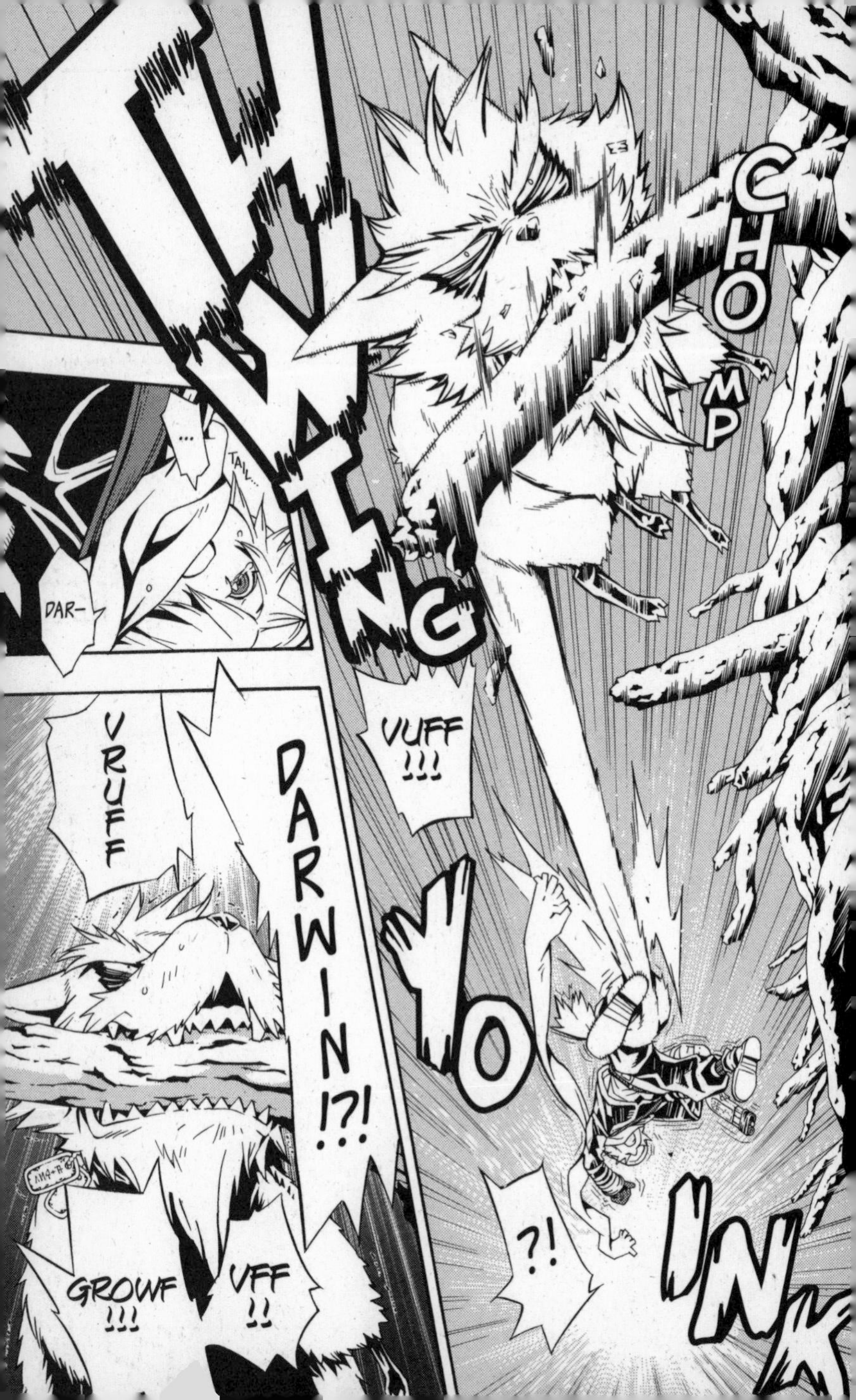
CHOMP
...
TAIL...
DAR-
VUFF !!!
DARWIN!?!
VRUFF
YO
INK
?!
UFF !!
GROWF !!!

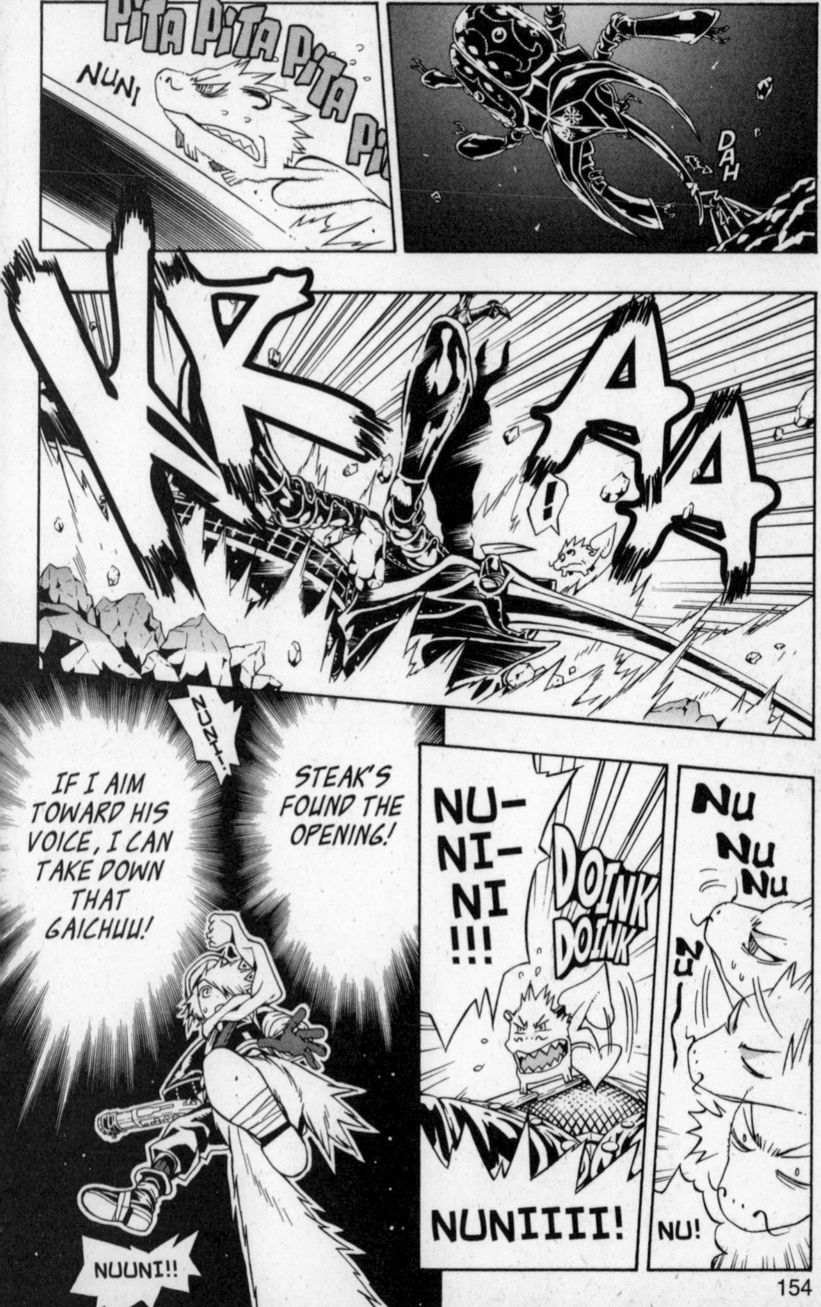
DAH
PITA PITA PITA PI
NUNI
KAA
!
NU
NU
NU
NU!
NU-
NI-
NI
!!!
DOINK
DOINK
NUNIIII!
NUNI!!
STEAK'S FOUND THE OPENING!
IF I AIM TOWARD HIS VOICE, I CAN TAKE DOWN THAT GAICHUU!
NUUNI!!

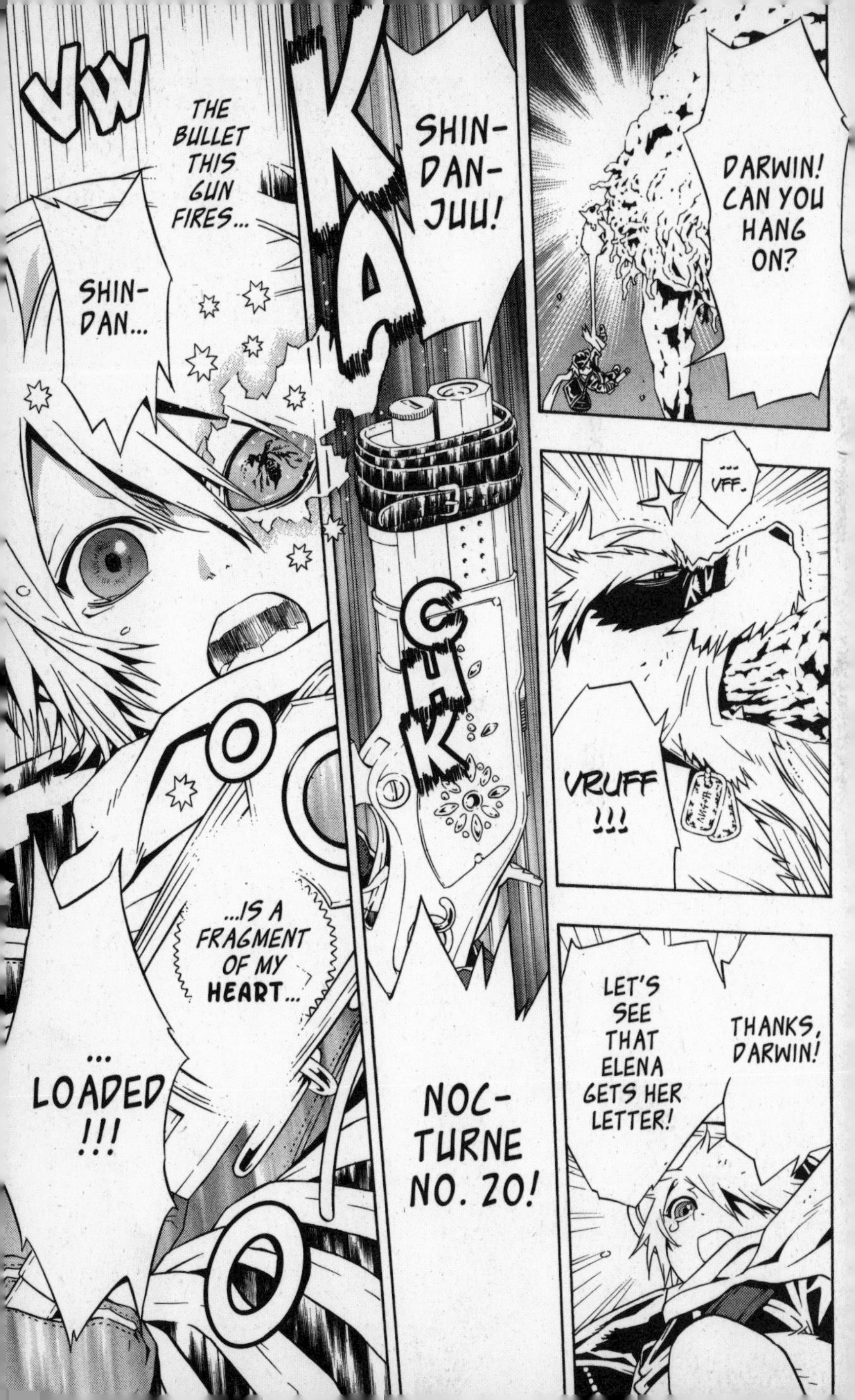
DARWIN! CAN YOU HANG ON?
... VFF..
VRUFF !!!
THANKS, DARWIN!
LET'S SEE THAT ELENA GETS HER LETTER!
KA
SHIN-DAN-JUU!
CHK
NOC-TURNE NO. 20!
VW
THE BULLET THIS GUN FIRES...
SHIN-DAN...
...IS A FRAGMENT OF MY HEART...
... LOADED !!!

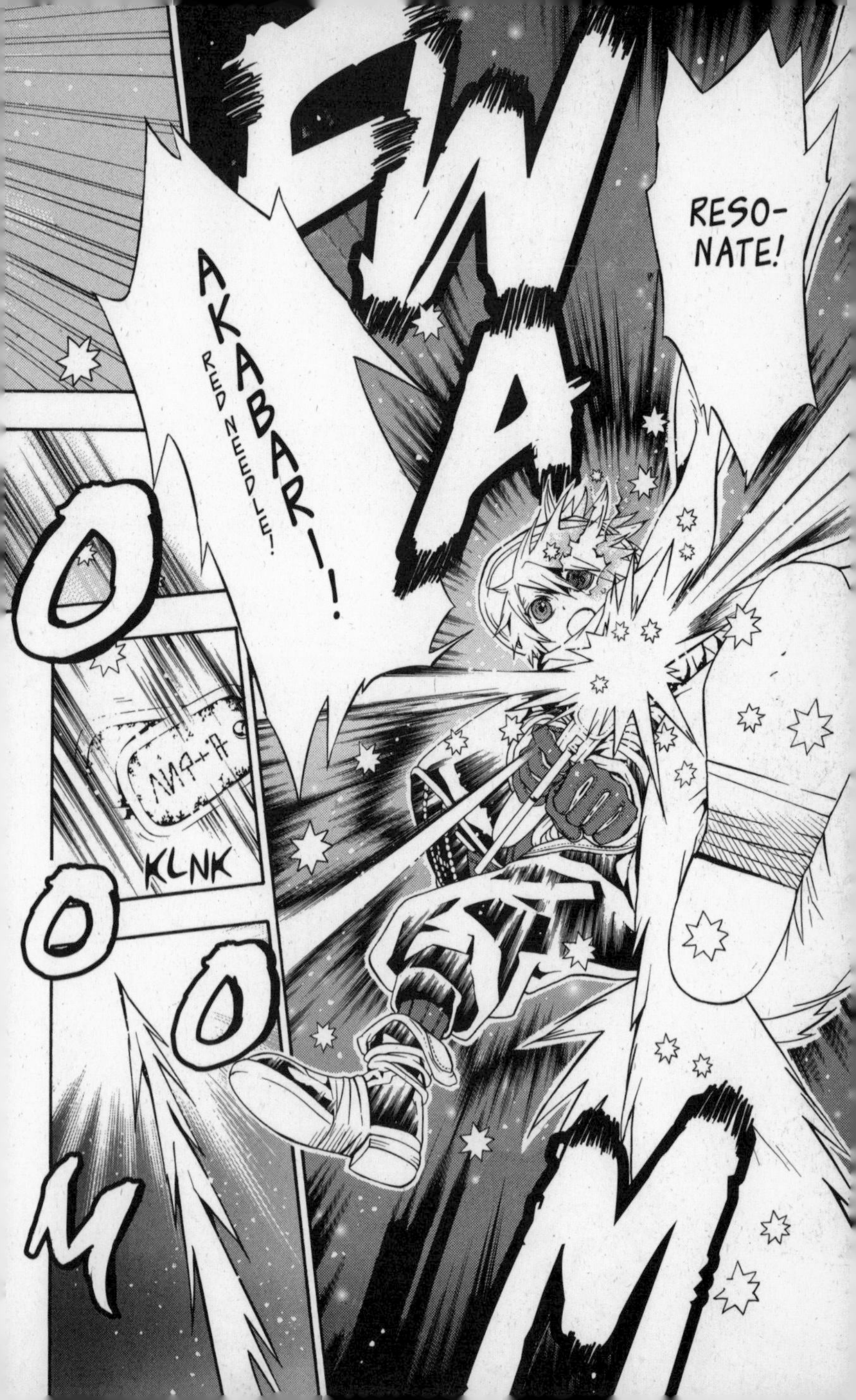
RESO-
NATE!
AKABARI!!
RED NEEDLE!
KLNK

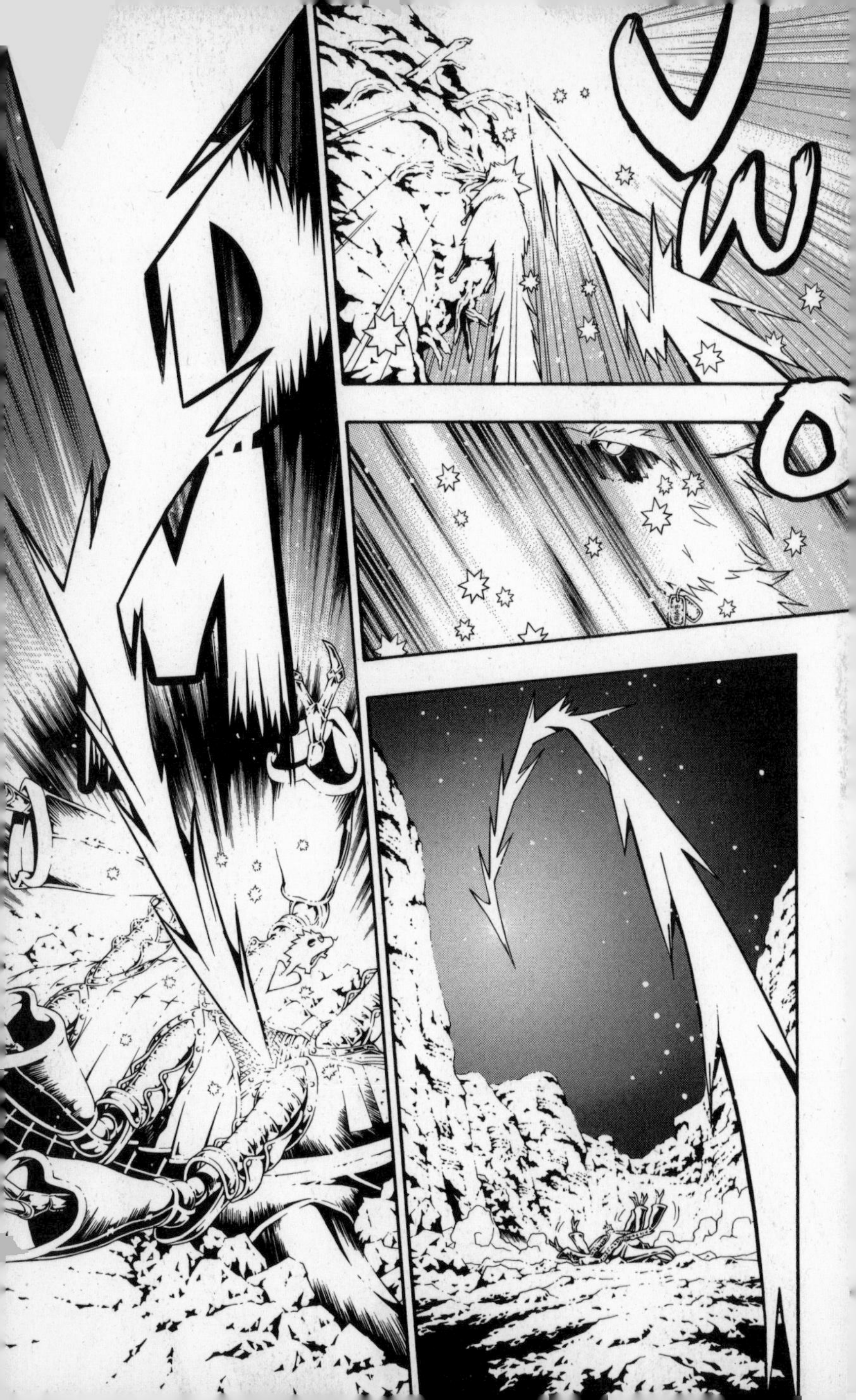

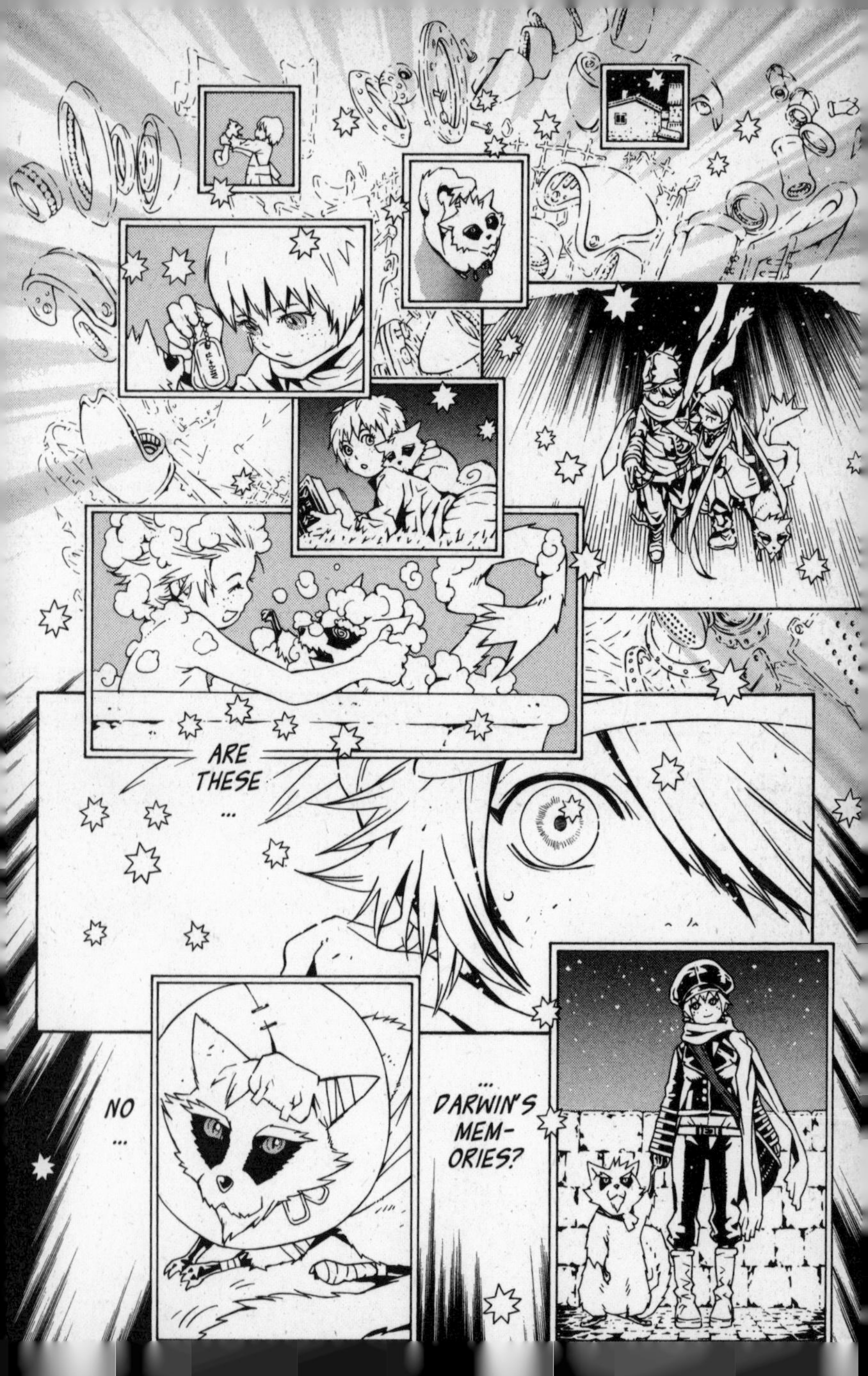
ARE THESE ...
NO ...
... DARWIN'S MEM-ORIES?

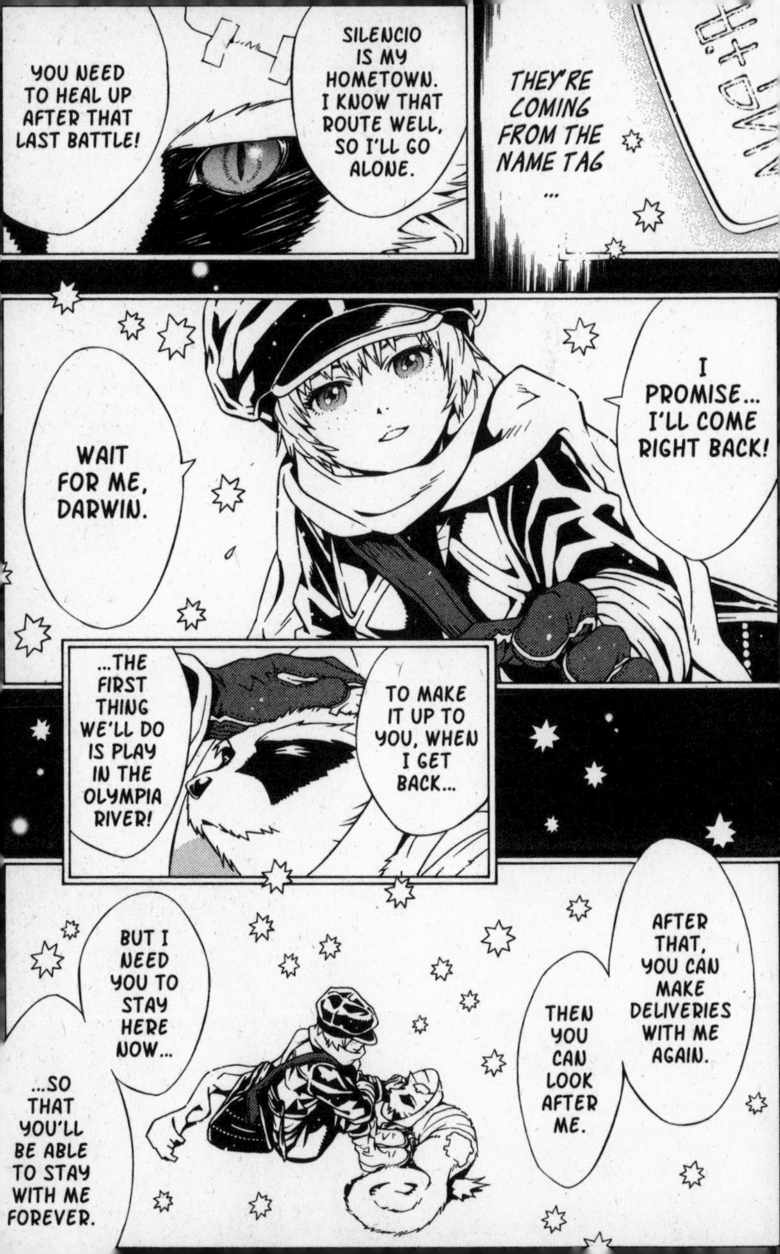

THEY'RE COMING FROM THE NAME TAG ...
SILENCIO IS MY HOMETOWN. I KNOW THAT ROUTE WELL, SO I'LL GO ALONE.
YOU NEED TO HEAL UP AFTER THAT LAST BATTLE!
I PROMISE... I'LL COME RIGHT BACK!
WAIT FOR ME, DARWIN.
TO MAKE IT UP TO YOU, WHEN I GET BACK...
...THE FIRST THING WE'LL DO IS PLAY IN THE OLYMPIA RIVER!
AFTER THAT, YOU CAN MAKE DELIVERIES WITH ME AGAIN.
THEN YOU CAN LOOK AFTER ME.
BUT I NEED YOU TO STAY HERE NOW...
...SO THAT YOU'LL BE ABLE TO STAY WITH ME FOREVER.

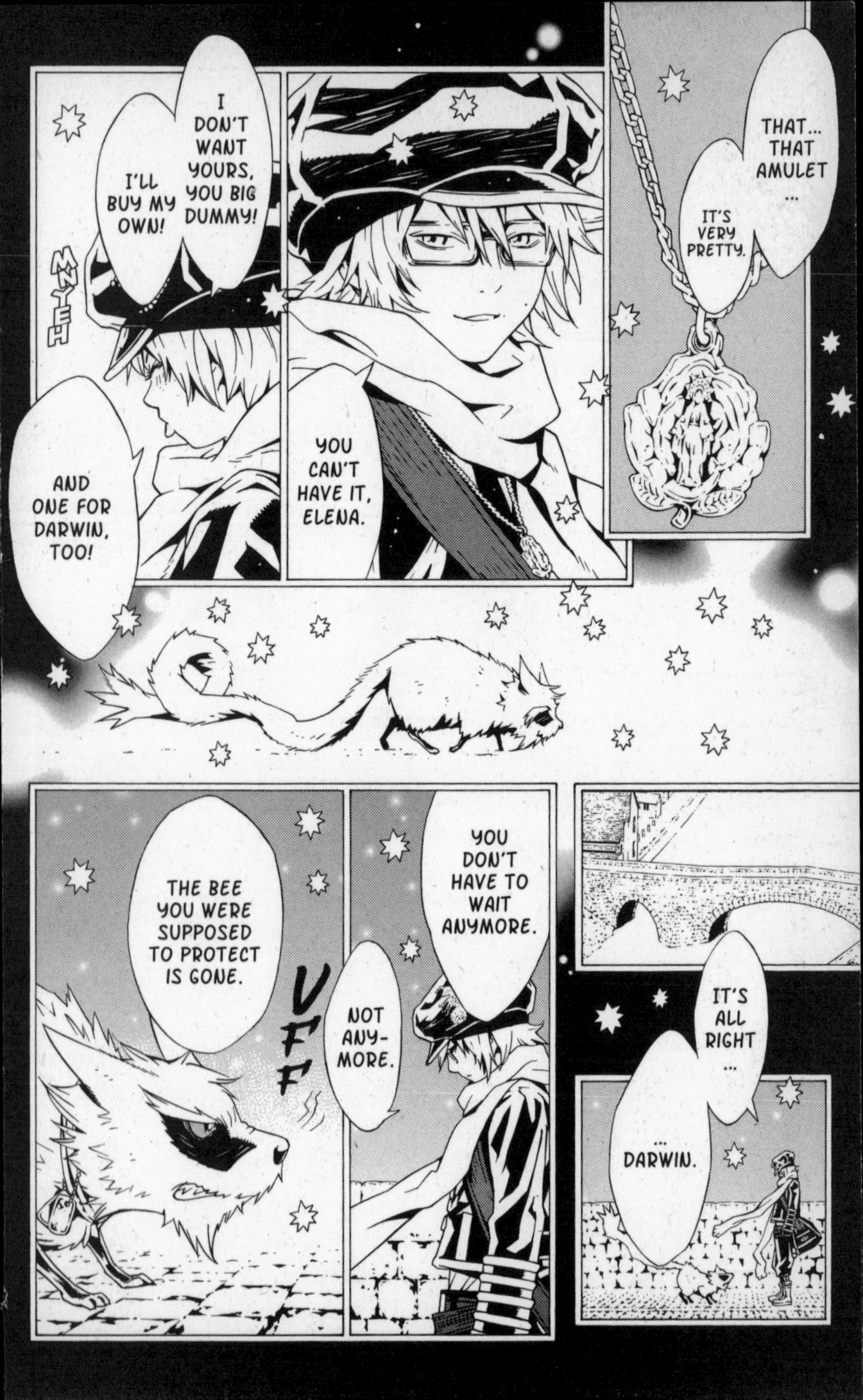
THAT... THAT AMULET ...
IT'S VERY PRETTY.
YOU CAN'T HAVE IT, ELENA.
I DON'T WANT YOURS, YOU BIG DUMMY!
I'LL BUY MY OWN!
MNYEH
AND ONE FOR DARWIN, TOO!
IT'S ALL RIGHT ...
... DARWIN.
YOU DON'T HAVE TO WAIT ANYMORE.
NOT ANY-MORE.
THE BEE YOU WERE SUPPOSED TO PROTECT IS GONE.
VFF

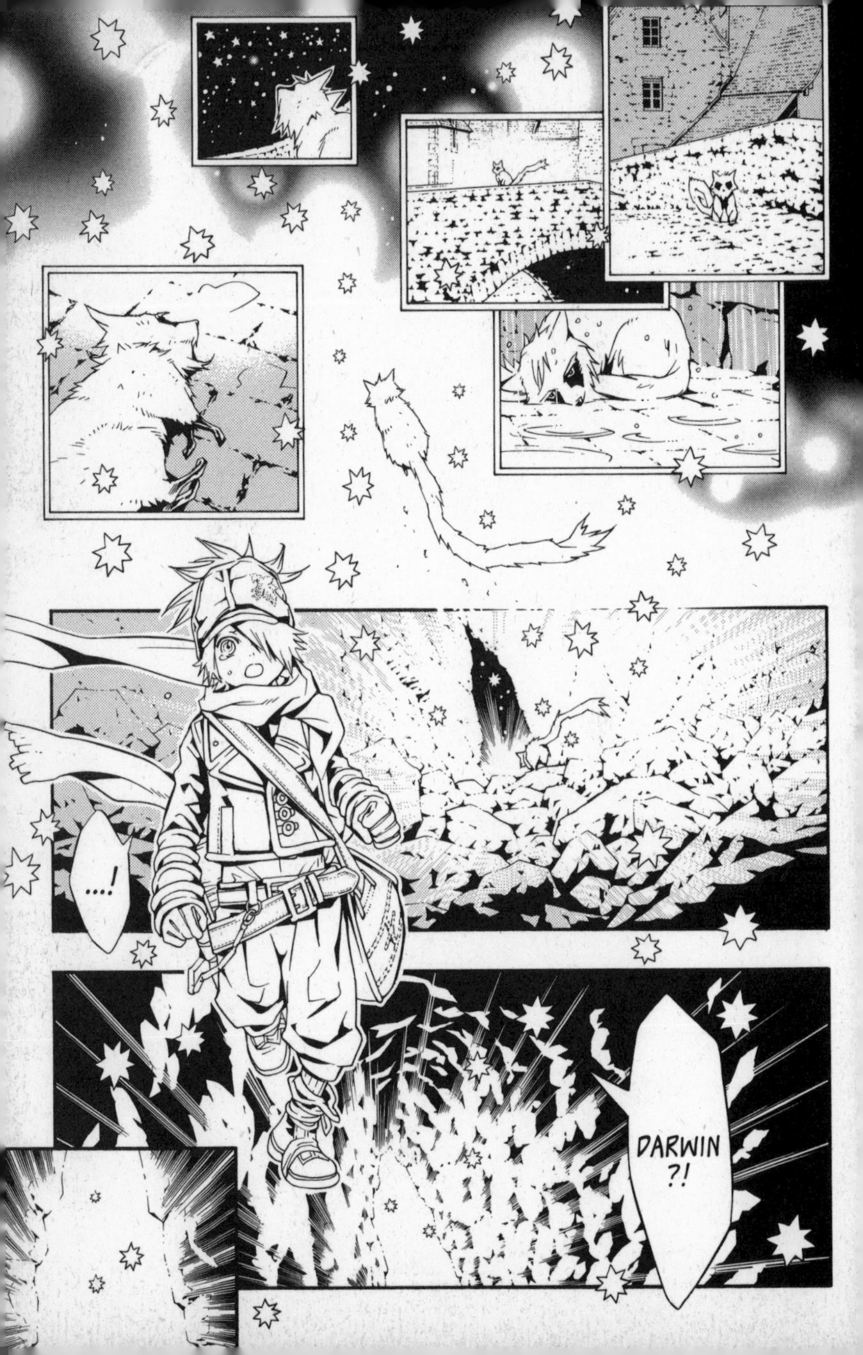
...!
DARWIN ?!

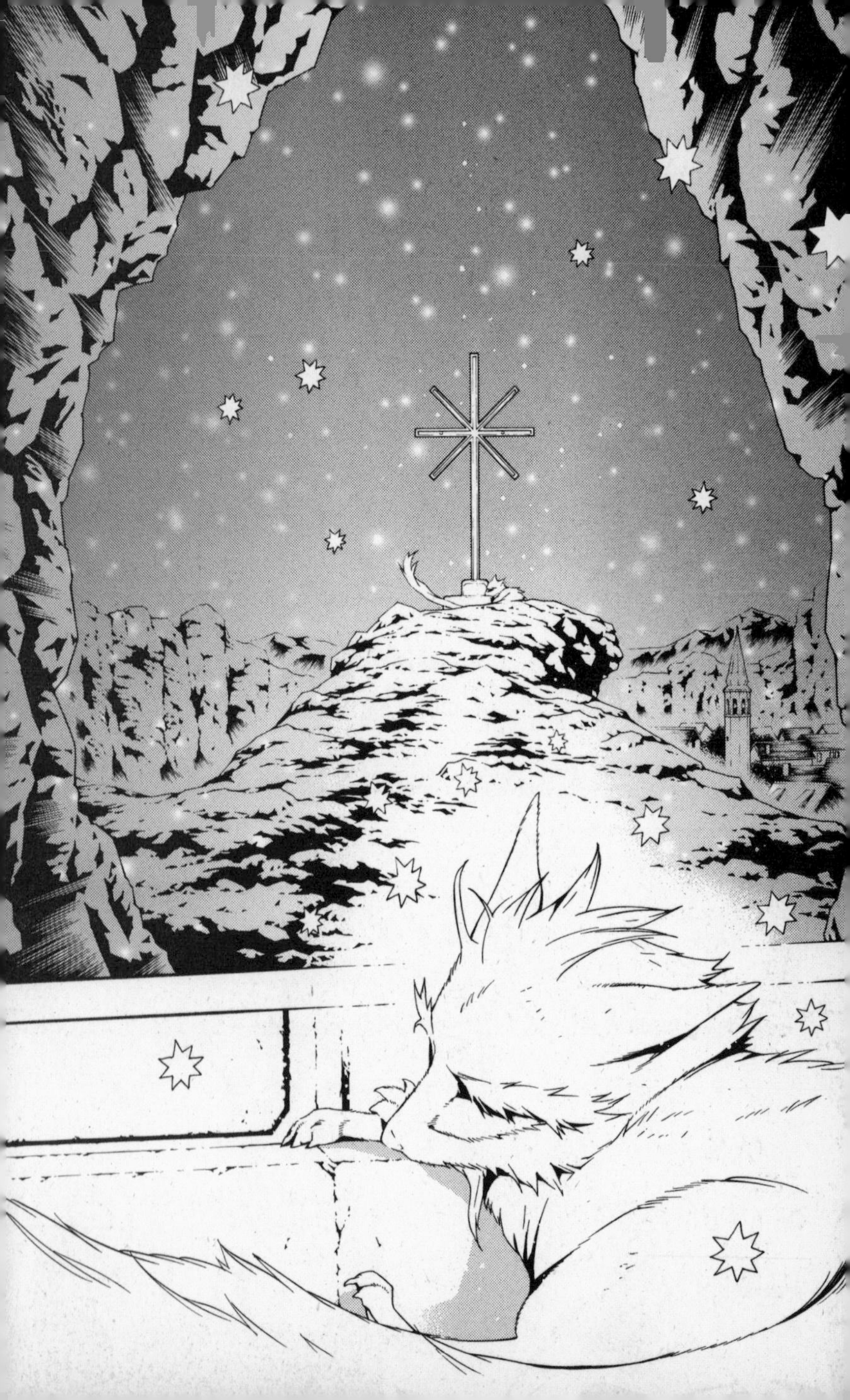

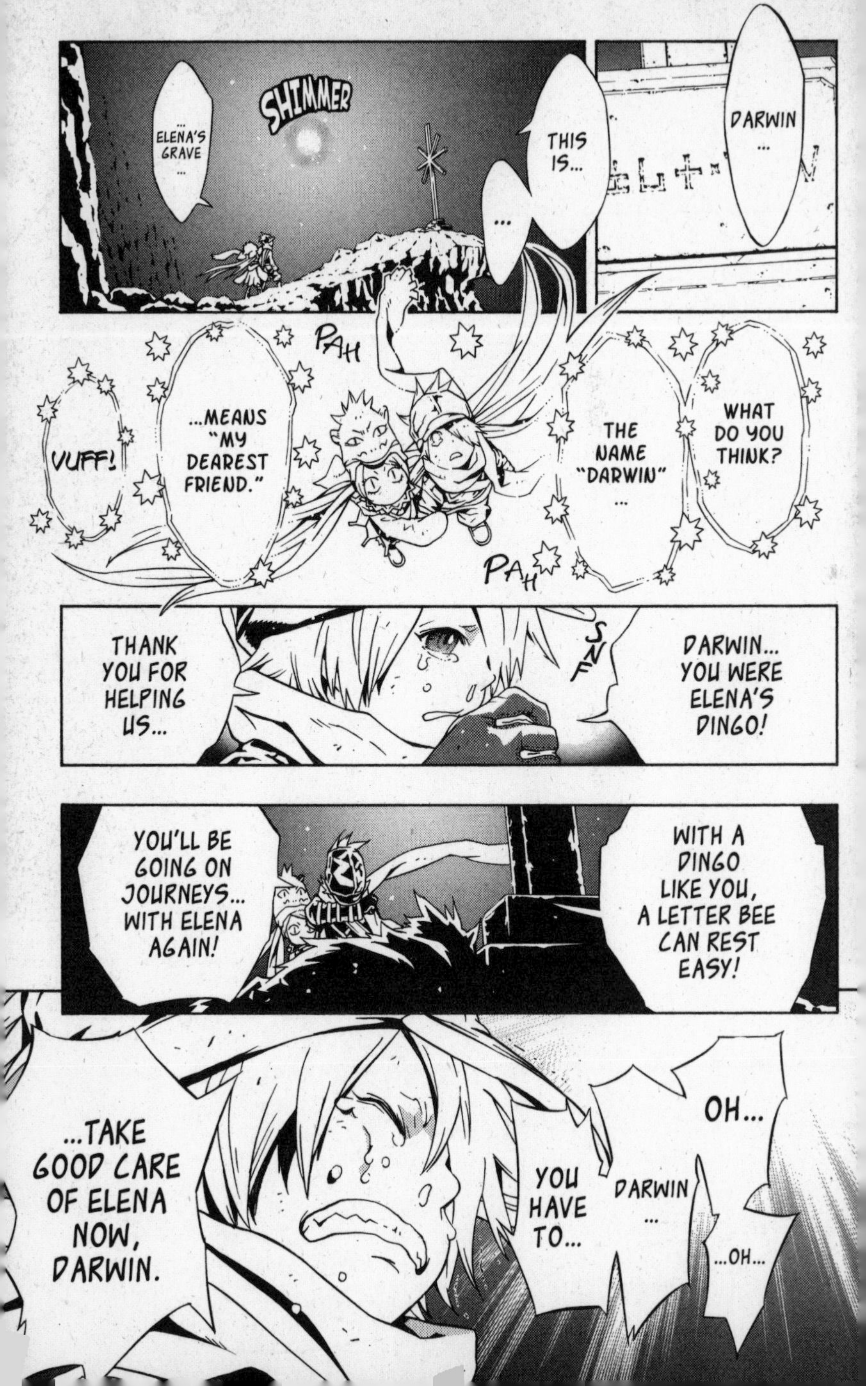
DARWIN...
...
THIS IS...
...ELENA'S GRAVE...
SHIMMER
WHAT DO YOU THINK?
THE NAME "DARWIN"...
...MEANS "MY DEAREST FRIEND."
VUFF!
PAH
PAH
DARWIN... YOU WERE ELENA'S DINGO!
SNF
THANK YOU FOR HELPING US...
WITH A DINGO LIKE YOU, A LETTER BEE CAN REST EASY!
YOU'LL BE GOING ON JOURNEYS... WITH ELENA AGAIN!
OH...
DARWIN...
...OH...
YOU HAVE TO...
...TAKE GOOD CARE OF ELENA NOW, DARWIN.

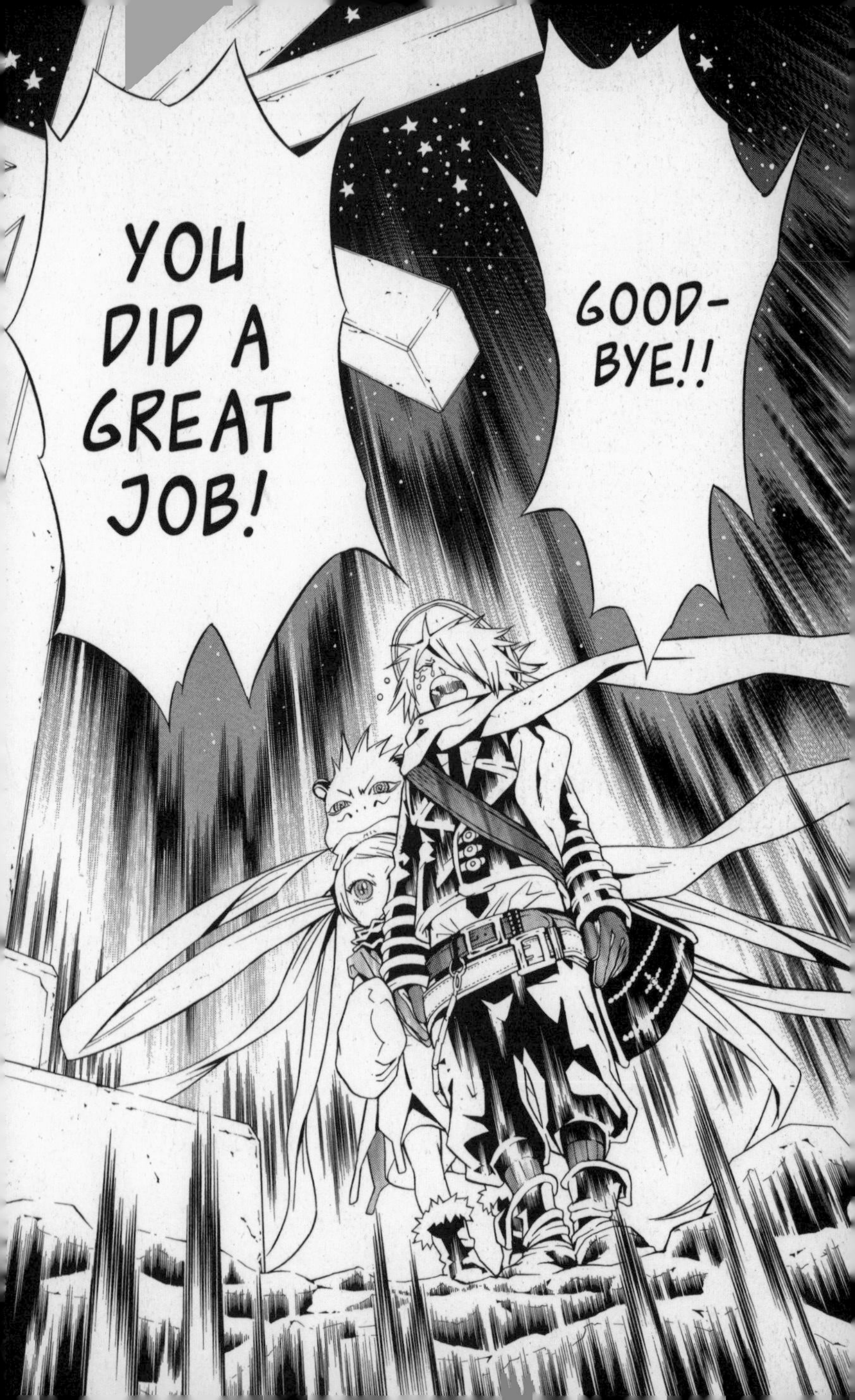
GOOD-BYE!!
YOU DID A GREAT JOB!

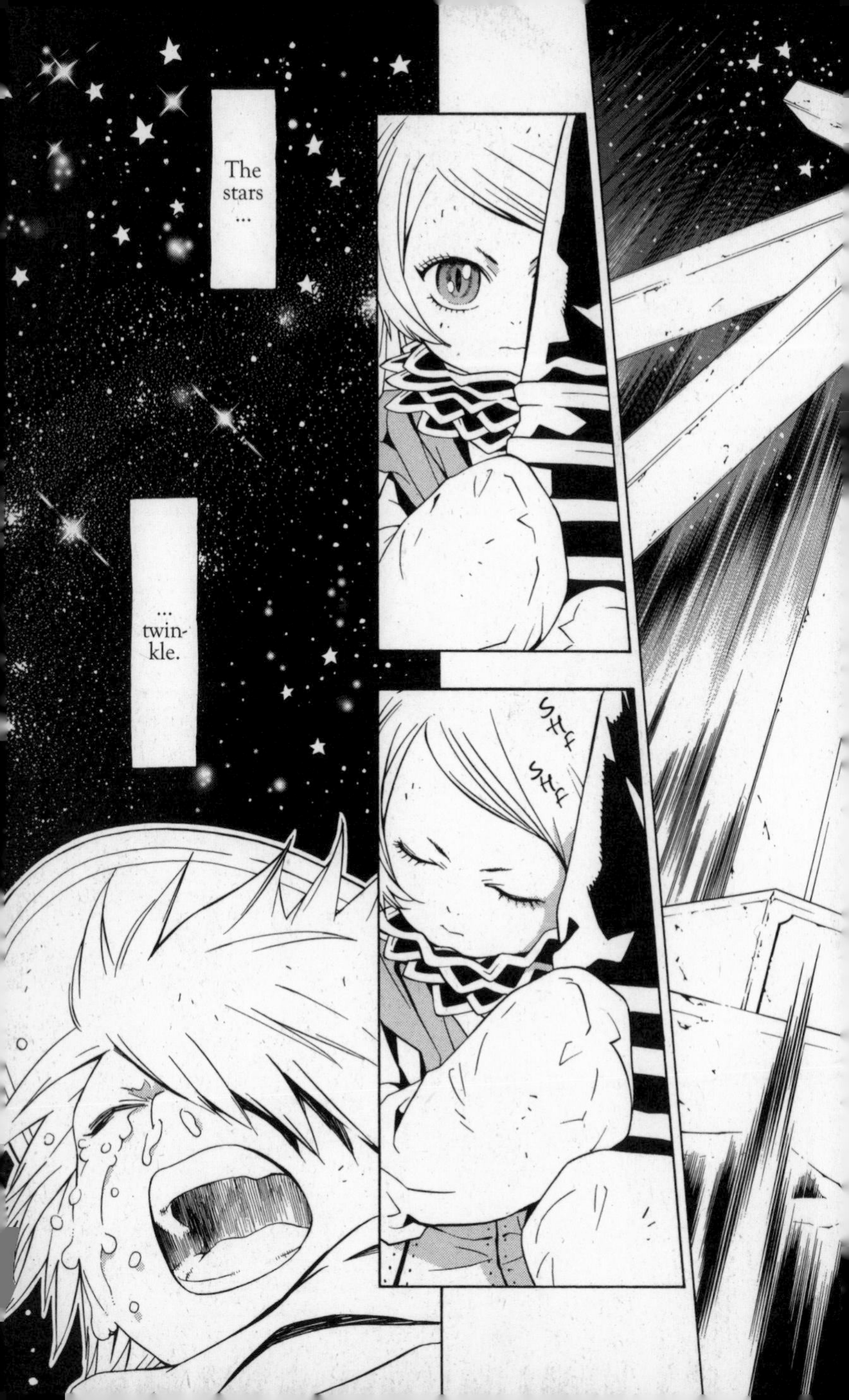
The stars ...
... twinkle.
SHff
SHff

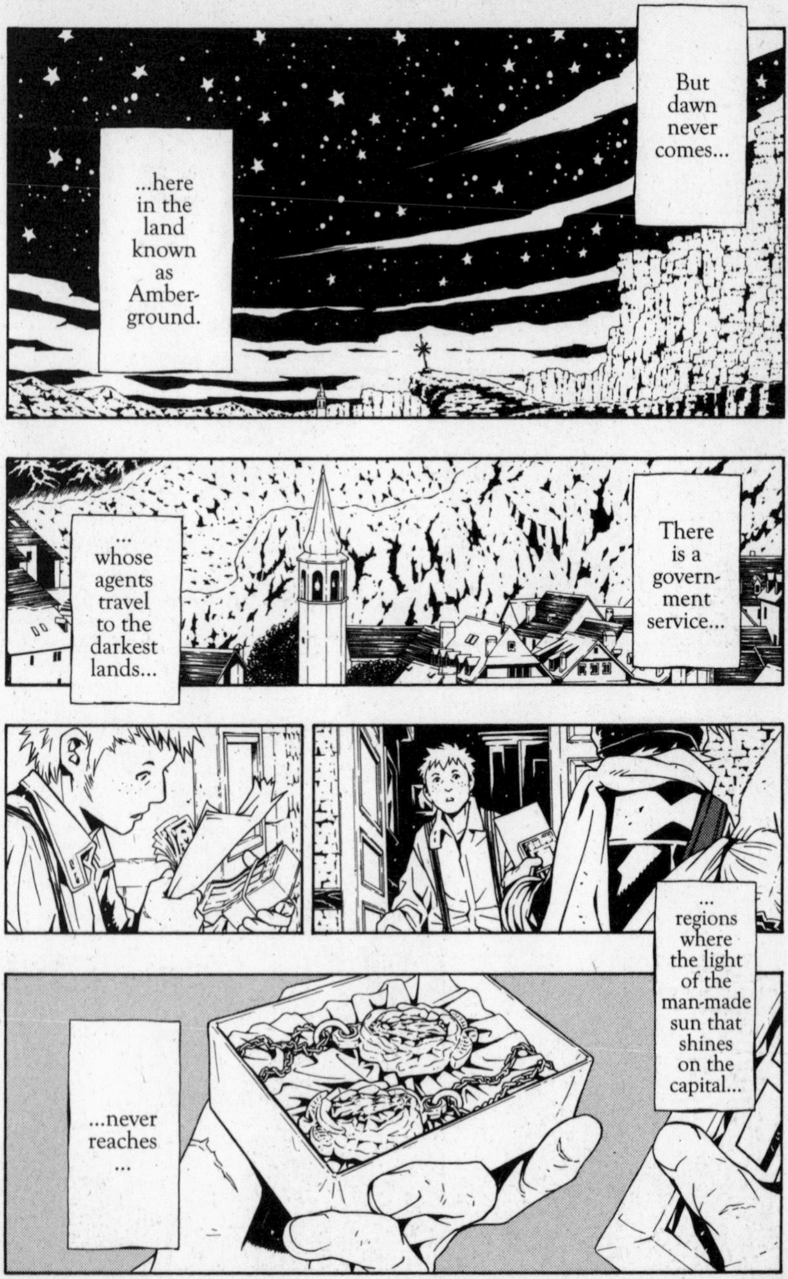
But dawn never comes...
...here in the land known as Amber-ground.
There is a govern-ment service...
...whose agents travel to the darkest lands...
...regions where the light of the man-made sun that shines on the capital...
...never reaches...

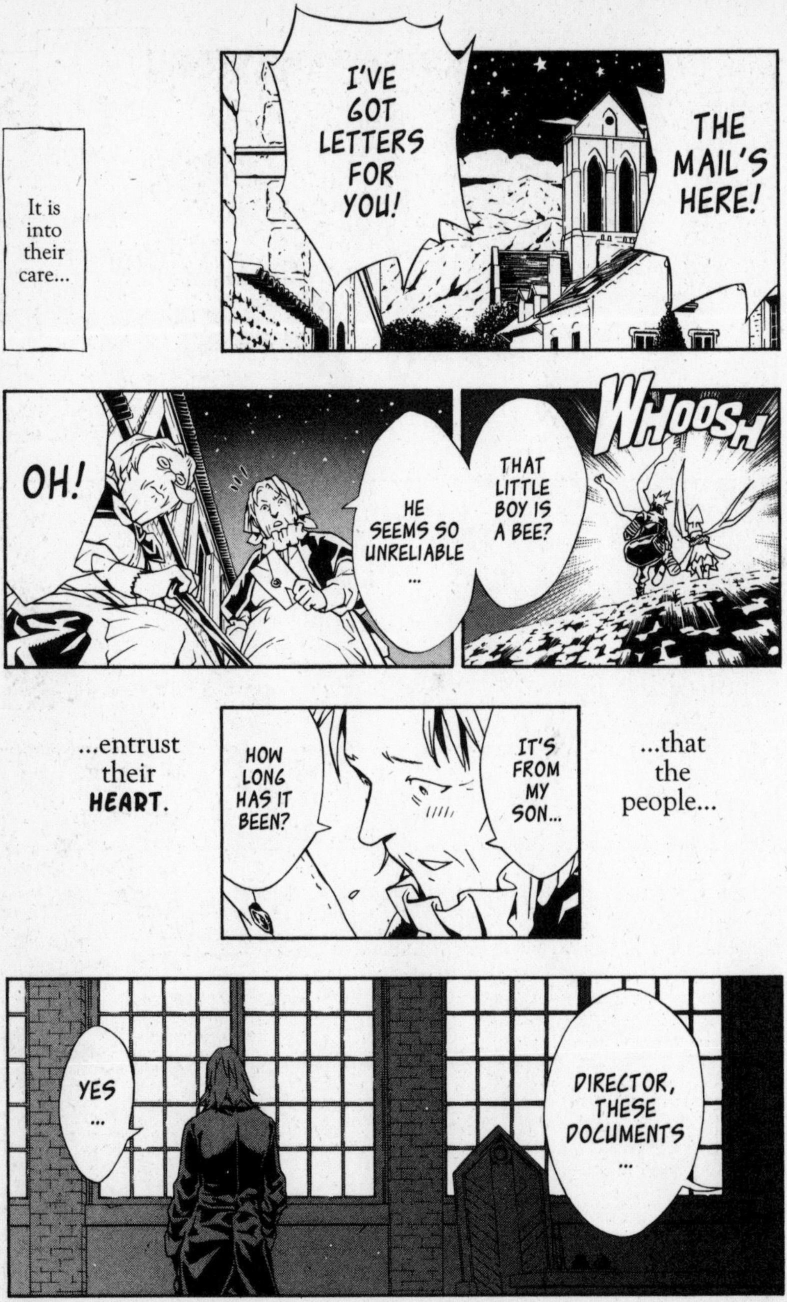
THE MAIL'S HERE!
I'VE GOT LETTERS FOR YOU!
It is into their care...
WHOOSH
THAT LITTLE BOY IS A BEE?
HE SEEMS SO UNRELIABLE...
OH!
...that the people...
IT'S FROM MY SON...
HOW LONG HAS IT BEEN?
...entrust their HEART.
DIRECTOR, THESE DOCUMENTS...
YES...

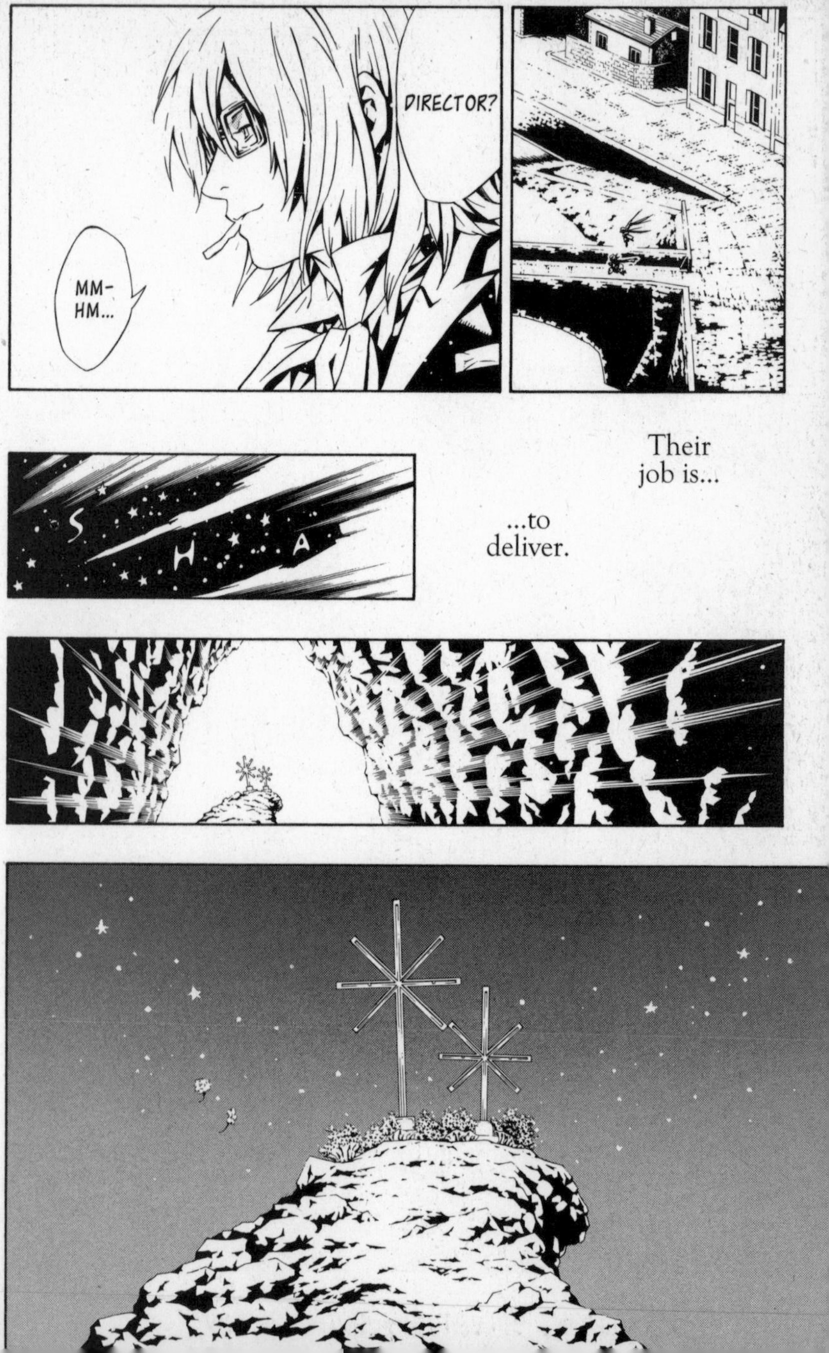
DIRECTOR?
MM-HM...
Their job is...
...to deliver.
SHA

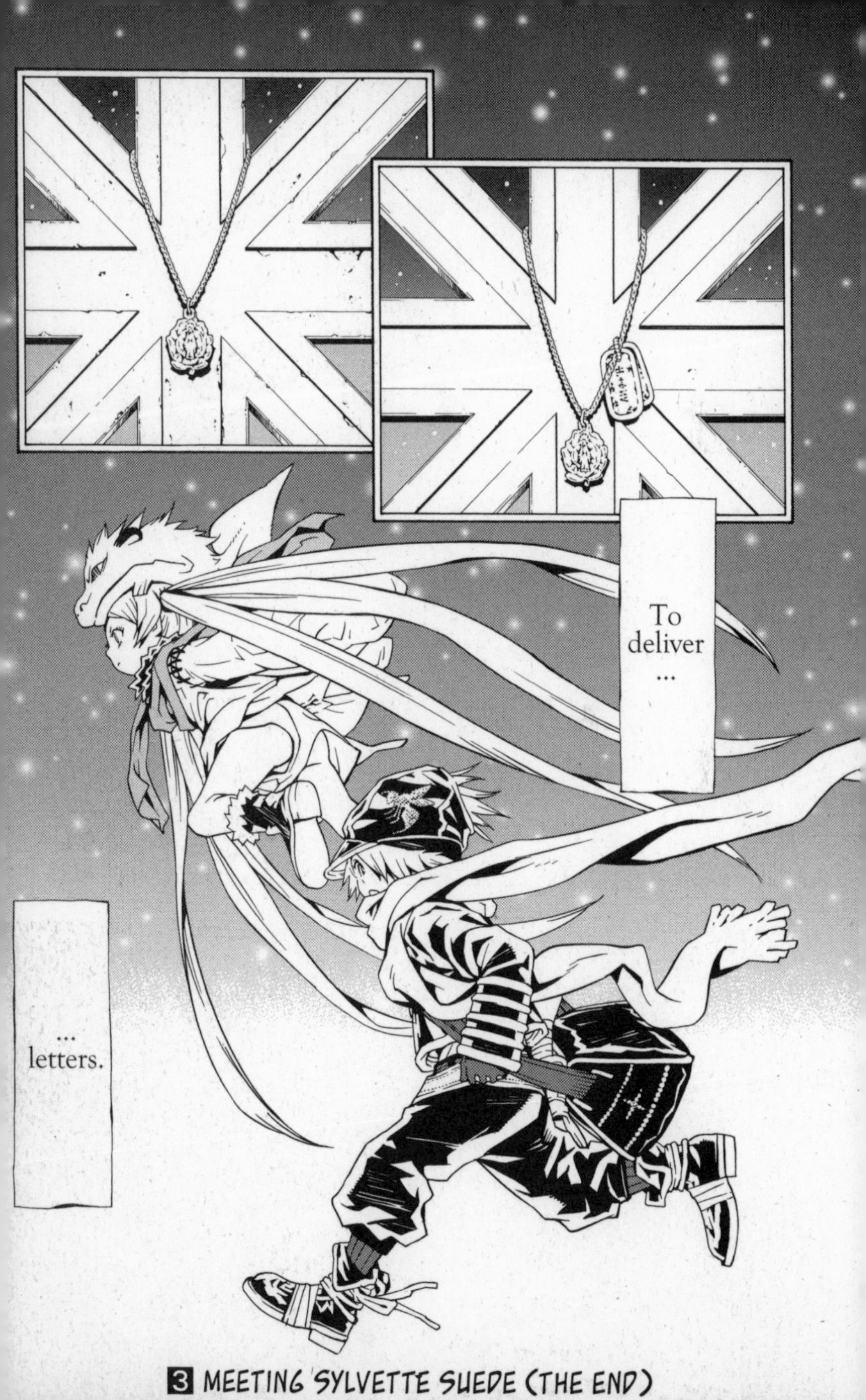
To deliver ...
... letters.

3 MEETING SYLVETTE SUEDE (THE END)

Dr. Thunderland's Reference Desk

I am Dr. Thunderland.

Thunderland!!

I heard that my son appeared in this volume—or something to that effect.

Ah, at last it seems my long preface is done. I'll make my appearance very soon, or so I think. I'm ready, so… Please?

I work at the Beehive in Yuusari, researching all manner of things.

For today's lesson, let's discuss the items I've compiled about Amberground and its environs.

Oh, but how I envy my son… Why did he get to appear before me? He takes after his mother. She never had any patience either.

■ FLAT

This is a kind of apartment. Sylvette's home is a two-story maisonnette type. (A maisonnette is a self-contained apartment, usually on two floors of a larger house with its own entrance.) It seems Gauche's room was on the upper floor since Sylvette's legs prohibit her from using the stairs. They may cause her more worries, but for now Lag and Niche will keep things lively for her.

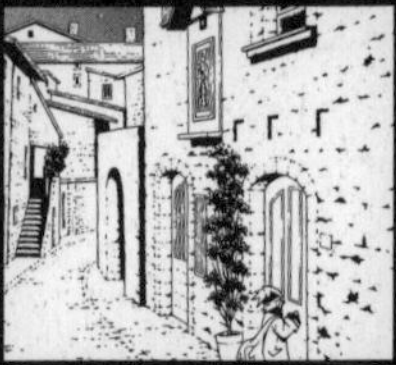

■ SINNERS WEAPONS AND BAKE SHOP

This shop is in Central Yuusari. When it was first opened, it seems it dealt exclusively in weapons, but now, in Mr. Gobeni's generation, it is mainly a bakery. But didn't you think it was strange for Gauche to say the bread was tasty? He must have weird tastes. There must be something wrong with the Suedes' taste buds.

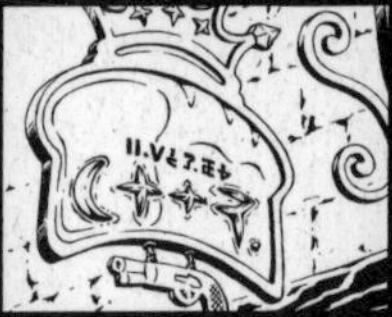

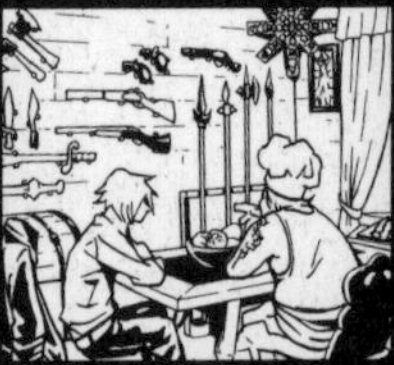

■ NOCTURNE NO. 20 (SHINDANJUU)

This rather old model of gun is a masterpiece created by Frederick Chopin in his legendary workshop. Many workshops produce guns and other weapons, but few have attained the status of legend. Each weapon's foundry has its own particular specialty. A Letter Bee's weapon is vitally important, for he entrusts his life and his heart to it. Selecting the right weapon maker is important, but there seem to be fewer good artisans lately. It's quite a sad situation really.

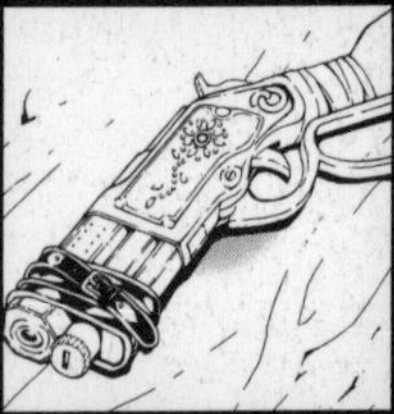

nb: *Nocturne:* 19th-century European musical compositions. Chopin developed nocturnes into romantic pieces. Nocturne No. 20 in C# Minor premiered posthumously. Frederic Francois Chopin (1810–1849); Fryderyk Franciszek Szopen in Polish.

■ DAY OF THE FLICKER

Twelve years ago, the man-made sun flickered. The public was given no details about the occurrence. Though its light is weak, it is constant— at least it was until that moment. For one instant, the world was thrown into utter darkness. Throughout Akatsuki and Yuusari, people feared for a moment that the light was lost forever. Strange effects were reported throughout Amberground, as you saw with Gauche, who witnessed the flicker firsthand. The official word was that the sun was undergoing routine maintenance work. It's no surprise that people distrust the government!

There were survivors from the crash of the investigation airship, but they aren't saying anything about the case. My son is one of them actually. But what a surprise to find that Lag and Sylvette were both born on that day! Hmm. There's probably something to it. I think this case needs further study.

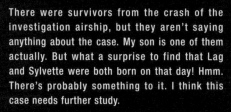

Incidentally, the 311th day of each year is celebrated as the Day of the Flicker. Even in Central Yuusari, this day is a holiday, and the citizens remain quietly at home to mark the occasion.

■ GEORGE'S LITTLE VILLAGE

This village, the hometown of the female writer George Sandstorm, rose to fame when she used it as a motif in her novels. Soon no one referred to it by its real name. Why, even the locals call it George's Little Village. The story of the love, elopement and tragic breakup of George and the weaponsmith Frederick is the stuff of legend. As the name suggests, this is a small village. The priest also serves as a doctor and looks after the village's infrequent visitors.

■ THE EMPRESS PENDANT (MEDALLION)

The design carved on this pendant is a religious image familiar throughout Amberground. Many wear it to focus their religious beliefs, but most commonly it's worn as a simple ornament. Elena was so thoughtful, wasn't she? So was Darwin, and even the Director. I'm not sure what the relationship was between them, but I have a feeling the Director had bought the pendants even before he heard about Elena's death. I'm sure he wishes he'd given her his pendant before all this happened. Not that he could have known, mind you. It's just how I would have felt. And to think how long he must have kept those feelings to himself. So sad! You know what else is sad? That I haven't even shown up in this manga yet!

nb: *The old tunnel at Dacquoise Cliffs:* a sloped passage dug in order to bury a coffin; a burial path; a path built into a mountainside.

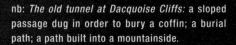

■ RAVINE TOWN SILENCIO

This town surrounded by mountains was Elena's hometown. She left it for Yuusari with Darwin in order to become a Letter Bee. The memories of those who came from Yodaka before them have probably left a mark on Lag's and Niche's hearts.

Her headstone overlooks her hometown. She now rests with her dearest friend.

nb: *Silencio:* Spanish for silence, quiet. One meaning is to pray silently.

Route Map

Finally, I am including a map indicating the route followed in this volume, created by the mapmaker Lonely Goatherd Map Station of Central Yuusari. This map is almost completely of Central Yuusari.

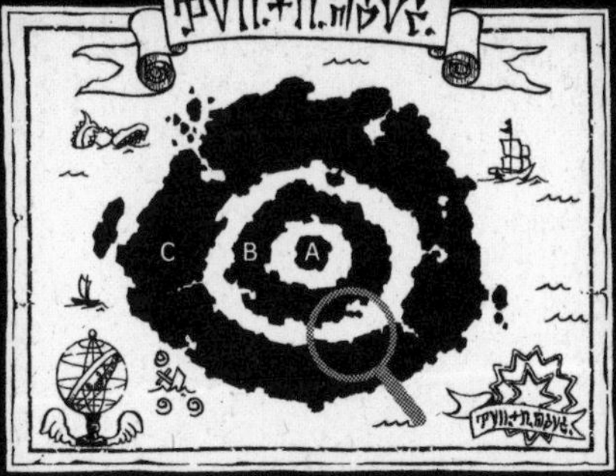
C
B
A

A: Akatsuki B: Yuusari C: Yodaka

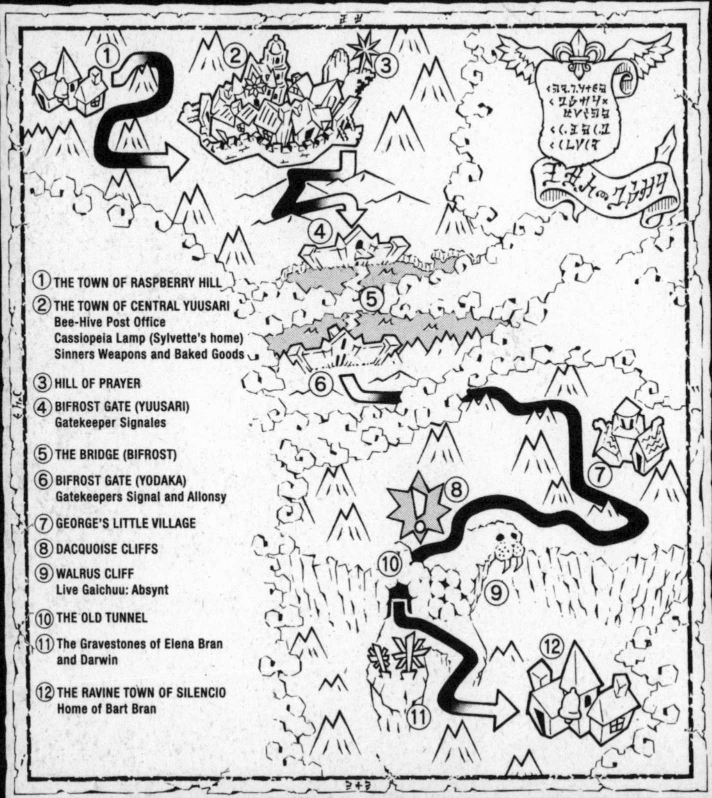
1 THE TOWN OF RASPBERRY HILL
2 THE TOWN OF CENTRAL YUUSARI
Bee-Hive Post Office
Cassiopeia Lamp (Sylvette's home)
Sinners Weapons and Baked Goods
3 HILL OF PRAYER
4 BIFROST GATE (YUUSARI)
Gatekeeper Signales
5 THE BRIDGE (BIFROST)
6 BIFROST GATE (YODAKA)
Gatekeepers Signal and Allonsy
7 GEORGE'S LITTLE VILLAGE
8 DACQUOISE CLIFFS
9 WALRUS CLIFF
Live Gaichuu: Absynt
10 THE OLD TUNNEL
11 The Gravestones of Elena Bran
and Darwin
12 THE RAVINE TOWN OF SILENCIO
Home of Bart Bran

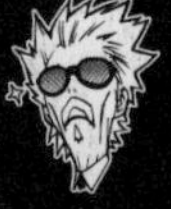

How was the lesson? It seems so trivial in comparison to my grand entrance, which is sure to be soon. I'm so nervous. I'll probably be on the cover of the volume after next. Oh my! The cover... me!

Tegami Bachi
LETTER · BEE

Volume 3

SHONEN JUMP Manga Edition
This manga contains material that was originally published in English in
SHONEN JUMP #84–87.

Story and Art by Hiroyuki Asada

English Adaptation/Rich Amtower
Translation/JN Productions
Touch-up & Lettering/Annaliese Christman
Design/Frances O. Liddell
Editor/Daniel Gillespie

VP, Production/Alvin Lu
VP, Sales & Product Marketing/Gonzalo Ferreyra
VP, Creative/Linda Espinosa
Publisher/Hyoe Narita

Published by VIZ Media, LLC
P.O. Box 77010
San Francisco, CA 94107

10 9 8 7 6 5 4 3 2 1
First printing, September 2010

www.viz.com

www.shonenjump.com

In the next volume...

In volume 4, new facts come to light about Gauche's
mysterious disappearance! As Lag continues his
deliveries in Yuusari, he comes across a clue to Gauche's
whereabouts. It all starts with the sinister-seeming
scientist known as "the Corpse Doctor," then leads Gauche
to seek "the One Who Could Not Become Spirit."

February 2011 will bring the answers to all your burning questions!